PENGUIN BOOKS

THE MASK OF COMMAND

John Keegan was for many years Senior Lecturer at Sandhurst and is now Defense Correspondent of the *Daily Telegraph*. He is the author of many books on military history, including *Six Armies in Normandy* and *The Face of Battle*.

THE MASK
OF COMMAND

JOHN KEEGAN

PENGUIN BOOKS

PENGUIN BOOKS
Published by the Penguin Group
Viking Penguin Inc., 40 West 23rd Street,
New York, New York 10010, U.S.A.
Penguin Books Ltd, 27 Wrights Lane,
London W8 5TZ, England
Penguin Books Australia Ltd, Ringwood,
Victoria, Australia
Penguin Books Canada Ltd, 2801 John Street,
Markham, Ontario, Canada L3R 1B4
Penguin Books (N.Z.) Ltd, 182–190 Wairau Road,
Auckland 10, New Zealand

Penguin Books Ltd, Registered Offices:
Harmondsworth, Middlesex, England

First published in the United States of America by
Viking Penguin Inc. 1987
Published in Penguin Books 1988

LIBRARY OF CONGRESS CATALOGING IN PUBLICATION DATA
Keegan, John, 1934–
The mask of command/John Keegan.
p.   cm.
Bibliography: p.
Includes index.
ISBN 0 14 01.1406 8
1. Command of troops—History.   I. Title.
[UB210.K44   1988]
355.3'3041—dc19   88-5429

Printed in the United States of America by
R. R. Donnelley & Sons Company, Harrisonburg, VA
Set in Janson

To Susanne

Contents

Illustrations

PLATES

between pages 68 and 69

between pages 132 and 133

between pages 196 and 197

Acknowledgement is made to the following publishers, picture libraries and archives for the use of plates: Weidenfeld & Nicolson (1, 5, 6, 7); Radio Times Hulton Picture Library (2, 3, 4, 9, 10, 11, 16, 17); Robert Hunt Library (15, 18, 19, 20, 21, 22, 24, 28); Barnaby's Studio Ltd (23, 25, 26); Weimar Archive (27); Victoria and Albert Museum (8, 12, 13, 14).

Acknowledgements

This book was begun at the Royal Military Academy Sandhurst, continued while I was a Fellow of the Davis Centre at Princeton in 1984 and completed after I became Defence Correspondent of the *Daily Telegraph* in 1986. To my colleagues at all three I am grateful for much help and encouragement. I am particularly grateful to Dr Christopher Duffy, Dr Richard Holmes, Dr John Pimlott, Dr Patrick Griffith, Dr Anthony Clayton, Dr John Sweetman and Mr Keith Simpson at Sandhurst; to Professors Lawrence Stone, Theodore Rabb, Richard Challenor and Sean Wilentz at Princeton; and to Mr Max Hastings, Mr Andrew Hutchinson, Lord Deedes, Mr Nigel Wade, Mr James Allen, Mr Daniel Johnson and Miss Claire Jordan at the *Daily Telegraph*.

I owe special thanks to the staffs of several libraries: Mr John Hunt and his staff at the Central Library, Royal Military Academy Sandhurst, Mr Michael Sims and his staff at the Staff College Library, Mr John Andrews and Miss Mavis Simpson at the Ministry of Defence Library and the staffs of the Firestone Library, Princeton University and of the London Library.

Many soldiers, of senior and junior rank, have helped me to understand something of the nature of command, during twenty-five years largely spent in their company. I would particularly like to record thanks for conversations with Field-Marshal Lord Bramall, Lieutenant-General Sir George Gordon-Lennox, Lieutenant-General Sir John Chapple, Brigadier Peter Young, Colonel Michael Hardy, Colonel Giles Allen, Lieutenant-Colonel Alan Shepperd and Captain Desmond Lynch of the British army, Major-General David Butler of the Australian army, Colonel Berthold Schenk Graf von Stauffenberg of the German army, Lieutenant-Colonel Michel Camus of the French army and Generals Alfred C. Wedemeyer,

Mark Clark and William Westmoreland of the United States army.

The manuscript was deciphered and typed by Miss Monica Alexander, to whom as always I am deeply grateful. It would not have reached her hands but for the support, advice and encouragement of my literary agent and great friend, Anthony Sheil, and of his transatlantic partner, Lois Wallace, also a friend of now almost as many years. I am deeply grateful to my publishers, Liz Calder, Tony Colwell, Alan Williams and, in particular, Elisabeth Sifton, who largely edited the manuscript. I am most grateful to Alison Mansbridge for her skilful copy editing. I owe a particular debt to my friend Paul Murphy for his support and understanding.

My love and thanks finally to my children, Lucy, and her husband Brooks Newmark, Thomas, Rose and Matthew, and to my darling wife, Susanne, to whom I offer this book as a housewarming.

Kilmington Manor   JOHN KEEGAN
May 7, 1987

THE MASK OF COMMAND

INTRODUCTION

Pre-Heroic Leadership

This book is about generals, who they are, what they do, and how what they do affects the world in which men and women live. It might be expected to proceed by one or other method favoured by those who have approached the subject before: the 'traits' method or the 'behaviour' method. The first takes as its premise the assumption that those who exercise military authority will reveal under examination a certain set of common characteristics. The second attempts to identify patterns of behaviour which distinguish leader from follower. 'Trait' studies deal in the qualities of energy, decisiveness and self-confidence. 'Behaviour' studies explore roles: roles of encouragement, dissuasion and coercion.

Both are the methods of social scientists and, as with all social science, condemn those who practise them to the agony of making universal and general what is stubbornly local and particular. I am an historian, not a social scientist, and am therefore free to believe that the generalship of one age and place may not at all resemble that of another. Not only am I free thus to believe; I actually do so, and all the more certainly after thirty years' practice of my trade. Commonality of traits and behaviour I certainly see in commanders of all periods and places. But even more strongly do I perceive that the warfare of any one society may differ so sharply from that of another that commonality of trait and behaviour in those who direct it is overlaid altogether in importance by differences in the purposes they serve and the functions they perform.

For the general – the word itself is pregnant with ambiguity – may be many things besides the commander of an army, though he will certainly be that. He may be king or priest: Alexander the Great was both. He may be diplomat: in their different ways Marlborough and Eisenhower excelled as much at conciliation as at strategy. He may be thinker rather than doer: Moltke the Elder's qualities were intellectual rather than executive. He may command by surrogate authority of a monarch, as Wellington did, or by endorsement of a democratic assembly, which gave Grant his powers. He may be owed obedience only for as long as his decisions bring victory, the uneasy lot of generals in the Boer free states. He may be demagogue-turned-tyrant, and yet sustain his military authority, as Hitler did almost until five minutes past midnight.

Generalship is, in short, much more than command of armies in the field. For an army is, to resort to cliché, an expression of the society from which it issues. The purposes for which it fights and the way it does so will therefore be determined in large measure by what a society wants from a war and how far it expects its army to go in delivering that outcome. A general may, given strong character traits and effective behaviour, carry both society and army farther than they believed they wished to travel. But he too, even if, like Alexander, he both rules and commands, will in the last resort act as a man of his time and place: when Alexander learnt in India that his army yearned for Greece more strongly than for new worlds to conquer, he managed an appearance of good grace and turned his steps homeward.

In ignoring the particularity of leadership, social scientists have been encouraged by unlikely allies, the strategic theorists. Social science conceives itself as a benign discipline, one of whose purposes is to rob strategy of point by reasoning the causes of struggle away. But strategic theorists are, in their way, social scientists also. For their aim – and the aim is a recent one, since strategic theory in its pure form was unknown before the eighteenth century – is to reduce the chaotic phenomena of warfare to a system of essentials sufficiently few for an ordered mind to bend to its purpose. The process of its development has been akin to that of economics. Just as modern economists have learnt to perceive that the aims of the mercantilists – who perceived trade as a form of piecemeal conquest – were misconceived, so too have modern strategists come to teach that the methods and aspirations of earlier practitioners were rooted in false perception.

Ironically, economics and strategy have moved in exactly contrary directions. Modern economists preach moderation: all grow richer, they argue, when none seeks advantage. Modern strategists teach exactly the opposite. There is no place, they insist, for moderation in warfare, of the sort that seemed to suffuse the warfare of cabinets and kings. Its only justification is victory, and victory is won by methods of extreme ruthlessness – decision, concentration, offensive action. These are 'the principles of war' which we owe to the greatest of the strategic theorists, Karl von Clausewitz, who began to publish at the beginning of the nineteenth century.

The chronology of strategic theory-making is of acute significance. Clausewitz, like Marx, is commonly portrayed as free-floating in time, simply a mind more powerful than any which had applied itself to its chosen subject before. Rarely is either subjected to the rigour of contextualization. Yet context, when theories as powerful as theirs are at stake, is all. Marx was able to argue for the primacy of ownership of the means of production as a determinant of social relationships largely because, at the time when he wrote, finance and investment overshadowed all other forces in society, and the military class – exhausted by the Napoleonic wars and dispirited by the defeat of its interests in Russia in 1825 and in France in 1830 – was at an unnaturally low ebb of self-confidence. Yet military power, represented in its crudest form by the robber-baron principle, can, of course, at any time it chooses, make fools of the financier and investor, as the history of investment in unstable areas of the world makes unarguably evident. It can equally make fools of revolutionary leaders who put their trust in the force of 'historical' laws. Marx, in his heart, recognised both truths, feared more than any other the temperament – and the military class is ultimately self-choosing by temperament rather than material interest – that will seize arms simply for the pleasure that blood-letting gives, and constantly urged the politically conscious to learn the habits and discipline of the military class as the merest means of defending and furthering the revolution.

Clausewitz also belongs in context, though he is rarely put there. His famous 'principles of war' – written originally as a school text for the Prussian Crown Prince – are, in a sense, words to the unwise. It is inconceivable that Alexander or Caesar or Frederick the Great or even Wellington should have needed to be reminded that a general should husband his resources and expend them only for good purpose – which is what the principles of 'decision', 'concentration' and 'offensive action' counsel. It is even less conceivable that any should have needed reminding, from Clausewitz's later work, that 'war is the continuation of policy by other means'. Alexander,

Caesar, Frederick, even Wellington – who had sat as a member of parliament and minister – inhaled war and politics in the same breath. All accepted without conscious reflection the interrelationship of force and persuasion; all understood the limits to which the exercise of force may be usefully pushed; all lived with the reality that there is only so much moral sacrifice to be extracted from peoples, only so much material sacrifice from their economic lives.

The great texts of strategic theory that began to appear at the beginning of the nineteenth century, of which Clausewitz's *On War* is incomparably the most incisive, as well as the most influential, must therefore be seen as products of their time and place. Clausewitz is often called 'the interpreter of Napoleon'. But that description misleads because it is entirely circular: Napoleon, though achieving power rather than being born or thrust into it, both ruled and commanded, and in almost exactly the same way and for the same purposes as Alexander had done. He, too, knew that war is an extension of policy by other means and his emperorship was a sustained exercise in that duality. Clausewitz, who might as well be characterized as 'the interpreter of Alexander' or of Caesar, Wallenstein, Frederick the Great or any other statesman-general, was clearly not writing for his or for their like. On the contrary: he was writing for a new class of warrior, whose upbringing and way of life distanced its members from the realities of politics by deliberate purpose.

This class was the product of a division of labour in societies that were rapidly complexifying. Europe, almost until the end of the *ancien régime*, remained a society in which the ruling class was also a military class. The sword, accoutrement *de rigueur* of anyone pretending to the title of gentleman, was the outward symbol of that identification. But the growing wealth of *ancien régime* states produced classes – mercantile, legal, academic – that would not tolerate their exclusion from politics simply because of their swordless status. The Revolution was indeed, in one of its aspects, a revolt by the swordless against the swordbearers, and its success in that respect was unmistakable. Power did pass, as a result of the events of 1789, from those who held wealth as a result of ancestral feats of arms to those who produced, extracted, manipulated or lent it. In that strict but narrow sense, Marx's observation was an exact one. But the separation of the military from the ruling class and the diminution of its influence did not entail its extinction. On the contrary: military class merely ramified, and in two contrary directions. Following the first, military *status* migrated from the few to the many. 'Every man a soldier' had been one of the principal slogans of the Revolution, and one of the most powerful for all that it was unspoken. Following the second, military *command* devolved from amateurs to professionals. The old swordbearing class, which had justified its social primacy by its availability to lead in battle, gave up its monopoly of military leadership to a new class, drawn partly but not exclusively from it, whose sole purpose was officership.

These developments were not contradictory but complementary. Political liberation logically required that all citizens should bear an equal share of the state's military burdens. The enormous armies that universal service produced came to require by extension that they should be commanded by men whose business was war. The Revolution, however, had taught anyone connected with politics, whether in old monarchies or new republics, that professional soldiers in command of mass armies were not merely *a* menace but *the* principal menace to the stability of government. Napoleon's career – he, as a professional artilleryman, was an early member of the new officer class – was dramatic evidence of that danger, and the word coined to denote it, Bonapartism, was taken from his name.

If the new military class was not to hold governments under permanent threat of blackmail, displacement or supplantation – Professor Samuel Finer's famous categorization of the levels at which soldiers intervene in politics – it must, then, both be excluded from politics and denied political skills. The military academies which sprang up all over the Western world contemporaneously with the Revolution were dedicated to that end. Not only did they raise their inmates in monastic isolation from public life; they also sought to inculcate the belief – with very large success, it must be said – that politics is none of a soldier's business.

But that, of course, is a nonsense, as the most famous of Clausewitz's dicta points out. War is indeed an extension of politics and, if it is to be fought in a manner that serves political ends, soldiers must understand how the two interact. The Romans, masters in the exercise of power, had grasped the necessity and designed a training *cursus* which made its products adepts of both worlds. Nineteenth-century Europe, by saddling itself with armies and electorates far larger than republican Rome had thought constitutionally safe, denied itself the *cursus* solution. It sought instead to educate soldiers in the means by which war may serve politics, without risking sullying the soldier's mind by political theory or political fact.

The many books which imitated Clausewitz's *On War* are the classroom texts of that syllabus. And very strange, distorted and partial texts they are as a result. For, if soldiers were to be forbidden all part in the calculations of foreign or domestic policy, then they had to be taught a method of war-making into which calculation of the political effects of their doings came not at all. It was enough that they should know that war had political purpose and that wars which exceeded in cost the value that victory might bring were not politically worth fighting. That being the case, the texts on which pupil officers have been raised since the mid-nineteenth century – roughly the date when Clausewitzian ideas began to circulate – have preached a form of warfare that makes no room for political or diplomatic calculation at all. The commander's purpose, they have been taught, is to deliver victory by the quickest and cheapest means he can find, leaving it to statesmen to decide what 'cheapness' means in that context and how victory is to be used once it has been won.

Strategy, by this teaching, becomes a crude form of economic theory – investment in, earnings out – or little more than asset-stripping by force. Like asset-stripping, it works, at least in the sense that it produces returns. But, as those who follow in the wake of asset-strippers know to their cost, the returns of the technique benefit the few rather than the many. For there is life after asset-stripping, communities that must be remade, confidences that must be re-established, trading relationships that must be rebuilt, credits that must be rewon, currencies that must be coaxed to recirculate. It would not be possible to construct a general economic theory drawn from examples of asset-stripping, any more than from examples of gold rushes, South Sea Bubbles or the great Wall Street Crash.

Yet the strategic theory distilled from Clausewitz – not directly taught by him, for his was a mind too subtle to topple into exactitudes – depends exclusively on the military equivalents of such examples. Take up any military academy text of the last 150 years, and the illustrations of principle on which it draws will be found to come almost without exception from epics of triumph or disaster – the conquest of Gaul, the First Crusade, Marlborough's Bavarian campaign, Frederick the Great's manoeuvres before Rossbach and Leuthen, Napoleon's invasion of Italy, the retreat from Moscow, Waterloo, Gettysburg, the Franco-Prussian War, the 1940 Blitzkrieg and Pearl Harbor. Yet the reality of warfare is no more wholly conveyed by such episodes than the reality of economics is conveyed by the World Slump of 1929–31 or the reality of politics by the Watergate scandal.

For enormous periods of time, even in Western Europe, crucible of the conquering impulse, warfare was not triumphalist but a cautious, local, piecemeal, protracted and indecisive business. The urge to fortify, defend and deflect in that continent, and even more so in others, was quite as strong as that to campaign, make expeditions or win victories. Indeed, if it were possible to quantify in military history – no doubt it is, but few have made the effort – it would probably be revealed that altogether more money and human labour has been expended, over the whole period of collective military effort before the two world wars, in fortification than in fighting. And to no bad purpose: deprecated though it has been by military academy orthodoxies, fortification has served communities well, whenever its works have been kept in order and modernized to meet improvements in weapon manufacture and management. In that perspective, President Reagan's urge to realize a Strategic Defence Initiative, and so protect his United States against the threat of wholesale ballistic missile attack, belongs not to some utopian dream of the future but to one of the deepest and oldest of all human responses to military danger.

The phenomenon of the conqueror – Alexander, Caesar, Genghis, Napoleon, Hitler – cannot, however, be wished away simply because conquest is an exceptional result of the use of military force. 'Strategy', as we have come to understand the word, may well have been given far too wide a meaning. I am increasingly tempted towards the belief that there is no such thing as 'strategy' at all, and that international relations and military affairs would prove more manageable callings if it could be banished from their vocabularies. Certainly, if 'strategy' means what military academies have taught these last 150 years, it is a crippled concept of distorting effect. But even if 'strategist' is wrongly equated with 'conqueror' and 'conqueror' with 'general', Alexander, Caesar and Napoleon cannot be dematerialized. Not only did they exist in their time and do what they did; generations of commanders have sought to emulate their achievements and will continue to do so. The critical questions that pose themselves, therefore, are whether there is an alternative style of leadership to that which they practised, dedicated to a strategy not of conquest but of security, and, if so, how and why it came to be supplanted?

That such a style of leadership has pertained is certainly the case, though the historian must travel long distances in time and space to discover it. He must travel, for his most important discoveries, into the realms of what ethologists call 'primitive warfare', once the norm in inter-communal relations and still to be observed, as a means of resolving conflicts, among a few peoples in remote parts of the world. Primitive warfare should not be idealized. Ritual or game, which some ethologists have conceived it to be, it is now recognized as not. Primitives are almost universally treacherous in inter-communal fighting, and generally kill freely in the raids and ambushes which are their preferred form of warfare, when the penalty of suffering casualties in return is slight. Their warfare when fighting pitched battles is nevertheless commonly characterized by very low levels of lethality. 'In spite of the huge array of warriors involved,' explains W.T. Divale in *Warfare in Primitive Societies*, 'little killing took place. Because of the great distances between warriors and the relative inefficiency of primitive weapons, combined with a young warrior's agility to dodge arrows, direct hits rarely occurred. In the event that someone was badly wounded or slain, the battle would usually cease for that day.' Professor Divale's analysis requires some exegesis. The 'great distances' at which warriors fought were produced by their commonly choosing an agreed battle site. The termination of the battle on a wounding or a death was due to the intervention of elders, who stood ready to mediate with their opposite numbers on the other side.

The moderating influence of elders was a critical but also determining influence upon battles of this style. Their presence, and readiness to intervene, was a structural guarantee that fighting would not exceed in cost the price that the engaged parties were prepared to pay in settlement of their differences. 'Differences' is, of course, the crux: ethologists are not of one mind at all as to why primitives fight in the first place. Some insist on seeing primitive warfare as 'cultural', a channelling of masculine instincts to violence into collective form, as well as an expression of identity by the males who form a particular collectivity. Others regard fighting as a means of competition for scarce resources and point out that, though pitched battles appear to achieve little on the day, the stronger collectivities do, over time, appear to prevail over the weaker, by taking up the territory that they are unable to defend.

Such territories are, nevertheless, separated from each other by recognized no man's lands, at or in which battles normally take place. Even after the territory of a weaker has been absorbed by a stronger collectivity, no man's lands are re-established at the new margin. Evidence of respect for no man's lands also comes to us from the first post-primitive societies of which we have knowledge, the irrigation or 'hydraulic' kingdoms of the Middle East and the early city states of Greece. Neighbours established frontier markers, but were careful to see that one frontier did not abut upon another.

At some stage, however, the time came when no man's lands disappeared and frontiers assumed tripwire function. By that point we may presume that state formation was far advanced, and the mechanisms by which war is made well developed. Competition for Scarce Resources (CSR – a term coined by Professor Ronald Cohen of the University of Florida) would already have led to military specialization in some degree in primitive society; the individualistic display of primitive pitched battle, in which the participants staged long-range duels on a man-to-man basis, and not necessarily against the same man throughout, must have given way under competitive pressures to more unified effort. Unification predicates leadership, and the organization of hunting parties, which was central to primitive society, provided a model from which leadership could be translated to the battlefield.

Once leadership implanted itself in warmaking, the age of the hero stood close at hand. Clearly, on the primitive battlefield, there could be no heroes because, while heroism is exceptional, primitive warriordom required that all behave identically. Insofar as there was exceptional behaviour of any sort, it was that of the elders – whom we may call 'pre-heroic' leaders – standing ready to mediate when levels of violence exceeded accepted norms. Hunting-band leadership, when brought to the battlefield, would have initiated the process of distinguishing some warriors from others, perhaps by the additional degree of risk that such leaders showed themselves willing to bear: 'proto-heroes' they might be called. And when the location of battlefields was fixed not in a no man's land between frontiers but at or beyond them – the inevitable consequence of no man's lands disappearing – 'proto-heroic' leadership would have transformed itself rapidly into leadership of the heroic style: aggressive, invasive, exemplary, risk-taking.

There is considerable intrinsic logic to suggest that this was the manner in which the shift to heroic leadership took place. The abandonment of fixed for encounter battlefields would have precluded the participation of mediatory elders, whose safety could not be assured in hostile territory. Transgression into hostile territory would, moreover, of itself require the direction of a powerful central authority. Empirical evidence supports this scenario. In warfare between early states which had fixed contiguous frontiers between themselves, the point of battle seems to have been crop-seizing or crop-destruction at times close to harvest; such expeditions would have required narrow timing and quick results, possible only through dynamic direction. In an alternative form of warfare, when nomads travelled long distances to cross frontiers fixed at the boundary between cultivable land and wilderness,* leadership would also have been a necessary condition of success. In such circumstances it would have been fostered by the likely mastery of the means of travel – first driven chariots, then ridden horses – that the strong, the brave and the adventurous were likely to display. In either case, whether of short- or long-range warfare, leadership would have been at a premium, and those who possessed the necessary qualities would have achieved or been thrust into it.

To admit such an identification between qualities and function might seem to be to concede an explanation of leadership denied at the outset. It is, however, nonsensical indifferentism to suppose that individual human qualities count for nothing in the way the world works. Clearly they count for a very great deal. But just as pre-heroic society found a way of organizing itself which equalized, even deprecated, differences between individuals in the processes of combat, so too did heroic society work to accentuate and exaggerate the characteristics of those to whom it conceded leadership for war and conquest. What is interesting about heroic leaders – champions of display, of skill-at-arms, of bold speech but, above all, of

*Professor William McNeill suggests that such expeditions may have originally been excited by the wealth of traders from civilization who visited nomads seeking to exchange goods for metals or animals not found in settled territory.

exemplary risk-taking – is not to show that they possessed unusual qualities, since that may be taken for granted, but to ask how the societies to which they belonged expected such qualities to be presented. Heroic leadership – any leadership – is, like priesthood, statesmanship, even genius, a matter of externals almost as much as of internalities. The exceptional are both shown to and hidden from the mass of humankind, revealed by artifice, presented by theatre. The theatrical impulse will be strong in the successful politician, teacher, entrepreneur, athlete, or divine, and will be both expected and reinforced by the audiences to which they perform. In no exceptional human being will it be stronger than in the man who must carry forward others to the risk of their lives. What they know of him must be what they hope and require. What they should not know of him must be concealed at all cost. The leader of men in warfare can show himself to his followers only through a mask, a mask that he must make for himself, but a mask made in such form as will mark him to men of his time and place as the leader they want and need. What follows is an attempt, across time and place, to penetrate the mask of command.

CHAPTER 1

Alexander the Great and Heroic Leadership

Imagine a Highland Napoleon. Imagine a Bonny Prince Charlie with European ambitions who, having won back Scotland from King George II, sets off at the head of his clans not just to conquer England – a mere preliminary – but to cross the Channel, to meet and beat the French army on the River Somme, then journey south into Spain to besiege and subdue its principal fortresses, return north to challenge the Holy Roman Emperor, twice confront and defeat him at the head of his forces, seize his Crown, burn his capital, bury his corpse and finally depart eastward to cross swords with the Tsar of Russia or the Sultan of Turkey. Imagine all this compressed into, say, the years 1745–56, between the princeling's twenty-second and thirty-third birthdays. Imagine on his death, at the age of thirty-two, the crowns of Europe shared between his followers – Lord George Murray ruling in Madrid, the Duke of Perth in Paris, Lord Elcho in Vienna, John Roy Stewart in Berlin, Cameron of Lochiel in Warsaw, a gaggle of tartaned chieftains braying for whisky in the small courts of south Germany and London garrisoned by a crew of bare-kneed highlanders. Finally, imagine most of the Jacobite empire enduring into the nineteenth century, parts of it into the twentieth, and its last fragment into the twenty-first.

Or imagine, if you prefer, a George Washington Bolivar, a Founding Father who determines also to be the Liberator of Latin America; who, having endured the long winter of Valley Forge and the setbacks of the middle years of the War of Independence, to exult at last in the capitulation of Yorktown, conceives the ambition of ridding all the Americas of foreign government. Imagine him embarking the Continental Army in the ships of the new-born United States Navy to voyage south, clear Mexico of Spanish troops, garrison the West Indies with Virginians or New Englanders and make a landing on the shores of South America. Then, victorious in Peru, he crosses the Andes, defeats the Spanish army of the east, and expires on the approaches to the empire of Brazil.

Thus is it just possible to grasp how extraordinary was the career of Alexander the Great. The distances and obstacles of either enterprise defeat the imagination – and they have, indeed, no parallel in any reality except that of Alexander's own life. The world has, of course, known conquerors of extraordinary ambition in its time: Attila the Hun whose horsemen rode from Central Asia to the gates of Rome in the fifth century; the Arab successors of Mahomet turned back into Spain by defeat on the banks of the Loire in the eighth century; and the sons of Genghis Khan, whose Mongols menaced Venice and Vienna in the thirteenth. Napoleon, a devotee of the Alexander epic, came close to re-enacting it in the years between Rivoli, 1797, and Moscow, 1812, as again did Hitler, in whom some gobbet of classical learning also nourished an admiration for Alexander. His orgy of victory was, of course, even more telescoped in time than Napoleon's, who in turn gave battle oftener than Alexander ever did. Yet the achievements of none of these earthshakers quite match those of the original. Napoleon and Hitler scarcely ventured beyond their own continent. Attila, the Arabs and the Mongols broke the boundaries of Asia but only scratched the heartland of Europe. Alexander, by contrast, first made himself master of the Greek world, then translated himself to another, the Persian Empire, and finally ventured into a third in India. At his death in June 323 BC, he had subdued the largest tract of the earth's surface ever to be conquered by a single individual – Genghis Khan's short-lived empire excepted – and ruled as overlord, emperor or king from Mount Olympus to the Himalaya. Who was Alexander and how did he do what he did?

Alexander: the Father of the Man

Alexander, whose birthday probably fell in July 356 BC, was the son of Philip II of Macedon and his wife Olympias; he was not the King's first son, any more than Olympias was the King's first wife.

Philip, an intensely physical man in every aspect of his being, had already married three times and fathered three legitimate children. He was later to marry another three times, and the tally of his offspring, legitimate and by-blows, has never been agreed. He took women where he found them, and, as he spent his life on the move and in impressing his will on the world, the women were many and the outcome of his encounters with them unreckoned.

But the marriage with Olympias was a love match, the love contracted at a celebration of certain mysterious and orgiastic religious ceremonies held a year before Alexander's birth on the Aegean island of Samothrace, which no girl of demure character would have attended. Olympias, already divorced, had no demure reputation and would not acquire one as time passed. Though she and Philip were soon to fall out, the attraction between them was probably that of equivalent, rather than complementary, spirits – wild, carnal and contemptuous of convention. Both were of royal blood and neither, in an age when royalty claimed kinship with the gods, would have thought matchmakers or courtiers necessary intermediaries in what they felt for each other.

Alexander was the immediate outcome of their passion, and perhaps the only one. For war, politics and the death of love quickly drew Philip away from Olympias into whose exclusive care Alexander seems to have fallen in infancy and boyhood. Not until he was twelve or so do we hear of his father taking an interest in the upbringing his son was given. It had run so far the normal course given any young prince of his day: he had been taught to sing and play the lyre, accomplishments that were to be his lifelong pleasures; he had learnt to hunt, and he would hunt bear, lion, birds or foxes every day he was free to do so throughout life; he had been schooled in the rituals of hospitality and as a boy of ten was already noted for the charm and poise with which he received visitors at court; he had, of course, learnt to ride (his taming of the intractable horse, Bucephalus, which would carry him into battle for twenty years, was almost the first element in the Alexander legend); and he had begun his formal education in debate and epic poetry.

Epic poetry meant Homer, whose celebration of the Greek heroic past was to determine Alexander's approach to life. Disregard for personal danger, the running of risk for its own sake, the dramatic challenge of single combat, the display of life-and-death courage under the eyes of men equal in their masculinity if not in social rank

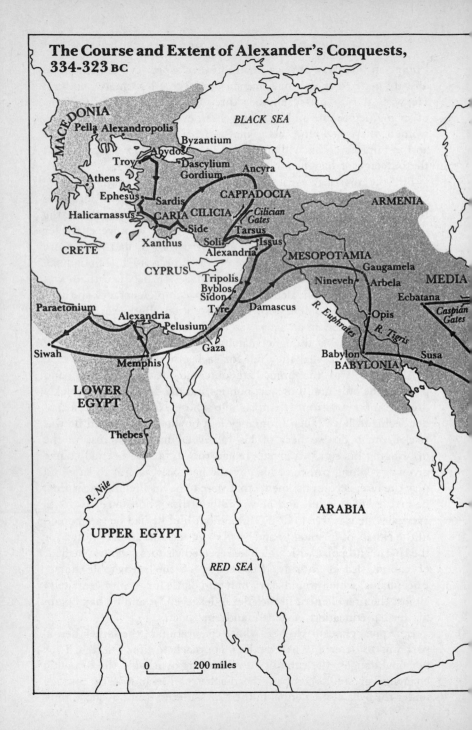

The Course and Extent of Alexander's Conquests, 334-323 BC

MACEDONIA

Pella Alexandropolis

Abydos

Byzantium

BLACK SEA

Troy

Dascylium

Athens

Gordium

Ancyra

Ephesus

Sardis

CAPPADOCIA

ARMENIA

Halicarnassus

CARIA CILICIA

Cilician Gates

CRETE

Side

Tarsus

Xanthus

Soli

Issus

Alexandria

MESOPOTAMIA

CYPRUS

Gaugamela

Tripolis

Nineveh

Arbela

MEDIA

Byblos

Ecbatana

Sidon

Tyre

Damascus

R. Euphrates

Opis

Caspian Gates

Paraetonium

Alexandria

R. Tigris

Pelusium

Siwah

Gaza

Babylon

Susa

Memphis

BABYLONIA

LOWER EGYPT

Thebes

R. Nile

ARABIA

UPPER EGYPT

RED SEA

0   200 miles

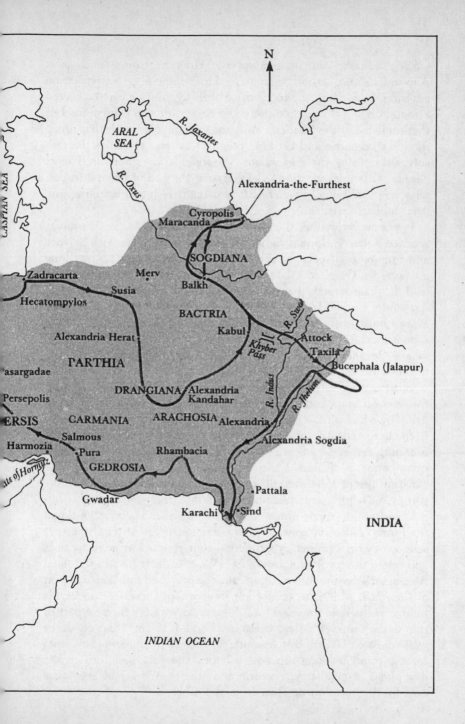

– such was the raw material of the Homeric canon, and on it Alexander's imagination began to feed in childhood. His first act, on entering Asia, would be to sacrifice at Troy, and he carried sacred armour kept in the temple there away with him on campaign. But the influence of the Homeric epic was intermingled with that of his mother's eccentric and extreme religious beliefs. Hercules the task solver was to be the god whom Alexander always honoured most closely; Olympias worshipped Dionysus, the god of natural forces, who was traditionally venerated by slaughter, blood drinking and even human sacrifice.

It was unsurprising, therefore, that Philip should, as Alexander reached puberty, think it right to invest his upbringing with balance and rationality. Isocrates, the Athenian philosopher who had long advocated a Greek 'crusade' against Persia and looked to Philip to lead it, had hoped that one of his circle might be chosen as Alexander's tutor. Instead Philip chose Aristotle, already famous as Plato's most brilliant pupil, brought him to his court and set up a school for him at Mieza, a beauty spot near the capital of Pella, where Alexander and a group of young Macedonian noblemen spent the next three years under his care.

What can have been the influence of one of the world's greatest thinkers on one of the world's foremost men of action is a conundrum by which almost every biographer of either figure has naturally been fascinated. Aristotle, to the modern world, is a philosopher, the founding father of empiricism. In his own time he was universal man, who, as Robin Lane Fox lists it, 'wrote books on the constitutions of 158 different states, edited a list of the victors in the games at Delphi, discussed music and medicine, astronomy, magnets and optics, made notes on Homer, analysed rhetoric, outlined the forms of poetry, considered the irrational side of men's nature, set zoology on a proper experimental course, was intrigued by bees and began the study of embryology'. We know that he also indulged Alexander's existing interests, because he prepared him a special text of the *Iliad*, which Alexander apparently kept thereafter under his pillow. Homer, in any case, would necessarily have formed part of the curriculum at Mieza because he did so in that of every well-educated Greek. But Aristotle also wrote pamphlets (now lost) for his pupil on kingship and colonies and schooled him in the disciplines of geometry, rhetoric and eristics, the art of arguing a case first from one side then from the other.

Alexander in short was given at Mieza the conventionally formal education of a contemporary son of privilege. And, as whenever the grand are set at the feet of the clever, probably as much of it stuck as could or would be grasped. Walter Pater's tutoring of Douglas Haig no more formed the future Field-Marshal into an aesthetic than Clausewitz's syllabus of instruction made the Prussian Crown Prince a strategic thinker. The exceptional fascination of the Aristotle–Alexander encounter has to do not with a meeting of minds but with a juxtaposition of opposites.

'Aristotle,' Victor Ehrenburg has concluded, 'never succeeded in exercising definite political and philosophical influence upon Alexander. The meeting of genius with genius remained without a deeper meaning. The great creations of either were conceived and grew and took effect without any mutual impressions worth mentioning.'

If we are looking for an impression that did take effect, we will find it in the achievements, example and direct personal influence of his father. Philip II, but for his untimely death, might have been Alexander himself. He was violent enough, as grandiose in his ambitions and quite as calculating. But his energies were consumed by the effort to unify the Kingdom of Macedon, subjugate its barbarian neighbours and impose its control over civilized Greece. Those were the preliminaries absolutely essential to any assault on Persia, the conquest of which Philip, forty-six years old in 336, was still young and capable enough to undertake on his own account.

What he had done thus far would have been sufficient to persuade his son that the Persian expedition was no more than a natural extension of the course of Macedonian imperialism, itself chiefly an undertaking of will and courage. Philip had acceded to the throne of a kingdom long under the thumb of the great Greek states, Athens, Sparta and, more recently, Thebes, and chronically disturbed by the attacks of its uncivilized northern neighbours. In twenty years of continuous campaigning he had brought the northerners to heel; imposed Macedonian power over Thrace, Persia's traditional foothold in Greece, Thessaly, and along the eastern Greek coast; had had himself nominated overlord of an invented alliance of Greek states; and finally, when Thebes and Athens rebelled, had definitively crushed their power in the battle of Chaeronea. Internally, meanwhile, he had carried through a social revolution among the Macedonian military class, in a fashion akin to that Frederick the Great would impose on Prussia during his epic of aggrandizement.

The old nobility were laid under an obligation of regular military service; to it a new nobility of military adventurers was added, recruited and promoted on the basis of professional excellence. The result was an army 'open to talents', in which the king's new and old followers competed for position in demonstrations of loyalty and self-disregard.

Alexander would have watched narrowly how his father manipulated the ambitions and antipathies of his followers. But the deepest of paternal effects upon him flowed from exposure to responsibility. At the age of sixteen, immediately after the three-year seclusion of Mieza, Alexander went to war. He could, of course, ride a warhorse, wear armour and wield a sword. Philip, however, presumed altogether greater powers in his son. Alexander was appointed regent, while Philip went off campaigning against Byzantium, and as regent Alexander led an expedition to subdue and expel a dissident allied tribe from Macedonian territory. Two years later, at Chaeronea, Philip gave Alexander a major command in a crucial battle against a formidable enemy, the combined Athenian–Theban army. Convention required Philip to take the right wing; he gave Alexander the left and it was there, as it happened, that the decision was struck. Opposite him Alexander found the Sacred Band, the Theban élite, and he destroyed it in a single, headlong cavalry charge.

Alexander's achievement at Chaeronea was important for his future in more ways than one: not only did it demonstrate his power of command, it also thereby validated his claim to the succession. That claim rested on his position as eldest son of the king's acknowledged wife; but a battle-shy crown prince would have found himself edged aside. Even as things stood, there were other candidates, and the unpopularity the Greek Olympias enjoyed among Macedonian courtiers affronted by her overbearing nature favoured their claims. But Chaeronea, for the time being, extinguished all other candidatures.

In 337, however, the issue of the succession was suddenly revived. Philip repudiated Olympias and took as his new wife a Macedonian girl who had already borne him a daughter and might now be expecting a son. Alexander was outraged, both on his spurned mother's account and on his own. He knew that, though respected at court for his warrior prowess, he was also resented as a half-Greek and a prince whose manner was too like that of a king. Within a year,

Philip was dead, stabbed through the ribs by a traitorous bodyguard on his way, unarmed, to the wedding ceremony of Alexander's sister, Cleopatra.

What part Alexander might have had in his father's assassination divides all who are fascinated by his character to this day. Those who see him as possessed simply by a passion for power take his complicity for granted. Father and son had certainly quarrelled, violently and publicly, over Philip's most recent marriage. But there are other explanations of motive, and they partially or wholly exclude him from guilt. Aristotle, for example, later wrote that Pausanias, the murderer, was revenging the slight of a terminated homosexual affair – Philip, like any nobleman of the Greek world, took love from both sexes. Alexander himself propagated the view that the murder was a political one, organized by the Persians as the shortest way to squash the expedition against them threatened by Philip's recent lodgement of an army on the Asia Minor coast. And then there is the interest of Olympias herself. Not only did the new marriage humiliate and disadvantage her: it spelt her permanent exclusion from court, and it menaced the prospects of her cherished son. Moreover, she was certainly sufficiently violent in temperament and commanding in character to have laid the plot and seen it through. She is said to have had the body of Pausanias taken down from its murderer's stake, cremated with honour and the ashes ceremonially interred as soon as she returned to Macedonia as dowager Queen.

Her return was swift. For whether or not Alexander had the ruthlessness to be a parricide, his ruthlessness as an heir apparent with a claim to establish was unconfined. The Macedonian kingship was elective. Those supporting a candidate donned their breast-plates, moved to his side and clashed their spears as a sign of their readiness to shed the blood of their challengers. Alexander did his own blood-letting: a deposed predecessor of Philip's was murdered instantly, two potential pretenders shortly afterwards and, as soon as an assassin could be got to Asia Minor, also one of the joint commanders of the expeditionary army whom Alexander had reason to suspect as an enemy. It may have been Olympias who planted the seed of suspicion. The victim, Attalus, was the guardian of Philip's last wife whose infant child, one source says, Olympias had killed in its mother's arms, thus driving the woman to suicide.

This bloody settling of accounts is shocking to modern susceptibilities. But the culling of rivals and the execution of the relatives of enemies of the régime – what the Nazis would call *Sippenhaft* – was common practice in Alexander's world, a policy of prudence in a society where the sword spoke more mightily than the law. The blood-bath that followed Philip's murder was not as complete as it might have been. Alexander had grounds, for example, to fear the other commander of the Asia Minor army, Parmenio, who was the murdered general's father-in-law. A cautious refusal to make more enemies than necessary – Parmenio's family was extensive – prompted him not only to spare Parmenio but to retain his services and promote his relatives. One of them, Parmenio's son Philotas, was to prove a superb leader of cavalry but also to figure in a plot against the king four years later deep in the heart of Persia. The politics of succession were to follow Alexander almost to the end of his own life.

Alexander's management of those politics, like his command of strategy, mastery of logistics and skill in diplomacy, were to be the raw material of his epic. But there was as yet, in his twenty-first year, no sign that his future held anything much different from that promised to any headstrong young king with an urge to be – his favourite quotation from the *Iliad* – 'a mighty warrior'. Brains he had, grace, charm, skill at arms, and more self-confidence than was usual even in one deliberately raised to believe in himself. Looks favoured him. Though not tall, he was well proportioned and handsome in a strikingly distinctive way: his brow, the jut of his nose and the set of his lips were characteristically 'noble', his curling hair grew in a peak on his forehead, his skin was smooth and slightly florid, and he had a habit of carrying his head and casting his eyes upwards and to the right, as if he were constantly communing with some unseen presence. Contemporaries spoke of a sweet aroma that surrounded him, but that may have been a conventional compliment. His quickness of speech and gait are better verified: they were imitated by his circle, as was his beardlessness. The total effect was of an urgent, impatient boyishness, which was to determine the style in which heroes would be depicted in Western art from his day to ours.

Looks, quality and character already set him apart from the common man as he stood poised in the summer of 336 to embark on his extraordinary life. Its sequence and pace not even he could guess. What was he to achieve?

The Achievement

First, the course or chronology of his campaign: campaign it can be called, for Alexander was constantly, with only the briefest of pauses, on the march between 335 and 325 BC, and conducted a major battle or siege at least once in almost every one of those years. Beginning in 335, the year after that in which he succeeded his father, Philip, on the throne of Macedon – of which more later – he campaigned first of all on the northern border against old tribal enemies, the Triballians, Getae and Illyrians, who had escaped from Macedonian lordship during Philip's recent struggle to subject Greece to his power. The tribes subdued, Alexander immediately found himself menaced by rebellion in his rear, where the city-state of Thebes had broken with the Hellenic League, a Macedonian medium of control over Greece, and encouraged others to do likewise. He hurried south, 250 miles in thirteen days, gave those who wished to leave the city before blood was shed the chance and time to do so, and then broke a way in and massacred the defenders; 6,000 were killed and 30,000 enslaved.

These were but preliminaries. Alexander's real purpose from the outset of his reign was to invade the Persian empire. How far he initially intended his invasion to go is still debated. It was enough for his Greek contemporaries that he intended to go at all. Persia, the most powerful state in the known world, stretching from the Mediterranean to the Indian Ocean, permanently menaced and had twice invaded Greece. But Greek antipathy for Persia was based not merely on menace and military history. Greek states were frequently at war with each other; indeed Greek political theory held the 'state of war' to be the normal relationship between neighbours. The feeling of Greeks towards Persians, however, was harsher than that. Free Greeks feared and hated the Persians as instruments of a despotic power bent on robbing them of liberty and reducing them to subject status. A war against Persia therefore partook of the character of 'crusade', and Alexander, as war leader, of the role of his civilization's champion.

A vanguard of his army was already established across the Bosphorus on the shore of Asia Minor. It had been sent thither by Philip in 336 and, under the veteran General Parmenio, had already occupied several of the Greek-populated cities of the coast. Parmenio had encountered the local Persian forces, suffered minor set-backs but not yet fought a major engagement. Alexander crossed to join him in the early spring of 334, bringing a following that raised the army's combined strength to 40,000 infantry and 5,000 cavalry.

He called first at Troy to pay homage to the Homeric heroes and sacrifice to the gods, and then set out to bring the local Persian commander and his army to battle. The commander was Memnon, on whom the emperor Darius had devolved responsibility for securing the region against invasion, providing support for his Mediterranean fleet and maintaining contact with his Greek allies, notably Sparta; Alexander was no more loved by all Greeks than Washington was by all Americans in 1778. He found Memnon some fifty miles inland, at the head of 40,000 cavalry and infantry who were lining the banks of a small river, the Granicus.

The infantry was Greek, as was Memnon himself; mercenary service in the Persian army was a natural source of employment for the thousands of landless and masterless men of whom the changing fortunes of war in Greece during the previous century had left a permanent surplus. They, however, stood in second line at the Granicus. The first was formed of Persian cavalry, poised to charge into Alexander's ranks as and when he ventured into the streambed at their feet. As an 'opposed' river crossing always gives the advantage to the defender, whose position in this case overtopped the attacker's, the Granicus should have resulted in an easy Persian victory. Alexander, however, noting that the Persians seemed to be counting on the steepness of the river bank to defeat his effort, rightly concluded that he enjoyed a moral advantage. He charged across precisely at the point where the Persian line was strongest, at least in appearance, and drove into it by brute force. In the struggle of hand strokes that ensued the Greek will overcame the Persian and the beaten cavalry streamed to the rear. The Greek mercenary infantry, summarily exposed to a concentrated Macedonian cavalry charge from which flight meant certain death, stood their ground, fought it out but were overcome. A remnant were eventually able to give their surrender; but in the blood lust of the preceding hand-to-hand combat the majority had been slaughtered.

The battle was to set the stereotype of Alexandrian generalship: precipitate, apparently reckless and highly personal. He lost the crest of his helmet to a sword stroke in the first charge and had his horse killed under him in the second. These close encounters shook him not the slightest. In the immediate aftermath of the victory, having rendered appropriate honours to the dead, he set off to consolidate his grip on Western Asia Minor. Several of the Greek cities which had timorously refused to be liberated before the Granicus now opened their gates to him. Only at Miletus and Halicarnassus, ports off which hovered Persia's Mediterranean fleet, did the garrisons show resistance. The Persian fleet was too slow to save Miletus, however, where Alexander's own smaller navy blocked the seaward approaches while he conducted a whirlwind siege. Parmenio urged that the Macedonian fleet be used again against Halicarnassus. But Alexander, rightly fearing that the Persian admiral was unlikely to be surprised a second time, sent his own ships home and stuck to a landward approach for the reduction of the next city. More strongly built and garrisoned than Miletus, it resisted his siege longer, falling eventually only with heavy loss of life on both sides.

The Macedonian army was now freed to undertake the conquest of Asia Minor proper – the high upland plateau of Anatolia which today forms most of the territory of the Turkish republic. Inhabited by a mixture of peoples – tribesmen in the interior, city-dwellers, many of them Greek, along the Mediterranean coast – it presented Alexander with a variety of problems. No large Persian field army remained in the operational area, but the hill people menaced his axis of advance from the landward, while the port cities along the coast offered the Persian fleet a chain of bases from which it might intercept his line of supply. Both dangers would have to be tackled simultaneously. So dividing his forces, he sent Parmenio inland while he took the pick of the army to campaign along the seaward flank. Both halves of the army were successful in their missions and in April 333, about fifteen months after Alexander had left Greece, they were reunited at Gordium, near the modern Turkish capital of Ankara.

Alexander's next concern was to occupy the two angles of the northern and eastern Mediterranean coasts, the region known as Cilicia, from which he could move either south to conquer Syria and Egypt or east to strike at the headwaters of the River Euphrates, on and beyond which lay the heartland of the Persian empire. The topography of the region confronted him with an acute military problem, since choice of movement through it was determined by mountain passes easily held by small enemy forces. Even more serious, however, the emperor Darius had now taken the field at the head of the imperial army and was manoeuvring to bring him to battle. A climax of the campaign was at hand.

Darius had marched up from Babylon (near modern Baghdad) with 140,000 men, planning to confront Alexander in Cilicia. The young king was successfully subduing the hill tribes which controlled the passes, in a brisk passage of irregular warfare, when he heard of the emperor's approach. The general engagement he had sought since entering Asia clearly impended and he felt as confident of winning as Darius of defeating him. But two means of bringing it about presented themselves: he might either await battle on the border of Cilicia or move southward into Syria so as to place himself across Darius's rear. He chose the latter.

It was to prove one of his few major misjudgements, perhaps his only one. Darius, acting on the belief that Alexander's forces were still scattered about Cilicia, decided to enter the region from the north, where he knew the key passes were unguarded, and to destroy the Greeks 'in detail'. His belief was wrong but the outcome of the decision based on it appeared perfectly calculated. Since Alexander had gone south, Darius now sat across his lines of communication and supply, thus ensuring that the Macedonians must turn and fight him or starve. Better still, he had given himself the time to choose the battleground. The site he picked was, like that of the Granicus, on a river, the Pinarus, which runs into the Gulf of Issus, after which the battle is named. As at the Granicus the river banks on the side chosen by the Persians stood high, until the river ran off into hillier ground supporting the Persian's left flank. On the right, their flank rested on the sea. The position was immensely strong and Darius may be excused for believing it impregnable.

Alexander, recovering briskly from the shock of finding Darius behind him, chose to believe differently. Turning his army about he marched straight for the Persian position, arriving some thirty-six hours after Darius had secured it. The exact date is unknown, probably early in November 333. He paused briefly, then led his army to the attack 'off the line of march'. Formations were adjusted as Alexander assessed the enemy's strength and deployment, so that the best of his line might be committed where the enemy's was weakest. Again as at the Granicus, he detected evidence of Persian moral infirmity. Not only were they clearly trusting to the steepness of the river banks to keep the Greeks at bay, but, where the banks were less steep, they had fenced them with palisades, thereby revealing that they would not advance to the fight and would probably shrink from man-to-man combat. It was all the sign Alexander needed. Placing himself (unusually, dismounted) at the head of his guard infantry, he led them across the streambed into the enemy ranks, carefully choosing to attack the Persian rather than Greek mercenary infantry.

Brute force, in short, was his tool. Admittedly there were complexities to his battle plan, worked out elsewhere on the field. But the crucial action took place exactly where he chose to fight, resulted in the collapse of the Persian line, the headlong flight of Darius, the consequent collapse of his army and its large-scale destruction in the brutalities of the Greek pursuit. Issus turned out a shattering victory.

Alexander was thus impropriated of almost half the Persian empire, a cool return on eighteen months' campaigning at no great distance from base. Darius nevertheless declared himself willing to legitimize the conquest, if only Alexander would return him his mother, wives and children, captured after Issus, and would promise to campaign no further. It was an offer rejected with scorn and without hesitation. 'In future,' Alexander's answering letter read, 'send to me as the King of Asia and tell me of your needs addressing me not as an equal but as master of all your possessions. Otherwise I will deal with you as a miscreant. If you challenge for the Kingship, stand and fight and do not run away since I shall go wherever you are.'

Darius, who had regained the safety of the eastern half of the empire, made no move to take up the challenge. And Alexander, for the next two years (332–331), left him alone. This period was filled with intense and violent activity, but directed chiefly at the destruction of Persian naval power in the Mediterranean. He had told Parmenio a year before that he intended 'to conquer the Persian fleet from the land', a mysterious phrase to modern ears but instantly comprehensible once the essential nature of galley warfare is understood. Galleys were not, as sailing ships are, an extension of the elements. Being instruments of muscular exertion, like the swords and bows of the crews that manned them, they were an arm of land power at sea, and usually hinged from it at a port. In the confined waters of an inland sea or an archipelago, army and galley fleet may indeed have been essential to each other – John Guilmartin suggests

so in his brilliant analysis of the sixteenth-century Turkish wars –
and were certainly a formidable combination when working in
concert. The combination's point of vulnerability was the hinge,
hence the fortification lavished on ports during the early years of
Mediterranean naval warfare. It was these points that Alexander
chose to attack in the months after Issus.

At Tyre, in modern Lebanon, Alexander reduced what was then
the strongest port in the eastern Mediterranean. The operation
lasted seven bloody months and culminated in the mass slaughter of
the inhabitants. Immediately the city had fallen, he moved on to
Gaza, bringing his siege engines with him, and reduced that place in
two months. These victories decisively defeated the Persian fleet
from the land, while a brief cavalry campaign in the interior gave
him control of the hinterland. The date was November 332.

A strange episode now intervened: the expedition into Egypt.
Egypt was a jewel in the Persian empire's crown, and a natural target
for Alexander's campaign of conquest. To venture thither while the
Persian field army remained undefeated in his rear was to run acute
risk. Alexander nevertheless decided to accept it and spent the first
few months of 331 there, founding Alexandria – greatest of his
'Alexander' cities – assuming the Egyptian kingship and making a
desert pilgrimage to the shrine of the god Ammon at Siwah oasis.
The pilgrimage was clearly of the deepest psychological significance
in his life, though the exact nature of the experience he underwent
there remains unexplained.

By the summer he was back on the eastern Mediterranean coast,
consolidating his growing empire and securing his rear, where the
Spartans and the remnants of the Persian fleet were still actively
hostile. But he was also gathering his forces for the descent into the
Persian heartland. While Darius and his field army retained their
freedom of action, the Macedonians remained interlopers in the
Persian empire, and their acquisitions of territory were windfalls
that might be dissipated in a single calamity. Alexander needed a
crowning victory and was now resolved to seek one. The second and
central climax of his epic was at hand.

The danger of its miscarriage was very great. The Persian army
outnumbered the Macedonian three times, was supplied directly
from the established quartermaster resources of the empire and
would operate at close hand to its centre. Alexander, by contrast,
had now to detach himself from the sea coast, a fertile zone in itself

and also one into which supplies could be run by ship more or less at need, to set off into territory hostile at several levels – economic, human, climatic – and to risk his army, his kingdom, the liberty of the Greeks, his reputation and almost certainly his life in a single throw of the dice: success in battle.

He hesitated not a moment. Parmenio, his right hand, had already urged him to settle for the partial victory implicit in the terms Darius had offered: half the empire if he would stay where he was. Alexander rejected that half-heartedness. Whatever his initial vision, he was now hellbent on displacing Darius as 'Great King' and making himself master of the world. He saw that the Persians for all their material superiority were vulnerable to the confrontation of a superior will, and of the strength of his will he had no doubt. In June he sent to Macedonia for reinforcements to join him in the Middle East. Shortly afterwards he set out to march into Mesopotamia – modern Iraq – for the culminating engagement.

Mesopotamia, the 'land between the two rivers' of the Euphrates and the Tigris, was the heartland both of the empire and of the oldest civilization in the known world, west of India and China. Naturally fertile, and made more fertile still because of the irrigation systems of which the imperial government was the controlling authority, it was a natural magnet for the Macedonian army. Darius and his generals understandably expected that, should they wait between the two rivers, Alexander would come to them, hoping to live off the land. He would then run across a difficult river line and expose himself to defeat, before, during or immediately after a risky water crossing. Great though the humiliation inflicted by the Macedonian king in Persia thus far had been, it seemed that a dramatic reversal of fortunes must inevitably follow.

Such calculations were not difficult to divine. Alexander certainly seems to have been able to unravel them. He struck through difficult upland country and across the headwaters first of the Euphrates and then of the Tigris. The 'land between the two rivers' thus by-passed, he began a descent on the eastern bank of the Tigris. With every mile that he advanced, consolidating his conquests as he went, yet more of the territory of Persia was eroded. Darius, who had apparently also thought of scorching the earth before him or of a further retreat into the inaccessible depths of the empire, was stung to action by the collapse of his immediate strategy of defending the river line. For all that his army had twice suffered defeat in pitched battle at Alexander's hands, he now summoned his resolution and marched north to put his crown to the test of the sword.

In late September, the Persians and Macedonians had marched to within striking distance of each other in open country just east of the modern city of Mosul. Darius had the advantage of time. Far closer to home-base than was his enemy, he could now pause and await battle at leisure. The ground he chose, near a place called Gaugamela, was open plain, part plough, part pasture, eminently suitable for the clash of cavalry, his strong suit; he further improved it by clearing the scrub and obstructions. On this occasion he would not make the mistake of limiting his forces' freedom of action either by depending on natural barriers or by building artificial defences to protect his front.

He had, nevertheless, a picture of how he expected the battle to develop. His army being much larger than Alexander's, its line would naturally overlap the advancing Macedonians at both ends. There he stationed masses of cavalry, whose role would be to charge down and envelop the Macedonians as soon as their order was broken. The breaking was to be done by squadrons of scythed chariots, deployed in advance of the Persian line, and perhaps to be supported by the charge of elephants. Finally, of course, the infantry – here, too, as at the Granicus and Issus, much of it mercenary Greek – was to advance to its front and complete the destruction of the surrounded enemy.

Given that edged weapons tend to force those wielding them into continuous lines, since they must stand both within arm's touch of the enemy and shoulder-to-shoulder with each other, Darius's linear plan was perfectly sound. Did geometry determine the outcome of battles, he would probably have won. There is, however, a variation on linear confrontation which, though difficult to implement, is open to well-drilled troops and can be deadly if delivered unexpectedly. It was to become the hallmark of Frederick the Great's battlecraft in the eighteenth century when it was known as the 'Oblique Order'. It had first been employed by the Thebans against the Spartans at Leuctra in 371, and across the intervening forty years it now recommended itself to Alexander. Its essence was that the advancing line should, at a moment when the enemy no longer had time to adjust the layout of his own force, shift the angle of its march to one flank or the other, thus threatening to overwhelm it.

That was how Alexander now acted. He himself took station with the best of his cavalry on the right wing and bore down obliquely on the left end of the Persian line. Darius, who was in the centre of his own line, was slow to detect what was happening; when he did, he sent orders for the Bactrian and Scythian cavalry squadrons on his left wing – horse people of the steppe, and probably his best mounted soldiers – to charge Alexander and his Companion Cavalry. Meanwhile, he set in motion a general advance and launched his three groups of charioteers at the meat of the Macedonian line.

None of his measures sufficed. The charioteers were either javelined into confusion or allowed to pass through gaps hastily opened in the Macedonian ranks – a technique Alexander had tried before; the general advance merely resulted in a large-scale, hand-to-hand brawl; while the Bactrian and Scythian cavalry charge at Alexander itself provoked him into counter-charging. Into the gap the Bactrians and Scythians, in coming forward to meet him, inevitably opened at the end of the Persian line Alexander and his Companion Cavalry poured, pivoting as they made contact with the enemy and driving left-handed towards the chariot of Darius, conspicuous by its imperial banner. The emperor, who had fled from Alexander once before, turned his horses and rode pell mell from the field.

Alexander might have caught up with Darius and made him prisoner on the spot. But a sudden crisis of the battle obliged him to turn about and lend the weight of his contingent to his hard-pressed infantry in the centre. By the time he was able to resume the chase, Darius had been given a head start and was beyond reach. Of his irrecoverable defeat, however, there was no doubt. Forty thousand Persians dead is the estimate given in one of the accounts; for once, an ancient historian's figures may not have been written merely for effect. The destruction of Darius's army – his last army – was total. The Great Kingship had definitively passed from him. In the aftermath, the new crown-holder made sacrifice for 'having mastered Darius in battle and become Lord of Asia'.

It would not be until July 330, ten months ahead, that Alexander would finally run Darius to ground – and their face-to-face meeting, so long delayed, was frustrated at the last instant by the defeated emperor's murder at the hands of traitors. These intervening ten months would be filled with activity as intense as any of the period since May 334, when Alexander had first set foot in Asia. Beyond the death of Darius, the conquest of new worlds beckoned – the

remnants of the empire itself, the mountains and valleys of Afghanistan and the plains of India. In October 331, as he rode away from his
field of victory at Gaugamela, Alexander's life of campaign still had
eight years to run. Those eight years were to test his military skills
even more vigorously than the previous four had done, impose far
greater strains on his capacity to manage his court and his army,
confront him with political challenges as difficult as any he had yet
met in Greece and Asia. Yet, in the strictest sense, that of having
met and overcome the most powerful king of the known world, his
epic was complete. It had lasted forty-two months, had entailed a
march of at least 3,500 miles by horse and foot over mountain and
desert and had required three great battles, two bloody and protracted sieges and dozens of smaller sieges and minor engagements to
achieve. How do we begin to understand the nature and methods of
the youth who was now Hegemon of Greece and King of Asia?

The Kingdom of Macedon

Capital is the raw material of achievement; if not material capital
itself, then the moral, intellectual or social resources on which the
man of ambition may draw to set his enterprise in train. Alexander's
material resources were few, certainly quite disproportionate to the
achievement he was to win with them, but considerable nevertheless. He had inherited the Kingdom of Macedon which his father,
Philip II, had in the twenty years before he succeeded to the throne
made the premier state of the Greek world.

Not that the Greeks regarded the Macedonians as truly ethnic
brothers. Greek they spoke, but in a rustic, uncultivated style; the
Greeks of the southern cities affected not to understand it at all.
Their traditions, moreover, were entirely un-Greek. The citizens of
the city states held their political culture – of equality between free
men and of democratic self-government – an essential element in the
quality of Greekness. No such culture obtained in the Kingdom of
Macedon. Its monarchy admittedly was elective in theory, but it was
hereditary in practice, and a monarchy first and last. Monarchy was
not a system Athenians, for example, could tolerate – all the less so
when the monarch, as in Macedonia, was also chief intermediary
between his people and the gods, a role that tilted monarchy towards
theocracy.

But it was in some sense the very un-Greekness of the Macedonians that made them such formidable actors on the Greek stage. The Greeks of the city states, with their 'passion for discord', lacked the capacity for common undertakings, yet belonged to states too weak in manpower and resources to achieve a great deal by themselves. The Macedonians had had their heads knocked together by Philip; he had 'formed one Kingdom and one people out of many tribes and races'. Unity really had brought strength, moreover; unlike the Greeks of the peninsula, whose acutely developed sense of worth derived from individualism and was diminished by any degree of subordination, the Macedonians had enlarged their self-confidence by merging the identity of their scattered and mutually suspicious highland clans in a larger nationality. 'Nationality' is, of course, a dangerous concept to apply to the ancient world; but if it knew nationalities, then the Macedonians were one of them. Under Alexander's father, Philip, and his predecessors, they had overcome neighbours who had long dominated and preyed on them, incorporated the defeated into the Macedonian state and generated the impetus for advance which Alexander was to harness to his breath taking scheme of victory over the Persians. Analogies with other future military powers suggest themselves in profusion – with the Sikhs of the Punjab, the Gurkhas of Nepal and the Ashanti of the Gold Coast. None rose to power on anything more substantial than success, feeding itself self-sustainingly by its own enlargement.

Yet Macedonia yielded resources that were material as well as human. The country was rich in natural resources: timber and minerals, both exportable and cash-producing commodities; livestock, particularly horses, which mounted Philip's and Alexander's formidable cavalry; and grains, the production of which was greatly increased by Philip's introduction of systematic irrigation. High, healthy, fertile and well watered, the soil of Macedonia was a factor of cardinal importance in underpinning the rise of its royal house.

The Macedonian Army

The powerhouse of Macedonian imperialism lay in its army. Alexander's inheritance of Philip's armed forces was as crucial to his achievement as the future Frederick the Great of Prussia's inheritance of his father's would be to his. The Macedonian was a different army from those of the Greek states. These were essentially citizen militias in which the duty but also the right to bear arms was constitutionally determined. Politically this feature of their character was highly desirable, for it eliminated all danger of the army troubling the freedoms the Greeks valued so highly. But militarily it imposed severe drawbacks on their operational capacity. For their size was thereby severely restricted, because the overwhelming servile majority in city polities, like those of Athens and Thebes, were legally disbarred from bearing arms. As long as the nature of Greek warfare was confined to inter-city conflict, this limitation on numbers was of secondary account; the larger states were not put at risk by it, while the smaller could compensate for their inferiority by clientage or prudent alliance-making. And, in a crisis, if cash availed, it was possible temporarily to pad out numbers by the hire of mercenaries, whose ranks the internecine warfare of the fifth and fourth centuries constantly enlarged.

But once the divided and contentious states of Greece found themselves confronted by an expansionist northern neighbour, which imposed on itself none of the limitations of military obligations under which they laboured, all the justification for their militia system evaporated. They found they could neither match the numbers Macedonia stood ready to put into the field, nor enlarge their pools of domestic military manpower with an equivalent flexibility, nor mobilize the sums of cash necessary to enlist mercenary assistance at haste and in quantity. Like the small states of north Germany confronted by the behemoth of Prussia in 1866, their choices were limited. They had either to acquiesce in Macedonian ambitions or undergo summary, if heroic, defeat in defiant opposition.

The Macedonian army was, in the strictest sense, a dynastic one, in that it comprised an inner core of warriors whose relationship to its royal leader was a personal, ultimately a blood one; the outer tiers were made up of less élite though still formidable troops whose loyalty was determined by more mundane factors – political obligation, pay, custom and calculations of self-advantage. Some of the outer tiers were 'new' Macedonians, brought within the kingdom by Philip's campaign of conquest in the southern Balkans; others were allies, to whom he had left varied degrees of independence, among the Greeks nominally one of autonomy; the remainder were mercenaries whom the house of Macedon was as ready to employ as the city-states, and better able to keep because of its ample cash resources and proven ability to generate plunder.

The innermost core of the army was the Companion Cavalry. The Macedonians, like the peoples who would overwhelm the Western Roman Empire in the fifth century AD, were a heroic society, at the centre of which stood the war leader and his band of fellow-warriors. At their closest, the ties between the leader and his companions would be those of blood. But the heart of their relationship was an ethical one, the equality that persists between those who share risks and vie to outdo each other in the display of courage, the more reckless the better. To keep the regard of such men, the war leader had constantly to excel – not only in battle but in the hunting field, in horsemanship or skill at arms, in love, in conversation, in boast and challenge, and in the marathon bouts of feasting and drinking that were the hero's *repos du guerrier*. Such Companions are the *dramatis personae* of the *Iliad* and the *Odyssey*, the texts on which Alexander had been raised and by which he set the star of his course through life. 'Busy and steadfast,' says Robin Lane Fox, 'they dine in his tent or listen as he plays the lyre; they tend his bronze-rimmed chariot and drive his hoofed horses into battle, they fight by his side, hand him his spear and carry him, wounded, back to their camp.' (Alexander was to suffer wounds with the frequency that the modern prizefighter accepts blows to the head and body.) 'With the collapse of kings and heroes, it is as if the Companions withdrew to the north, surviving only in Macedonia on the fringe of Europe. Driven thence when Alexander's conquests bring the Macedonians up to date, they retreat still further from a changing world and dodge into the swamps and forests of the Germans, only to reappear as the squires of early German kings and the retinues of courts in the tough beginnings of knighthood and chivalry.'

Alexander's Companions differed from those of Homer in arms and style of combat. The Greeks of the Trojan wars had been charioteers. Alexander's were horsemen, for the 'cavalry revolution' had intervened between the twelfth century and the fourth. But in approach to life and cast of mind they were beings of the same blood, men whose worth in their own eyes and those of their equals was determined by disregard for danger and contempt for the future. To do the right thing in the present moment, and to suffer the consequences as they might be, was the code by which the Companions lived. Sword and steed were their armour against fate. Thus equipped, they 'dashed in among the enemy', wrote Thucydides of their ancestors, 'and no one withstood their onset'.

Alexander had some 3,000 Companion Cavalry, of which he took 2,000 with him into Asia. They provided the battle-winning shock force of his army and he almost always took station at their head. But, unlike the oriental hosts of élites and feeble followers which the European empire-builders of the eighteenth century were to demolish with such ease, the Macedonian army was not a head without a body. It was a carefully balanced force, in which the secondary components were treated with an esteem by their leader proper to their quality. It contained, for example, an important body of infantry, accorded the title of Foot Companions, which Alexander's predecessors had trained up to provide solidity to the line of battle. Armoured on the head and body and equipped with the long spear known as a sarissa, the distinctive Macedonian tool of war, the Foot Companions' role was to withstand the shock of the enemy's offensive while the Cavalry delivered the decisive stroke elsewhere. Out of the Foot Companions, Philip had formed an even more select group of infantry, the Shield Bearers, whose title to status derived from that of the king's personal squire. In an earlier age, he had carried the king's shield into battle, so as to leave him unencumbered for single combat. The Shield Bearers (*hyspaspisti*) collectively fulfilled this duty on the larger fields of action Alexander was to stake out for them. All in all, the heavy infantry of the expeditionary army probably numbered some 9,000.

Cavalry and Foot Companions were drawn from the nucleus of the Macedonian nation. But they were not the only elements of Alexander's army of conquest. There were also light cavalry, mainly recruited from Macedonia's neighbours – Thracians, Paeonians and a group called 'scouts' of mixed stock – which operated on the flanks of the Companions against the enemy's light troops. Neighbours also provided contingents of light infantry, notably the Agrianians, Alexander's loyal allies in his Balkan wars. Specialist troops – archers, siege artillerymen, engineers, surveyors, supply and transport servicemen – were drawn from both Macedonia and Greece proper. The Greek allies furnished sailors, infantry and cavalry, among whom the Thessalian heavy cavalrymen made a key contribution; the total of troops provided by the Greek states may actually have exceeded in numbers that found by Macedonia itself. And, finally, there was Alexander's complement of Greek mercenaries. As so often with mercenaries, earlier contingents had fulfilled a critical function under Philip in introducing the Macedonians to the most up-to-date military techniques. Their usefulness on the field of battle, where professional pride and sheer force of habit worked to keep them in place, was undeniable. Alexander was therefore content to include some 4,000 of them in the expeditionary force. For all his appreciation of the mercenary ethic, however, he would, as we have seen, harden his heart against Greeks who had taken paid service under the Persian king.

The army that gathered at Amphipolis, at the head of the Aegean, in the spring of 334 numbered altogether about 50,000, of which 6,000 were cavalry. How was it equipped, armed and trained for war?

Like all those of the pre-gunpowder age, it was a muscle-power army, its offensive power depending on the strength of its soldiers' bodies, their defensive apparel in turn designed to withstand blows that were limited in force by the physical energy of their opponents. Bronze, elastic and comparatively easy to work, was still favoured for some protective equipment; the infantry's shields, particularly the button-shaped shield carried by the *hyspaspisti*, were made of it. But iron had almost entirely replaced bronze in weapon-making, so that swords, arrow-heads and spear-points were all of iron or forged steel. The primitive metallurgy of the period kept swords short, so that swordsmanship was an affair of hacking and stabbing rather than lethal thrusting; but the inflexibility of the blade made the wounds such swords inflicted deep and gaping. The sword blow to the crest of Alexander's helmet at the Granicus left it dented. Delivered to the unprotected skull, it would have cloven to the brain. Spears, those at least carried by the Macedonians, were compensatorily long. The sarissa, a pike made of tough cornel wood tipped with a foot of iron, was up to eighteen feet in length. Quite unsuited for use in single combat, it made the Macedonian phalanx, from which it bristled in sheaves, unapproachable by either infantry or cavalry as long as the phalangists kept their nerve and cohesion.

Cohesion was the foundation of phalanx warfare. Since muscular strength offered the only means by which a formation determined to resist could be shaken, tactical logic demanded that infantry stand in the closest possible formation, shoulder to shoulder, armed with weapons that kept the enemy at the greatest possible distance. The more ranks the better, too, since the weight of a man behind is the best assurance that the man in front will not flinch when the enemy's spear-point levels at his breast; it is weapon length alone that imposes a restriction on the number of ranks it is useful to deploy. Eight ranks appears to have been the normal depth of the Macedonian phalanx, which meant that, even with the eighteen-foot sarissa in their hands, the rearmost men must have acted as stiffening rather than as spearmen. On the move, particularly when the phalanx went over to the attack, the depth might be increased. Its manoeuvrability is difficult to estimate. On the face of it, the density of such large masses of men defies easy change of direction. On the other hand, accounts of the fighting at Issus make it clear that the phalanx varied its depth on the move, and, admittedly during a deliberately cautious advance, pivoted on a flank to approach the enemy and extended its length to approximate that of the opposing line. The phalanx then must have had a greater flexibility than its appearance suggests; certainly it was trained to manoeuvre in action, was sub-divided and sub-officered to that end, and, of course, was already a combat-tested and experienced force before it set foot in Asia.

Cavalry is by definition more manoeuvrable than infantry though notoriously more difficult to control. Alexandrian cavalry, like all that of the ancient world, lacked moreover the means of control thought essential by modern horsemen: the stirrup was unknown to the Greeks; it had not even started its evolutionary migration, as a simple toe loop, from far-away India, where it was to be invented about the first century AD. Because friend and foe alike lacked the stirrup, its absence was a self-cancelling disadvantage; disadvantage none the less it was, since a rider had to impose his will on his mount through an otherwise unnecessarily fierce bit and by bestriding him on a flimsy saddle which made no sort of platform for heavy weapon handling. The charge with couched lance by which the cavalry of feudal Europe would sweep battlefields clear of the enemy 1,500 years later was thus not a technique either open to or even to be guessed at by Alexander and his cavalry leaders; despite his portrayal wielding a lance from horseback, it seems more probable that a short spear or javelin was the cavalryman's weapon, to be thrown or thrust by choice, complemented by a curved slashing sword.

The Macedonian horse was of pony size, about fourteen hands at the shoulder, but strong enough to carry a man long distances and to work up to a trot in the charge. In action Alexander's heavy cavalry were trained to ride in a wedge-shaped formation designed to allow both penetration of gaps should they open in the enemy's line to the front and easy inclination to right or left. The Companion horsemen were practised rigorously in these manoeuvres, whose smoothness required that all kept their eye on the leader at the apex of the wedge – 'as happens in the flight of cranes', explained a tactical theorist of antiquity. The light cavalry operated in a different style, characteristic of their kind throughout the ages: hanging about the enemy's flanks, harrying and skirmishing when the chance offered, milling through the ranks of unsteady or shaken infantry and riding down those who broke. The heavy cavalry naturally joined in any sustained pursuit.

Of the other troops in Alexander's army, none of the ancient writers supplies precise detail. Some of the siege engineers and artillerymen may have been specialists; but the brute labour of siege engineering would have been performed by infantrymen doubling as sappers and miners. Alexander's supply arrangements, the complexity and smoothness of which offers 'one of the clearest signs of his genius', were in the hands of his baggage train and baggage-masters. His system, none the less, seems to have been an inherited one, originally devised by his father to unshackle his army from the bonds that limited the mobility of his Greek opponents. They, as free citizens, disdained to march under the burden of foodstuffs and logistic necessaries, bringing slaves with them to do the porterage. They further encumbered themselves with ox-drawn carts, notoriously slow and heavy consumers of their own payloads. Philip trained his soldiers to march long distances under heavy weights – as much as a month's supply of flour – and to shun dependence on wheeled baggage columns. As a result his army – like that of the Vietnamese enemies of the French and Americans in the Indo-China war of 1946–72 – acquired the ability to arrive unexpectedly at battlefields in defiance of all orthodox logistic calculation. Alexander extended and perfected his father's arrangements, allowing only pack animals – horses, donkeys and camels – to follow the line of march and ruthlessly burning waggons that his subordinates attached to the column. Yet his army rarely went short; careful calculations of the range over which it was possible for the army to operate, efficient local purchase or requisition, discreet suborning of Persian officials in the areas he intended to occupy and exact co-ordination of landward marches with the movement of maritime

cargoes allowed him to take a well-fed army wherever he chose –
until the very end of his wanderings, when ambition got the better of
his judgement.

Alexander's Staff

How did Alexander form his military judgements? It is dangerous,
in any age much before our own, to speak of a 'general staff', because
to do so is to imply a bureaucratization of society quite at odds with
reality. The general staff, officered by men selected and trained to
perform intelligence, supply and crisis-management tasks, was a
nineteenth-century Prussian invention. The Romans, via the *cursus
honorum*, anticipated something akin to it. But mediaeval armies
knew it not at all, while even the Renaissance and dynastic armies of
early modern Europe were staffed at best by gifted amateurs, usually
the friends or favourites of the commander.

Alexander commanded alone, certainly maintaining nothing like
the 'three bureaux' system – operations, intelligence, logistics –
through which European armies of the last hundred years have been
articulated. Nevertheless, he needed and used subordinate commanders, if only to control his detached armies, such as those sent ahead
into Asia Minor before the invasion and left behind in Greece after
it. He took surveyors, secretaries, clerks, doctors, scientists and an
official historian – Callisthenes, a nephew of Aristotle – in his
entourage, and he consulted anyone whose expert knowledge promised to enlarge his own picture of how the future could be made to
fall out. As a boy at his father's court he had closely questioned
visitors from distant places about the topography of their home-
lands, and on the eve of his march into Asia was certainly one of the
best-informed men in the Greek world. But between information
and decision falls the shadow. Did Alexander find his way through
the dark alone, or did he require the minds of others to guide him to
the right choice of action?

Alexander's intimate friends, the inner circle of Companions,
were by no means all hard-drinking highlanders, boastful and
empty-headed. Ptolemy, the future ruler of Egypt, would write a
history of the conquests; Marysas also became an author. Hephais-
tion, Alexander's favourite, was the friend of scholars, and Peucestas, who was to govern Persia, took the trouble to learn the language

and cultivate a knowledge of Persian customs. But our main sources give no real hint that Alexander used his circle of friends as a sounding-board for his plans. That was not their function: it was personality and character that were under test when Alexander was among his close Companions, the test of quickness of wit, sharpness of retort, memory for an apt phrase, skill in masking insult, boast or flattery, capacity to see deep into the bottom of a glass, and no heeltaps. When in doubt – and Alexander probably took the trouble to disguise doubt though he felt it but rarely – he turned to the most experienced professional at the court, Parmenio, to help him fix his ideas, using the old general's temperamental prudence as a catalyst to precipitate his preference for the bold and immediate option.

Arrian, whose biography is the most important surviving source, provides four specific examples of how debate was conducted at court, when Alexander locked minds with Parmenio and overcame his objections to pressing forward rather than holding back. Arrian's testimony is of the greatest value; writing though he did 400 years after Alexander's death, he worked from biographies and histories, now lost to us, written by Alexander's contemporaries. Moreover, being a Greek himself, who as a high Roman official had governed and campaigned in exactly the area in which Alexander began his conquests, he was in close sympathy with both his subject's character and his problems.

Two of the reported Alexander–Parmenio debates are strategic in character, two tactical. At the strategic level the first concerned the policy to be adopted against the Persian Mediterranean fleet after the victory of the Granicus. The choice lay between a continental and a maritime campaign. Such a choice is a constant, recurring in all campaigns where sea- and land-power intermingle, as they must do in inland seas, as they have always done in the Mediterranean, as they notably did in Macedonia's struggle against Persia. Persia, though maintaining a large Mediterranean fleet, was essentially a continental empire, whose control of its territory depended in the last resort on the superior strength of its army. Macedonia, though almost land-locked and only a recent entrant to the world of the Greek states, had thereby joined the ranks of maritime powers, in which strategists' thoughts always turned on how superior land force might be negated by a stroke from the sea.

After the victory of the Granicus, Alexander proceeded on a mopping-up campaign of those ancient Greek cities along the western coast of Asia Minor that had fallen into Persian hands. Ephesus – to whose future Christian congregation Saint Paul would write one of his epistles – and Miletus quickly fell to him. Three days after his small fleet had anchored offshore, however, the much larger Persian fleet arrived. Not only did its presence threaten his freedom of manoeuvre, it also menaced his communications with Greece, where the militant Spartans remained Persia's firm allies. Parmenio therefore urged Alexander to seek a naval battle. 'If they won,' he said, 'it would be a great help to the expedition generally; a defeat would not be very serious; [and] he was willing to embark himself and share all the perils.' Brave words from a 67-year-old. But Alexander would not have it. Parmenio had not grasped the overarching range of the young king's vision. The old general's thoughts were of immediate advantage in a local campaign, Alexander's of ultimate victory on the stage of the world. That could be won only by feeding success with success. 'He would not risk sacrificing the skill and courage of the Macedonians; should they lose the engagement it would be a serious blow to their warlike prestige.' He would instead proceed with his reduction of the Persian naval bases along the coast and so 'defeat the Persian fleet from the land'.

This was an extraordinarily incisive piece of strategic judgement; an obvious analogy is with MacArthur's scheme at the outset of the South Pacific campaign to outflank Japan's naval advantage by seizing only those islands that he needed as stepping-stones north-ward, leaving the rest 'to wither on the vine'. Alexander's decision, like MacArthur's, was justified by results. After the reduction of the last great Persian fortified ports at Tyre and Gaza in 332, the Persian fleet began to disintegrate. Its squadrons were recruited from precisely those Phoenician cities that Alexander had made his targets and, as one after another fell, the crews lost heart and made for home. As winter approached, Alexander's admirals were no longer outnumbered and had regained control of the whole of the Aegean.

By then, of course, Alexander had also won his first direct engagement with Darius, at Issus, in November 333. The shock of defeat had so unsettled the Great King that he had offered the invader a bribe well calculated to buy him off: the whole of Asia Minor, not only a territory of great wealth but also the homeland of all those Greek colonists whose subjection by Darius had supplied the initial motivation for the Persian expedition. Isocrates, its ideologue, had actually urged that the capture merely of Asia Minor would be justification enough of the risk entailed, but Alexander had already rejected this in the most insulting terms. After the fall of Tyre, when Darius improved his bid, offering the whole of his empire up to the Euphrates, from which Alexander was still 500 miles distant, and also threw in the offer of a large cash sum and his daughter's hand in marriage, Parmenio at once urged Alexander to accept. Alexander's famous reply was that 'he would indeed have done this were he Parmenio but, being Alexander, he would do no such thing'. He had already told Darius that since Issus he was Lord of Asia, that the Great King's money and lands were therefore already his, and his daughter's hand also, if he chose to take it.

Alexander could never have been accused of lack of boldness. After Issus, however, he had reason to feel bold. More impressive, and more indicative of his fundamental character, was his boldness at the Granicus, where he and Parmenio differed over the tactical scheme for the battle. The Persians, holding a river position, had brought their line right down to the river's edge, thereby, as Parmenio warned, threatening a Macedonian attack with disaster. 'As we emerge in disorder, the weakest of formations, the enemy cavalry in good solid order will charge.' Better, he proposed, to camp for the night, wait until the enemy had done likewise, and get across the watercourse when it was unguarded.

Alexander would have none of it. 'I should feel ashamed,' he said, 'after crossing the sea from Europe to Asia so easily if this little stream should hinder us . . . I consider it unworthy either of the Macedonians or of my own brisk way with danger. Moreover the Persians would pluck up courage and think themselves fighters as good as we are . . . ' And so, clapping spurs to horse, he ordered the advance and plunged into the Granicus.

Parmenio, of course, was proved wrong and he right (though as we shall see, there was perhaps as much acute tactical insight as moral wilfulness in Alexander's decision). Before Gaugamela, when he and Parmenio differed again over tactics, it was almost, perhaps wholly, the issue of moral courage that divided them. Parmenio, seeing the Persian army drawn up in overwhelmingly preponderant force, urged Alexander to wait until darkness fell and make a night attack. Curtius, another of the Romans who wrote from the lost sources, has Parmenio argue that, 'in the silence of the night, the enemy may be overwhelmed. For nations so discordant in language and customs, attacked in their sleep, terrified by unexpected danger and by formidable darkness, will plunge tumultuously together, unable to form.' Alexander did not answer Parmenio directly but spoke to one of the nobles he had brought with him for moral support. 'Darkness,' he said, 'belongs to robbers and waylayers. But my glory shall not be diminished by stealing a victory . . . I am determined on an open attack.'

Arrian, the old campaigner, whose account tallies closely, thoroughly approved. Alexander, he says, had good military reasons for shunning a night operation. But, more important, 'the secret attack by the Greeks under cover of night would excuse Darius from any confession of being a worse general with worse troops'. Alexander, now deep in the heart of the enemy's empire, had not only to win but to be seen to win unequivocally if the campaign were not to protract itself interminably. All or nothing: Alexander played for all, and won.

Alexander and his Soldiers

Thus with his staff: peremptory and headstrong but usually with good reason, and rarely deaf to counsels of caution well argued. On the approach to Gaugamela he summoned 'the Companions, the generals, the Cavalry commanders, and the commandants of the allies and mercenary troops [to discuss] the question whether he should advance his phalanx at once, as most of them urged, or, as Parmenio thought best, camp for the time being, make a complete survey of the ground, in case there should be any part suspicious or impassable – ditches or hidden stakes – and make a thorough reconnaissance of the enemy's dispositions.' Parmenio's advice prevailed, and quite rightly, for Darius had prepared the field of Gaugamela as a killing-ground.

If so with his staff, how with his soldiers? They formed, it is important to remember, neither a tribal war band nor a royal regular army, nor were they conscripts or mercenaries (though there were mercenaries among them). They were, insofar as such a body can be said to have existed before the rise of conscious nationalism, a sort of nation-in-arms, recruited from those classes deemed socially eligible for military service in Macedonia and, though undoubtedly paid, following their king as much out of comradeship as obligation. It was the assembled army, after all, that elected the king ('a real choice,' says his biographer, N. E. L. Hammond, 'even if the candidates were restricted to members of the Temenid house') and, though the election was irreversible, the authority thereby invested in him did not entitle him to abuse or misuse them. It may have been that Alexander's officers flogged or struck their soldiers. But, if so, we do not read of it in the sources. It would have been contrary to the ethos of that army of warriors – as it was, for example, in the high-caste regiments of the British Indian Army, or among the Bedouin who followed Lawrence of Arabia and became the soldiers of the Jordanian Arab Legion. To such men a blow from a superior was a deadly insult, a denial of manhood, which could be expunged only by violence in return. Hence the relative frequency with which British officers in Indian or Arab regiments were murdered by subordinates. The explanation was almost always an ill-considered affront to a man's dignity.

Alexander in a rage could strike a man down. Insulted by his cavalry general, Cleitus, during a camp dinner on the march to India, he first punched his personal trumpeter for refusing to summon the guard – presumably to arrest the old man – and then, when the quarrel worsened, seized a spear and ran Cleitus through the body, killing him dead. But the act was out of character, at least out of the character with which he had begun his epic. And perhaps out of character altogether: later, when his soldiers indicated that they were weary of conquest and longed for home, Arrian has their spokesman preface his deposition with the words, 'seeing that you, sir, do not yourself desire to command the Macedonians tyranni- cally, but expressly state that you will lead them on only by gaining their approval, and failing this you will not compel them . . .'

Alexander, in short, sought to lead by indulgence as well as by example. Indulgence could take various forms. Early in the Asia Minor campaign, after the Granicus but before Issus, he made a block grant of what today the British army would call 'compassion- ate leave': 'some of the Macedonians had been recently married; Alexander sent them off to spend the winter with their wives in Macedonia . . . He gained as much popularity by this act as by any other.' Much later, during the Indian campaign, he decreed a general cancellation of debts; 'nervous lest Alexander had merely tried an experiment to see who had not lived on their pay,' few at first registered. But, when it became clear that he genuinely intended to spend the army's accumulated wealth on a moratorium, without enquiring who paid what, the soldiers queued up at the accountants' tables to clear their slates, 'more gratified by the concealment of their names than by the cancellation'.

Leave and debt clearance are easily granted when a leader is not under pressure, and on neither occasion was Alexander. Concern for subordinates' welfare comes less naturally when the leader is distracted by impending danger or celebrating release from it. Alexander was notably thoughtful even at such times. Before Issus he made sure his men had eaten – better than Wellington could manage before Waterloo, when much of his army fought on stomachs empty for two days – and before Gaugamela 'he bade his army take their meal and rest'. He had already rested the army for four days and so arranged his base that his men could advance to battle 'burdened with nothing but their arms'. After Issus, 'despite a sword wound in his thigh', he 'went round to see the wounded . . . He promised all who, by his own personal witness or by the agreed report of others [an exact anticipation of the modern practice in citation for medals], he knew had done valorous deeds in the battle – these one and all he honoured by a donation suitable to their desert.' It was a repetition of his behaviour after the Granicus when 'he showed much concern about the wounded, visiting each, examining their wounds, asking how they were received, and encouraging each to recount and even to boast of his exploits' (excellent psychotherapy, however wearisome for the listener).

He was also, of course, meticulous about disposing decently of those who succumbed to their wounds, friend and foe alike. 'To make sure the dead were buried on the day following a battle . . . was a first, sacred duty,' the historian Yvon Garlan tells us. Alexander fulfilled it to the letter. After the Granicus, he 'buried [the Macedonian dead] with their arms and other accoutrements; to their parents and children he gave remission of local taxes and of all other personal taxes and property taxes . . .' He buried also the Persian commanders and the mercenary Greeks who fell in the ranks of the foe' (the common Persian soldiery may have been too numerous to honour properly); after Issus, 'he gathered the dead together and gave them a splendid military funeral, the whole army marshalled in their finest battle array'; and, certainly after the Granicus and probably also after his other battles, he raised memorials to the fallen and sent trophies taken from the enemy home 'to be hung in the temples to Athena [with] this inscription attached: "Alexander son of Philip and the Greeks (except the Spartans) [send] these spoils from the Persians in Asia".'

Ceremony and Theatre

To send spoils from the Persian War to Athens, greatest of the Greek states but also Macedonia's least certain ally in the Hellenic League, was a calculated stroke of public relations; to associate his Greek followers with the Macedonians whom he proclaimed himself to personify – 'Alexander son of Philip and the Greeks' was an epitome of his army – but specifically to exclude the Spartans was a breathtakingly arrogant rescripting of the course of recent Greek history. For historically it was the Spartans who had championed the cause of Greek liberty against Persia, who had fought the hopeless epic of Thermopylae to check the invasion of the Emperor Xerxes 150 years before, but who had subsequently and cynically made their peace with the Persians for reasons of state. Alexander's donation of the Persian armour was a brilliantly theatrical announcement of his assumption of the heroic role of King Leonidas and displacement of the Spartans as standard-bearers of Greek civilization against Asiatic barbarism.

But theatricality was at the very heart of Alexander's style of leadership, as it perhaps must be of any leadership style. Throughout the Alexander story, acts of theatre recur at regular intervals. Daily, of course, he had to make sacrifice to the gods; in Macedonian culture, only the king could perform that central religious act. Bizarre though it seems to us, therefore, his day began with his plunging of a blade into the living body of an animal and his uttering of prayer as the blood flowed. Before Gaugamela, uniquely in his whole kingship, he performed sacrifice in honour of Fear.

Irregularly, but whenever he had a victory to celebrate or the overcoming of an ordeal for which to give thanks, he staged literary and athletic ceremonies. On his arrival in Egypt, after crossing the desert of Sinai, 'he held a contest, both athletic and literary; the most famous artists in these branches came to him there from Greece'. After his return from the desert pilgrimage to Siwah, he 'sacrificed to Zeus the King, held a procession with his force under arms and held an athletic and literary contest'. Very Greek, and a reassurance to men far from home that military values need not obliterate the customs on which their culture centred. And he staged a similar ceremony after the ordeal of the desert crossing in Sind, making thanks offerings for his conquests in India.

Analogies could be made here of a cruder sort, with the camp theatre, football matches and horse-shows with which the British army in France during the First World War sought to preserve the illusion of normality in the minds of men assaulted by the horrors of the trenches. But Alexander's recourse to ceremony and theatre went far beyond the use of mere device. He was in the strongest sense a brilliant theatrical performer in his own right. Not only were his appearances in the field of battle dramatic stage entries, tellingly timed and significantly costumed, but he also had the artist's sense of how to dramatize his own behaviour when the mood of his followers failed to respond to reason, argument, threat or the offer of material inducement, or when he detected the opportunity to play the prima donna as a means of enhancing his legend.

Two of his *coups de théâtre* are known to anyone who knows anything at all about Alexander: his cutting of the Gordian Knot and his taming of Bucephalus. The significance of the knot-cutting remains elusive. Alexander took his sword to a famously tangled skein no man had been able to unravel, thus presumably demonstrating a radical impatience: the more complicated commentaries are for ancient historians. The taming of Bucephalus is an episode of universally straightforward appeal. This horse – 'in stature tall, in spirit courageous; his mark was an ox-head branded upon him', as Arrian tells us – was one of those fractious beasts whose breaking by a young unknown is a favourite staple of Western movies. Given to Philip by one of his generals, he defied the king, shying and stamping whenever approached. Alexander announced that he would mount him, seized his halter, turned him and leapt into the saddle, to the applause of courtiers and his father's tears of joy. The son's trick was to have noticed that Bucephalus shied at his own shadow and to turn him towards the sun.

The two were to be inseparable for twenty years – though Alexander commonly rode another horse to the edge of battle, mounting Bucephalus only for the fray, another ingredient of his theatricality. But he was equally adept at the extempore performance, word of each one of which – since he was never really alone – spread rapidly through camp and army to add to his myth. An excellent example is his entrustment of his life to the doctor Philip the Acarnian when he fell into a fever before Issus. The other doctors despaired of his life, but Philip claimed that he knew the cure. However, as he handed Alexander the medicine, a note arrived from Parmenio which read, 'Beware Philip; I learn that Darius has bribed him to murder you.' Alexander handed the note to Philip and simultaneously downed the draught, thus giving 'proof to Philip that he was his firm friend, to his suite generally that he trusted his friends, and showing also his bravery in the face of death'.

The relationship of the great with their doctors is one of the most interesting in the whole study of power; Alexander avoids the alternatives of paranoid suspicion and hypochondriac dependency in impressive style. There is also a glittering element of self-control in this exchange. In other scenes, however, his performance could topple over into melodrama. The notable episodes of over-acting follow crises in his relationships with his followers, the first when he fell into the notorious blood-rage with Cleitus, the second when he failed to persuade the army to follow him across the last river into the interior of India.

His rage with Cleitus was in itself the product of a long-standing dispute over theatrical court ceremony. After the defeat of Darius and seizure of the Persian throne, Alexander had begun to exact from his courtiers the performance of obeisances; these Asiatic customs were deeply repugnant to the egalitarian Macedonians. Cleitus, a bluff old cavalryman, outspokenly resented being required to bow and scrape. That did not provide the pretext for the quarrel between them that broke out one evening of heavy drinking, but it was the underlying cause. When harsh words were exchanged over who had done what, and who was the better man – Philip, Alexander, or, indeed, Cleitus, whose hand had once saved Alexander's life – the king's festering irritation boiled over. Its bloody and terrible result instantly sobered him. He was racked with self-reproach.

But he was not stumped for means to display it in the most theatrical manner possible. Justin tells us that, 'bursting into tears, he embraced the dead man, laid his hand on his wounds and confessed his madness to him as if he could hear; then, snatching up a weapon, he pointed it against his breast, and would have committed suicide, had friends not interposed'. Foiled, he retired to his tent, and took to his bed, according to Arrian, 'and lay there lamenting, crying out the name of Cleitus and of Cleitus's sister . . . who had nursed him. "What a fine gift of nursing he had given her . . . she had seen her sons die fighting and now with his own hand he had murdered her brother". He kept again and again calling himself the slayer of his friends, and lay three days without food and drink, and careless of all other bodily needs.'

Eventually, 'with some difficulty Alexander was brought by his friends to take food,' then to wash and dress, finally to perform certain ritual acts of sacrifice that he also reproached himself with neglecting. All in all his performance achieved a superbly effective transformation of focus from the crime to his repentance, and from that to others' concern for his own well-being.

In the episode on the river Beas three years later, when the army refused to follow farther, he replayed the act but this time without result. Words failed, though he pitched his appeal high, perhaps too high ('those who wished to return home might do so and could tell their friends that they had left their king surrounded by foes'). Realizing this, he retired to his tent, where he stayed alone, again for three days, 'waiting to see if the Macedonians would change their minds . . . But . . . there continued dead silence through the camp, and it was clear that the men were annoyed at his temper'. Prima donna and army had mismatched their moods.

Alexander found a graceful escape – that gift, too, was in his repertoire. But his crowd management was usually better calculated. At Opis, when he and the army again fell out after the return from India, the cause on this occasion being his alleged preference for his new Persian subjects over his old Macedonian trusties, he actually threatened to send home anyone who had a complaint about his leadership, reminded them in embarrassing detail how good he had been to each one of them – debts cancelled, parents provided for, the dead honoured, the brave decorated – and then flounced offstage (he actually spoke from a platform) once again to stay in his quarters for three days alone, until he deigned to admit his unquarrelsome Persian followers for a distribution of promotions and rewards. Melodrama this time almost overpaid its performance. His country-men besieged the palace like besotted fans at the stage door of a matinée idol, shedding tears and announcing that they would stay all night unless Alexander took them back into his favour; complained that the Persians were allowed to kiss Alexander – exactly what Cleitus and Callisthenes, another victim of his rages, had objected to, as they all had themselves – and demanded that Macedonians be admitted to the privilege; and finally showered him with kisses, while he managed tears of his own, they going back to camp afterwards 'shouting and singing their victory song'. This orgy of emotion culminated in a feast of reconciliation, at which the Macedonians were given the places closest to him and the Persians were seated farther down the table. Who exactly was fooling whom at this extravaganza, since all parties had by this stage got a considerable measure of what they wanted – the Macedonians a homeward turn, Alexander a full measure of untraditional obeisance – is difficult to judge.

He was also a master of the full-blown formal encounter between royal equals. Almost nothing in dynastic relationships matches the magnanimity shown by Alexander to the captured queen, brother and household of Darius after Issus. The women – Darius's wife was said to be the most beautiful woman in Asia, and Persians were noted for the purity of their looks – trembled in their tents awaiting outrage at the hands of the victors. Hearing their cries of mourning, for they had good reason to believe that Darius was dead, he sent a courtier to assure them that the Great King was still alive and that they would continue to enjoy royal status and the title of princesses of the blood. He was equally magnanimous seven years later to the Indian King Porus after the battle of the Hydaspes. He had beaten Porus fair and square after the hardest battle of his career. When his vanquished opponent was led before him, he asked what Porus wanted to be done with him. 'Treat me, Alexander, like a king,' was the reply. Alexander immediately restored him to authority, added to his territory and took future friendship between them as understood, a brilliantly calculated act of generosity that had exactly the effect intended.

At the very top of Alexander's range of theatrical performances was his dramatization of the natural occurrences of sickness and sleep. After the enforced decision to return from India, Alexander was wounded in a local engagement with an Indian tribe. The wound, though serious, was not mortal but gave rise to the rumour that he had died. The army fell into a panic, which, the accounts give good reason for suspecting, Alexander deliberately allowed to protract. 'Everything seemed to them hopeless and helpless,' Arrian tells us, 'if they had lost Alexander' – an entirely satisfactory mood for a leader to encourage in an army that had recently defied his will.

He did nothing to disabuse his soldiers' fears peremptorily. First he sent word that he was alive, which was not unnaturally disbelieved. Then he sent a letter to say they would soon see him again; 'even then most of them could not believe this for excess of fear . . . they thought that it was made up by his bodyguards and officers'. Finally, he had himself carried aboard ship, floated down-river and brought into sight of the army and his person exposed to view. 'But the troops even now disbelieved, saying to themselves that Alexander's dead body was being brought down, till at length . . . Alexander held up his hand to the multitude; and they shouted aloud, holding up their hands to heaven and crying tears of joy and relief.'

This extraordinary resurrection scene – little wonder that secular anthropologists find anticipations of the Christ story in the Alexander legend – has a parallel in his behaviour before Gaugamela. There, having made his plans and disposed his army as best he could in the face of the overwhelming Persian host, he retired to his tent and fell into a deep sleep. 'At the dawn of day,' Curtius tells us, 'the officers, repairing to his tent to receive orders, witnessed with astonishment unusual silence. He had been accustomed to send for them, sometimes reproving their delay. Now, the decisive crisis impending, he was not risen. Some suspected that he was oppressed not by sleep but by fear. None of his guards presumed to enter his tent, although the moment of action was at hand; nor dared the troops take arms or form into ranks without their leader's order . . .' Parmenio at length went into the tent. Having pronounced the king's name repeatedly, without effect, he awakened him with his hand. ' "It is broad day, Sir! The enemy approaches us, arrayed for battle; your soldiers, not under arms, await your orders." Alexander immediately directed the signal to be made for battle. And when Parmenio went on to express amazement that the king could have slept so soundly,' Alexander explained that he had been worried while Darius refused battle but now that he had been brought to offer it, he was perfectly at ease, because battle was what he wanted. It brought things to a head – and, though he did not say so, he was sure of winning.

Sleep in the face of danger, even if feigned, is a magnificent gesture of reassurance to subordinates. This episode before Gaugamela is one of Alexander's most sublime theatrical passages. The masterstroke, however, was his visit to the shrine of the God Ammon at Siwah. As Robin Lane Fox explains in a brilliantly exegetic passage of his biography, the shrine of Ammon marked the convergence of three Mediterranean cultures. Originally the home of a Carthaginian deity, it had subsequently been adopted by the Egyptians, who proclaimed Ammon the father of the universe. Alexander, the new Pharaoh after his conquest of Egypt, was therefore making a pilgrimage to the fount of his pharaonic kingship in visiting Siwah. But he was also paying homage to a shrine of his own favourite Greek gods, for the legendary Hercules, his chosen hero, had allegedly been there before him to worship the Ammon whom local Greek settlers venerated as a manifestation of Zeus, master of the universe in their pantheon. Ammon-Zeus was thus as powerful a totem as any Alexander would have attached to his own name.

What its oracle spoke as Alexander approached the place where its voice could be heard was consequently of central importance to the outcome of his epic. The lengthy detour the consultation entailed – that to Troy was the only other undertaken in the course of his anabasis – was justified only if Ammon-Zeus said the right thing. In the event the right thing was said, so fittingly right that it is churlishly alleged by some that Alexander had pre-arranged it. That seems unlikely; Alexander was devout, and the priests were in no sense beholden to him. Both sides, by the written accounts, seemed anxious only to play their proper parts; Alexander to pose his questions, the priests to see that Ammon-Zeus replied in the customary way, that is, by the shaking of the portable shrine in which his oracle resided. Alexander is rumoured to have asked if he would conquer the world. But that is only rumour. What is recorded by the best source is that the chief priest, deliberately or by a slip of the tongue, addressed him as 'Son of Zeus'.

This salutation may have been overheard by his entourage. It was certainly reported by his court historian, Callisthenes, and so transmitted to the army waiting in fertile Egypt for the return of its leader from his wilderness pilgrimage. He returned to it having 'received the answer his soul desired,' says Arrian, but it was also an answer that must have enormously enhanced the dimensions of his leadership and profoundly heartened his followers for the ordeal that lay ahead. 'The kings and heroes of myth and of Homer's epic', writes Robin Lane Fox, 'were agreed to be children of Zeus.' Alexander had identified himself from childhood with the heroes of the *Iliad*, the power of which over the Greek mind was general, not particular. By his dramatic journey to Siwah, therefore, he had promoted himself to a special relationship with the overlord of the universe. 'Zeus', Alexander was believed later to have said, 'is the common father of men, but he makes the best peculiarly his own.' In heroic warfare the best of men are rewarded by victory.

Alexander's Oratory

If Alexander was a supreme theatrical performer to the point achieved by the greatest of actors – not consciously calculating the impact of his performances, but letting its force transcend both his own and his audience's emotions – he was at the same time the most calculating of dramatic orators. Oratory, whose public importance in our own time has been overtaken by the small intricate skills of the electronic conversationalist, retained its power to move hearts and sway minds even into the age of the printed word. Two of the greatest orators of history, Lincoln and Gladstone, certainly derived part of their power from the familiarity which their graven images and reported speech imparted to their appearance and style on the platform. But the power of the spoken word in the pre-literate world is now difficult to retrieve. Story-telling and verse-speaking were callings by which men made a living; the *Iliad* and the *Odyssey*, for example, were both spoken texts for centuries before they were written down and were actually elaborated extempore to audiences which must have almost literally hung on the poet's word. Before the book, before even the theatre, the gift of speaking in a forceful and collected style to an assembled gathering was thought a semi-divine gift. It brought a livelihood to those who hoped only to divert or entertain; to those who sought or held power it multiplied manifold their ambition and authority.

Alexander certainly possessed the envied power of oratory to a supreme degree. How he exercised it we can now only guess. Before artificial amplification, speakers could be sure of carrying their voice to large numbers only by careful pre-arrangement. The Greek amphitheatre, carved from the backdrop of a steep hillside, was a device for ensuring that the audience not merely saw but also heard. A human mass absorbs and diffuses sound, and the more so the more densely packed. Armour perhaps helped to reflect and disseminate speech, though perhaps not. Certainly an army even of the comparatively modest size commanded by Alexander – 50,000 – was too large to hear him when addressed on open, level ground. Lincoln, for example, addressed 15,000 at Gettysburg and was heard badly; Gladstone was heard well by crowds of 5,000 or 6,000 but usually spoke indoors. Can we presume that Alexander took the trouble to parade his men in something like a natural amphitheatre, or at least against a steep hillside, before he spoke?

There were other devices he could have used to project his oratory. In the famous speech at Opis, during a crisis of his authority, he spoke from a platform; and before Issus he rode along the front of the army, presumably making the same short speech at several stops; he bade his soldiers 'be good men and true, calling aloud the names with all proper distinctions, not only of the commanders, but even squadron leaders and captains, as well as of any of the mercenaries who were conspicuous for rank or any deed of valour'. He must have judged the intervals just right – given 50,000 men ranked perhaps ten deep, he would have had to stop only ten times to be heard by 5,000 at a time – and, as his message was simple, it could have been relayed by almost simultaneous transmission from front to rear, a sort of Chinese whisper whose import would have actually enhanced the force of what he had to say. At any rate, 'there came an answering cry to him from all sides to tarry no longer but to charge the foe'. The roll of endorsing shouts running with his progress along the front would also have keyed his listeners to hear his words of encouragement. Sometimes he spoke only to a select group. During the Gaugamela preliminaries, for example, his pre-battle exhortation was an 'officers only' occasion, what the British army calls an 'Orders Group', from which subordinate leaders take back the word of the commander to their own units. Then he had a short and lighter message for each of the component contingents, which he perhaps thought best interpreted by the men who understood their own people.

But often Alexander's speeches were not simple or short. What did he say? The speech before battle was a rhetorical form well known and appreciated in the Greek world. Those that have come down to us from Alexander – through Arrian, Justin and Diodorus – reflect the conventions which those writers knew an Alexander speech ought to observe. It is doubtful if we can hear through them Alexander's actual words. But we can possibly catch the echo of his voice and probably the import of his message.

Thus, before the Granicus, his exhortation took the form of a dialogue with Parmenio. Dismissing the old general's counsel of caution and sensible warning that a river crossing in the teeth of the enemy courted disaster, Alexander declared that the only advantage the Macedonians enjoyed was their reputation for risk-taking and ferocity. Boldness was all. If they showed Persian prudence, they would suffer a Persian fate. 'Who dares wins' might perfectly encapsulate his message.

Before Issus he cast the net of his appeal much wider, in a speech embracing the local advantage the Macedonians enjoyed, their racial superiority and the special qualities of their allies. He dwelt on their tradition of victory and that of their predecessors in Persia, Xenophon's Ten Thousand, and urged on them the argument of 'one last push':

> We Macedonians are to fight Medes and Persians, nations long steeped in luxury, while we have long been hardened by warlike toils and dangers; and above all it will be a fight of free men against slaves. And as far as Greek will meet Greek [Darius's mercenaries] we shall not be fighting for similar causes; those with Darius will risk their lives for pay, and poor pay too; our troops will fight as volunteers from Greece. As for our foreign troops, Thracians, Paeonians, Illyrians, Agrianes, the stoutest in Europe and the most warlike, will be ranged against the feeblest and softest hordes of Asia; nay, further, you have an Alexander engaging in a duel of strategy against a Darius.

The challenge was arrogantly personal; follow *me* – and remember how I have led you into action before – against *him* the contemptible Darius and his haughty but hollow minions, and victory will result. Bare your breasts, stifle your fears, risk the chill of steel and the whole of Asia will fall into your grasp. You have done it before – 'he reminded them of all they had already achieved . . . any noble act of bravery he cited, both the deed and the man' – you can do it again. After that, 'nothing remained but to lord it over all Asia and set an end to their many heroic labours'. Little wonder that 'they crowded round and clasped their king's hand, and cheering him to the echo bade him lead on'.

But Alexander could fail as an orator. On the river Hyphasis (the modern Beas, a tributary of one of the five rivers of the Punjab),

which was to mark his farthest penetration into India, he invoked
any argument available to him: a review of their common successes,
the decreasing will of any enemy to resist them, the trifling extra
effort required to complete the conquest of the known world, the
superfluity of riches that would then fall to each of them – 'By
Heaven, I will not merely satisfy you, but will surpass the utmost of
good things for each of you' – and, finally, the ignominy of turning
back on the threshold of final victory: 'those who stay I shall make to
be envied by those who go back'.

But he was out-argued by the army's spokesman, Coenus, who
had the crowd with him from his opening words. The retreat from
India that followed may be counted Alexander's only real defeat, all
the more telling for being inflicted by his own men. Yet, shaken
though his confidence in his hold on the army must have been, it was
not destroyed. Two years later, at Opis, in Mesopotamia, when he
was faced by mutiny again, his silver tongue found the formulae that
had been wanting in the Punjab.

The difficulty to be overcome was, admittedly, different. In India
it was the army which wished to go, he to stay. At Opis, he tried to
rid himself of part of his army, the troublemaking veterans who had
been with him from the first, while they tried to turn the whole army
against him rather than bear the disgrace of dismissal. He sugared
the pill: those sent home were to be paid off handsomely. But the
bribe – and Alexander was a master of the technique of bribery – on
this occasion did not avail. His old-and-bold threw his bribe back in
his teeth, shouted that if he wanted them to go he should send the
whole army home and taunted him to carry on the fight with his
father-god, Ammon-Zeus.

The effect of their insolence was electric. In an uncharacteristic
outburst, Alexander fingered thirteen of the veterans for instant
death. They were 'to be marched off to die'. He jumped down from
his speaking platform to point out the victims to his entourage.
While the dumbstruck crowd watched the condemned men being led
away, he remounted his podium and launched into a harangue
almost unparalleled in nationalistic demagoguery. It is one of the
supreme performances of political theatre. He began by turning the
screw of the debt they owed to his father:

Philip found you vagabonds and helpless, most of you clothed
in sheepskins, pasturing a few sheep on the mountain sides,

and fighting for those against Illyrians, and Triballians and Thracians; Philip brought you down from the hills to the plains, made you doughty opponents of your enemies, so that you trusted not to the natural strength of your own villages but to your own courage. More, he made you city dwellers and civilised you.

The tribes who had been their former masters, he went on, became their servants and across their territory Philip opened a high road into Greece, down which he led the Macedonians to victory over Athens and Thebes – a victory of the weak over the strong scarcely to have been anticipated in the course of Greek history.

But, even so, it was a minor victory on the world stage on which Alexander himself operated:

I inherited from my father a few gold and silver cups, and more debts than assets. By borrowing he had managed to fit out the army for war; and then he had led it in a campaign of conquest without parallel. He had crossed the sea in the teeth of Persian naval superiority, taken Asia Minor and the cities of Phoenicia. All good things from Egypt which I took without striking a blow came to you.

Syria, Palestine and Mesopotamia, the treasures of the imperial capitals and the wealth of western India had all become Macedonian property; and that was true in a real sense, for his men knew that he lived no better than they did, woke earlier, worried worse and suffered wounds more frequently than any of them:

I have no part of my body, in front at least, that is left without scars; there is no weapon, used at close quarters, or hurled from afar, of which I do not carry the mark. I have been wounded by the sword, shot with arrows, struck from a catapult, smitten many times with stones and clubs – for you, for your glory, for your wealth.

He had cancelled their debts, loaded them with rewards and decorations, buried their dead, provided for their bereaved families. And now, because he wished to repatriate those no longer fit for war – a neat circumlocution of his more complex motives – they all wished to leave him. Well, then:

depart all of you. And when you reach home, tell them there

that your king, Alexander, victor over the Persians, Medes and Bactrians [then followed a long litany of his victories, ordeals and achievements] . . . tell them, I say, that you deserted him, that you took yourselves off, leaving him to the care of the wild tribes you conquered. This, when you declare it, will be no doubt glorious among men and pious in the sight of heaven. Begone!

This superbly dismissive speech was only the opening act of a three-day drama. Alexander, leaping from his speaking platform, returned to his quarters and shut himself in. After three days' seclusion, he announced that the high command appointments in the army were to be distributed among the Persians whom he had taken into his following, and that Persians were to be mustered as royal guards and some even nominated as Companions, most cherished of Macedonian relationships with the royal house. His old faithfuls, who had hung round the speaking platform since he had left it, were now unable to contain themselves. Running to his door they threw down their weapons, begged to be let in and shouted that they would stay there day and night until 'Alexander had some pity on them'.

Alexander now relented, came out, shed tears when they burst into tears and, as an ultimate concession, allowed those who complained that Persians were allowed to kiss him while they were not to give him kisses also.

To kiss the king was a right enjoyed only by his immediate kinsmen. In accepting kisses from Persians – the famous *proskynesis* of Persian court ceremony   he had therefore deliberately wounded his commoner followers, a hurt he now healed by making the right universal. Then, to seal the bond between the new kinsmen of such disparate backgrounds, he ordered a feast, sat Macedonians and Persians around him, with the former in nicely calculated positions of honour and the Persians beyond. He was careful to see, moreover, that they all drank from the same festive bowl and poured the same libations to the gods, 'especially for harmony and fellowship in the empire between Macedonians and Persians. They say that those who shared the feast were nine thousand and that they all . . . sang the same song of victory.'

Alexander on the Battlefield

Victory was the end to which Alexander's kingship, leadership of his army, management of his staff, mastery of theatre and command of oratory were all ultimately directed. Each one of his skills was an ingredient in the elaborate edifice of personality that was his generalship. But how did Alexander actually translate his talents into overlordship of his soldiers and subjection of the enemy?

His daily routine, unvarying even on days he awaited battle, was of key importance in assuring his followers that the mechanisms of control were in place and in operation. He rose early, having slept alone; the subject of his sex life obsesses his biographers but all are agreed that sex, whether hetero- or homosexual, was peripheral to him. Though he married, it was for reasons of state and there was no great passion, no Olympias, in his life.

After rising, he sacrificed, offering the body and flowing blood of animals to the gods in a ceremony only he, as their king, could perform for Macedonians. Then perhaps he conducted the business of the day, receiving his generals and officers of state; there was justice to be dispensed, taxes to be levied and distributed as pay, subsistence and court expenses, appointments to be made and revoked, the movements of the army and strategy of the campaign in hand to be discussed and arranged. At noon he took a short siesta and then undertook the rituals (to him also the pleasures) of the hunt, riding with his hounds after deer, wild horned sheep, wolves, bears or, if it could be found, the mountain lion; and he would also practise skill at arms with sword, shield and lance, against his companions. Alexander, unusually in a Greek, did not care for any athletic contest except wrestling.

Late in the day (though he also bathed on rising) came his bath; after Issus he made straight for the magnificent imperial bath in Darius's travelling palace. Finally, the day's climax, came dinner among his companions. The dinner among friends, important to all upper-class Greeks, was central to the life of the hero. It was an enjoyment and a relaxation, when the lyre was played, songs sung, verses declaimed, but also the forum in which personality was tested, wits sharpened, the limits of boasting and taunting measured, reputations assessed and challenges thrown down; on the more sober evenings, dinner was the time for an exchange of news and a consideration of the future; on wilder nights, talk could turn to quarrel, quarrel to violence, violence even to murder. Alexander, of course, was the arbiter of mood, and he knew and would impose the decencies. But, when blood was in the air and drink flowed, as it did on the terrible night of his assault on Cleitus, dinner could take a form that let no one forget he belonged to a society of passion whose ultimate expression was death.

It was from evenings such as these that Alexander was to go forth to battle. For an encounter with the enemy he dressed in a special and conspicuous style. Leaders of a later age – Frederick the Great, Napoleon when emperor (though not as the young general with a reputation to make), Wellington, Grant – affected an unostentatious appearance, but theirs was a style of leadership reflective and managerial rather than heroic; they were to 'lead' from the rear. Alexander, who led in the precise sense of the word, needed to be seen and to be recognized instantaneously, and he dressed accordingly. 'His helmet,' Curtius tells us, 'was of iron but so polished that it shone like the brightest silver; of its lofty, graceful crest, the nodding plumes were remarkable for their snowy whiteness. His body-armour was formed of double layers of linen, strongly quilted; a throat-piece of iron, enriched with sparkling gems, connected this with the helmet. From a superb belt hung a sword famed both for edge and temper . . . it was light and easy to wield. Under the breast-plate he sometimes wore a short military coat of the Sicilian fashion.' Over all, he slung a magnificent cloak and usually he had carried near him the sacred armour he had taken from the temple of Athena at Troy, reputed to be relics of the Trojan war.

Alexander was therefore unmistakable, all the more so when he changed horses for the famous Bucephalus. But he did not, of course, always fight mounted. Confronted by cavalry armies, as in the three great engagements with the Persians at the Granicus, Issus and Gaugamela, he rode. But in the small early battles on the northern Macedonian border he may not have done, and in his siege fights he went on foot, to share the labour of the siege engineering and lead his men where no horse could go; hence the frequency with which he was wounded at his sieges.

Alexander's wound history is a sort of shorthand index of his style of leadership. We have a record of eight wounds, four slight, three serious and one nearly mortal. Two of the slight wounds were inflicted later on in his epic, both by arrows shot during siege operations. Either might have been serious, since siege warfare is of its nature a close-range business. Two of the earlier wounds, both suffered in sieges, were severe. The last almost killed him.

By the end of his fighting career, Alexander was, as he chided the mutineers at Opis, literally covered by the scars of old wounds. We can document the nature of his wounding almost exactly; indeed, we know more about his traumatic history than we do of any other ingredient of his personal life. He had, so he said at Opis, been struck by almost every weapon available to an enemy: sword, lance, dart, arrow and catapult missile. He does not appear to have been touched at Chaeronea; we should certainly have heard of it. He was hurt slightly in one of the early Balkan battles but not at the taking of Thebes (where Perdiccas, one of the nearest Companions, was so seriously wounded) or even at the Granicus, where he certainly risked wounding: a Persian called Rhoesaces launched a blow at his head with a cleaver that took off part of his helmet. He was wounded for the second time at Issus by a sword in the thigh, though not badly enough to stop him visiting the gravely disabled immediately the battle was over.

Thereafter the wounds came thick and fast. At the siege of Gaza in the autumn of 332 he was struck in the shoulder by a shot from a catapult (presumably a large arrow) that penetrated both his shield and his quilted breastplate, suffering a wound for which he 'was not easily treated'. In 329, campaigning against mountain tribesmen on the River Jaxartes to the north of Afghanistan, he was 'shot right through the leg with an arrow and part of the small bone of the leg was broken'. Later in that year, besieging the city of Cyropolis in the same region, he was 'struck violently with a stone upon his head and neck'. In 326, in the siege of a city near the River Indus, he was slightly wounded by an arrow: 'the breastplate prevented the dart passing through his shoulder'. Shortly afterwards, in another siege, he was wounded on the ankle, 'not seriously, by an arrow from the wall'.

The increasing frequency with which Alexander was wounded as he led the army towards the limits of the known world implies a growing quality of desperation in his leadership and anticipated the probability of a serious wound (the arrow shot in the leg had been bad enough). At Multan in early 325 probabilities caught up with him. Multan, which was to undergo a ferocious British assault during the Sikh Wars 2,200 years later, was a city of formidable strength, encircled by a double ring of walls and towers. Impatient at the slowness with which his siege engineers commenced their deliberate procedures, Alexander put himself at the head of a small storming party and rushed the inner wall. He got to the top, found himself cut off and had to fight for his life. Over-exposed on the crest of the wall, he leapt down inside, put his back to the mudbrick beside a small fig tree and began to lay about him with his sword at a swelling body of attackers. For some moments he held his own, slashing and throwing stones. His attackers, deterred by his spitfire bravery, drew off and began to shower him with 'whatever anyone had in his hand or could lay his hands upon'. Three of his storm party jumped down to join him. One was shot in the face with an arrow. Shortly afterwards an arrow struck Alexander also. It penetrated 'right through the breastplate into the lung, so that', according to Ptolemy, 'breath together with blood shot forth from the wound'. Such a 'sucking wound' is extremely serious. Alexander contrived to resist for a while, 'but when a good deal of blood came forth, in a thick stream, as would be with the breath, he was overcome by dizziness and faintness, and fell there where he stood bending over his shield'.

The frantic intervention of his followers saved the king from immediate death. They slaughtered all the Indians within sword distance and managed to carry their stricken leader away on a shield. But his life still hung in the balance. The arrow was lodged in his lung and its extraction might have killed him; whether it was just pulled out, or whether the wound was enlarged with a sword – Arrian cites two accounts – the surgery was of the crudest. The result was 'a great rush of blood', while Alexander fainted again.

He was lucky. No large blood vessel had been touched, and the wound remained clean. But it took time to heal and the after-effect was permanent and disabling. 'He would never escape from it,' Robin Lane Fox points out. 'It would hamper him for the rest of his life and make walking, let alone fighting, an act of extreme courage. Never again after Multan is he known to have exposed himself so bravely in battle. True, no more sieges are described in detail, but when Alexander is mentioned he is almost always travelling by horse, chariot or boat. The pain from a wound, perhaps the lesions from a punctured lung, are a hindrance with which he had to learn to live.'

What this wound history suggests is a rising temperature of

commitment, almost as if Alexander's fever for victory rose with the tide of difficulty. For the difficulty did increase. Nothing succeeds like success goes the saying – true enough, no doubt, when a man sets himself targets within the value system of an established society. But Alexander sought his success not only in Macedonia, but in the greater world of Greece, then in the Persian empire – itself an assemblage of cultures – and finally in the far kingdoms of India. Along with the difficulties of mastering cultural variety was the sheer physical difficulty imposed by the increasing separation of the army from its base. Alexander's fighting force, it must be remembered, remained essentially Macedonian from beginning to end. It contained both allied and mercenary contingents from the start and was later enlarged to include substantial Persian elements. But its core was Macedonian, which had to be reinforced, relieved and replaced in accordance with unvarying military requirements. Men were killed, fell sick and had to be left on the line of march, demanded and were given leave, passed out of service by nature of age or unfitness. Twice at least Alexander sent large contingents home: after the Granicus in 334, when he granted home leave to all the men who had married before setting out; and on his return to Persia from India, when he discharged his veterans, the latter episode prompting the mutiny of Opis in 324. He equally received large increments of reinforcements and returning leave-men, particularly at Gordium in 333, at Susa in 331 and on the Jhelum in India in 326.

The marching of large contingents from home base to the field army was a major administrative feat, but an intermittent one and far less testing than his need to keep his men and animals supplied with provender on a day-to-day basis. Any hope of doing so by a chain of resupply points between Greece and his point of operations would have been quite unfeasible. As Donald Engels has pointed out in his brilliant and wholly original *Logistics of the Macedonian Army*, the supply animals would have consumed their own loads long before they were delivered to the men in the field, since eight days' worth of its own grain supply was as much as an ox could carry or pull. That span of time also fixed the distance from a port at which Alexander could operate when dependent on sea communications, as he often was. For much of the time, however, he was out of touch with both ships and home, and had to improvise supply as he moved. He did so by a system of makeshifts, involving 'prodigious long- and short-range planning. Preparations included the forming of alliances, often combined with the installing of garrisons or the surrender of hostages, to ensure the installation of magazines or provisions in desolate regions . . . the division of the army into several units when supplies would be difficult to obtain, forced marching to conserve supplies and the synchronizing of the march with the harvest dates throughout the conquered regions.'

Alexander greatly minimized the supply problems by enforcing the rules of movement that Philip had introduced. The Macedonians, unlike the Greeks (and many other epicene hosts which would come to grief at the hands of hardier enemies), were trained to carry their necessities on their own persons and to travel without servants, or women, or indeed any camp-followers who would have unnecessarily expanded the number of 'useless mouths'. As a result the number of animals in the column could also be kept low, since their burden-carrying could be confined to loads too bulky to split up into man loads – principally siege equipment, fodder and weapon reserves.

But the effort to drive his army forward, against the resistance of fears and uncertainties, as well as the sheer physical difficulties of the task, clearly made increasing demands on Alexander's reserves of spiritual strength. 'In sustained pursuit,' wrote General A. P. Wavell, 'mobility is dependent mainly on the personal will and determination of the commander-in-chief, which alone can keep alive the impetus of the troops.' Alexander's anabasis amounted to a continuous campaign of pursuit sustained by an even greater output of his own will-power, of which the increasing frequency and gravity of his wounds is the index. Unlike Napoleon, who shunned exposure as success permitted him to delegate personal leadership to subordinates, or Caesar, who risked exposure only in supreme crises, or the generals of the wholly post-heroic era, who actually deprecated resort to the dramatic, Alexander was forced to give more and more of himself to the prosecution of his epic as its dangers and difficulties increased. In that sense Alexander is the supreme hero. Nowhere do the dimensions of his heroic effort show more clearly than in his personal conduct on the battlefield.

Alexander's battles may be divided into four groups: the Balkan punitive strikes before the departure for Asia; the battles inside Persia and eastward of its borders after the defeat of Darius; the sieges; and the three great battles – the Granicus, Issus and Gaugamela – which brought Darius down. Too little is known of the second group, except for the Hydaspes, for much light to be shed from them on Alexander's methods of command. The first group is interesting as an example of Alexander's experimentation with his skills. The sieges tell us a great deal about his philosophy of risk-taking, self-exposure, example-setting and relentless output of energy. The fourth group demonstrates his genius for victory. Let us look at the three last groups in turn.

1 The Balkan Battles

The Balkan battles were fought against enemies – Triballians, Thracians and Celts – who were irritating rather than dangerous. In the past, before Macedon's rise, they had bullied and extorted tribute from Alexander's forefathers. That power was now denied them, but they could still make sufficient trouble in his rear for their suppression to be necessary before he could risk departing to Asia. Because of their diminished power, however, it was unlikely that they would allow themselves to be manoeuvred into positions where they had no alternative but to fight. It would be necessary, therefore, to put them at a disadvantage, one of the most difficult of all military operations. The prerequisites for success were speed, deception and the exploitation of the unexpected.

Alexander's first encounter was with the Thracians, who occupied land in what today are the mountains of southern Bulgaria. Its conformation prompted him to choose the Shipka pass as his point of entry into their territory; geography, of course, does not change, and it was in this same pass that the Turks sought from the opposite direction to block the advance of the Russians to the siege of Plevna in 1877. The Thracians, alerted to Alexander's intention, blocked the pass with waggons which they intended, if he pressed the attack, to roll down into the tight-pressed ranks of his phalanx.

Alexander summarily made what modern staff officers would call an 'appreciation' (*Lagebeurteilung*, as the Prussian staff officers, who later invented the term, would have said). Eliminating the possibility of 'turning' the position, he sent his phalanx onward, but with orders to the hoplites to open passages in the path of the waggons as they hurtled down, or to fall to the ground under the protection of their shields if the waggons could not be avoided. He himself did not lead the advance. as he might have done later, but waited to observe. As soon as the phalanx had survived the waggon

onslaught – the analogy with Roland at Roncesvalles is unavoidable –
he sent his archers to the left flank and took his 'shock troops', his
Foot Guards and the semi-barbarian Agrianians, in behind them.
The deployment of the archers – whose volleys would not have
carried more than 200 yards – tells us that he must have kept close to
the phalanx while it was under attack, else he would not have got to
hand strokes with the Thracians before they abandoned their
positions. In the event, they were too soon in breaking contact, were
caught by the more heavily armed Macedonians and 'casting away
their weapons fled helter-skelter down the mountain-side' (presumably the reverse slope).

Fifteen hundred men perished. They had made the mistake, to be
repeated time and again the world over by mountaineers in the
presence of really determined professional soldiers, of thinking that a
little artificial embellishment of the natural difficulties of their native
habitat permitted them to show defiance to an intruder at no risk to
themselves. Alexander, we may guess from his later reactions,
guessed from their attempt to strengthen their position that they had
no stomach for a fight and could be devastated if brought under
physical attack. Certainly it would be the case in all his subsequent
engagements that he took any improvisation of field defences as an
invitation to boldness and always attacked precisely at the point the
enemy had sought to make attack most difficult.

The next enemy against whom he marched, the Triballians, were
stouter folk. Their king, Syrmus, sent the tribe's women and
children to safety on an island in the Danube and then doubled back
with his warriors across Alexander's rear. He followed, caught them
pitching camp in a narrow valley and instantly improvised a plan: it
was to use the archers and slingers to provoke them into attacking
while he positioned his cavalry to left and right and stationed the
infantry in the centre under his own command. The plan worked
like a drill manual. Stung into leaving the safety of the glen by
showers of arrows and slingstones, the Triballians advanced, were
pincered by the foot and horse troops – the latter using bows from
the saddle until close enough actually to bump them with their
horses – and fled to the river. Some escaped into the dense
surrounding woodland but 3,000 died. Alexander's losses – as always
in edged-weapon warfare when one side suddenly gave way – were
trifling by comparison.

The third engagement of his Balkan campaign was an essay in

psychological warfare. The remnants of the Thracians and Triballians had taken refuge with Triballian women and children on the island in the Danube. Failing to get a foothold on its steep banks, he decided instead to cross the river to overawe the Getae, one of the troublesome northern tribes who lived on the far bank. He was joined by a small detachment of his fleet from the Black Sea, but this was too small to convey his army across the Danube, 'greatest of rivers', so he improvised rafts by stuffing leather tent covers with straw and commandeered a large number of the local dug-out boats. Choosing a landing place under a field of thick corn, he bivouacked his men for the night in the standing grain – 1,500 cavalry, and 4,000 infantry – and next morning led them out of hiding to attack the Getae. They were terrified by his materialization, discrediting anyone's capacity to cross the Danube in a single night at the unbridged point. They first took refuge in a nearby but weakly fortified town, then abandoned it altogether as he pressed onwards and finally fled into the wastes behind. Alexander destroyed the town and returned to camp. His point was made. In many ways the operation anticipated the German crossing of the Meuse at Sedan on May 13, 1940. Its success depended upon the enemy's incautious reliance on the natural strength of the position they were defending, their neglect to overwatch a vulnerable point and their failure to react resolutely against the enemy's foothold as soon as it had been secured. The Sedan crossing was to lead, of course, to the Blitzkrieg of France. South of the Danube there was nothing that justified Alexander making Blitzkrieg, and from its shores he therefore turned away.

The punitive expedition was not quite over and was to be concluded with the most difficult of the engagements so far ventured. The Danubian *coup de main* had induced the Triballians' neighbours hurriedly to offer promises of good behaviour. Others farther away, particularly the formidable Illyrians of the north-west, living in and near what is today Albania, seem to have been provoked by the news of Alexander's repressions to challenge his right to impose the Macedonian peace. They had raided into Macedonia as recently as Philip's reign and killed 4,000 Macedonians in battle only twenty-five years earlier. Alexander was therefore now obliged to take them on suddenly, to shift his axis of operations from right to left after four months of what he must have hoped would have been decisive action, and to make forced marches into their territory. The

1 Alexander the Great, portrait head from Pergamon, second century B.C.
The turn of the head and upward cast of the eyes are described by
Alexander's ancient biographers; the open brow, clean-shaven face, crisp
curls and intensity of expression set the pattern for 'heroic' portraiture in
European art ever after.

2 Alexander taming Bucephalus: nineteenth-century Italian engraving of antique sculpture.

3 *Above* Alexander and Darius at the Battle of Issus: Pompeian mosaic, second century B.C., copy of fourth-century B.C. painting.

4 *Below* Alexander at the Granicus: nineteenth-century Italian reconstruction.

5 Alexander and his mother, Olympias:
cameo, third century B.C.

6 Philip II of Macedon, Alexander's father:
attributed portrait bust, fourth century
B.C.

7 Alexander riding Bucephalus in battle: detail from the Alexander
Sarcophagus commissioned by King Abdalonymus of Sidon, fourth
century B.C. Alexander is wearing the lion-crest helmet associated with the
god Hercules.

king of the Agrianians promised to deal with one of the Illyrian tribes. Alexander therefore concentrated his effort against the most threatening of the others, a tribe called the Dardanians.

His first encounter with the enemy nearly ended in disaster. Though the Dardanians hastily withdrew into the city of Pelium (modern Gorice), leaving the grisly relic of three sacrificed boys, girls and rams as evidence of their initial intention to fight had the speed of his advance not shaken them, Alexander almost immediately found himself caught between two fires. A third tribe, the Taulantians, whom his Agrianian allies had not pinned down, suddenly appeared across his rear.

The safe decision would have been to retreat, particularly as he was now short of food: the prolongation of the campaign had exhausted the stores with which he had started, his army had eaten out the surrounding countryside and his men and animals were hungry. It was a decision he nevertheless rejected. Instead he sent out a foraging party to collect the harvest and graze the horses in a rich agricultural district some distance away, intending to plan his next move when re-supplied. The Taulantian chief prepared an ambush to trap the foraging party on its return, but Alexander, detecting the danger, drove him off by a rapid assault of picked troops which he led himself.

Though now fed, his army was still surrounded by troops holding positions – the fortified city to his front, high ground to his rear – too strong to attack. Willy-nilly he had to break out if he was not shortly to starve again, but his reputation would not stand a stampede or a *sauve qui peut*. He had therefore to devise that most difficult of operations, a fighting disengagement. He surveyed the lines of retreat that offered and, as he was so often to do in the future, opted for the most difficult piece of ground. His thinking clearly was that the enemy would presume the contrary, take time to react and so confer on him a moment of initiative. And at the exploitation of an initiative he was already becoming a master.

The escape route he decided upon was the Wolf's Pass, through which the small river on which Pelium stood flowed in a defile between high ground. To conceal his intention, he first formed up the army, 25,000 strong, in review order 'and manoeuvred various formations for a brief time'. The Illyrians may have thought they were watching some ceremonial performance. Alexander was, in fact, ordering his ranks for a breakthrough. When he suddenly unleashed his phalanx of spearmen, the nearest enemy took to their heels, abandoning the first line of obstacles they manned. He now ordered the army to 'clang their spears upon their shields' and raise. the Macedonian war cry, a deep-throated ululating *Alalalalai*, which frightened more of the enemy out of his path.

The army was now close to the Wolf's Pass and, though both its flanks were cleared, still had its line of escape blocked by the enemy holding the neck of the choke point. In mountain warfare, the rule is always to seize the high ground. Whether Alexander had been taught the rule or grasped it by intuition we cannot say, but, reacting as if he knew it, he struck to open an escape route by taking a mixed force of cavalry and infantry up the steep slope on the bank of the river, ordering the rest of the army to cross to the other bank in the confusion. Once it had secured a foothold, the archers and siege engines with it turned their fire back across the river, and under cover of that rain of missiles the mixed cavalry-infantry force disengaged, crossed the river themselves and rejoined the main party.

The brilliance of this all-arms operation, dependent as it had been on the nicest combination of shock and missile action, did not end here. His enemies again miscalculated, this time in the judgement that he would relax in gratitude for a lucky escape. Moreover he had abandoned his waggon train on territory they still held. They compensated by over-relaxing themselves, neither posting sentries nor entrenching their positions, and abandoned tactical formation. Hearing of their incaution, Alexander three days later recrossed the river under cover of darkness with his favourite striking force of Foot Guards, Agrianians and archers, made a surprise attack on their camp and, surprised himself by its success, countermanded orders he had left for the rest of the army to follow. The Dardanians and Taulantians scattered into the hills, burning Pelium behind them, leaving the waggon train to be repossessed, crowning Alexander's recovery from threatened disaster with the ignominy of their own ineptitude, and leaving themselves no political recourse but to make peace later on what terms they could get.

What to make of this five months of whirlwind mountain warfare? Alexander had advantages on his side: a splendid professional army, a clear aim and divided enemies. But advantages they too possessed: intimate knowledge of their own terrain, ready access to supply and the knowledge that they had more time and less to lose than he. Yet they had thrown away their advantages and he had maximized his. The besetting weakness of highland warriors, to be demonstrated over the centuries from Alexander's day to our own, and in places as far apart as Inverness-shire and Afghanistan, is that they over-estimate the difficulties that tackling their native peaks and passes present to heavy-footed but disciplined outsiders. Occasionally the outsiders get it wrong – as Charlemagne did in the Pyrenees in AD 778, the British at Gandamak in 1842, the Italians at Adowa in 1896 and the Spanish at Anual in 1921; over time, however, the re-morselessness of drill and heavy equipment almost always prevails. To those 'permanently operating factors', as Soviet military jargon characterizes them, Alexander added the entirely extraneous and personal variables of quite extraordinary boldness, flexibility of mind and quickness of decision. Whence he drew his dependency on choosing the apparently most difficult option as the most rewarding we cannot now guess. It may have been temperamental, it may have been intuitive, it may have been intellectual, it may have derived from observation of his father's own considerable penchant for the bald-headed and bloody spurred approach to the solution of military difficulty as the best. Whichever is not now important. The point to be observed throughout his subsequent generalship is that Alexan-der preferred the more to the less difficult among options and regarded evidence that the enemy had sought to increase the difficulty of a difficult option – by choosing a naturally strong position – as evidence of infirmity of purpose in the opposition. When he detected that the enemy had artificially enhanced the strength of a strong position – by fortification or the emplacement of obstacles – those signs seem to have clinched his conviction that it was there he should attack, since they signified that there the enemy was most vulnerable to attack, in psychic if not material terms. It is perhaps not going too far to say that Alexander, without benefit of Adlerian theory, had hit upon the concept of the inferiority complex and made its exploitation the kernel of his war-making philosophy.

2 The Sieges

Siege warfare, until the advent of rapid-firing weapons, was always – and rightly – judged the most dangerous of military operations. Indeed, in retrospect we can now see that the tragedy of the First World War was that the waging of siege warfare and the proliferation of rapid-firing weapons had suddenly coincided without the military establishment of the Western world having had time to detect their coincidence or draw the appropriate conclusions from it.

Siege warfare in the ancient world derived its danger from three factors: it was necessarily fought at close range, where muscle-power weapons were at their most effective; it equally necessarily demanded a high degree of bodily exposure from the attacking side; and it was intrinsically time-consuming. The impact of the first two factors could be minimized by the organization of counter-fire and the improvisation of siege shelters – towers, bulwarks and portable roofs. But nothing outside epidemic, treachery or collapse of will could shorten the 'natural' length of a siege – 'natural' here being a factor of the investment previously made in the bulk and complexity of the defences. Vauban, Louis XIV's great siege engineer, claimed that he could calculate to the day when a fortress would fall. No such certainties attached to siege engineering in the pre-artillery age, since the inherent strength of masonry far exceeded the power of human energy – whether stored in torsion siege artillery or expended in pick-and-shovel work – to bring it down. Siegecraft, therefore, took the form of navvying, itself exhausting and dangerous, to the dangers of which were added assault by missiles of every sort.

Alexander conducted more than twenty recorded sieges, and probably others as well: Thebes, 335; Miletus and Halicarnassus, both in Asia Minor, 334; Tyre and Gaza, on the eastern Mediterranean coast, 332; some six sieges in north-eastern Persia, 329; the Sogdian Rock and Rock of Chorienes, 328; an Aspasian city, Ora and the Rock of Aornos, all in the Upper Indus Valley, 327–6; Sangala, an unnamed Mallian city and Multan, all in modern Pakistan, 326; and three Brahmin cities on the lower Indus, 325. Because of the essentially stereotyped nature of siege warfare, however – 'deliberate siege' of the walls and headlong 'escalade' over them are the only available forms – only three of these deserve close attention: Thebes, Tyre and Multan.

Thebes is significant because it was the first of Alexander's sieges, at which he may have learnt an important lesson. It was not one he had sought. News of the rebellion at Thebes, which the Macedonians had garrisoned since it had accepted Philip's hegemony in 327, reached him on the Balkan border in October 335. The outbreak just missed coinciding with the successfully conducted Illyrian uprising, so that, by a forced march of 240 miles in thirteen days, he was able to reach the city before it had disseminated revolt any wider in Greece proper. What he found was a military conundrum: some Thebans at once showed they were ready to make peace; but the war party was not and had surrounded the citadel, the strongest part of the fortifications, with a double stockade. The stockade may have completely encircled the citadel, inside as well as outside the main walls, or merely have stood beyond the walls proper. In either case, Alexander could not make contact with the Macedonian citadel garrison except by breaching the temporary fortifications.

He decided to temporize, hoping that the will of the Theban peace party would prevail. But a hot-tempered subordinate, Perdiccas, who was occupying an advance post, decided to force the issue. Breaking through the first stockade, he was soon so heavily engaged that Alexander had to order a general assault. Advantage swayed one way and another in the narrowly constricted battle zone between the stockades and the walls, but eventually went Alexander's way. In their panic, the Thebans fled inside the city but were unable to close the gates behind them. The garrison in the citadel broke out to join the Macedonians flooding in through the abandoned gateways, and very shortly an appalling massacre began both inside the city and out, as many Thebans sought escape in open country.

This massacre in what had once been the foremost military city in Greece, as well as a cultural centre second only to Athens, thunderstruck the rest of the Hellenic League. Athens, in particular, which had a war party akin to Thebes's, performed the diplomatic kow-tow in its efforts to dispel Alexander's anticipated displeasure. And every other state – except, of course, for intransigent and pro-Persian Sparta – was equally placatory. Intend it though he had not – his initial impulse, as we have seen, was conciliatory – Alexander had thus learnt the heady lesson that frightfulness pays. He had not ordered the atrocities that filled the gutters of Thebes with blood and babies' bodies. But atrocity had won him the subservience of the Greeks with a peremptoriness that no amount of diplomacy or military menace could have achieved.

The siege may have taught him a tactical as well as a strategic lesson: that boldness can be rewarded as generously in siegecraft as in open warfare. Perdiccas, who recovered from the grave wound he suffered inside the Theban stockade to become one of Alexander's foremost commanders in Asia, had abbreviated what threatened to be a protracted and costly stand-off by yielding, in effect, to a rush of blood to the head. The spectacle of the danger to which he thereby exposed himself had fired the neighbouring Macedonians likewise, and the city had fallen to a torrent of bloodlust rather than tedious technique. The memory of Perdiccas at Thebes may have come back to Alexander ten years later and 2,500 miles away while his once-bold Macedonians procrastinated under the mud-brick walls of Multan in the Punjab.

Tyre, the city which he was to besiege in the fraught period between his initial success over Darius at Issus and culminating victory at Gaugamela, never looked to yield to the berserk approach, nor did Alexander contemplate it. An inhabited place to this day, scene of some of the bloodiest fighting in the Lebanese tragedy these last ten years, Tyre was important because its two harbours, located on the offshore island of New Tyre, gave anchorage to one of the strongest of Persia's fleets. Alexander could not continue his coastwise march into Egypt leaving the menace that force presented to his home base across his rear. From it the Persians could co-ordinate operations designed to dominate the eastern Mediterranean and Aegean or even rekindle the war in Greece.

But, as Arrian says, 'the plain fact is that anyone could see that the siege of Tyre would be a big business' – marvellously modern words that might come to us from MacArthur's Pacific or Margaret Thatcher's Falklands campaign. And absolutely true: New Tyre lay 1,000 yards offshore on a rocky island, was surrounded by walls 150 feet high, had a garrison of perhaps 15,000 'exceptionally able and brave' warriors, and was stocked with ample provisions. It was therefore unlikely to fall to treachery, starvation, disease or amphibious landing. Alexander came quickly to that conclusion himself and decided on an entirely Alexandrian alternative. He would alter geography.

Tyre today is joined to the coastline by an isthmus. Its core is the mole, 200 feet wide, which the Macedonians began to build under the orders of their king in January 332. They 'were eager for the work', Arrian tells us, but Alexander kept them personally to it. 'He was himself present, explained each step, and encouraged the workers, besides rewarding with a gift those who did any specially good work.' The description might be of Louis XIV's Vauban, supreme master not only of siege engineering but also of the psychology of siegecraft. The contradiction of siege engineering, as Vauban knew and Arrian succinctly puts it, is that the front-line men must be 'clad rather for work than for warfare'. Siege warfare is navvying under fire; armour must be laid aside; half-naked and sweating bodies are exposed to the enemy at close range, pick and shovel wielded in the closest proximity to men handling missiles and edged weapons. In circumstances like these, the example of leadership is not enough; men must be bribed and rewarded to run the risks. Alexander, running risks with the boldest, bribed and rewarded as the best of siegemasters were to do for centuries afterwards.

He also improvised ripostes to all the shifts and devices with which the Tyrians, indeed 'exceptionally able and brave people' (the characterization is that of N.E.L. Hammond, who campaigned in those parts himself), continued to delay the inexorable progress of the Macedonian works. A fireship was tried; it successfully incinerated the two siege towers, apparently the highest ever built, which Alexander 'had had pushed to the working end of the mole'. When Alexander assembled his fleet, the Tyrians sailed out theirs to give battle, withdrawing only when they found themselves hopelessly outnumbered. They countered his efforts to broaden the attack on the wall – with battering rams mounted on ships – by sending armoured ships of their own to sink them. They built towers and catapults with which to neutralize those of the Macedonians. They made a successful naval sortie, prepared behind a screen of sails in one of the harbours, to sink part of the Macedonian fleet.

Eventually, in July 332, after some months of unrelenting effort, Alexander succeeded in breaching the Tyrian fortification. He synchronized the assault with diversionary attacks elsewhere on the circumference, dropped bridges from his assault ships into the breach and poured troops into the city. A massacre ensued. Some 8,000 Tyrians died in the siege, presumably most by atrocity, since Macedonian losses throughout were only 400. The 30,000 Tyrians who survived were sold into slavery.

At Tyre Alexander had perfected his skill as a siege engineer already practised against Miletus and Halicarnassus, and he was to drag his siege train with him across the length of Asia (perhaps only the metal components; the timber parts could be improvised). But, as time pressed towards the climax of his anabasis, the army's reluctance to be drawn farther towards the end of the earth grew, Alexander's temper worsened and his patience for deliberate siege diminished. At the Rocks of Chorienes and Aornos (327–26), in and near modern Afghanistan, he undertook earth-moving operations akin to those of the Romans at Masada 400 years later. But in India proper (326–25), his siege tactics became peremptory and personal. At Sangala, he terminated a brief deliberate siege with a bloody assault. At the 'city of the Mallians' he simply attacked the wall himself, his followers in his wake, and was then 'here, there and everywhere in the action'. Finally, at Multan, he attempted to take the city virtually single-handed. It was thus that he suffered his nearly fatal wound.

How he came to brush so closely with death is worth attention in detail. Loss of strategic equilibrium – what Montgomery liked to call being 'off balance' – was part of the explanation. He was not, when he set out down the river Hydaspes (the modern Jhelum), in November 326, expecting an opposed passage. He anticipated a voyage of exploration which was to be the first stage of his return to the West. News that the Mallians, a people who controlled its lower reaches, intended to oppose his passage came as an unpleasant surprise. It was one to which earlier he would have improvised a businesslike countermove without discomposure. But he himself was probably also in a disturbed and frustrated mood. He was descending the Jhelum because his soldiers had refused to follow him to 'the end of the world', thereby opposing the *pothos* (headstrong desire) which was one of his most powerful springs of character.

When he came to make his assault on Multan, therefore, he was in no mind for 'deliberate siege' (easily arranged, with water transport at hand for his battering train) or for any delay in 'escalade'. He led an immediate assault in person on the outer walls and then led on against the inner citadel to which the Mallians fled. The main Macedonian body straggled after him, some with ladders, some without, most apparently believing that the city was now taken. Discovering their mistake, they began a disorganized assault, some digging at the citadel's foundations, others putting up ladders where they could.

Alexander now lost his temper. 'Thinking that the Macedonians who were bringing up the ladders were malingering', he seized one himself, set it against the wall, held his shield over his head and started up. On his heels were Peucestas, a Companion since child-hood, carrying part of the sacred armour taken from Troy as a token, and Leonnatus, the commander of the bodyguard. Both, no doubt, were terrified at the risk Alexander was running. He, however, was running almost amok. Reaching the battlements, he pushed some of the Indians off it with his shield, killed others with his sword and waited for his followers to join him in the foothold he had won.

They were so anxious to reach him – the crisis might have been contrived at an officer candidate school – that they overcrowded the ladder, which broke, decanting those at the top on to those at the bottom and so stopping anyone getting to Alexander's help. He, 'conspicuous both by the splendour of his arms and by his miraculous courage', was now under attack by bowmen at close range. He could not remain where he was. He would not jump down to safety. He therefore jumped into the city and began to lay about him with his sword as if Gulliver among the Lilliputians.

The sequel is known to us. He was nearly killed, rescued from death almost at his last heartbeat and never the same man thereafter. But, as we have seen, he thereby terrified his army into the most extreme display of 'Alexander worship' of which we have record, stage-managed a bizarre resurrection ritual and succeeded through it in bringing about a reconciliation between his 'old' (Macedonian) and 'new' (Persian) army which he might not have been able to achieve in any other way. His ability to turn almost any shift of fortune to his advantage had survived undiminished.

3 The Great Battles

If Alexander's sieges tell us a great deal about the inner nature of heroic leadership – exemplary, risk-taking, physical, passionate – the experience of leadership in siege warfare undoubtedly taught Alexander a great deal also. Halicarnassus, Tyre and Gaza were stages in his apprenticeship for the climactic struggle with Darius that had begun with his little Balkan battles against the Thracians and Illyrians in 335.

But mountain skirmishing and siege warfare cannot substitute tutorially for the test of leadership in pitched battle. It is on the open field, when armies clash face to face in the grip of those terrible unities of time, place and action, that a man's real powers of anticipation, flexibility, quick-thinking, patience, spatial perception, thrift and prodigality with resources, physical courage and moral strength are tried to the extreme. The trial is potentially destructive for any leader; perhaps no fate on earth is worse than that of the defeated general who must live out his days with the burden of

wasted life on his conscience. For the heroic leader it is destructive
in the most direct sense. To know when and how to risk his person
entails a narrowness of choice between death and triumph.

Alexander's three decisive pitched battles – decisive because they
attached to the central issue of defeating the Persian empire – fell out
for him in extraordinarily fortunate sequence. He was able to fight
the first, the Granicus, at the nearest periphery of the empire and in
the absence of Darius, whose presence might have spurred his
subordinates to victory. At Issus he fought on equal terms against an
enemy of whom he had taken the measure. At Gaugamela, though
seriously outnumbered, he enjoyed the supreme advantage of having
once already driven the opposing king ignominiously from the field.
Had he had to fight a psychologically unshaken Darius at the head of
superior numbers at the Granicus, the anabasis might have terminated there.

Yet, for all that Alexander brought large and then enhanced
self-confidence to each of the decisive battles, he also brought an
integrated command technique. What was it?

It essentially partook of two elements: first, the belief that the
enemy would, if the signs were read aright, betray where he most
feared attack, thereby signalling a psychological vulnerability that
was more important than any imagined physical frailty; second, the
determination to place himself at the head of the culminating attack
at that point.

Both elements are clearly detectable in his conduct of the battle on
the Granicus. Parmenio, as we know, argued with him to postpone
battle. They had arrived not earlier than the middle of the day – it
was late May or early June 334 – after three days' march from the
landing at Abydus forty miles to the east. Parmenio disliked the
prospect of making an 'opposed river crossing' against an enemy
already drawn up for battle on the far bank. He disliked the risk of
losing cohesion as the army crossed a fast-flowing stream. Above all,
he disliked the lie of the land. 'There are many deep parts of the
river,' he pointed out. 'Its banks, as you see, are very high,
sometimes like cliffs.'

Alexander could not have failed to note exactly that. And it must
have told him something that he very much wanted to know: the
Persian commanders were trusting to terrain features to defeat the
enemy attack, rather than to their own tactical skills and powers.
Ten years later, at Opis, he would remind the mutinous Macedo-

nians that his father had taught them to trust not so much 'to the natural strength of your villages but to your own courage'; it was that transformation of attitude that had made them 'doughty opponents' of their neighbouring enemies. If the Macedonians had learnt that lesson, how much more so Alexander, who had been taught it at his father's knee. He dismissed Parmenio's objection peremptorily – and, significantly, in explicitly topographical terms: 'I should feel ashamed after crossing the sea from Europe to Asia if this little stream should hinder us.'

Lest delay encourage the Persians to think that for one moment, he gave orders immediately for an attack off the line of march. The phalanx was already in battle formation and he brought it up to the river bank. To its left he sent Parmenio with part of the cavalry; on the right he took station himself with the rest. For a while he allowed the Persians to contemplate the spectacle of the Macedonians arrayed for attack. They, who had left their infantry in second line on a ridge to their rear, now thickened their cavalry ranks opposite the spot where they could see Alexander in his magnificent battle costume.

What could Alexander see? For some time he held the army in check, perhaps waiting for the dust, raised by the deployment of some 40,000 horse and foot, to settle, probably also to deepen dread in the enemy cavalry's hearts. They, 20,000 strong, were drawn up along a front of some 2,000 yards, and so massed ten deep. If in close order, each file of horses would have occupied a strip of ground 100 feet from first nose to last tail. Only those in the front ranks could have seen anything but their immediate neighbours. Alexander's view, on the other hand, would have embraced the whole mass; he could even have kept their further flank under observation from his station on the opposite bank.

Did he wait for evidence of some tremor in their ranks? Horses experience fear, and are particularly suspectible to the sensation of fear in their riders. It may have been a ripple of movement, signifying indecision or momentary loss of nerve, that precipitated his order to advance. Whatever the trigger, at some moment Alexander 'flung himself on to his horse' – a page would have been holding Bucephalus's head – called his suite to follow, ordered a screen of foot skirmishers and Paeonian light cavalry to advance and followed in their wake.

Within seconds – the river is only 100 feet wide – action was joined. It fell into four phases: contact, cavalry engagement, infantry advance, culminating slaughter.

Contact was joined under a shower of javelins, launched by the Persians from their commanding position. The Greek light troops, inclining to their right against the flow of the current, suffered badly and were turned back at the far water's edge, to which the Persian cavalry began to crowd down.

It was at this point that Alexander intervened. Riding at the point of the leading heavy-cavalry rank, 'he charged into the press . . . where the Persian commanders were posted'. With a press of his own numbers building up behind him, the fight thickened. 'It was a cavalry struggle, though on infantry lines; horse pressed against horse . . . trying to push the Persians from the bank and force them on to the level ground, the Persians trying to bar their landing and hurl them back into the river.'

The Macedonians' equipment gave them an advantage, their lances having a longer thrust than the Persians' javelins. Alexander nevertheless ran a terrible risk. The enemy were out to kill and nearly did so. His lance broke and he fought with half of it until a subordinate passed him another. One Persian, as we know, got close enough to land a blow on his helmet; a second was raising an arm over him when a bodyguard got his thrust in quicker.

Conspicuous leadership was now a factor out of play; in the swirling mass of men and horses, Alexander was but one warrior lost among many. But his initial plunge had already done its work. The Macedonians had followed en masse and were pressing the Persians back by weight of numbers and frantic determination. The first collapse of their front occurred 'at the very point when Alexander was bearing the brunt of the affray'. A collapse in the centre, where the Macedonian phalanx was now engaged, followed. Soon the collapse was general. The Macedonians took possession of the level ground above the steep river bank, and the Persian cavalry 'turned to flight in earnest'.

They must have streamed off to the flanks leaving their Greek mercenary comrades on the ridge behind to fend for themselves. Those heavy infantrymen were shortly attacked in flank by the Macedonian cavalry and in face by the Macedonian phalanx. 'They stood,' says Arrian, 'rather rooted to the spot by the unexpected catastrophe than from serious resolution.' That is a phenomenon reported time and again from battlefields: the rabbit-like paralysis of soldiers in the face of a predator's unanticipated onslaught. They were shortly surrounded and hacked down on the spot. If reputed figures are accurate, some 18,000 died. It is not impossible. Some 60,000 Romans are said to have been killed in the encirclement battle of Cannae 150 years later.

Alexander's victory not only was thus complete, but had wholly vindicated his initial appreciation and operational method of command; in the modern sense, there had been none at all. After making his dispositions and issuing his orders, he had exercised no general control over the battle, nor could he have done so, being thrust so deep into the action that he had no time or thought for anything but a fight for life; 'heroic' leadership had nevertheless done its work. The knowledge that their king was taking the supreme risk drove capable and well-briefed subordinates, at the head of drilled and self-confident troops, to fight as hard and skilfully as if he had been at the elbow of each one of them.

At Issus Alexander was to confront his antagonist for the first time in person – literally, in the later stage, face-to-face. It differed from the Granicus in its strategic prodrome; at the former battle, the Persians, having made the mistake of letting the Macedonians get ashore unopposed, merely stood to receive them athwart the first defensible position on their natural line of advance. By the winter of 333, after Alexander had been abroad in Asia for eighteen months, they had learnt to take him more seriously. They were determined to manoeuvre for an advantage, just as Alexander was himself. In early November, therefore, Darius, who had come up with a large army from Babylon, was putting out feelers across the Taurus mountains, which fringe the Mediterranean shore at its corner between Asia Minor and Syria. Alexander, who had just recovered from a serious illness, was probing westwards along the coast, looking for Darius either in the hinterland or beyond in Syria proper.

False information prompted him to make his ill-judged dash into Syria. By the time he was better informed, Darius had got across his rear, captured the heavy equipment and hospitals he had left on the banks of the Pinarus river and was awaiting battle there. Alexander now had to fight, like it or not, to recover his prestige, his siege train, his line of communication with home and, most important of all, access to immediate re-supply. Fight or starve. It was all the more reason to make Issus the decisive battle he had sought since entering Asia.

The sequence that had preceded action at the Granicus now unrolled. The Persians, who had been in position for thirty-six hours, were already in line of battle; their number, inflated as in all accounts of war coming down to us from antiquity, was certainly larger than Alexander's (about 40,000). Consisting of Greek mercenary infantry, Persian élite cavalry and more humdrum foot and horse units from the empire at large, they may have numbered 100,000 or 200,000; Engels, unsurpassably the most exact of the commentators, suggests 160,000. Darius had arrayed them – there was not much choice in pre-gunpowder times – with cavalry on each flank, slingers on the right, and infantry in the centre, across a front of some 4,000 yards. He and his entourage had taken station behind his best troops, the Greek mercenaries, towards the left wing.

Alexander, having addressed his officers in stirring terms, conformed; he also put cavalry on each flank and infantry in the centre, himself taking post himself on the wing nearest Darius. Because the Persians had occupied high ground on his right, he also threw out a series of archers, horsemen and light infantry in that direction; 'refusing' that flank would be the technical term. He then ordered the advance, but at a slow pace, despite shouts from the ranks 'to charge the foe', 'with halts, so that their advance seemed a leisurely affair'.

Commentators have generally explained these stops and starts as part of a plan to smuggle forces unperceived to the right wing, or to provide an opportunity to assess the Persian order of battle. It seems much more likely that, as at the Granicus, Alexander sought to inspire dread in the ranks of the enemy who, he once again detected, were 'trusting to the natural strength' of the position rather than to their own courage. The evidence, indeed, was unmistakable. For, rather than just lining the high banks of the river, as at the Granicus, here the Persians had actually improved on nature, 'in some parts building up palisades' where the banks were not 'precipitous'. 'It was here,' says Arrian, 'that Alexander's staff perceived Darius to be a man of no spirit.' This was a harsh, indeed contemptuous judgement, but it went straight to the point. Two thousand years later, when the North European 'Philhellenes' came to help the Greeks fight their war of independence against the Turks, they would take it as evidence of how far Alexander's kinsmen had degenerated into servility that they were prepared to face their oppressors only after they had constructed just such palisades on their chosen field of battle. Another ancient writer expresses the idea of servility even more exactly: 'It was at this point [seeing the stockades] that those around Alexander realised quite clearly that Darius was slavish in his ways of thought.'

Given his initial moral superiority, Alexander's chance of victory in the battle to come was far better than the disparity of numbers implies. He himself was unshaken by doubt. When within charging distance he had ridden along the ranks to urge his men to be brave, hailing the officers and any well-known fighters by name. Then, followed by shouts that can be summarized as 'Get on with it', he returned to his command position and led on.

The battle that followed, though altogether larger in scale than the Granicus, was cruder in form and quicker in conclusion. 'All fell out as Alexander had guessed.' He simply charged across the river at a moment of his choosing, passed rapidly through the Persian archers' impact zone and struck the cavalry formation around Darius so hard that it gave way 'the moment the battle joined'. Darius took to flight and Alexander followed.

In the centre, where the Persians' Greek mercenary infantry had locked spears at the outset with their Macedonian counterparts, the fighting was 'severe'; the Greeks tried to push the Macedonians into the river – and had some success; not all the Macedonians got 'to work with like enthusiasm' (an unusual incidence of ragged morale); some were impeded by the steepness of the banks; the whole phalanx lost touch on the right with its cavalry supports as Alexander charged deep into the Persian line. This brutal scrimmage – the unusually high total of 130 Macedonian spearmen were killed in what must have been quite a prolonged, noisy, angry, fear-smelling bout of shoving and thrusting – was resolved only when part of the Macedonian right-hand cavalry wing managed to overlap the Greek mercenary left. They were charged in turn by Persian cavalry but held their own, sustained the outflanking move and so eventually 'rolled up' the Persian line. Once it began to concertina, it gave way along its whole length and took to flight.

Persian losses in the rout that ensued were heavy; the chase extended over twenty-five miles to the foothills of the Taurus, and strewed the plain with dead, many of them élite Persian cavalrymen whom the Macedonians had singled out as their target. The purpose was to break the strength of the class on which Darius directly depended for support. He himself managed to keep ahead of the chase. Abandoning his family, his travelling palace, eventually even the royal chariot, Darius was able to find a pass through the mountains which eventually led to safety on the far side of the Euphrates. Alexander was not to confront him again for twenty-three months. In the intervening period he conducted the great sieges of Tyre and Gaza, thereby destroying the basis of Persian naval power in the Mediterranean, incorporated Egypt into his growing empire, visited Siwah and subdued resistance in Syria and what today is northern Iraq. Darius meanwhile lay doggo, reconstructing his army, gathering supplies for a major campaign and waiting for Alexander to make a wrong move. Ultimately, he knew, Alexander must come to him, in the heartland of the empire, and he was prepared to use space and time to offset the advantage of superior operational ability that the young king demonstrably possessed. If we were looking for an historical analogy, it might be found in Stalin's strategy in Russia in 1942: that of letting distance exhaust the enemy until 'overstretch' in unfamiliar terrain exposed his élite formations to a decisive counterstroke. In November 1942 that counterstroke was to be at Stalingrad, in October 331 BC at Gaugamela.

Alexander was, however, to prove better at making space and time work for him than was Darius. The emperor had calculated that the Macedonians, from their base in Lebanon, would march through the top quadrant of the Fertile crescent to the headquarters of the Euphrates and then descend through the central Mesopotamian valley towards Babylon, the emperor's winter capital and current base. It was a reasonable prognosis, but it was wrong. Alexander decided, perhaps because of the appalling summer temperatures that prevail there (110 degrees Fahrenheit is common), to avoid the 'land between the two rivers', cross *both*, and march southwards along the eastern bank of the Tigris.

News of this unexpected turn-out threw Darius into precipitate action. Breaking camp at Babylon he marched northwards, sending scouts ahead to locate the Macedonian army. Some of those fell into Alexander's hands. From them he learned of the movements of Darius, while the latter remained in ignorance of his. Because that was so, but knowing that Alexander must cling to the Tigris for reasons of supply, Darius decided to choose a strong position across its upper reach and await Alexander there.

The site he chose at Gaugamela, on a tributary of the Tigris called the Boumelus (Greater Zab), is an absolutely level plain some eight miles square, which Darius improved as a cavalry arena by levelling it further, and, one account says, even making three 'runways' for his chariot force.

This engineering may have been necessitated by the truly enormous size of his army; even disallowing the familiar exaggerations of ancient writers, it must have outnumbered Alexander's 50,000 several times, for Darius had assembled troops from every remaining corner of his empire. Arrian mentions twenty-four nationalities, of whom some, like the Scythian steppe horsemen, had formidable reputations.

Many of the rest did not. Darius had over-insured by including too many contingents of inferior or negligible worth, who in action would merely get in the way of the serious warriors. But the latter's number was large enough seriously to concern Alexander. That factor, and the care Darius took to prepare the ground, caused him to approach battle at Gaugamela with altogether more caution than he had ever displayed before. His caution showed in four ways: reconnaissance, timing, psychological preparation and tactical method.

Having identified where Darius stood, Alexander spent four days resting his army and building a secure base; the baggage train was emplaced inside an entrenchment. Then on the night of September 29 he advanced the army in order of battle to within attacking distance, halted again, and held a staff conference. Most of his officers were for attacking at once, although Parmenio argued for making 'a complete survey of the whole ground . . . and a thorough reconnaissance of the enemy's dispositions'. It is evidence of how determined Alexander was to get this battle right that he now yielded to the advice of his prudent old general, so different in temperament from himself, and overruled the others.

He would not, however, accept Parmenio's suggestion, made the following evening after a day spent spying out the land, that he should lead the army in a night attack. There were sound military reasons for rejecting it: that, if the night attack went wrong, the Macedonians would be lost in terrain familiar to the Persians but not to themselves. There were wiser commonsense reasons. Alexander was resolved neither to 'steal a victory' nor to chance anything 'too risky'. For all his achievements so far, he was still a highland prince from the hinterland of Greece. If he won in a night attack, Darius might cry 'foul' and continue to rule; if he lost in a night attack, the more fool he and goodbye to him.

So much then for timing; he would fight by light of uncommon day. As for psychological preparation, it was excellent sense to keep the Persians standing to arms throughout the night of September 30, as they did in expectation of a night attack which 'they had feared all along', with a fear 'not suddenly created from the crisis of the moment, but long dwelt on' so that it 'unnerved their minds'. It was even better sense to keep his speech before battle short. He merely urged his officers to 'think of discipline in danger'; to keep 'complete silence when they must go forward in silence'; to 'cheer when it was right to cheer'; to raise 'the most frightful battle-cry when it was time to raise it'; to obey orders and to pass them on smartly; and to remember that in the individual's 'neglect there was universal danger, in his own diligent achievement universal success'.

This model address but briefly anticipated Alexander's initiation of the first truly unstereotyped tactical plan he had ventured so far. At the Granicus and Issus he had simply charged to glory. At Gaugamela, where he was both outnumbered and irremediably overlapped, he had to devise a more subtle means to win victory. His adoption of the revolutionary tactics used by the Theban general Epaminondas against the Spartans at Leuctra was so creative that it may be judged an innovation in its own right. Epaminondas had merely, in defiance of convention, overmassed one of his wings against one of the Spartans'. Alexander went much further. By arranging his army in conformity to the Persian order of battle – infantry in the centre, cavalry to left and right – and then marching it *obliquely* across the enemy's front until his right wing made contact with their left, he anticipated by 2,000 years the tactics that would make Frederick the Great the most celebrated soldier of Europe in his time. It was a supreme risk to take in the gamble for a supreme prize.

The gamble paid off. Darius, instead of ordering his army forward to assail the Macedonians while their left sides were turned to his front, inertly awaited their assault. As soon as the head of Alexander's column – he was, naturally, there – touched the Persian line, their cavalrymen indulged him by charging to outflank it. As they did so, they lost contact with their infantry centre, opening the gap for which Alexander had been looking. He charged into it at the head of his Companion squadrons, 'actually hustling the Persians, and striking their faces with their spears', exactly as had happened at the Granicus. The psychological shock was too much to bear. 'Darius,' at whose position behind the centre Alexander had struck, 'nervous as he had been all along' and seeing 'nothing but terrors all around . . . was himself the first to turn and ride away.'

That was the end of his emperorship, though it was ten more months before Alexander cast eyes on his corpse. A few moments' resolution at Gaugamela might have spared him all the indignity and suffering that lay ahead. For, even as he turned to make his escape, the Macedonian phalanx fell into trouble. Perhaps in trying too hard to keep pace with Alexander's mounted advance, something infantrymen cannot do, it lost cohesion in the centre. At any rate, a gap opened in its front through which some Persian and Indian cavalry poured, galloping on to reach Alexander's entrenched baggage camp, where a body of Persian prisoners joined in the action. (A very similar incident occurred during the battle of Agincourt.) Parmenio sent a galloper to beseech Alexander's return and he, temporarily abandoning the pursuit, turned back to join in what for a time was a very bloody cavalry fight indeed: 'there was no javelin-throwing and no manoeuvring of horses . . . but each tried to break his way through . . . as men now no longer fighting for someone else's victory but for their very own lives'. Sixty of the Companion cavalry fell in this struggle, the resolution of which delayed the resumption of the pursuit for some time. When Alexander was free to take it up again, Darius had put enough distance between himself and the ruin of his kingship to get clear away. In his wake he strewed the panoply of glory: his treasure, his spear, his bows and his chariot. With them, the fire and burning gold of power passed to the new Lord of Asia.

Alexander and the Mask of Command

Gaugamela, though leaving Alexander much campaigning to complete in the recesses of the Persian empire, was that rarest of events, a truly decisive battle. It substituted, by right of conquest, the legitimacy of his rule for that of Darius, and, after Darius's death at the hands of treacherous courtiers in July 330, reduced all who opposed him to the status of rebels. By the summer of 328, at the end of a campaign that had telescoped into two years' fighting as much pacification as it took the British in India a century to achieve after Plassey, he had established his authority over the whole of the empire and was poised to march 'to the end of the earth'.

Alexander's triumph was, therefore, complete by the evening of October 1, 331. He was not materially to add to his extraordinary – in the truest sense unique – success. How had he achieved what he had?

Historians and biographers by the hundred, would-be imitators by the dozen, have sought the answer to that question. At two extremes, Sir William Tarn, who devoted his life to Alexander's, ultimately conceived him to be a sort of pre-Christian saint; Ernst Badian, a refugee from twentieth-century totalitarianism, saw him as a sort of Hitler in prefiguration. Among fellow conquerors, Pompey called himself a second Alexander, Caesar wept at not having accomplished by the same age a fraction of his achievements, Augustus worshipped at his tomb, Trajan claimed to have surpassed him, Napoleon thought the study of his life the supreme military education. None of his imitators – not even Napoleon – equalled or even approached him in conquests, while both Tarn's and Badian's characterizations are travesties (even if the latter is nearer the truth than the former).

It may be that both imitators and analysts have failed to 'find' Alexander because they have been searching for an 'inner', an 'essential', a 'real' Alexander which did not exist. Alexander's inner life is almost entirely unknown to us. We have no word-for-word record of anything that he said or of anything that he wrote. He left no code of laws, no theory of war, no philosophy of kingship. He certainly kept no diary and, if he communed with himself, he confided in no one. Alexander may not have been a mystery to himself, but he is a mystery to us. All that we have as clues to the wellspring of his achievement are the accounts of the technique he employed to establish his mastery over men – his friends, followers and enemies – and a sketch of his self-presentation to the world.

His technique, though characterized above all by violent, impetuous and apparently unreflecting action, was by no means entirely impulsive. He was an incisive strategist – as his meticulous logistic arrangements, now reconstructed, and the consultative format of his staff conferences, recorded by Arrian, demonstrate. In the management of his army he was materially practical and psychologically acute: his men were well fed and promptly paid, rested, entertained, flattered, rewarded and granted leave. The brave were decorated, the sick tended, the wounded praised and comforted. Alexander punished when he had to, bribed when he had to, never forgot that homesickness and the strain of celibacy were afflictions he had imposed on his followers. Superhuman though he sought to appear, he accepted and indulged the ordinary human nature of his soldiers.

In the management of his immediate circle he could not assume the Olympian manner he often chose to present to his men. Some of the circle had known him from childhood; all dined and drank with him in the intimacy of the evening feast. But precisely because they knew him so well and competed so strongly for his attention and favour he had to show them a harder and more calculating face than he offered to the common run. Power corrupts, but its real corruption is among those who wait upon it, seeking place, jostling with rivals, nursing jealousies, forming expedient cabals, flaunting preferment, crowing at the humiliation of a demoted favourite. The life of the camp corrupts less than that of the court: battle tests the real worth of a man as politics never can. But even in Alexander's warrior circle resentment seethed. Thrice it boiled over into plots against him: that of Philotas, Parmenio's son, in 330; that of the 'Old Companions' at Samarkand in 328; and that of the pages in 327. In each case Alexander moved with ferocious rapidity to preserve his authority. In 330 he used torture to extract confessions, then had the conspirators stoned to death, finally sent agents to kill the principal's father, his old general, whom he probably unjustly suspected of complicity. In 328 the quarrel with the 'Old Companions' led to the appalling murder of Cleitus over the dinner table. In 327 he had the pages – one of whom resented a public beating – stoned to death and his court historian, Callisthenes, imprisoned on suspicion.

Significantly all three plots postdate the great battles: they fomented in the period when Alexander had come into the plenitude of his power, not while he was still striving after it. Alexander the young general was not troubled by conspiracy. All eyes were then focused on his extraordinary battlefield performances, attent to see how he would next humiliate the Persians. His technique in the face of danger we have already established. Reconnaissance and a staff discussion preceded the advance to contact. Then he addressed his men, sometimes the whole army, sometimes only their officers. Finally, when the light troops and cavalry had made touch with the enemy's line, Alexander, clothed in his unmistakably conspicuous battle garb, charged into the brown. At that moment his power to command the battle passed from him. He lost sight of the line, lost all means to send orders, could think only of saving his own life and taking that of as many of the enemy as put themselves within reach of his sword-arm. But the knowledge that he was risking his skin with theirs was enough to ensure that the whole army, from that moment onwards, fought with an energy equal to his. Total exposure to risk was his secret of total victory.

Over more protracted periods, he employed exactly the same technique in his siegecraft (at least until the later sieges, when desperation began to displace calculated performance). And it is in his conduct of sieges, rather than battles, that we are best able to perceive his presentation of self. Alexander, it is clear, was an actor of the most consummate theatrical skill. His courtly upbringing, first at the knee of his histrionic mother, then at the saddle-bow of his equally sensationalist father, amounted to a complete thespian apprenticeship. It had been refined through his schooling in rhetoric by Aristotle and reinforced by the unrelenting close-quarters scrutiny of his mannerisms, traits and reactions during the years when as heir apparent he was the centre of attraction at court. All princes have to learn to guard their tongues and mask their expressions. Alexander, blessed with beauty, physical grace and quick intelligence, was fortunate in having to do so less than most. He was 'princely' by nature.

But so too have been dozens of other princes who achieved not one whit. His ferocious energy was one of the dimensions of character that transformed his physical and intellectual gifts into practical capacity. His unblinking courage was another. Alexander was brave with the bravery of the man who disbelieves his own mortality. He had a sort of godlike certainty in his survival whatever risk he chose to run. There is no hint, in any of the ancient biographies, that he ever showed fear at all, or that he appeared to feel it. This absolution from fear may have stemmed from his intimate identification with the gods of the Greek pantheon. He claimed descent from Hercules, the supreme hero-god; assumed kinship with Zeus, after the pilgrimage to Siwah; and – this is a much disputed point – may have actually allowed, even encouraged, his worship as a god after his assumption of the Lordship of Asia.

Whether he actually thought of himself as a god in the last stage of his life is to return, by a different way, to the question of who the 'inner', 'essential' or 'real' Alexander was. It is a question that can perhaps be answered about no human being. But it is particularly inappropriate in Alexander's case. In his life, the private and public self, thought and action, reflection and execution, so entwine and interpenetrate that the one cannot be disentangled from the other. Like a great actor in a great role, being and performance merged in his person. His life was lived upon a stage – that of court, camp and battlefield – and the unrolling of the plot which he presented to the world was determined by the theme he had chosen for his life. 'It is those who endure toil and who dare dangers that achieve glorious deeds,' Arrian has him say at Opis. 'It is a lovely thing to live with courage and to die leaving behind an everlasting renown.'

But simply because Alexander chose to pursue glory within the dramatic unities of time, place and action that warfare imposes upon those who practise it, the perfection of his performance should not blind us to the harshly limited nature of his achievement. He destroyed much and created little or nothing. The Persian empire, a force for order in the ancient world, to summarize its function at its lowest, did not survive the Alexandrian conquest. Within a generation of his death, it had been torn to pieces by the quarrels of his successors, the Diadochi. The conquest itself was made at the cost of great suffering to many, not only to the Persians who opposed the Macedonian invasion but to the disparate peoples of the empires whose lives were disrupted by it and who reacted to disruption in what Alexander called insurrection and rebellion.

One of his most perceptive biographers, N.E.L. Hammond, juxtaposes with a list of his good qualities a list of his bad: 'his overweening ambition, his remorseless will, his passionate indulgence in unrestrained emotion, his readiness to kill in combat, in passion and in cold blood and to have rebellious communities destroyed. He had many of the qualities of the noble savage.' And that, perhaps, is the 'real' Alexander that the mask of his command of himself conceals. There is the nobility of self-forgetting in his life – danger forgotten, fatigue forgotten, hunger and thirst forgotten, wounds forgotten. But they were forgotten with the amnesia of savagery, to which all who opposed his will were subject. His dreadful legacy was to ennoble savagery in the name of glory and to leave a model of command that far too many men of ambition sought to act out in the centuries to come.

CHAPTER 2

Wellington: The Anti-Hero

'I never', said Wellington after Waterloo, 'took so much trouble about any battle.' It was a large assertion. Wellington's battles were so many that by 1815 even he might have had trouble to enumerate them. Sixteen battles and eight sieges as a commander, several more as a subordinate, might have been the tally. As he had first been shot at on September 15, 1794, in Holland, the score averaged out at more than one battle or siege a year; subtracting several years of peace or staff duty, the annual incidence was actually higher. In 1811 he had fought four small actions in March alone, in 1812 conducted two sieges and won the great victory of Salamanca – regarded by those who like to write about battles in such language as his 'masterpiece'. But it was Waterloo that counted – for the history of Europe, for his reputation, in his own memory. 'It was the most desperate business I ever was in . . . [I] never was so near being beat.'

If he was not beaten, much indeed had to do with the trouble he had taken. Wellington's energy was legendary; so too was his attention to detail, unwillingness to delegate, ability to do without sleep or food, disregard for personal comfort, contempt for danger. But in the four days of the Waterloo campaign he surpassed even his own stringent standards of courage and asceticism.

He slept, for example, hardly at all. Beginning on Thursday, June 15, when news of Napoleon's attack on his Prussian allies first reached him just before the Duchess of Richmond's ball in Brussels, he did not go to bed until 3 the next morning and then rose again at 5. He went to bed at midnight that night, June 16, in the Roi d'Espagne inn at Genappe, but was up by 3 the next morning. That evening he went to bed in Waterloo village between 11 and 12, but on Sunday, June 18, the day of the battle itself, he was writing letters by 3 in the morning. Apart from a short nap on the morning of June 17, therefore, he thus slept only nine hours between rising early on June 15 and retiring at midnight on June 18–19, when he lay down on a pallet in his field headquarters, having surrendered his bed to one of his dying staff officers. Nine hours' sleep in ninety; Wellington's own explanation to Lady Shelley a month later of how he bore the strain must suffice: 'While in the thick of it, I am too occupied to feel anything.'

How occupied? Very occupied indeed; his first reaction to the news of Napoleon's advance was to ask the Duke of Richmond, at a moment which would not distract his host from the duties of hospitality, if he had 'a good map in the house'. From it he deduced the dangers of the situation ('Napoleon has *humbugged* me, by God! He has gained twenty-four hours' march on me.') and returned in haste to his lodgings. He fell instantly asleep. 'I don't like lying awake, it does no good. I make a point never to lie awake.' But his rest was short. At 5 he was woken by a message from Blücher, the Prussian general on whose co-operation he counted for success, and at 5.30 he was issuing orders.

By 8 he was on the road, at the head of his staff of forty or fifty functionaries and messengers, for the Quatre Bras crossroads on the highway from France to Brussels. It was there that he intended to make his first stand. He arrived at 10, dictated a despatch to Blücher and then at midday decided he must confer with his ally in person. The six-mile ride to Ligny took an hour, a brief conference and telescope survey of the surrounding countryside from a windmill a few minutes, and he was then off back to Quatre Bras, which he reached at 2.20 p.m.

He found the beginnings of a battle in progress. At 3 it was in full swing. For the next two hours he was engaged at close range to the French in deploying his battalions, hurrying forward reinforcements, rallying shaken units, siting his artillery positions and, at one moment, galloping to escape French cavalry. He just won the race, jumping the bayonets of the 92nd Gordon Highlanders ('Ninety-second, lie down!') to land out of reach of the French lances. At 5 he organized the fire of his best infantry to drive off a concerted cavalry attack and at 6.30 began hurrying fresh reinforcements into line. Shortly afterwards he was able to order the advance and by 9 the French, who had anyhow received orders from Napoleon to leave the battlefield, were gone. Wellington had been under fire for six hours and constantly in motion across a front of some 2,000 yards, riding back and forth as the ebb and flow of fighting called him, for longer. It had been a physically tiring, to say nothing of nervously exhausting, afternoon.

But of rest he was to have almost none. As soon as the last shots had been fired, he rode back three miles with his staff to the Roi d'Espagne, supped and was in bed by midnight. He was up again at 3 and on the field of Quatre Bras again at 4.30 a.m. At 6 he was waiting for news of the Prussians in a little hut made of branches, by which the 92nd Highlanders had lit him a fire. When news came of the Prussians' defeat at Ligny the day before, he recognized he must retreat, spent half an hour consulting his map and then between 8 and 9 walked up and down outside his hut – the 'forty paces' he had learnt to take as exercise in his Indian years – one hand behind his back, the other swinging a riding-switch at which a Highlander noticed he occasionally took a 'ruminative bite'.

By 10 the news from the Prussians was worse and Wellington was issuing orders for the army to make a stand on the Waterloo position eight miles to the rear. While its rearguards departed he rode forward from time to time to keep the French line of advance under surveillance. Between times he read the newspapers, chuckling over the London gossip and once taking a brief nap on the ground with a copy of the *Sun* spread over his face; was it deliberate sang-froid or his own natural imperturbability?

By 2 he had joined the retreat. It lapsed suddenly into a wretched affair, tempestuous rain following a violent thunderstorm, and the roads, bad at all times, suddenly turning to streams. He got out of the wet to take food again at the Roi d'Espagne, then rode past La Belle Alliance where he and Blücher would meet after the battle but which would be Napoleon's headquarters during it, and on up the ridge he had chosen to be the British army's defensive line. The road took him past the tree ('Wellington's Elm') which would be his own post of vantage next day and so to Waterloo, the village two miles in rear, where he prepared to spend the night in a modest house in the main street.

He went to bed between 11 and midnight and was awake again at 3 in the morning of Sunday, June 18, writing letters to people in Brussels: one to the British ambassador, one to the Duke of Berry, one to an English lady friend ('I will give you the earliest information of any danger that may come to my knowledge; at present I know of

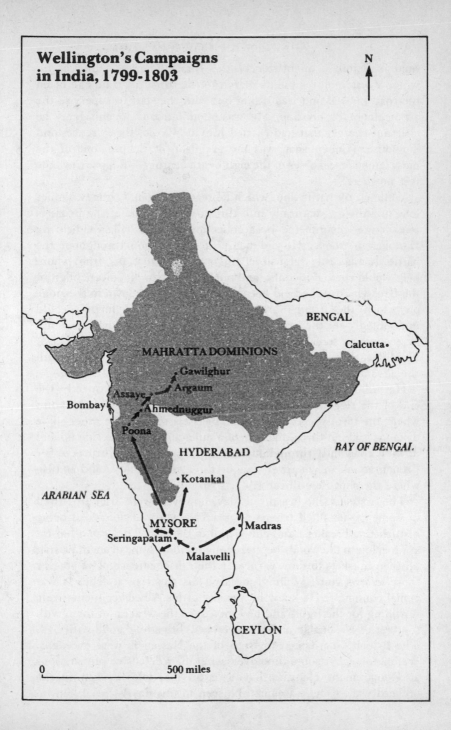

Wellington's Campaigns
in India, 1799-1803

N

BENGAL

Calcutta•

MAHRATTA DOMINIONS

Gawilghur

Argaum

Assaye•

Bombay•   Ahmednuggur

Poona

HYDERABAD   *BAY OF BENGAL*

ARABIAN SEA

•Kotankal

MYSORE   Madras

Seringapatam•

Malavelli

CEYLON

0   500 miles

none'). Before 6 an officer of the Inniskillings saw him at his window watching regiments march to the front. By 6 he had taken the road himself and was riding out with the staff to supervise the arrangement of his line. He was mounted on Copenhagen, the chestnut charger that had carried him at Vitoria, the Pyrenees and Toulouse. (Copenhagen was the grandson of Eclipse, one of the most famous racehorses of the eighteenth century – 'Eclipse first, the rest nowhere!')

Wellington's battle line, which he reached about 7, was two miles long and divided naturally into three sections. East of the Brussels road it was encumbered by a collection of small villages, held by Hanoverian troops. He did not visit that section throughout the battle. It was easily defensible, closest to the Prussians, from whom help would come if it could, and not attractive to Napoleon. West of the Brussels road the field becomes open, sloping down to the ridge on which the French army was drawn up. Wellington could undoubtedly see the French massed in review order for Napoleon's inspection as soon as he arrived on the crest of his own ridge. Finally, at the far end of the ridge, orchards connected the spur with the advanced strongpoint of Hougoumont château.

His radius of action during the battlefield was to be defined by the end of the ridge about Hougoumont at one extreme and the point where the farm track crossed the Brussels road at the other. The distance is about three-quarters of a mile, and he was to ride up and down it constantly throughout the day, drawn by the thrusts of the French attack to wherever danger threatened worst – and so also where the shot flew thickest.

The first shots he heard that day, however, were 'friendly', fired by some of his allied troops, Nassauers, who did not relish being disturbed at breakfast and chivvied into the line. They ran off at his approach into the woods behind Hougoumont, some of them loosing off their muskets to show earnest in their disobedience. 'Did you see those fellows run?' Wellington asked his Austrian attaché. It was genial contempt. He knew how many of his Allied regiments were unwilling for the fight, and had mixed up the weakest of them with the best of his British and Hanoverians, 'brigading' good with bad. The British Guardsmen in front of the Nassauers were excellent. Wellington spent some time overseeing their defensive preparations at Hougoumont château, having extra loopholes broken in the orchard wall. (The traces can be seen to this day.)

The hour was now about 10. Wellington had been seen by almost the whole army as he had ridden along the ridge. Kincaid, of the Rifle Brigade, had sent him a cup of sweet tea from the kettle he was brewing near the crossroads, perhaps the only nourishment taken by the Commander-in-Chief throughout the battle. Gronow, a Guardsman, had been struck by the coolness of his entourage: 'They all seemed as gay and unconcerned as if they were riding to meet the hounds in some quiet English country.' Surgeon James, of the Household Cavalry, also thought they looked as if they were 'riding for pleasure'. The impression was reinforced by Wellington's appearance. As had become his custom, he was wearing civilian clothes: a blue coat over white buckskin breeches, short boots, a white neckerchief. His only military appurtenances were the knotted sash of a Spanish marshal and, in his low cocked hat, the cockades of Britain, Spain, Portugal and the Netherlands. At his saddle bow was folded a blue riding cloak which he was to remember putting on and off fifty times during the day. July 18, 1815, was to be interrupted by frequent showers.

Showers and mist made for poor visibility, which worsened as soon as cannonade and musketry began to fill the windless air with clouds of dense, white smoke. By early evening Wellington, then by his elm, could not see the farmhouse of La Haye Sainte just 250 yards to his front. But in the early morning his view carried across the valley to the ridge occupied by the French and, though he later denied having seen Napoleon as some British officers claimed to have done, he could clearly see the beginning of the French attack which, at 11.30, began to head down the slope to Hougoumont in front of him.

It had been preceded by a heavy cannonade from the hundred guns of Napoleon's 'grand battery', and some of the shots came his way as he sat his horse on the ridge behind the château. He remained there for the next two hours, watching the course of the fighting from the buildings and sending forward reinforcements as he judged he must. Husbanding what few he had in reserve was to be most of his work throughout the day. When he saw the orchard fall he sent down four companies of Coldstreamers, who recaptured it. When the French broke into the château courtyard, he sent down another four to join the terrible fight within the walls, which ended with all the French dead but for a drummer boy.

Hougoumont then looked to be secure, had a French shell not

landed in the farmyard and set fire to the buildings. Soon much of the château was in flames and the conflagration threatened to drive the British defenders out into the open. The time was about 1. Wellington, still watching from the ridge to the rear, though action was now intensifying near the crossroads, was acutely concerned. Taking one of the slips of parchment he kept folded in the buttonholes of his waistcoat, he pencilled a note which is preserved today in a showcase at his London residence, Apsley House. It reads:

> I see that the fire has communicated from the haystack to the roof of the château. You must however still keep your men in those parts to which the fire does not reach. Take care that no men are lost by the falling in of the roof, or floors. After they will have fallen in, occupy the ruined walls inside of the garden, particularly if it should be possible for the enemy to pass through the embers to the inside of the House.

Wellington's clarity of mind and conciseness of expression were famed. To have written such purposeful and accurate prose (the note contains both a future subjunctive and future perfect construction), on horseback, under enemy fire, in the midst of a raging military crisis is evidence of quite exceptional powers of mind and self-control. Soon after he had sent the note off by messenger, he turned his horse and rode back the three-quarters of a mile to the crossroads where the centre of his line was about to be attacked by dense columns of French infantry.

He arrived at his tree soon after 1.30 p.m., rode forward to a sandpit on the Brussels road held by the Rifle Brigade to get a closer look at the approaching French columns, 18,000 strong, which were crossing the 1,000 yards of valley forward of his ridge, and then returned to the crossroads to direct the defence. A Belgian brigade, left by its commander under direct French cannon fire, had been almost destroyed by the ordeal. He summoned reinforcements to repair the line and then waited – he could do nothing else – to see if his British battalions' firepower could destroy the weight of the French attack.

Firepower, in a terrible exchange of killing, saved the line, though the Duke did intervene at one moment to replace a Hanoverian battalion overrun by an undetected French cavalry assault with fresh brigades. He also had to watch powerless as Uxbridge, his subordinate commander of the cavalry, released, on his own ill-judged initiative, a cavalry counter-attack that came to grief in the valley bottom. As the survivors straggled back, Wellington rode forward to the sandpit, which had been lost and retaken by its Rifle Brigade defenders, inspected their positions and sent orders to the King's German Legion at La Haye Sainte just to their front to barricade the farm buildings more stoutly.

It was by now about 3. Wellington brought forward infantry and artillery reinforcements to stand behind his right and left wings but was more concerned for his right-centre. There, between Hougoumont and the crossroads, the ridge was held by a string of inexperienced British battalions which it was clear were about to be assaulted by French cavalry charging en masse. To their sector the Duke now rode. He felt time pressing hard. While near his tree he had just caught a glimpse of the Prussian spearheads moving to his support from Wavre, whither Blücher had retired after Ligny. Their arrival meant salvation. But, as he told Sir John Jones years afterwards, 'The time they occupied in approaching seemed interminable. Both they and my watch seemed to have stuck fast.'

While they crawled forward, the headlong onset of the French cavalry columns might throw his careful defence into ruins and give the battle to Napoleon. The Emperor had chosen to take no part in its tactics. He was watching from the height on the far side of the valley. Wellington, by contrast, kept at the closest quarters to his infantry, riding among them, uttering brief words of encouragement, occasionally taking refuge in a square when the French cavalry boiled about. More often he 'relied on his dexterity as a horseman and the speed of Copenhagen' to keep him out of danger. He was constantly in his soldiers' range of vision. Wheatley of the King's German Legion saw him waving some reinforcements forward with his hat; Norris of the 73rd saw him talking to General Halkett and then breaking off to enter the regimental square as a French charge arrived. Gronow of the Guards observed him sitting pale but 'perfectly composed' immediately behind the front. One of his own staff recalled that 'between 3 and 4 o'clock he remained for many minutes exposed to a heavy fire of musketry. All the staff except a single A.D.C. had received a signal to keep back in order not to attract the enemy's fire . . . and the better to keep out of observation dismounted. As I looked over my saddle I could just trace the outlines of the Duke and his horse amidst the smoke, while the balls

– and they came thickly – hissed harmlessly over our heads. It was a time of intense anxiety, for had the Duke fallen, heaven only knows what might have been the result.'

At 4.20 he asked an aide-de-camp the time. The French cavalry attacks were becoming less frequent and Wellington's hopes of surviving until the Prussians appeared were rising. He now brought forward one of the last but best brigades he had in reserve, stationing it between the inexperienced British battalions – now able to call themselves veterans – and Hougoumont. It was an excellently judged decision, as the impending 'Crisis of Waterloo' would prove.

Before the 'Crisis' could supervene and while the French cavalry attacks petered out in impotence about 5.30, he was, however, called away by a crisis at another point. Renewed infantry fighting around Hougoumont had forced him to commit reserves there while refusing others to one of the generals whose men had just barely survived the cavalry onslaught. 'Tell him what he wishes is impossible,' he said. 'He and I and every Englishman in the field must die on the spot which we now occupy.' While making his refusal, he was brought the news that La Haye Sainte had fallen.

He at once issued another of his perfectly articulated and purposeful orders: 'I shall order the Brunswick troops behind Maitland to the spot, and other troops besides. Go you and get all the German troops of the division to the spot that you can, and all the guns that you can find.' He left on the heels of his orders to rally some Brunswickers who were running from behind La Haye Sainte and brought them back into line; Cathcart, one of his A.D.Cs, remembered that he looked 'much vexed' at the time. He may have been cross with the King's German Legion light battalion for losing the farmhouse, or with himself for letting them run out of ammunition.

But this lesser crisis, temporarily solved, now gave way to the greater. A French deserter is said about this time to have brought him word that Napoleon was ready to release the Imperial Guard. Whether he had warning or not, he soon had the evidence of his own eyes. After dealing with the La Haye Sainte reverse he had ridden back along the line towards Hougoumont, ordering reserves of infantry and guns forward wherever he spotted gaps or weaknesses. About 7 he was on the ground above the château, with the Foot Guards and the 52nd Light Infantry in front of him. Through his telescope (an observer had watched him sliding the tube in and out abstractedly) he now caught sight of the French guardsmen beginning to descend the slope across the valley, advancing in dense columns to the beat of drum. They had never been defeated in battle.

Wellington had made the British guards lie down. As the French came within musket range, he ordered, 'Stand up, Guards. Make ready. Fire!' The volley struck the head of the French column with an effect that an observer noted as forcing it bodily backwards. Some of the French managed to return fire. But then the British advanced with the bayonet, the 52nd Light Infantry meanwhile volleying from the flank. The Imperial Guard column began to disintegrate from the rear and soon the whole of it was streaming back to its point of departure. Wellington, who had ridden across to the 52nd, gave their colonel a concluding order: 'Go on, go on. Don't give them time to rally. They won't stand.'

Then he spurred Copenhagen back to the crossroads where through his telescope he shortly afterwards detected unmistakable signs that the Prussians were attacking the French main body on the ridge opposite in force. A Highlander watched him standing in his stirrups, an 'almost superhuman' expression on his face. 'Oh, damn it,' he was heard to say to himself. 'In for a penny, in for a pound.' Taking off his hat he waved it three times towards the French in a signal for the general advance.

In the gloom – part smoke, part mist – that now hung over the battlefield, the Duke rode forward with his troops, through unspeakable sights. Forty thousand soldiers, several thousand horses, had been killed or wounded in the preceding ten hours and their bodies lay in an area of ground not much more than a mile square. The living literally stepped over the dying and the dead as they crossed the battlefield in advance or retreat. It was now that Uxbridge lost his leg to a cannon shot at Wellington's side. The ball passed under Copenhagen's neck. Wellington supported his second-in-command until others came to carry him away, then continued to ride forward, issuing orders as he went: 'Form companies and move on immediately' – 'You must dislodge those fellows' – 'Right ahead'.

As he pressed on closer to the retreating enemy, one of his staff urged him not to take any more risks. 'Never mind,' he answered. 'Let them fire away. The battle's gained. My life's of no consequence now.' About 10 his progress across the battlefield brought him close to La Belle Alliance. There Blücher, reeking of gin and liniment, was waiting to throw an embrace round him. '*Mein lieber Kamerad,*' he exclaimed, 'quelle affaire.' The old Prussian's few words of French were the only language they had in common.

It was now nearly dark and Wellington turned back to recross the battlefield to his lodging. The way home was not the carefree ride of that morning. His party, pitifully reduced, went at a walk, and 'during the ride back,' recorded one of them, 'I did not observe the Duke speak to any of his little suite; indeed he was evidently sombre and dejected . . . the few individuals who attended him wore, too, rather the aspect of a little funeral train than that of victors in one of the most important battles ever fought.'

At Waterloo he dismounted, gave Copenhagen a pat, answered by the thoroughbred with a nearly disabling kick, and then went in to the dinner his French cook had ready. It was about 11. He ate in silence. Perhaps even more than the strain of the day and the horror of the battlefield it was by the loss of close subordinates that he was most consciously affected. 'Thank God I have seen him,' he repeated as one after another of the survivors put a head round the door. They were few enough. Gordon was dying in the Duke's bed, de Lancey not far away. Canning had been killed, Barnes and Fitzroy Somerset wounded. Wellington himself, sitting with a single officer to keep him company, was afflicted by the sense of his own survival. He drank one glass of wine with his companion, 'To the memory of the Peninsular War,' then, holding up both hands 'in an imploring attitude', exclaimed, 'The hand of Almighty God has been upon me this day,' jumped up, and went to a couch, to fall instantly asleep.

He was to be left only a few hours. At 3 he was woken by the surgeon, Hume, with the news that Gordon, whose leg he had amputated earlier that night, had just died in his arms. The Duke was instantly wide awake. 'He had, as usual,' wrote Hume, 'taken off all his clothes but had not washed himself [an almost unique omission, since Wellington was exceptionally fastidious]. As I entered the room he sat up, his face covered with the sweat and dust of the previous day, and extended his hand to me, which I took and held in mine, whilst I told him of Gordon's death, and related such of the casualties as had come to my knowledge. He was much affected. I felt his tears dropping fast on my hands, and looking towards him, saw them chasing one another in furrows over his dusty cheeks.'

But, however affected, the Duke was now awake and so the duties of another day were upon him. He rose, washed, dressed, shaved,

had a cup of tea and some toast, his unvarying breakfast, and then
sat down to compose his Waterloo Despatch. When published four
days later in the London *Times* it would fill four columns of print.
News of casualties so affected him that he broke off at 5, but it was
completed later the same day in Brussels. There, sitting at an hotel
window, pen in hand, he recognised the diarist, Creevey, in the
crowd below and called him up to his room. 'It has been a damned
serious business,' he related, walking up and down. 'Blücher and I
have lost 30,000 men [the real total was much higher]. It has been a
damned nice thing – the nearest run thing in your life.' And then,
still pacing, he burst out, 'By God! I don't think it would have done
if I had not been there!'

Wellington the Man

What had prepared this extraordinary man for the mental, moral and
physical ordeal of the four days of Waterloo – days that left those
who had merely fought, without any of the strain of command
Wellington had borne and perhaps less of the danger, shocked into
pallor and silence by the horrors of the slaughter, drugged by fatigue
and physically deafened by the close-range discharge of musketry?
That Wellington had borne a greater share of danger than his
subordinates is unarguable. Whenever the pressure of attack had
flowed from one section of the line to another, he had followed it,
leaving the units he had been supervising to a respite of which he had
none at all. If he told his sister-in-law a day later, 'The finger of God
was on me all day – nothing else could have saved me,' he spoke close
to the virtual truth.

' "A sprig of nobility" who came into the army more for ornament
than use', was how this God-fingered man characterized his standing
at the start of his military life. 'They [his brother officers] looked on
me with a kind of jealousy because I was a lord's son.' If they so
thought of him, it tells us more about the limited social horizons of
British officers of the 1790s – sons of officers themselves or
clergymen or small landowners – than it does of Wellington, for his
father was a marginal lord, one of the peers of the Irish parliament
and, like most of them, without much money, estate or family
history. Arthur Wesley (the spelling was later changed to Wellesley)
was, moreover, a younger son and could expect no bequest from his

father's estate. If he enjoyed any inheritance, it was that the eldest son, his brother Richard, was endowed with quite outstanding political qualities, self-esteem foremost among them. Richard's rise to position, first as Governor-General of Bengal under the East India Company, gave Arthur his start in life.

He certainly had none at home or school. When we make our estimate of Alexander, even rightly allowing for his intelligence, physical strength and beauty, and unrelentingly 'forward' character, we have to recognize that his upbringing at court as the heir apparent, or at least presumptive, of a reigning king and conqueror was of decisive effect on the development of his personality. Alexander enjoyed, first, the whole-hearted and doting attention of a tempestuous mother, and later the exemplary affection of an out-standingly kingly father. He was next, at an age when puberty invests the attentiveness of coevals with life-long effect, placed at the centre of a group of lively, intelligent and athletic contemporaries who were ready to follow any lead he would give them. To excel in such company – and Alexander's innate bias towards the pursuit of excellence, to which all observers testified, would have been warmly endorsed by Aristotle – is to acquire expectations that nothing but success in later life will satisfy. All élite institutions understand and operate on that principle. Wellington, who went to Eton at the age of twelve, was the product of such an élite institution, but it had none of the effect on him that Philip's little school for princes had on Alexander. 'His habits,' a Victorian biographer wrote, 'were those of a dreamy, idle and shy lad . . . He walked generally alone, often bathed alone, and seldom took part either in the cricket matches or the "boat races".' Eighteenth-century Eton offered, of course, scarcely the same environment as Aristotle's academy. There was no heady hunting for big game, no cult of nakedness and the body, which robbed Alexander of all false shame in physical competition and made his tactical leadership so electric on the battlefield, no tutorial intimacy, no warm endorsement of mental and athletic achievement. Wellington's Eton was too impersonal and arbitrary a place to have enlarged the personality of any but the most robust spirit. And the young Wellington was the opposite of that.

So neither at Eton nor at the French schools he apparently attended did he shine. No more did he as a young soldier. His early military career followed the pattern common to any junior officer with just enough money to buy 'steps', as purchased commissions were then called, in regiments with vacancies or good postings to offer. He served successfully as an ensign in the 73rd Foot, lieutenant in the 76th and 41st, captain in the 58th, captain in the 18th Light Dragoons, finally major and then lieutenant-colonel in the 33rd, all in the period 1787–93. As lieutenant-colonel of the 33rd he saw action in Flanders in the early stages of the war of the French Revolution and there achieved his first experience of generalship as commander of a brigade. He also tasted politics when sitting as member for the family seat of Trim in the Irish parliament.

But there was nothing to mark him out from dozens of other 'sprigs of nobility' before he took ship for India with the 33rd Foot in 1796. His decision to risk Indian exile – it would last eight years – was decisive. It entailed large dangers, personal and professional. Eighteenth-century India was a graveyard of European lives. It was also a graveyard of ambition, for service there removed an officer from the eye of those who preferred and promoted. But he had the luck to arrive at a moment when India was suddenly about to accelerate rather than obliterate fortunes. For thirty years British power in India had stagnated – since 1763 and the end of the Seven Years' War, the feudatories of the moribund Moghul court had skirmished with the East India Company, sometimes surrendering a little territory but generally playing British off against French to their own advantage. The outbreak of the French revolutionary war in Europe now invested these distant squabbles with strategic importance. The British determined to supplant French influence with their own wherever it operated in the sub-continent. Soldiers with the wit necessary to manoeuvre armies in Indian conditions – bad roads, intermittent supply, epidemic sickness, appalling climate – and to win battles when the enemy could be brought to fight were guaranteed reputation. The challenge Wellington faced was to prove himself a soldier of that quality.

He rose to it as if his whole life had been a preparation for nothing else. A Calcutta contemporary, George Elers, cousin of the feminist Maria Edgeworth, describes the impression he made on his arrival:

He was all life and spirits. In height he was about 5 feet 7 inches [in fact nearer 5 feet 10 inches] with a long pale face, a remarkably large aquiline nose, a clear blue eye and the blackest beard I ever saw. He was remarkably clean in his person and I have known him shave twice in one day, which I

Wellington's Campaigns
in the Peninsula, 1808-14

N

FRANCE

BAY OF BISCAY

Toulouse

Bayonne • Orthez
Santander   San Sebastián   R. Nivelle
Corunna   R. Nive
                      Vitoria •   Sorauren
                            • Pamplona
                    • Burgos

                R. Douro
Oporto   SPAIN
            • Salamanca
    Almeida
R.   • Ciudad Rodrigo
  Mondego • El Bodon   MADRID
Bussaco Fuentes de Onoro   R. Tagus
PORTUGAL
Rolica   Almaraz   Talavera
  • Santarem Arroyomolinos R. Guadiana
Vimeiro
Sobral   • Badajoz
LISBON   Álbuera
R. Calo
Torres Vedras

ATLANTIC
OCEAN

MEDITERRANEAN SEA

0   100 miles

believe was his constant practice. He spoke at this time
remarkably quickly with, I think, a very very slight lisp. He
had very narrow jawbones, and there was a great peculiarity in
his ear, which I never observed but in one other person, Lord
Byron – the lobe of the ear uniting to the cheek. He had a
particular way when pleased of pursing up his mouth. I have
often observed it when he has been thinking abstractedly.

He must have thought abstractedly a great deal in his Indian
years, for the campaigns he now undertook were of the greatest
complexity. Britain, which ruled its Indian possessions through the
East India Company, controlled only the three enclaves that had
grown up around the Company's original trading bridgeheads at
Calcutta, Bombay and Madras, in eastern, western and southern
India respectively. Of these the Calcutta enclave had been enlarged
by conquest to considerable size, but the others remained footholds.
Britain's strategic problem therefore resembled in some respects
those of Alexander before he embarked on the conquest of Asia
Minor. Just as the existence of the Greek cities on the fringes of the
Persian empire gave him the potentiality to operate here and there
from a firm base, so too did possession of the trading forts and their
hinterland confer that advantage on the British. And, like Alexander, the British were confronted by an imperial presence, the
Moghul dynasty, whose powers were in decline. But there the
analogy almost ends. Britain, for all the strength of the Royal Navy,
was operating effectively much farther from home than Alexander
ever did. And its available military force, of which European troops
formed but a fraction, was a far weaker instrument than the
homogeneous Macedonian-Greek army at Alexander's disposal.

All that favoured Wellington, or any other British general committed to the campaign, was the disunity of his enemies. The French
had sought to throw a web of alliances across the fissiparous
principalities owing allegiance to the Moghuls, but all had tasted the
pleasures of autonomy too deeply to co-operate trustfully among
themselves. The British were thus presented with the opportunity to
defeat them 'in detail', which they proceeded to do. In 1799
Wellington took part in the overthrow of the leading southern ruler,
Tippoo Sultan, at Seringapatam, and in the following year, in
independent command, hunted down a local warlord, Dhundia
Wagh, who was terrorising Tippoo's former kingdom.

Indian operations then lapsed for three years until in 1803 war broke out with renewed intensity in the Mahratta Confederacy. The fighting in that assemblage of Moghul dependencies was to give Wellington his supreme chance and make his reputation (at least as a 'Sepoy General'). It fell for him into two stages. In the first he defeated the major Mahratta ruler, Sindhia, at the battle of Assaye, a ferocious affair in which he had two horses disabled under him. In the second he manoeuvred against Holkar, Sindhia's confederate, until recalled by his brother, the governor-general, to act as his military adviser in the conclusion of the war. It had marked a significant stage in the British conquest of the whole sub-continent.

He was now, having made his name and acquired enough prize money to give him modest financial independence, ready to go home and in 1805 did so. He came back as a knight and a major-general, anxious to be married, as he was in 1806, and keen to resume political life. His motive there was to defend the reputation of his brother, who had fallen foul of the scandalmongering that then beset the Indian government. But the effect of his return to parliament (at Westminster, not Dublin, the Irish house having been abolished in 1800) was to bring his talents to the attention of the then war minister. It was his incisiveness of mind and powers of expression that impressed Castlereagh; soon the minister was consulting the young general (in 1807 Wellington was thirty-seven) on one military scheme after another.

These schemes were designed to check the spread of Napoleon's power which was then extending, through his subordination of Spain and conquest of Prussia, from the shores of the Baltic to the coasts of South America. Wellington actually took part in two small such amphibious operations in northern Europe in 1806 and 1807, the latter, in Denmark, briskly successful.

But both were pinpricks on Napoleon's hide. It was the outbreak of risings in Portugal and Spain in 1808 that first offered the British the opportunity to wound him hurtfully. Two early attempts to open what would become the 'running sore' of the Peninsular War ended in fiasco, though in the first of them Wellington succeeded in defeating a small French army at the battle of Vimeiro (August 21, 1808). In the following year, however, Britain hit on the key to an effective Peninsular strategy. It was of Wellington's finding. 'I have always been of the opinion,' he wrote to Castlereagh in March 1809, 'that Portugal might be defended whatever the outcome of the contest in Spain.' Seapower was to be his means. With naval power, a firm base could be secured and supplied at the mouth of the Tagus, from which a British army could safely operate within the protective girdle of Portugal's mountain frontiers. Via the five exits that led through the mountains into Spain the British could mount strategic penetration as they chose; should the French venture back in riposte, they could be stopped and defeated in ground that wholly favoured the defence. Castlereagh not only accepted the force of Wellington's exposition in its entirety. He also decided to implement his plan and give him command of the expeditionary force.

So began Wellington's – and the British army's – Peninsular epic; which was to last until the spring in 1814. It fell, with much ebb and flow of advantage, into six phases. In 1809 Wellington established his base near Lisbon, on the estuary of the Tagus, won the battle of Oporto, drove the French out of Portugal, followed them into Spain and fought the bitter but successful battle of Talavera. In 1810 he was forced on to the defensive, undertook the construction of a fortified system around Lisbon, the Lines of Torres Vedras, to ensure its impregnability, and fought the battle of Bussaco to cover his retreat inside the Lines. Starvation outside drove the French back across the Spanish frontier, on which the armies fought inconclusively against each other throughout 1811. Wellington, by the victories of Fuentes de Onoro and Albuera (his subordinate Beresford's victory) had the better of things strategically.

The trend of the campaign led him in 1812 to break into Spain, by his capture of the frontier fortresses of Ciudad Rodrigo and Badajoz, to fight the brilliant manoeuvre battle of Salamanca and in August to enter Madrid. But he had overstretched himself – the French, who always outnumbered him, achieved a superior concentration of force – and he was obliged to retreat to the Portuguese frontier where he spent the winter. In the spring of 1813, however, reinforcement allowed him to resume the offensive, retake Madrid, win the victories of Vitoria and Sorauren and so drive the French across the Pyrenees into France. In the spring of 1814, with Napoleon's fortunes collapsing at home, Wellington fought and won the battles of Orthez and Toulouse, destroying French military power in southern France. Four days before Toulouse – so slowly did news travel in those days – the hopelessness of his situation had driven Napoleon to abdicate.

Wellington was now a European figure. His Peninsular victories

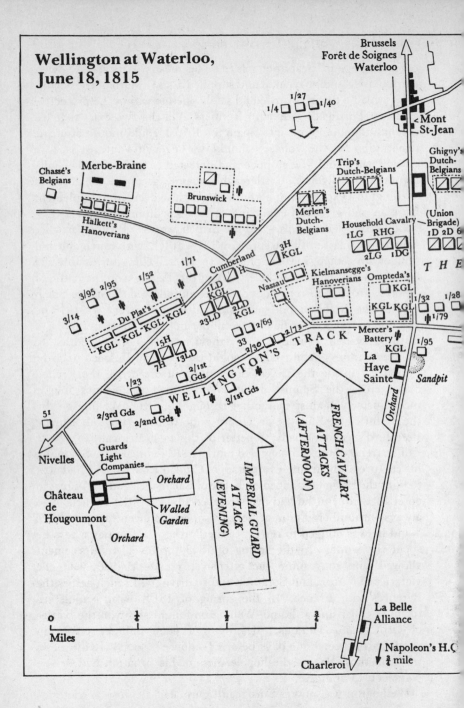

Wellington at Waterloo, June 18, 1815

Brussels
Forêt de Soignes
Waterloo

Mont St-Jean

1/4 1/27 1/40

Chassé's Belgians

Merbe-Braine

Trip's Dutch-Belgians

Ghigny's Dutch-Belgians

Brunswick

Halkett's Hanoverians

Merlen's Dutch-Belgians

Household Cavalry
1LG RHG
2LG 1DG

1D 2D 6
(Union Brigade)

THE

3/95 2/95 1/52

1/71

Cumberland

3H KGL

3/14

Du Plat's
KGL · KGL · KGL · KGL

1LD KGL

23LD 2LD KGL

Nassau

Kielmansegge's Hanoverians

Ompteda's
KGL
KGL KGL

1/32 1/28

1/79

1/5H
7H 13LD

33

2/69

2/73

2/30

Mercer's Battery

KGL

1/95

1/23

2/1st Gds

WELLINGTON'S TRACK

La Haye Sainte

Orchard

Sandpit

3/1st Gds

5I

2/3rd Gds

2/2nd Gds

Nivelles

Guards Light Companies

Orchard

Château de Hougoumont

Walled Garden

Orchard

FRENCH CAVALRY ATTACKS (AFTERNOON)

IMPERIAL GUARD ATTACK (EVENING)

0   ¼   ½   ¾
Miles

La Belle Alliance

Napoleon's H.Q
¾ mile

Charleroi

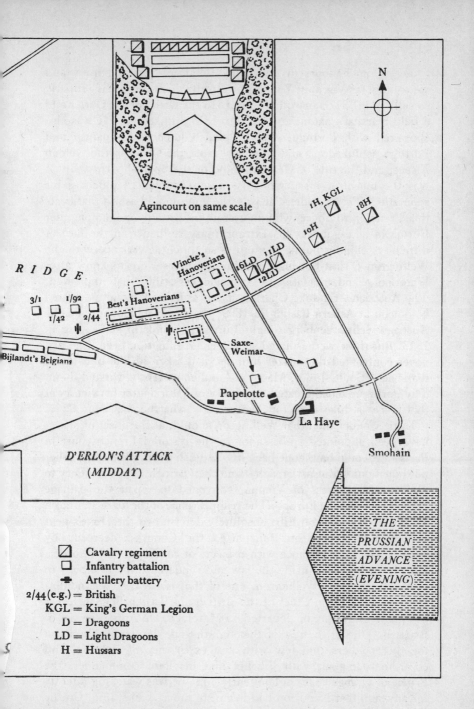

Agincourt on same scale

N

RIDGE

1H, KGL

18H

16H

Vincke's
Hanoverians

16LD   11LD
12LD

3/1   1/92

Best's Hanoverians

1/42   2/44

Saxe-
Weimar

Bijlandt's Belgians

Papelotte

La Haye

D'ERLON'S ATTACK
(MIDDAY)

Smohain

THE
PRUSSIAN
ADVANCE
(EVENING)

☒ Cavalry regiment
◻ Infantry battalion
⬤ Artillery battery
2/44 (e.g.) = British
    KGL = King's German Legion
      D = Dragoons
     LD = Light Dragoons
      H = Hussars

brought him honours in a swelling flood; in 1809 a barony and viscountcy (as Viscount Wellington, from which time he is properly so called), in 1812 a marquisate, in 1813 the Order of the Garter and a field marshal's baton, and in May 1814 a dukedom. He was also showered with Portuguese and Spanish honours – Spanish and Portuguese dukedoms and marshals' rank, the Order of the Golden Fleece, and the title of Generalissimo of the Spanish Army. But it was the image of his personality which counted as much as his reputation. To his soldiers he was 'the long-nosed bastard that beats the French'; to those who mattered in Britain and among her European allies, it was his extraordinary resilience in the face of difficulty, chilling public hauteur – so much at variance with the Wellington of fast-flowing tears his intimates were to know after Waterloo – and indefatigable strategic versatility that impressed. The Austrian Archduke Charles, it was true, had actually defeated Napoleon at Aspern-Essling in 1809; the Prussian Blücher and the Austrian Schwarzenberg fought him to a standstill at Leipzig in 1813. But those were isolated successes. Wellington, even if he had never confronted the master himself, had taken on the best of his marshals – Soult, Junot, Masséna – and consistently worsted them. The Portuguese had created him Duke of Vitoria after his victory at that place; a duke of victory was exactly what he was.

Little wonder then that Wellington should, at the onset of peace, have been appointed ambassador to the restored French court in Paris – he would have gone back into English politics had his brother not fallen out with Castlereagh – and then British Plenipotentiary to the Allied Congress of Vienna, convened to repair the damage Napoleon had done Europe. The reappearance of the 'ogre' in March 1815 from his exile on Elba absolutely determined the Duke's next appointment. 'Napoleon Bonaparte,' the Congress decreed, 'by again appearing in France with projects of confusion and disorder, has placed himself outside the law and rendered himself subject to public vengeance.' Wellington, one of the signatories, was nominated Commander-in-Chief of the British and Dutch-Belgian forces in Flanders, whither he departed on March 28. On April 4 he was in Brussels. During the rest of that month and May he was scraping together soldiers, too few with any experience of fighting, and co-ordinating plans with Blücher and his joint commander, the Prince of Orange. Throughout early June he was watching intently for any sign that Napoleon had begun to move against him. On the evening of June 15, while he was eating dinner before the Duchess of Richmond's ball, the sign came. The consequences we know.

Wellington and Western Military Society

Wellington's conduct in the four days that followed – exceptional though it was even by prevailing standards of generalship – tells us a great deal about the nature of command at the end of the era of black-powder warfare. It was heroic in a truly Alexandrian sense. This comparison – even in a book about comparisons – may seem unjustifiably, even perversely, wide. So much had confusingly worked to alter the equipment of armies in the period between Gaugamela and Waterloo, so much to alter the nature and composition of armies themselves. And the terrain over which they operated had been changed too, by the construction of road networks, the bridging of rivers, the fortification of nodal points, the enlargement of towns, the provisioning of magazines and supply depots, the centralization and semi-industrialization of military manufacture – everything that is connoted by the term 'infrastructure' in its military sense. Given merely these military changes – quite beside the larger social developments of which they were an expression and on which they had a reciprocal influence – can it be said that these are grounds for drawing threads of comparison between Alexander and Wellington with any confidence at all?

I think it can. For this is a book not about the evolution of warfare but about the technique and ethos of leadership and command. And there the pace and intensity of change had been far less marked than in warfare generally, so much less marked as regards technique, indeed, if not ethos, as to amount to scarcely any change at all.

Take, for example, the critical question of the distance at which Alexander and Wellington respectively placed themselves from the enemy on the battlefield. Alexander, bound and inspired by the heroic ideal, placed himself initially very close to and finally in the forefront of the battle line. Wellington also commanded from close at hand. In this, he was perhaps exceeding contemporary expectations of risk-taking. Though he suffered nothing like Alexander's succession of wounds, being in fact hurt only once, at Orthez in 1814, the French musket ball which hit his sword-belt buckle and badly bruised his thigh might well have killed him; it must have been fired from less than 200 yards, the limit of a musket's lethality. And he had bullets through his cloak and holsters at Salamanca and Talavera, two horses were disabled under him at Assaye, and he was often struck too . . . 'struck,' he said to his friend Stanhope, 'is from a spent ball, which may often be able to knock a man over and yet do him no other injury'. This list of narrow escapes is not the record of a general who shunned danger (even if sensitivity to that whispered slur apparently helped to motivate his near-foolhardiness in 1815).

Wellington, like it or not, had to command from close at hand for many of the same reasons that impelled Alexander to do so. It was only by keeping close to the action that he could see what was happening in time to react to events, his means of communication on the battlefield being no better than those available 2,000 years earlier: mounted messengers and trumpet calls. Wellington, of course, occasionally sent written orders, which Alexander probably did not, and it is arguable that his chain of command was tighter than Alexander's, though even that may not be true. Visibility actually disfavoured him: though General J.F.C. Fuller, who had served with cavalry on the dusty plains of India, argues that Alexander often commanded inside a haze impenetrable at a few yards, the dust upthrown by horses' hooves cannot limit vision to the same extent as gunpowder smoke, which often hid combatants from each other as if in a London pea-souper.

Strategic distances, likewise, were no greater for Wellington than they had been for Alexander. While in India he was at a further remove from home than Alexander ever placed himself; but his effective base there was Calcutta, not London. In Spain he was nearer London than Alexander was to Macedon when in Babylon. And when Alexander was campaigning in Afghanistan he was operating at the end of lines of communication far more extended than any Wellington ever had to manipulate. Wellington's means of maritime resupply, in ships carrying hundreds rather than dozens of tons, may have been better than Alexander's. But forward of the trans-shipment point, both depended upon exactly the same means of transport. Wellington's despatches from India and from Spain alike are monotonously concerned with four-footed beasts of burden, the animals he called bullocks and Alexander's translators call oxen. When he wrote from Madras in August 1804 that 'rapid movement cannot be made without good cattle, well driven and well taken care of', he was expressing a thought that must often have been as close to Alexander's heart as his own.

'The success of military operations [in India],' he had written earlier, 'depends upon supplies; there is no difficulty in fighting, and in finding the means of beating your enemy either with or without loss; but to gain your object you must feed.' Both Wellington and Alexander succeeded masterfully in keeping their troops fed, by methods that had scarcely altered over 2,000 years. Less discernibly to modern eyes, their 'means of beating your enemy with or without loss' were also remarkably congruent. For despite the universality of firearms in European armies by 1800, which substituted chemical energy for the muscular efforts that pre-gunpowder armies had had to make, the energy supplied by gunpowder was still too feeble to allow armies to fight at any much greater distance from each other than they had in the 3,000 years of edged-weapon battle that preceded it. Cannon, it is true, could kill at a mile. But cannon were rarely present on a battlefield even in 1800 in a proportion of more than two or three per 1,000 men. The musket was the workaday instrument of death. It dealt death, however, in doses strictly limited by space and time. Above fifty yards its aim was erratic, and at about 150 quite undependable. And, in the hands of the best-drilled battalion, it would not be fired more than three times a minute. As a man can run 150 yards in twenty seconds – the reloading interval between musket volleys – brave, fit and well-led infantry could charge home with the bayonet after an initial exchange of volleys to drive the enemy from the field. The British Guards and 52nd Light Infantry had done something like that against the Imperial Guard in the 'Crisis' of Waterloo. Well-trained and mounted cavalry, charging weak and irresolute infantry, could do even better. If their horses survived serious loss from the opening volley, they could toss the foot into ruin in the space of a few seconds. Such happenings were rare but, when they occurred, decisive.

A battle like Waterloo was, therefore, not very different in its opposition of essential forces from Gaugamela. Alexander's soldiers had suffered a great deal less than Wellington's from missile strike. They had laid out a great deal more muscular effort, having to hack and thrust with a desperation few at Waterloo felt. But the two experiences of combat were closely similar. Both were close-range almost to the point of intimacy, noisy, physically fatiguing, nervously exhausting and, in consequence of that physical and nervous strain they imposed, narrowly compressed in time.

If we translate the ingredients of individual combatant experience into factors constraining the commanders of the men involved, one may better grasp how closely their respective difficulties resembled each other. Both Alexander and Wellington had to extend their armies in line to the greatest possible length, since it was only by matching the enemy almost man for man that the short-range weapons available to either could be made to have their effect. Both had to avert the danger of having the end of the line so deployed 'turned', that is to say overlapped by the enemy's line, since 'turning' exposed a few men, facing the wrong way, to attack by many facing the right way. Each equally sought to outflank the enemy if he could. But, failing that, neither could hope to achieve anything better than to cause a break at some point in the face of the enemy's line by superior savagery. Alexander broke Darius's line at Gaugamela by the ferocity of his cavalry onrush, Wellington Napoleon's line at Waterloo by the intensity of the Guards' volleying followed by a charge with the bayonet. In both cases the decisive stroke was delivered at speaking, if not spitting distance, and in both cases the commanders were close enough to the enemy for their lives to be at extreme risk.

The similarities to be drawn between Gaugamela and Waterloo may be thought to imply that Waterloo was a military aberration or throw-back. It is certainly the case that Wellington exposed himself a great deal more than was then common practice, and it is also true that Waterloo, given the number of troops involved, was unusually compressed in both space and time. But the death of generals in action was, as it would remain until after the American Civil War, still frequent. We know, for example, that in Napoleon's army one general was killed and thirteen wounded at Austerlitz, eight killed and fifteen wounded at Eylau, twelve killed and thirty-seven wounded at Borodino and sixteen killed and fifty wounded at Leipzig. How, indeed, could generals who hoped to win avoid these dangers, as long as short-range weaponry imposed linear tactics on the armies they commanded?

Had the military historian a time-machine at his disposal, in which he might travel backwards from Waterloo to Gaugamela stopping at whichever battlefield he chose in order to survey the course of action (a grisly tour, but what is military history about?), he would be struck above all by how little difference was to be found between the Alexandrian-Wellingtonian style of command and that of any other general of quality in the intervening centuries. Roman tactics were rigidly linear and Roman commanders notably interventionist; Caesar, in the crisis of the battle against the Nervii on the Sambre in 57 BC, seized a legionary's shield and, flaunting his distinctive red battle cloak, rushed into the front line to hearten his flagging troops. The tactics of armies of the Dark Ages are obscured from us but mediaeval tactics were linear and the prevailing ethos of command intensely heroic; the rise of the chivalric ideal made it more so. We have only to think, among reputable rulers, of Harold of England dying among his housecarls at Hastings, Malcolm III of Scotland's death at Alnwick or John of Bohemia's self-sought end at Crécy to recognize how 'forward' the style of leadership remained among warriors who had certainly never read the *Iliad* and might not even have heard of Alexander.

It is true that if we look at the only method of warfare to compete with linear tactics in the military repertoire of conquering peoples before the industrial age – the light cavalry swarm of the Arabs in the era of Mahomet, and later of the Mongols, Tartars and Turks – we find a different command style at work. In those Moslem and pagan armies, which overwhelmed their enemies by mounted archery, harassment and terror, chieftains did not normally take station in the vanguard. The place they chose was on the flanks, and in the rear of the centre. But since the preferred method of those armies was to wear their enemies down by hit-and-run attacks, feints and encirclements, all depending on the nimbleness of their strings of frequently exchanged ponies, exemplary leadership was not the necessity it was in the brutal, face-to-face, sledge-hammer warfare of Greeks, Persians, Romans and their European successors.

Genghis Khan, for example, seems to have articulated his tribal horde (the word, Turkish in derivation, implies an organizational form, not a preponderance of numbers, the steppe armies being quite small) almost as a post-Napoleonic commander might have done. He remained at a distance from the action, communicating and receiving information by an extremely efficient system of messengers, scouts and spies, and imposing his will by a ferocious code of discipline. The Moslem rulers, who learnt to recruit steppe peoples into their armies from the ninth century onwards, actually evaded the demands of direct leadership altogether by making their soldiers slaves. This mameluke system, a unique military institution, originally recommended itself to Islam as a means of avoiding the religious tabu on Moslem fighting Moslem. And though in the long run it defeated its own purpose, when slave soldiers drew the appropriate conclusions from the force they exercised and usurped power in Iraq and Egypt, in the short term it proved as effective as would Genghis Khan's in sparing political rulers the need to exercise direct military leadership.

But the steppe and Islamic armies, ferocious though they were, ultimately failed to translate their light cavalry power from the semi-temperate and desert regions where it flourished into the high-rainfall zone of Western Europe. Whenever it encountered, on their own territory, peoples who lived by intensive agriculture, accumulating thereby food surpluses which enabled them to sustain campaigns longer than the foraging nomads ever could, and breeding on their rich grasslands horses which outmatched the nomad pony in battle, it had to admit defeat. Light cavalry conquerors were in time either forced back into the arid environment where nomadism flourished, as on the borders of Western Europe, or, as in China, corrupted by the softness of agricultural civilization and absorbed by it.

In the long run, therefore, the only warriors to succeed in rooting their power in the land, in consolidating their military instructions as stable states, and, when they learnt the skills of oceanic expeditions, in exporting their conquering capabilities far from home, were to be Europeans. But it was not merely material factors which determined their success, but also those of time. Peoples, however favoured by soil and climate, however enriched by ready accessibility to mineral resources and the skills to work them, however united by social tradition, however sharpened by literacy and numeracy, need leadership if their advantages and qualities are to be directed into the power of conquest over others. It was to be a decisive ingredient of European mastery of the world that the continent's culture worked to produce leaders, so much separated in time but so little differentiated in motive and method, like Alexander and Wellington.

But though culture was to be the decisive factor in determining Europe's distinctive leadership style, it was not to operate over 2,000 years with uniform effect. The historian in his time-machine, descending at intervals to scrutinize how Napoleon behaved at Lodi in 1796 (leading a bayonet charge across the bridge on the Adda),

Gustavus Adolphus at Lützen in 1632 (dying at the point of a cavalry charge), Henry V at Agincourt in 1415 (thrusting deep into the French line at the head of his armoured knights), the Roman Emperor Valens at Adrianople in 378 (succumbing to wounds received at the hands of the Goths), or Caesar at Pharsalus in 48 BC (leading a legion against Pompey's flank), might conclude that he was the spectator at an unvarying event, characterized by the determination of the leading actor present, on one side or the other, to interpose his own body between the enemy and the foremost ranks of those who looked to him for example in danger.

Such observation would be only superficially accurate. The ethos of example would indeed persist throughout the centuries that separate Gaugamela from Waterloo. But the 'when' and 'how' of examples would prove, at closer inspection, to have undergone over the period a subtle but important shift. In front always? In front sometimes? In front never? Here were the key questions. They were questions, moreover, of which the Greeks themselves, to return to Alexander, were already acutely aware and to which, in his own time, they had begun to formulate answers.

The warfare of the *Iliad*, so influential as we have seen in teaching Alexander how a king of the Greeks should comport himself in battle, is ringingly unambiguous about the leader's role:

> The Trojans came on in a mass, with Hector in the van sweeping forward like a boulder bounding down a rocky slope . . . Thus [he] threatened for a while to reach the sea with ease through the Greek huts and ships, killing as he went. But when he ran into that solid block of men, he stopped short, hard against them; and the Greeks facing him lunged hard with their swords and double-pointed spears and thrust him off. Hector was shaken and fell back, but in a loud voice he called upon his men: 'Stand by me Trojans and Lycians, and you Dardanians who like your fighting to be hand to hand. The Greeks will not hold me up for long, packed together though they are, like stones in a wall. They will give before my spear.'

Alexander led, both at the Granicus and at Gaugamela, just as Homer had Hector do, wielding a spear in the van of his army. Unlike Hector, who dies at the hand of Achilles in single combat at the end of the siege of Troy, Alexander escaped death in battle, though – as we have seen – only just. To him the voice of victory uttered demands that overlaid altogether counsels of prudence and delegation. But, even before he had embarked on his anabasis, Xenophon, another Greek who had beaten Persians, had begun to debate the merits of a modification of the heroic style. 'He asked himself,' writes Yvon Garlan, 'whether the foremost quality of a general is bravery, as was thought in ancient times, or reflection which may enable the weaker to triumph over the stronger . . . Torn as he was between his attachment to tradition and his feeling for new developments, he inevitably arrived at a compromise . . . His answer is that it is best to be brave, for the example it gives, but not rash, so as not to endanger the general safety for reasons of personal glory. In this way the commander would be able to win by making the most of circumstances.'

The 'new developments' to which Garlan refers are, in particular, the intensification of drill and the emergence of reserve formations. The first, though associated latterly with Philip, probably had its origins in the readier availability of metals and so of armour from about the eighth century BC. That made it possible to equip large numbers of men uniformly, and so worthwhile to orchestrate their skill-at-arms. The second development was an extension of the first: as armies grew bigger generals discovered that not all men had to be committed to a single line of battle; some could be retained in the rear to reinforce a weakness or exploit a success.

Philo of Byzantium, writing 200 years after Xenophon but working from the same premises, shunned the compromise in which Xenophon had taken refuge. The reasons for that may have been social. City statehood, fundamental to Xenophon's belief in personal responsibility and by extension to the duty of example it laid on the general, was in irreversible decline by the second century BC. The larger polities to which it had lost ground were unfree in ethos, and with the loss of political liberty went also the right of the citizen-soldier to be led rather than commanded. Philo's advice to a second-century general underlines this transvaluation of warriordom in unmistakable language:

> It is your duty not to take part in the battle, for whatever you may accomplish by spilling your own blood could not compare with the harm you would do to your interests as a whole if anything happened to you . . . Keeping yourself out of range of missiles, or moving along the line without exposing yourself,

exhort the soldiers, distribute praise and honours to those who
prove their courage and berate and punish the cowards; in this
way all your soldiers will confront danger as well as possible.

That Philo was not merely giving advice but describing exactly
that 'shift' in leadership style already mentioned is confirmed by the
account given by his near contemporary, Polybius, of the behaviour
of Scipio Africanus at the siege of Carthage in 202 BC: 'Though
throwing himself heartily into the struggle he took all possible
precautions to protect his life. He had three men with him, carrying
large shields which they held in such a position as to protect him
completely from the side of the wall; and accordingly he went along
the lines, or mounted on elevated ground and contributed greatly to
the success of the day.'

Here, in both battle and siege, are descriptions of generalship
which differ significantly from Alexander's style: 'Keeping yourself
out of range of missiles' (recall Alexander's four missile wounds);
'moving along the line without exposing yourself' (Alexander chose
the most exposed position in the line he could find and, once he had
taken it, stayed there); 'protect him completely from the side of the
wall' (Alexander, at his sieges, joined in the attack on the wall and, at
Multan, was the first man over it). Something significant, it is clear,
had occurred between the fourth century BC and the second. The
methods and material of warfare had altered not a jot. But to the key
questions, in front always, sometimes or never? – which Alexander
would have answered 'always' – his successors at an interval of only
200 years were certainly answering 'sometimes' and perhaps feeling
the temptation to say 'never'.

'Never' may have been the answer heard in the theocracies of the
Egyptian Old Kingdom, Sung dynasty China, Abbasid Arabia and
Ottoman Turkey. There the religious role of rulers precluded their
soiling their hands with blood, even their seeing it shed. The
reverent immurement of the Japanese emperors in the era of the
Shogunate, from the thirteenth to the nineteenth centuries, is an
extreme example of that attitude. But 'never' was the exceptional
answer rather than the rule. The idea that the sovereign authority
required military validation has always tended to wither with
increasing political sophistication, but the idea that the sovereign's
military delegate might absolve himself from the risks of leadership,
might adopt a purely 'command' style, might take station 'behind'

and never 'in front' was more difficult to sell to any common soldier worth his salt. Generals as far apart in time as Caesar (merely a delegate of the Roman Senate when he conquered Gaul), Gaston de Foix (killed at the head of the French king's army at the battle of Ravenna in 1512), Tilly (the Habsburg emperor's leading general, killed fighting Gustavus in 1632), Seydlitz (Frederick the Great's commander of cavalry at the head of which he was twice severely wounded in 1757 and 1759) and, as we have seen, Wellington himself – all were driven by an ethic, of which the heroic was still a strong element, to share the common soldier's predicament and, if bullet hit or steel scored, to undergo his fate.

What we are looking at, then, is the adaptation of a value system, not its supplantation. Wellington, like Alexander, was moved by the demands of heroism; but he was not so moved all the time and, when he was, he was moved in a different way. What had changed on the battlefield to transmute the requirement for confrontation with the enemy from 'always' into 'sometimes' and to shift the general's proper station from the point of assault itself to a place merely near the location of crisis?

We may identify two factors: the first is a change in the nature and composition of armies; the second is a change in the relationship of armies to sovereign authority. Let us take the second first. Alexander and his Macedonians were members of a warrior society. Not all Macedonians, of course, were warriors. Age, health and wealth were determinants of who could and who could not bear arms. The old were exempt; the propertyless, who could afford neither the time, sustenance nor equipment necessary to serve, were ineligible. These determinants are found in all societies of the warrior type. They include the Teutonic war bands that overwhelmed the defences of the Western Roman Empire in the fifth century AD, their Meroving-ian and Carolingian successors, the knightly kingdoms of the high Middle Ages in Europe and, at a greater distance from the heartland of warriordom, such peoples as the Ashanti and Hausa of West Africa, the Amharic-speakers of the Ethiopian highlands, the Mos-lem Sudanese, the Rajputs of North-West India and their Mahratta associates (both descended from the original Aryan conquerors), the Sikhs of the Punjab, the Pathans of Afghanistan and the Gurkhas of Nepal.

Such societies may evolve into warriordom or may achieve it precipitately. The evolutionary process is obscure, precipitation less so, often seeming to connect with the adoption or revival of some dynamic ethical or religious creed, of which its adherents conceive themselves to be chosen propagators. The outbreak of Mahdism in nineteenth-century Sudan and the militarization of Sikhism in the eighteenth-century Punjab both exemplify the 'chosen people' effect. But, whether warriordom evolves or is precipitated, leadership is always found to play a key role in its working. Such leadership is commonly called 'charismatic', a word meaning no more than 'graced' or 'favoured', usually by God or the gods. In religious leadership, the charismatic is graced with the power to display extraordinary virtues: resistance to temptation, liberation from the bodily needs for food, drink and sleep and apparent indifference to physical pain and emotional suffering. In secular leadership, these qualities are transvalued: they appear as the 'military virtues' of courage and hardihood. When, as often happens in warrior societies, religious and secular leadership inhere in the same individual, as they did in Alexander, the two manifestations of virtue complement and reinforce each other.

It is perhaps now possible to see why from such a leader as Alexander the question 'in front always?' would have evoked an automatic 'yes'. For, however much his survival may seem to us necessary for the good government of the Kingdom of Macedon, a good but prudent king would have appeared both to him and to his followers a contradiction in terms. His headquarters might be a seat of government. But what Macedonian worth the name would choose to be governed by a king who shirked risk in battle? The very means by which Macedonians endorsed the accession of a new king were military; his supporters put on their breastplates and ranked themselves at his side. When their number constituted a clear majority, the assembly signified acceptance of its will by clashing their spears on their shields. Military force thus validated his kingship; but he was thenceforth bound to validate his authority by an unrelenting display of military virtue.

Such warrior sovereignties were to persist or frequently re-emerge in the Western world and its rimlands from Alexander's time until the coming of the nation state in the seventeenth century. But the heroic society had already acquired in Alexander's day an important competitive model. That was the political system in which rulers had found means, separate from the theocratic, to avoid the injunction 'in front always' through the separation of military from political functions. Those means were, in fact, already present in Philip's army, though he had not drawn the appropriate inferences from them. They were equally ignored by Alexander. Shortly afterwards, however, they were to institute one of the most important political revolutions in world history.

The means were those of military hierarchy and military manoeuvre, whose interdependent evolution had its origins in the armies of the Greek city states. They, as we have seen, were assemblies of free property-owning electors who went to war as equals. But the proliferation of metals in the last millennium BC which created the citizen armies by making affordable by the many what previously had been available only to the few (particularly the chariot aristocracies of the millennium before that), tended by inexorable logic to enlarge armies to a point where the ethic of equality defeated their purpose. Small armies, like small anythings, can operate effectively at the behest of a single leader chosen by all. Large armies require articulation through a pyramid of command which a leader must ultimately construct himself. All the more does that become necessary when the discovery is made, as it will be, that large armies can and should perform complex evolutions in the face of the enemy.

The first military event at which complex rather than simple evolutions seem to have been attempted was, as we have seen, at Leuctra in 371 BC, where an army of Greek allies under the Theban general Epaminondas overthrew the long-dominant army of Sparta. The Spartans, a people who had taken to extremes the city-state principle of limiting citizenship to an arms-bearing élite, had long terrorized their neighbours. At Mantinea in 418 BC they had achieved the unprecedented effect of defeating their enemies by overlapping the left wing. But it was an accidental occurrence caused by the tendency of a shield-carrier to seek shelter from the men on his unshielded right. At the battles of the Nemea and Coronea, both in 394, they had, however, repeated their success, having practised massing on the right in the military exercises which were a Spartan freeman's principal occupation. Drill was essential in Spartan society, because it ensured the dominance of the military class over the much larger and prominently discontented slave population. It could not always remain their secret. The Thebans, who had held their own at Coronea when their disorganized allies had run away, drew the conclusion from the course of that battle that they must drill also. When, at Leuctra, they came to confront the Spartans again, their drilled phalanx overmassed the Spartans' right and won the day.

It was thus that the principles of drill and manoeuvre infiltrated the Greek world at large. But there was another infiltrator: hierarchy. No Spartan resented, as other Greeks did, the superordination of officers, for their role was exclusively military. Officers were those at the head of a file of five or six men which, by combination, formed sections, platoons, companies and regiments. A group of files normally constituted also, it appears, a voting unit in the Spartan constitution. And since all were equal for electoral purposes, none felt subordinate to the man who took rank first in military formation and passed on orders from those higher up.

Once the practice of drill and manoeuvre took root outside the egalitarian army of Sparta, officer rank acquired a different status. Instead of expressing the will of the rank-and-file to accept authority for a common purpose, it came to exemplify the subordination of the man in the ranks to the power of those above him. Elsewhere in the Mediterranean world, and otably in the Roman republic, officer-ship was already associated with economic status. The Roman army, though in theory a citizen militia, had certainly been directed since the fifth century BC by aristocrats. That trend intensified in the later republic, as did the tendency for the better-off to take a decreasing share of military obligation, until the Roman army became professional, and so a mercenary force in all but name. The mercenary had been a familiar figure in the Greek military world from early times and in Alexander's day was, as we have seen, a mainstay both of his own and of the Persian army. By definition the mercenary was a man under authority. Though his loyalty to his ultimate employer was bought, and could be assured only as long as that paymaster paid, his subordination to his mercenary commander was imposed. It was through the mercenary captain that the man in the ranks received wage and rations; to him he owed the normal duties of any employee, reinforced by the military sanctions of fine, flogging, imprisonment or death if he disobeyed, depending on the heinousness of his crime. In the mercenary, a master of drill and manoeuvre (Alexander always rated them highest among his opponents), and at the same time an instrument of purely military hierarchy, we encounter the separation of citizenship from warrior-dom in its most extreme form.

With the emergence of the mercenary, and his near-relation the

full-time professional soldier, ancient armies completed the transformation both of their nature and of their relationship with the
state. They also, as it happened, rehearsed and anticipated identical
transformations to those that the armies of Western Europe would
undergo when they emerged from warriordom at the end of the
Middle Ages, passing for the second time through the heroic stage,
which resurrected itself after imperial rule by the Romans. And
Europe's early modern armies were to display exactly that mixture of
soldier-types so characteristic of those of the Mediterranean world
before Roman power beat all into the same shape on its legionary anvil.
Mercenaries and professionals, officered by warrior aristocrats,
formed the backbone of the French and Habsburg armies from the
sixteenth to the eighteenth centuries. Town militias, equivalents of the
city-state armies of Greece, succeeded in surviving for much of the
same period. It was not until the 1790s that these multiform bodies
were to encounter, in the conscript levies of the Revolution, a military
model which first challenged and then overcame their dominance.
Wellington was to prove himself one of the very few *ancien régime*
officers with the talent to meet Revolutionary armies on their own
terms and defeat them in battle. The British army was to be his
instrument. What was it like?

Wellington's Army

'There,' said Wellington, sitting in the park at Brussels two weeks
before Waterloo, and answering Creevey's question about how well
he hoped the coming campaign would go, 'it all depends upon that
article whether we do the business or not.' He had seen a private
soldier of one of the infantry regiments enter the park, gaping about
at the statues. 'Give me enough of it,' he went on, 'and I am sure.'

Wellington's opinion of his soldiers is commonly thought to be
entirely otherwise. 'The scum of the earth – the mere scum of the
earth,' is one of those rare quotations instantly attributable to both
speaker and subject. Almost as well known is how the judgement
goes on: 'It is only wonderful that we should be able to make so
much out of them afterwards. The English soldiers are fellows who
have all enlisted for drink – that is the plain fact – they have all
enlisted for drink.' This to Lord Mahon in 1831: to his confidant
Lord Stanhope he reflected in 1840 that his army at Waterloo was 'an

infamously bad one – and the enemy knew it. But, however, it beat them.' He himself knew the 'difference in the composition of [and] therefore the feeling of the French army and ours. The French system of conscription brings together a fair sample of all classes; ours is composed of the mere scum of the earth', and so on.

There is the voice of the Iron Duke the world knows, icy, distant, loftily contemptuous, the voice of someone speaking across an unbridgeable gap set between him and the groundlings. Even the hint of approval spoken in the Brussels park is detached and impersonal – 'that article . . . give me enough of it.' Wellington really did not seem to love his soldiers, or perhaps even to know them.

We should not jump to conclusions on slender evidence. Almost all these judgements yield kinder meanings when put in context. 'An infamously bad army', for example: that was a comment not on the British army, nor even all the British troops at Waterloo, but on the newly recruited regiments and their counterparts in the Allied contingent. His Peninsular veterans he specifically excluded. 'There are no men in Europe that can fight like [them] . . . [they] and I know one another exactly. We have a mutual confidence and are never disappointed.' It was the admixture of inexperienced British, Dutch and Belgians that made the Waterloo army 'infamous'. But, 'I had discovered the secret of mixing them up together. Had I employed them in separate corps I should have lost the battle.'

'Enlisted for drink' also requires exegesis, which Wellington supplies. His condemnation was in fact larger. 'People talk of their enlisting from their fine military feeling – all stuff – no such thing. Some of our men enlist from having got bastard children – some for minor offences . . . you can hardly conceive such a set brought together.' But he had a perfectly sensible explanation of what selects such men for the regular army and an even wiser remedy. 'It is expected that people will become soldiers in the line' (and so liable for foreign service) and 'leave their families to starve when, if they become soldiers in the [home service] militia, their families are provided for . . . What is the consequence? That none but the worst description of men enter the regular service.' The remedy, he pointed out, was to transfer the allowance paid from the militiamen's to the regulars' families.

For all their infamy he could warmly praise the quality of his soldiers once they were trained, and provided they were disciplined and properly led. 'Bravery,' he wrote from St Helena in 1805 (the voyage home from India landed him in that place of Napoleon's future exile), 'is the characteristic of the British army in all quarters of the world. An instance of their misbehaviour in the field has never been known; and particularly those who have been for some time [in India] cannot be ordered upon any Service, however dangerous or arduous, that they will not effect, not only with bravery, but with a degree of skill not often witnessed in persons of their description in other parts of the world.' Discipline, by his philosophy, was essential and, given the 'description' of his soldiers, had to be harsh. He was a wholehearted flogger. 'Who would', he asked rhetorically in 1831. 'bear to be billed up [confined to barracks, as Guardsmen were] but for the fear of a stronger punishment?' He would knock down the sentry and walk out. The 'stronger punishment' was, of course, the cat o' nine tails which would remain in use in the British army until 1881 (a century after it had been abolished in France, Prussia and Austria) with the support of strong majorities in Parliament. Soldiers in Wellington's armies, in both Spain and Flanders, were flogged extravagantly; as late as 1834 he would argue, 'I do not see how you can have an army at all unless you preserve it in a state of discipline, nor how you can have discipline unless you have some punishment . . . There is no punishment which makes an impression upon anybody except corporal punishment.'

He also hanged and shot. Like every army of which we have records from the sixteenth century onwards, Wellington's carried on its books a body of executioners. During the Peninsular War they shot or hanged fifty-two British and twenty-eight non-British soldiers. Larpent, his Judge Advocate General, reckoned that forty-one were executed between November 1811 and February 1813. In an army usually less than 100,000 strong, when the offences concerned were desertion to the enemy, violent mutiny or armed robbery, these figures were perhaps not large. It was flogging that terrorized the men in the ranks into submission – though it never stopped them drinking themselves insensible when the chance offered. 'I remember once at Badajoz,' Wellington recalled of the end of that terrible siege, 'entering a cellar and seeing some soldiers so dead drunk that the wine was actually flowing from their mouths! Yet others were coming in not at all disgusted . . . and going to do the same. Our soldiers could not resist wine.'

His officers, equally, could not resist time-wasting, idleness and frivolity. Their habits put their punctual, businesslike, painstaking commander-in-chief beside himself. 'Must I do everything myself?' is the rhetorical *leitmotiv* of much of his correspondence from the Peninsula, rhetorical only because some at least of his staff officers were, when not ill or absent, willing servants of his relentlessly efficient mind. 'We may gain the greatest victories,' he complained to Lord Bathurst in June 1813, 'but we shall do no good until we shall so far alter our system as to force the officers of the junior ranks to perform their duty and shall have some mode of punishing them for their neglect.' Two weeks later he was writing on the same theme: 'Nobody ever thinks of obeying an order; and all the regulations . . . of the War Office and all the orders of the Army applicable to this peculiar service are so much waste paper.' Worse, officers actively defied his authority. Ponsonby, one of Wellington's trusted subordinates, described the offenders as 'croakers . . . gentlemen who like their ease and comfort . . . they exaggerate the numbers of the French army and diminish our own.' Wellington himself complained in 1810 that 'there is a system of croaking in the army'. He ascribed it particularly to those of high rank who, he thought, 'ought to keep their opinions to themselves'. Of many of his generals his own opinion was withering: 'When I reflect upon the character or attainments of some of the General Officers of this army, and consider that these are the persons on whom I am to rely to lead my columns against the French Generals, and who are to carry my instructions into execution, I tremble.'

No wonder that Wellington, while despising them for shirking, was only too happy to accept from officers like these their excuse to quit for home comforts. McGrigor, Wellington's chief surgeon, describes his morning audience in Spain in 1812. 'A general officer, of a noble family . . . next advanced, saying, "My lord, I have of late been suffering much from rheumatism – ". Without allowing him time to proceed further, Lord Wellington rapidly said, "and you must go to England to get cured of it. By all means. Go there immediately." ' But too few of his bad officers would go of their own accord. Their commissions, which they had bought, were their livelihoods. But they were equally, because private property, their defence against the displeasure of their superiors. Hence Wellington's frustrated rage against 'the utter incapacity of some officers at the heads of regiments to perform the duties of their situation, and the apathy and unwillingness of others'. Court-martial served no purpose, he complained, because officers would not find fellow commission-owners guilty. And a Commander-in-Chief's reprimand 'is just so much waste paper; the more extended punishment of suspension from rank and pay . . . is considered another mode of being absent and generally idle; at the end of the period the officer returns to his regiment in as good a situation as ever'.

Wellington's sense of impotence was inevitable as long as English society persisted in indulging the claims of the propertied classes to monopolize military office, just as their equivalents had done in the Hellenistic world and late republican Rome. But his dissatisfactions dissolved when he brought his idlers within musket shot of the French. Then their sense of aristocratic obligation, whether their aristocratic origins were real or assumed, asserted itself in heroic style. 'There is not much difficulty,' he wrote in 1814, 'in posting a British army for a general action, or in getting the officers and men to do their duty in the action. The difficulty consists in bringing them to the point where the action can be fought.'

Through all this railing speaks the voice of a 'sprig of nobility' who had disciplined himself out of the bad habits of mind and body he knew came so easily to the lieutenant or captain assured of his rank as long as he did not run in the face of the enemy. It is the voice of a man who had mastered all the 'difficulty . . . in bringing them to the point' and who resented all the obstacles to that end his officers and soldiers put in the way. Idleness, drink, looting, improvidence were the worst of them. Irreligiosity was another; he deplored both the poor quality of the chaplains he was sent and the – seditious he thought – influence of Methodism on the lower ranks, the result of the chaplains' ineffectiveness. And he consistently berated the state itself, for its short-sightedness in paying the soldiers too little to encourage sobriety and the non-commissioned officers not enough to value their rank – 'they are as bad as the men, and too near them, in point of pay and situation . . . for us to expect them to do anything to keep their men in order.'

And yet he never complained about his army's fighting will or ability. What sort of military instrument was it and why did it perform so well in combat? The secret lay, as it still does, in the British regimental system. Wellington's army, like Napoleon's, was by 1815 organised in brigades and divisions. But the fundamental unit was the battalion of infantry or regiment of cavalry between 500 and 1,000 strong. The French army had moved onward from this form of organization, which had its origins in that of the mercenary bands of the late middle ages. Some British regiments had actually begun as mercenary units; the Royal Scots had served the French and Swedish kings before entering Charles II's service, a pattern of employment which would have been entirely familiar to Alexander the Great.

Though regimental officers transferred, by purchase, from one regiment to another, soldiers and N.C.Os did so rarely or never. Indeed it was uncommon for soldiers to move between the ten companies or four squadrons in which infantry and cavalry units respectively were organized. The effect was to produce a high degree of what today is called 'small unit cohesion'. The men knew each other well, their strengths and weaknesses were known by their leaders and vice versa, and all strove to avoid the taint of cowardice that would attach instantly to shirkers in such intimate societies. Motivation was reinforced by drill. Both infantry and cavalry fought in close order, knowing what the Germans call 'the feel of cloth', under strict supervision and to the rhythm of endlessly rehearsed commands.

Command was designed to achieve two effects: the first, applying particularly to the infantry, was the discharge of large volumes of well-aimed musketry, at steady intervals and close range to the enemy; the second was the orderly and uniform movement of the ranks, if necessary at speed, backwards, forwards, to a flank or into one of a number of prescribed formations – notably, for infantry, the self-defending square. Properly drilled, and reasonably hardened to the terrors of the battlefield (one battle was usually quite enough), an infantry battalion became, in combination with others, and under the hands of a resolute and decisive commander like Wellington, an instrument of appalling human destruction within its own radius of action. In defence, that is to say, no cavalry could break it when it was formed in square, no enemy infantry could approach within 100 yards of it except at heavy, perhaps unbearable loss; in attack, after proper preparation by musketry or artillery, it could charge with the bayonet distances of several hundred yards. Cavalry, an attacking arm except when ranked behind infantry to deter them from running, was more difficult to handle. British cavalry's besetting fault – the Union Brigade at Waterloo gave an example – was to charge too fast and far to re-form, a fault Wellington ascribed to its horses being of better quality than those of the French.

Artillery, of which Wellington never had enough, was the only constituent of his force which enlarged its striking power beyond that available to Alexander. Even so, its range was short – 1,000 yards was extreme – and its effects could be nullified by making the infantry lie down, if possible on a reverse slope, which was Wellington's favoured practice. The power of field artillery was not yet great enough to influence tactics, which remained strictly linear. The object of tactical practice, as in Alexander's day, was either to 'turn' a flank or cause a break in the face of the enemy's opposed line. Cavalry's chief role, though cavalry officers made larger claims for it which they were given to implementing with often disastrous results, was to inflict casualties on a broken enemy, usually in pursuit.

These, then, were the means by which Wellington's men did their 'duty in action' – much of it still muscular as in Alexander's day, though with chemical energy simplifying the missile effect. But his real difficulty, as he always emphasized, was to bring the instrument 'to the point where the action can be fought'. How did he do that?

Wellington's Staff

Napoleon, according to Wellington's recollection of a conversation with one of the emperor's subordinates, never had a plan of campaign. 'He always decided according to the circumstances of the moment. "It was always his object," added the Duke, "to fight a great battle; my object on the contrary was in general to avoid to fight a great battle." ' Wellington there does both Napoleon and himself injustice. In India the young Wellington had sought battle with the single-mindedness of the young Alexander, and for much the same reason: operating with a small élite army against a large, ill-assorted enemy army, he had no option but to attack. Napoleon, by contrast, attacked because he usually had numbers enough to ensure victory. 'There are in Europe,' he said, 'many good generals, but they see too many things at once. I see only one thing, namely the enemy's main body. I try to crush it.' To that extent his plans were simple. But to find the one thing he wanted to see took forethought and time. Much of it was spent with his operations officer, Bacler d'Albe, crawling over a large map spread on the floor of his campaign tent, sticking in pins to mark the morrow's destinations.

8 Wellington by Sir Thomas Lawrence, 1814; the 'heroic' elements of the composition are distinctive.

9 *Above* The Battle of Assaye, September 23, 1803: contemporary battle plan.

10 *Below* Wellington at Assaye, losing his wounded horse: contemporary engraving.

11 *Above* Wellington and his staff on the ridge at Salamanca: contemporary engraving.

12 *Below* The Battle of Salamanca, July 22, 1812: contemporary engraving.

13 *Above* Hougoumont and La Haye Sainte, Waterloo, immediately after the battle: contemporary engraving; Hougoumont is burnt out, the mounds opposite La Haye Sainte are graves.

14 *Opposite* Orders written by Wellington during the Battle of Waterloo, June 18, 1815, pencil on asses' skin; he kept the slips of skin in his waistcoat buttonholes.

Wellington's and Napoleon's methods, if not their objects, were therefore more similar than either would concede. Both laid plans; but Wellington more cautiously and with less help from others. 'I really have no assistance,' he despaired to his brother William in September 1810. 'I am left to myself, to my own exertions, to my own execution, the mode of execution, even the superintendence of that mode.' Vignettes of Wellington, sitting alone in the doorway of his tent, writing, writing, writing, are certainly a staple of Peninsular memoirs. He wrote well and knew he wrote well. 'They are as good as I could write now,' he said to the Marchioness of Salisbury in 1834 of his wartime despatches. 'They show the same attention to details – to the pursuit of all the means, however small, that could promote success.' But the sense of doing everything himself was a rare Wellingtonian vanity, which he shared with the sort of pompous busybody he absolutely was not. Afflicted though he often was by incompetents (General Dalrymple 'has no plan, or even an idea of a plan, nor do I believe he knows the meaning of the word Plan' – all the worse because Dalrymple then commanded him) and by bores ('still Admiral Berkeley bores me to death . . . his activity is unbounded . . . I never saw a man who had so good an education . . . whose understanding is so defective and who has such a passion for new invented modes of doing ordinary things'), he could generally count on intelligent and hard-working subordinates to aid him. Hudson Lowe, Napoleon's future gaoler, was not one of them. Appointed chief of staff in Flanders in 1815, he was got rid of by Wellington before too late. But Murray, his quartermaster-general and effective chief of staff, and, to a lesser extent, Stewart, his adjutant-general, were both valued by him. Many of their subordinates, particularly Gordon and de Lancey, were also able staff officers, conscientious and competent. There were personal shortcomings: Stewart was 'difficult', Gordon officious, de Lancey long-winded. They were not in the class of Murray, the 'perfect' staff officer. But they were up to their jobs.

They were, nevertheless, very few. No army as yet had the sort of modern staff college which, as today, annually graduates a class of carefully selected and meticulously trained military bureaucrats. The output of the recently founded Senior Department of the Royal Military College, whom he stigmatized as 'coxcombs and pedants', though a score served on his staff, was tiny. The total number of staff officers – as opposed to 'footmen, grooms, cooks, assistants, goatboys, carmen, huntsmen, batmen, orderlies, muleteers and farriers' – at his headquarters in Spain was rarely more than twelve. They were the commandant of his personal headquarters and the military secretary, the adjutant-general and six deputies or assistants and the quartermaster-general, an assistant and a sketching officer. Aides-de-camp, Spanish liaison officers and interpreters to all these numbered eighteen. In addition, there were nine officers in the medical department, three paymasters and a score of commissary, provost and judge-advocate officials. Most of those personally attached to Wellington, who excluded the commissaries and paymasters, performed office duties only, what his brother-in-law, Edward Pakenham, called 'this insignificant clerking business'.

The result of this understaffing – itself an effect of the want of training and experience in Wellington's subordinates – was that he did indeed have to be his own staff officer most of the time. There were, of course, routine matters that he left to subordinates: finance and officers' appointments (though he made the choice) to the military secretary, supply (though he was adamant about requirements) to the commissary-general, personnel to the adjutant-general and so on. But the essentials he kept under his own hand. They were movements, intelligence and operations.

Movement meant animals and foodstuffs. We have already seen his obsessive concern to acquire draught and pack animals and to keep them fit. Foodstuffs meant money. The British, unlike the French, did not live off the land, for two main reasons. His soldiers could not 'shift for themselves', he said; he meant that their foraging expeditions became drunken devastations. Moreover, in both India and the Peninsula, he sought to retain the goodwill of the locals. Therefore he bought rather than requisitioned, seeking, like a Victorian empire-builder, to create local markets. One of the consequences of looting, he complained in a general order of 1809, was that 'the people of the country fly their habitations, no market is opened and the soldiers suffer in the privation of every comfort and every necessary'. Four years later, at St-Jean de Luz, the effect of his policies was clearly seen: 'the town is now all a market or fair,' wrote Larpent. 'The French peasants are always on the road between this place and Bayonne, bringing in poultry, and smuggling out sugar in sacks on their heads.' Prices were high but supply abundant.

Intelligence was more difficult to acquire than supply since it could not all be bought. In both India and the Peninsula, Wellington campaigned in mapless country, almost as mapless as Alexander's Asia Minor. In the Peninsula he was to institute a mapping service of his own. In India, time and the enormity of space surrounding his army precluded that. He had to proceed as Alexander had done: by questioning locals, sending out spies and making reconnaissance.

His maplessness may not have been altogether the frustration we imagine. Good maps impose their own drawbacks, inflicting too much information on those who use them. To simplify what they tell requires direct observation of ground, which a commander may acquire himself or by questioning eyewitnesses. In that way he builds up a mental map of key points and their interconnections, of much the same sort as a chess master does of the nodal centres on his board. Alexander, whose mental map of the Persian empire probably had the Royal Road as its skeleton, undoubtedly operated by an inward vision. So, too, must Wellington have done agains Tippoo and the Mahrattas.

In Portugal and Spain he was better provided, though not much. Maps were few, incomplete and often very inaccurate. Fortunately the British army had outstanding mapping skills, developed in the making of the one-inch Ordnance Survey of England, of which the first edition had just been published (1801). At least six trained cartographic officers were therefore usually in the field, mapping at four inches to the mile. Others were actually infiltrated far behind French lines, where they mapped while maintaining liaison with a wide network of Spanish informers. In India Wellington had used the age-old network of professional double-agents (*hircarrahs*) to provide himself with the raw material of intelligence. In Spain, where the French were hated, intelligence came freely and plentifully; but it was his sifting and assessment that turned it into useful 'product'.

And, ultimately, he found no substitute for the evidence of his own eyes. Always well-mounted, and a tireless, bold and skilful horseman, Wellington commonly rode scores of miles a day: forty-five before Assaye, when he discovered the ford that was the key to the position, sixty on two successive nights in Spain to catch officers in dereliction of their duty. A Peninsula veteran testified, 'I have seen his fifteen valuable chargers led out by the grooms to exercise, with scarcely any flesh on their bones – so much were his horses used.' We have his own account of the reconnaissance before Assaye. His Indian guides had denied that there was a passage but he insisted in seeing for himself. Noticing the locations of two villages, 'I immediately said to myself that men could not have built two villages so close to one another on opposite sides of a stream without some habitual means of communication, either by boats or a ford – most probably by the latter.' His judgement proved right and it gave him the victory.

Stored information also supplemented Wellington's intelligence system. To both India and Spain he took a small library of topographical and historical books, which he enlarged in the country; on the way out to Spain he taught himself the rudiments of Spanish by reading the New Testament in that language (also to be Macaulay's method of adding to his linguistic repertoire) and was delighted on landing to receive an address of welcome of which 'to his own surprise he perfectly understood every word' (but he had also learnt Urdu in India). Wellington was not an intellect perhaps of the same stature as Napoleon. Methodical though he was, he never hit upon an equivalent of the emperor's remarkable means of storing essential information in a travelling filing cabinet, which kept him almost as instantly abreast of developments as does a modern data retrieval system. But his mental powers were very great indeed, in both assimilation and exposition. He gave his own description to his friend Stanhope of how his mind worked: ' "There is a curious thing that one feels sometimes. When you are considering a subject, suddenly a whole train of reasoning comes before you like a flash of light. You see it all," he went on, moving his hand as if something appeared before him, his eye with its brightest expression, "yet it takes you perhaps two hours to put on paper all that has occurred to your mind in an instant. Every part of the subject, the bearings of all its parts upon each other, and all the consequences are there before you." '

This is not self-congratulation. The enormous volume of Wellington's papers, impossible for him to have produced except by high-speed composition, testifies to the accuracy of the passage. Later in life he often drafted replies which he had fair-copied by another hand – the drafts being 'crossed' in the contemporary fashion on the letter to be answered, or written on the blank space if there were any. In India he seems to have written everything himself. In the Peninsula his methods were mixed. Sometimes he wrote, sometimes he spoke and expected his officers to render what he said into written form. It depended upon the time available.

In directing operations there was little time; and it was to operations that the movement of the army and the collection of intelligence both led. They were not ends in themselves. Wellington certainly often agonized long over whether to act or not; he himself spoke of his 'cautious system' during the Portuguese period, when inferiority of numbers kept him on the defensive for nearly three years. He certainly hesitated for weeks before Salamanca. Then, legend has it, he made the decision to attack while munching a chicken leg. Suddenly throwing the bone over his shoulder, he swept his telescope over the French position, and announced, 'By God! That'll do.' He had seen a gap opening in the French deployment, into which he ordered Pakenham's division.

Salamanca provided an unusual opportunity. Usually his discussions with his staff were more deliberative. We have an eye-witness account of his 'orders group' before the battle of the Nivelle in October 1813; the reporter is the famous Harry Smith, of the Rifle Brigade, then a divisional staff officer:

> The Duke was lying down (a favourite posture) and began a very earnest conversation. [We] were preparing to leave the Duke, when he says 'Oh, lie still.' After he had conversed for some time with Sir G. Murray (the chief of staff), Murray took out of his sabretache his writing materials and began to write the plan of attack for the whole army. When it was finished, so clearly had he understood the Duke, I do not think he erased one word. He says, 'My Lord, is this your desire?' It was one of the most interesting scenes I ever witnessed. As Murray read the Duke's eye was directed with his telescope to the spot in question. He never asked Sir G. Murray one question, but the muscles of his face evinced lines of the deepest thought. When Sir G. Murray had finished the Duke smiled and said, 'Ah, Murray, this will put us in possession of the fellows' lines. Shall we be ready tomorrow?' 'I fear not, my Lord, but next day.'

The scene is, indeed, of the greatest interest. It reveals exactly the division of labour in Wellington's entourage. He decides; his chief adviser translates decision into paperwork and makes a technical judgement. From it action flows. The telescope occupies Wellington's nervous energies while he thinks. Telescopes, unknown to Alexander, might appear an important addition to the commander's tools, but they were of such low magnification – only three or four – that they did not greatly extend his range of vision.* It was mental powers, not aids to them, which distinguished the true commander from the military functionary.

Wellington's Routine

Operations occupied only a few days in each of Wellington's years of campaigning. When battles and sieges occurred, he threw routine to the winds. But routine – 'method' as he called it – was essential to his operational success. It was almost unvarying. How did he organize his day and the surroundings in which he spent it?

Climate affected routine. Campaigning in southern India, where great heat prevails even during the monsoon season, he had to conduct the business of the day ('I always conduct the business of the day in the day') early. But in the Peninsula, where winters in the highlands of the interior can be Arctic and even summers sometimes freezing ('I never suffered more from cold than during the manoeuvres preceding Salamanca'), he maintained his habit of rising early and getting at once to work: 'When it's time to turn over it's time to turn out.' Wellington was up at 6 every day, wrote until breakfast at 9 – tea and toast, as throughout his life – and then interviewed his heads of department, one after the other, which took until 2 or 3. They were the adjutant-general, quartermaster-general, intelligence officer, commissary-general, inspector-general of hospitals, the artillery and engineer commanders and, if necessary, also the paymaster-general and judge-advocate.

McGrigor, his inspector-general of hospitals, an acute observer of human nature, describes the encounter:

> At first it was my custom to wait upon Lord Wellington with a paper in my hand, on which I had entered the heads of the business about which I wished to receive his orders, or to lay before him. But I shortly discovered that he disliked my coming with a written paper; he was fidgetty, and evidently displeased when I referred to my written notes. I therefore

---

*But telescopes probably did enhance precise calculation of distance on the battlefield. This was important because units were ranked at mathematical intervals from each other and moved at known speeds.

discontinued this, and came to him daily, having the heads of business arranged in my head, and discussed them after I had presented the states of the hospitals.

Larpent, his judge-advocate, may have failed to detect his impatience with subordinates who could not imprint fact into the appropriate slot in the mind as readily as he could himself. 'He is very ready and decisive and civil, though some complain a little of him at times and are much afraid of him. Going up with my charges and papers for instructions I feel something like a boy going to school.'

A French ambassador to London when Wellington was Prime Minister told an acquaintance in later life that he could transact as much business with him in thirty minutes as with a French minister in thirty hours. Napoleon possessed the same command of subjects. He, of course, had unusual mathematical gifts, which imply strong analytic powers. Wellington was musical, and deeply interested by mechanics and astronomy, which are also mentally ordering. Neither man, however, had had formal university training, a deficiency Wellington always regretted. Given their quite unusual capacity to absorb and organize information, the suggestion presents itself that both may have in some way been exposed to the mnemonic 'theatre of memory' technique so influential in the Europe of revived classical learning.

Whatever his method for mastering his subordinates' affairs, the work was soon done. By 2, and certainly not later than 4, he was out on horseback, riding both to take exercise and to see his army at close hand. At 9 he shut himself up to write again and at 12 he went to bed. In the interval he might have taken dinner in company. His was not a luxurious mess. Wellington ate little and insisted on rice with almost everything. He had largely subsisted on it for three years in India 'and those who knew his habits had it in readiness when he dined out'. He drank moderately, but less as time went on: in India, 'four or five glasses with people at dinner, and about a pint of claret afterwards,'; in Spain, 'no port wine, only thin claret, and the country wines and brandy'. He might sit down twenty-eight to dinner, but 'the conversation is commonplace . . . on his part he talked with apparent frankness . . . All however seemed unnecessarily in fear of the great man.' Nothing of Alexander's revelry among his companions here. The party was sober and broke up at the Duke's bedtime.

His headquarters were moved frequently and pitched wherever accommodation could be found. The billeting officers went ahead to find quarters and chalked names on doors as accommodation seemed appropriate (Saint-Simon describes an identical practice when Louis XIV went on campaign). At Bussaco in 1810, Wellington was billeted in a monastery. The abbot recorded that, 'we showed him his room. It did not please him, in spite of being the best, because it had only one door. He chose another more secure, for it had two. He ordered us to wash the place and dry it by lighting a fire.' The staff were scattered wherever there was lodging, sometimes in another village. Conditions were usually makeshift. McGrigor describes finding Wellington at Ciudad Rodrigo 'in a miserable small room, leaning over the fire'. Larpent describes headquarters near Irun, where they were from July to October 1813, as located in a 'small, dirty place . . . a curious scene of bustle . . . noises of all sorts . . . here a large pig being killed in the street . . . another near it with a straw fire singeing it . . . Sutlers and natives with their Don Quixote wineskins . . . pouring out wine to our half-boozy weary soldiers . . . perpetual quarrels take place about payment for these things.' Freneda, where headquarters rested in 1811 and 1812, was 'decayed and dirty with immense piles of stones in the streets, and holes and dung all about and houses like farm kitchens with this difference that there are the stables underneath'. Wellington would pace about in the market place, conversing with his staff. Sergeant Costello, when posted on guard, observed the Duke 'walking through the market place, leading by the hand a little Spanish girl, some five or six years old, and humming a short tune or dry whistle, and occasionally purchasing little sweets, at the child's request, from the paysannes of the stalls'. Even Wellington – 'there is but one way – to do as I did – to have a HAND OF IRON' – sometimes felt the need for the warm press of simple affection.

Wellington and the Presentation of Self

The vignette from Freneda implies a total unselfconsciousness in Wellington's presentation of himself to the world, and tallies with others' observations. He froze at the idea of self-dramatization. Alexander had been a master of theatre. Napoleon mimicked his art – to Wellington's scorn. The emperor's ability to recognize his soldiers by name, he said, was a contrivance; a staff officer supplied him with a list, he called out from it, and when the named men stepped forward Napoleon feigned recall. The Duke would not stoop to such devices.

His contemporaries testify to his untheatricality. One of them remarked on the remarkable contrast between the Duke and his governor-general brother: 'the one scorning all display, the other living for nothing else'. Wellington himself dismissed the appeal of rhetoric and deplored display.

Yet Wellington was certainly not unconscious of his appearance, with which he took a great deal of trouble. His brother officers in Spain called him 'the Beau' or 'the Peer' – a supreme compliment, as many were lords themselves, equivalent to Edwardian society's naming Lord Ribblesdale 'the Ancestor'. He was, as we have seen, scrupulously fastidious in his person, an almost obsessive washer and shaver. He was proud of his figure, which remained trim and muscular into old age. And there was a deliberate lack of ostentation in his dress. In youth he wore regimentals – scarlet coat and heavy sabre. As he grew older – though age was relative for he was only forty-four when promoted field-marshal – and honours accumulated, he seemed to take pride in not displaying them. Surgeon Burroughs recalls seeing him at Salamanca – 'the electric effect of the words "Here he comes" which spread from mouth to mouth . . . [he] passed our columns in review, as usual unaccompanied with any mark of distinction or splendour; his long horse cloak concealed his undergarment; his cocked hat soaked and disfigured with the rain.' A Light Division officer describes his normal round:

We know Lord Wellington at a great distance by his little flat cocked hat, being set on his head completely at right angles with his person, and sitting very upright in his hussar saddle, which is simply covered with a plain blue shabrack . . . Within the last year he has taken to wearing a white neckerchief instead of our black regulation, and in bad weather a French private dragoon's cloak of the same colour . . . Often he passes on in a brown study, or only returns the salute of the officers at their posts; but at other times he notices those he knows with a hasty 'Oh! how d'ye do,' or quizzes good-humouredly some of us with whom he is well acquainted. His staff come rattling after him, or stop and chat a few minutes with those they know, and the cortège is brought up by his lordship's orderly, an old Hussar of the First Germans who had been with him during the whole of the Peninsular war.

The man's name was Bleckermann, and the two were on gruffly affectionate terms.

Wellington's taciturnity grew with age and elevation. As a young officer he had been a tremendous talker (as he remained with friends in private company all his life), bursting with ideas he had picked up from his extensive reading. High command drove the loquacity out of him. In the Peninsula his mess was sedate, though he entertained almost as liberally as he had done in India, where his dinners and picnics were famous for fun:

> Lord Wellington carries himself with much dignity at table [George Eastlake recorded], and is treated with profound respect when addressed. Indeed it seems impossible to take a liberty with him. He drank wine with no one and I learned that this was his habit . . . Lord Wellington is silent rather than otherwise. At about a quarter before six he said, 'Canning, order coffee,' and Colonel Canning left the room for the purpose, there being no bells in Spain. Some very good coffee was served in dragon-china basons, and so soon as he had partaken of it Lord Wellington rose, and everybody did the same.

Wellington's reserve was reinforced by self-knowledge of his explosive temper. He once reduced Stewart, his adjutant-general, to tears, and other times left a Spanish general clinging to the banisters in terror at an outburst; it was further reinforced by his impatience with those who failed to meet his exacting standards. Hill, among his divisional commanders, was the only general to whom he both spoke and wrote freely. At the deepest level, he may have shunned speech because he met so few minds the equal of his own. 'I like,' he once said, 'to convince people rather than stand on mere authority.'

Hence his contempt for the arts of theatre and oratory which came so easily to Alexander, in whom there were no reservations about standing on 'mere authority'. Alexander was a king, Wellington a gentleman, perhaps the most perfect embodiment of the gentlemanly ideal England has ever produced. It had no counterpart in the Greek world because the values on which it rested – reticence, sensitivity, unselfseeking, personal discipline and sobriety in dress, conduct and speech, all married to total self-assurance – were at extreme variance with the extrovert style of the hero. Only in the ethic of *noblesse oblige* do the gentlemanly and heroic codes overlap. Sense of *noblesse* very much obliged Wellington; but from almost everything else in Alexander's personality – his bonhomie, familiarity, ostentation, display, knowingness, all the characteristics Napoleon mimicked – he would have recoiled. Wellington actually despised Napoleon for his false heroics. His mind, he said, 'was in its details low and ungentlemanlike. I suppose the narrowness of his early prospects and habit stuck to him. What we understand by gentlemanlike feelings he knew nothing at all about. He never seemed himself at his ease, and even in the boldest things he did there was a mixture of apprehension and meanness.' Napoleon's 'harangues' to his soldiers aroused Wellington's particular contempt.

He himself, as far as we know, never addressed his men and thought it futile to do so. 'As to speeches – what effect on the whole army can be made by a speech, since you cannot conveniently make it heard by more than a thousand men standing about you?' But his disdain for oratory – one of his few severe shortcomings as a politician in later life – drew on attitudes deeper than belief in its impracticality. Long before politics became his life, he already had a well-developed political philosophy which exactly complemented the austere personality he had been at such pains to construct.

Wellington accepted absolutely that separation of feeling from function which had given birth to the modern state. Alexander's system thrived on feeling; his kingship was as much an exercise of emotion as of deed, an identification which explained why 'in front always' was his automatic response to the unasked question of where the leader should station himself. He felt, just as his followers did, that he must always be seen to take the greatest risk, because risk-taking validated rule. Wellington deplored feeling; it was only by separating it from the act of government that equity and respect for law – the antithesis of the system prevailing under heroic kingship – had been established and could be maintained. He already saw the connection in India. 'Bengal,' he wrote in 1804, 'enjoys the advantage of a civil government [it was under British authority] and requires its military force only for its protection against foreign enemies. All the other barbarous establishments called governments [the 'heroic' warlordships of the Mahrattas] have no power beyond that of the sword. Take from them the exercise of that power . . . and they can collect no revenue, can give no protection and can exercise no government.' His distaste for revolution in Europe was founded on exactly the same analysis, what he recognised as the deplorable effects of confounding emotion and politics. As he wrote to Bentinck in 1811, in one of the most brilliant of his letters, dashed off amid the squalor of his headquarters at Freneda:

> The enthusiasm of the people is very fine and looks well in print; but I have never known it produce anything but confusion. In France what was called enthusiasm was power and tyranny, acting through the medium of popular societies, which have ended by overturning Europe and establishing the most powerful and dreadful tyranny that ever existed . . . I therefore urge you, wherever you go, to trust nothing to the enthusiasm of the people. Give them a strong, and just and, if possible, a good government; but, above all, a strong one, which shall enforce them to do their duty by themselves and their country.

Good government, by Wellington's prescription, meant government by gentlemen. Not Wellington himself: 'I am not very ambitious,' he had written with a little disingenuousness in 1805; in 1801 he had confessed his 'highest ambition' was 'to be a Major-General in His Majesty's Service'. But he had nevertheless fitted himself to exercise power. After denying his instincts for many years, he eventually married out of a sense of obligation someone who proved on near acquaintance to be far from his ideal of the equal companion. He was extremely careful about his health, keeping hounds in Spain to give himself enjoyable exercise and drinking and eating sparingly; although sometimes exhausted – he was confined to bed for several days at Lesaca in 1813 after riding his horses thin at the siege of San Sebastián – he suffered nothing more on campaign than fever and 'Malabar itch' in India and rheumatism in Spain. He never asked for promotion or honours ('not withstanding the numerous favours that I have received from the Crown, I have never solicited one . . . I recommend to you the same conduct and patience,' he wrote to a tuft-hunter in 1813). He had a just opinion of his own talents. 'I was the fit person to be selected,' he wrote when passed over (by his brother) for command of the expedition to Egypt in 1801; and, 'I alone in the Army can overcome their difficulties,' in 1808. He believed strongly in the value of financial independence and had taken trouble to acquire it by scrupulously honest means. He brought back from India his legitimate due in prize money, about £43,000, which made him 'independent of all office and employment'. He took a realistic view of the importance of knowing those who counted: 'I believe I should have been but little known, and should not be what I am, if I had not gone into Parliament,' he wrote to Malcolm, a man he admired, in 1813. But, in the last resort, it was a gentleman's modest self-regard that made him what he was and fitted him to exercise authority. To Malcolm again, 'you are big enough, unless much altered, to walk alone; and you will accomplish your object soonest in that way'.

Accomplishing his object – the defeat of Napoleonic tyranny – was, by the time he went to the Peninsula, Wellington's only aim. 'My die is cast,' he said on the eve of his departure; 'they may overwhelm me but I don't think they will outmanoeuvre me . . . I suspect all the continental armies were more than half beaten before the battle was begun – I, at least, will not be frightened beforehand.' Challenging the French would require at times, he recognized, a practice of heroic display from which in every other matter he instinctively shrank. But he was ready to accept that necessity.

Wellington in Battle

What also, besides conscious exposure to risk, did Wellington bring to the business of beating the French?

He had, of course, his mastery of the practice of military movement and supply. But, though bad logistics may lose a campaign, even good logistics will not win a battle. Wellington also knew, by 1808, how to win battles – at least against the sort of enemy he had met in India: 'Dash at the first fellows that make their appearance,' he wrote to his comrade Stevenson, 'and the campaign will be our own. A long defensive war will ruin us.' Both at Assaye and at Argaum, his two great victories in independent command, he had done just that.

Assaye, an insignificant village 200 miles inland from Bombay, happened to be the place where in September 1803 his army caught up with that of Sindhia and Berar, two of the most powerful of the

Mahratta warlords. The disparity between the forces was dauntingly great. At least 200,000 Mahrattas were found encamped on the river Kaitna; Wellington, who was expecting reinforcement by Stevenson, had only 7,000 under command. He decided, nevertheless, not to wait. The vast majority of the Mahratta force were light horsemen, irregular infantry and camp followers. The followers counted for nothing except to impede the light horsemen and irregulars, who in turn were an encumbrance to the only formidable fraction of the Mahratta army, its disciplined battalions of infantry and batteries of artillery under European mercenary officers. They numbered no more than 15,000 and, though they had eighty cannon against his twenty, his force formed a coherent and self-confident unit, which he believed theirs did not.

The confrontation resembled Alexander's with Darius at Issus and, by Wellington's intention, would be resolved in the same way: a headlong assault on the enemy line. First, however, he had to ensure that his force could not be swamped by superiority of numbers and its skills overwhelmed. It was here that his discovery of a ford across the river Kaitna was crucial. By crossing unexpectedly at that point, he might put his flanks between the Kaitna and its tributary the Juah. Thus protected, they would advance as if in a corridor and deliver the fatal blow.

All went exactly as forethought. Wellington had discovered the ford soon after 11 on the morning of September 23. He reckoned he had three hours in which to deliver battle. Galloping back to where he left the army – he was riding Diomed, an Arab he loved as much as he would Copenhagen – he led it on to the ford, into which he was the first to plunge. As he did so, a Mahratta cannonball took off the head of the orderly riding at his side. Wellington spurred on to make another reconnaissance, was chased back to his own lines by Mahrattas after he had seen what he wanted, and gave the orders for the army to deploy into line between the two rivers. That entailed a ride from commander to commander of each of his six battalions, two British, four Indian.

As they moved forward, he took station on the right, in line with the attackers and fully exposed to the enemy's fire. It played heavily and caused casualties, but Wellington was not touched, though his horse was. As the enemy retreated before the advance, however, he found that a covering force he had aligned farther to the right had got into trouble attacking Assaye village, which was not an element of his plan, and that it was in danger of annihilation. An independent action by his cavalry restored the situation, but the momentum of the advance had been lost. It was further interrupted when some Mahratta artillerymen returned to their guns, which had been overrun, and resumed firing. To check the damage they were doing, he rode back to fetch the only cavalry unit not engaged, led it forward and joined in hand-to-hand combat. It was here that Diomed was speared through the lung, causing Wellington to shift to his third horse of the day.

The battle was now nearly over. It remained only to put forward his infantry again towards the remnants of the Mahratta regulars, who had formed line with their backs to the River Juah. When they broke, resistance ended. Wellington spent a little time congratulating the winners and then retired to sleep in a straw-filled farmyard. His dead numbered about 450; but the strain of the day gave him a nightmare in which 'whenever I awakened it struck me I had lost all my friends, so many had I lost in that battle . . . In the morning I enquired anxiously after one and another; nor was I convinced that they were living till I saw them.'

Wellington, besides suffering the attack of guilt connected with responsibility for casualties, had been in the saddle for twelve hours continuously, had been in extreme danger of his life, had actually crossed swords with the enemy (perhaps the first of only two occasions he did so in his career), had eaten little or nothing, and had been deluged by gunfire noise at a range of 500 to 50 yards for long periods. Little wonder that, years later, when asked what was 'the best thing' he had ever done, he should have answered with the single word, 'Assaye'.

It was certainly a far worse experience than either of his major sieges, Seringapatam or Ahmednuggur. At the latter it was his subordinate, Colin Campbell, who replayed the Alexander epic at Multan by scaling the wall first and sweeping the battlements clear of defenders with his sword. Wellington, as befitted an anti-heroic commander, remained with the main body. He displayed a similar discretion at his other Indian pitched battle, Argaum, fought two months after Assaye. There, though he took the daring decision to attack a superior army in a prepared position with only three hours of daylight left, his personal boldness went no further. The battle was won by the steady advance of his infantry, supported by artillery, in the centre, and a cavalry charge on the right. Wellington himself does not seem to have been at significant risk, and the casualties in his army were small. The Mahrattas ran quickly, probably demoralized after the drubbing of Assaye.

Wellington brought to the Peninsula, therefore, a military philosophy little different from Alexander's – 'dash at the first fellows that make their appearance'. To that extent Napoleon was correct to dismiss him as a 'Sepoy general', for warfare in India, despite all the noise and smoke that firearms brought to Mahratta battlefields, had not changed in essentials since Alexander had campaigned in the Punjab 2,000 years earlier. The armies of Sindhia and Berar were, like those of Darius or Porus, vast travelling caravans of which the fighting element formed but a small part and the fighting élite a smaller element still. Alexander's and Wellington's recipes for defeating many with few in such circumstances were identical: to make the élite their target and break it by ferocious attack. Their methods differed only in that Alexander rode point, while Wellington directed from the rear.

But Wellington was not just a 'Sepoy general'. His wide reading and insistent questioning of veterans with European experience had persuaded him that, different in class though Napoleon's armies were from those of the Mahrattas, 'if what I hear of their system of manoeuvre is true, I think it a false one'. He went to the Peninsula with the germ of an alternative system burgeoning in his mind and, after the briefest experimentation, convinced himself that it was correct.

We have his own description of what that method was, outlined to his staff who had undergone with him a succession of those assaults by dense columns of infantry that were the hallmark of Napoleonic tactics:

> We place our main bodies, indeed our whole line, behind the heights, at least behind the summits of them, and cover our front with light troops. [The French] place their lines *on* the heights, covering them all with light troops. The consequence is that not only their light troops but their line is annoyed by our light troops and they make a bad defence. On the other hand, with us it is an action of light troops only, and if we want the line we bring it on in succession into the position or such points as is most wanted, still keeping it as a sort of reserve. A [French] general who is thus dealt with knows not where to

apply his force, or what is against him except the exposed part of the line; and it is not easy to make out where it is more vulnerable.

Such a method required, of course, an appropriate topographical context; but the Peninsula abounds in ridge lines. It also required a particularly intense 'managerial' style − 'taking trouble' with the battle, as Wellington himself would later put it. The general must make himself the eyes of his own army, from which the enemy is hidden as much as vice versa, must constantly change position to deal with crises as they occur along the front of his sheltered line, must remain at the point of crisis until it is resolved and must still keep alert to anticipate the development of crises elsewhere. Hence the distinctive 'in front sometimes' (but not always) style which Wellington, in the tradition of Caesar and again of Frederick the Great and of all other great post-heroic commanders, made distinctively his own.

The style was seen in full flowering at Waterloo, one of those rare ridge positions on the plains of northern Europe where the Wellingtonian method worked to perfection. But we may watch its step-by-step development during the actions in Portugal and Spain. It is not, of course, seen in the sieges − Ciudad Rodrigo, Badajoz or San Sebastián. There, quite unlike Alexander, Wellington left the leadership of the assault to his juniors, as he had to Colin Campbell at Ahmednuggur. He saw no point in playing the hero when he was served by scores of subordinates whom prize money, presentation swords, promotion or awards of honour would reward for simple bravery at the head of their men in the struggle for the walls. At all these sieges, but particularly Badajoz and San Sebastián, the loss of life was appalling. Siege warfare had been truly transformed by gunpowder; it made the blowing of a breach a matter of days, sometimes only of hours, as against the weeks and months such work had taken Alexander at Tyre and Gaza; but it made the assault on the breach an affair of horror. Wellington, who watched the final assault of Badajoz from a hilltop just beyond missile range, turned deadly pale as the reports were brought him of how badly the attack went and how grave the casualties were. His reception by his victorious troops in the aftermath was barbarian. 'Old boy, will you drink?' the swaying half-crazed survivors screamed at him. One fired a musket in a *feu de joie* that almost took off his head. Peninsular sieges reduced British soldiers, terror-struck before the assault, stricken by brutal catharsis afterwards, to a level of indiscipline that perhaps Alexander never saw in his men at any of his battles.

Peninsular battles, by contrast, were almost methodical affairs. Wellington certainly tried to make them so, and exerted himself to preserve the appearance of iron self-control throughout. At Vimeiro in 1808, his first major engagement in Portugal, he coolly re-aligned his army, deployed to meet the French from one direction, into another at right angles to the first when the enemy attack developed along an unexpected axis. So frightened, he recalled, was the cavalry scout who brought him the bad news, that his hair was actually standing on end. Wellington concealed his own anxieties, brought one infantry formation after another into action, deployed artillery to break a French assault, and launched cavalry to pursue French columns retreating in disorder. When the general in overall command refused him permission to order a final, concluding advance, Wellington rode away remarking to his staff that they would be better off shooting partridges.

Bussaco, where he commanded alone, was the first test of his system in something like its developed form. Fought to cover the retreat of his army into the Lines of Torres Vedras in September 1808, it entailed the defence of the ridge position, roughly eight miles long, by some 50,000 British and Portuguese troops against 65,000 French. Wellington had taken the trouble to improve a road that ran along the ridge, so as to facilitate the movement of reinforcements from one point of crisis to another. It would also facilitate his own. He took his initial stations on the left of the ridge where the crest stands some 1,000 feet above the surrounding countryside, but was poised to transfer his command post when danger threatened.

Action began at 6 in the morning, in thick mist. Wellington, who had slept in the nearby monastery and been up at 4, saw the French column break through the fog and ordered two six-pounders trained on it. That, and infantry musketry, held it at bay. Meanwhile, however, a parallel French column was attacking farther to the south. It was counter-attacked on the initiative of the local commander, Wallace, and driven back. 'Upon my honour, Wallace,' said Wellington, riding up on that moment, 'I never witnessed a more gallant charge than that made by your regiment.'

Both men were probably within musket range of the retreating

French at that moment. The danger affected Wellington not at all. A German observer, Schaumann, reports the impression he made: '[Wellington] displayed extraordinary circumspection, calm coolness and presence of mind. His orders were communicated in a loud voice, and were short and precise.' A third French attack now developed. It came on with greater impulsion than the first, reached the crest of the ridge and threatened to bisect the British position. Wellington's lateral road, and orders he had given to Leith, commanding farther south, came into play at this critical moment. While the commander-in-chief galloped south, Leith marched north and, as the French reached the crest, took them in flank with a concentrated volley. They fell back down the slopes, Wellington rode on the southern end of the line, where General Hill was stationed, and issued the necessary orders to deal with an attack should it spread that far. 'If they attempt this point again, Hill, you will give them a volley, and charge with bayonets; but don't let your people follow them too far down the hill.' Captain Moyle Sherer, who overheard the exchange, remembered that 'He has nothing of the truncheon about him; nothing foul-mouthed, important or fussy; his orders are all short, quick, clear, and to the purpose.'

The ride south had taken him too far from the end of the ridge where he had set his command post. It was the key sector because there his position could be turned; at the other it rested on the River Mendego. Suspecting trouble could not be delayed, he turned and rode back the mile he had come. The battle had been in progress for more than two hours. It was now after 8. As he reached his original station, the spearheads of a large column of French infantry reached the crest. They belonged to the corps of Ney, who would direct the battle for Napoleon at Waterloo. Their numbers were strong, their advance unhesitating. In their path, however, Wellington had concealed a division of his best infantry. The French drove his light troops ahead of them. But when they reached his reserve position, the British main body jumped up, volleyed and charged with the bayonet and drove them down the hill. A parallel column was treated likewise. By 11 o'clock the French survivors had rallied on their line of departure and the battle was over.

Its course had exactly fitted the pattern outlined in the description of Wellington's method: the French had failed to find where his line was 'most vulnerable', if it was vulnerable at all, and had been defeated. He had conducted the battle in the 'trouble-taking' way which, since his return from India, he had designed to match his method. The combination of the two proved decisive.

He demonstrated the combination again two years later at Salamanca. In the interval, he retreated into the Lines of Torres Vedras, watched a French army starve itself into inanition outside, won the small victory of Fuentes de Onoro, and recovered the two exits from Portugal at Ciudad Rodrigo and Badajoz. Salamanca stood on the high road into Spain proper, whither Wellington was determined to transfer his campaign. It had been fortified by the French and as a preliminary Wellington laid successful siege to it. That operation prompted the French commander, Marmont, who was awaiting reinforcements from elsewhere in central Spain, to manoeuvre in a fashion he hoped would frighten Wellington back the way he had come.

Wellington matched manoeuvre with manoeuvre: for two days, he and Marmont – each commanding some 50,000 men – marched their armies parallel to each other, watching for an advantage. It was the culmination of three weeks' balletics which Wellington remembered had tired him as much as anything in his military experience. As usual it was the result of 'having to do everything himself'. 'I was never so fagged. My gallant officers will kill me,' he recorded. 'If I detach one of them, he is not satisfied unless I go to him or send the whole Army; and I am obliged to superintend every operation of the troops.' Up at 4 every morning, no rest before 9 at night and all day on horseback was enough to try a constitution even as ferrous as Wellington's. He relapsed into cat-napping more frequently than usual. 'Watch the French through your glass, Fitzroy,' he ordered on one day of march and counter-march. 'When they reach that copse near the gap in the hill, call me.' Then he settled down in distinctive pose, newspaper over his head. On another day an expedition with one of his quartermaster-general's staff cast him among French cavalry, from whom he only escaped at the gallop, sword in hand. Kincaid, who had been out posting his riflemen, saw his return. 'Lord Wellington, with his staff and a cloud of French and English dragoons and horse artillery intermixed, came over the hill at full cry and all hammering at each other's heads in one confused mass.' The general appeared to have enjoyed the adventure. 'He did not look more than half-pleased.'

On the morning of July 22, the frenzy of manoeuvre reached a climax and was brought to an end. Wellington had actually been ready to give Marmont best and beat a retreat to Portugal when, watching their outposts and his own skirmishing around the high ground beyond Salamanca, he was heard suddenly to exclaim, 'By God, they are extending their line; order my horses.' As he galloped off to his right to unleash the attack, he told his Spanish liaison officer that the French were 'lost'. The division poised to take advantage of their over-extension was that of his brother-in-law, Edward Pakenham. Riding up, Wellington – who had outdistanced his staff – tapped him on the shoulder and said, 'Ned, d'ye see those fellows on the hill? Throw your division into column; at them! and drive them off the hill.' A bystander recalled that his orders came 'like the incantations of a wizard'. Ned Pakenham answered, 'I will, my lord, if you will give me your hand,' and rode away to open the battle. 'Did you ever see a man who understood so clearly what he had to do?' asked Wellington of his staff at large.

While Pakenham's division started down the slope to take the French in flank – the time was about 3.30 p.m. – Wellington turned his horse to ride right to left along his front, some four miles, giving orders to his seven other divisional commanders. The gist was simple. The six infantry divisions were to advance 'in echelon' – inclining to their right. The cavalry division, under Stapleton Cotton, was to charge if and when opportunity offered. The exact sequence would be decided by Wellington himself.

In the first half-hour the battle was almost won. Pakenham's successful advance was flanked by the attack of its two neighbours and three French divisions were dispersed beyond hope of re-forming. Into the chaos of this infantry fight Wellington at the critical moment released his heavy cavalry. 'By God,' he shouted to Cotton as the two rode to watch the effect of the charge, 'I never saw anything so beautiful in my life. The day is *yours*.'

But the battle was not yet concluded. The British attack on the left, launched against the steeper ground on the battlefield, was checked and then repelled by the French, who proceeded to a counter-attack. The time was about 5.30 and, should the counter-attack succeed, the remaining daylight would not suffice for Wellington to develop his own counter-move. A drawn result would be the best for which he could hope.

He had, however, foreseen that topography on his left flank might favour the French and had predisposed two divisions to guard against a crisis there. As the French counter-attacks developed, he rode himself to the nearer and sent his staff officer, Beresford, to the farther. Both stood close enough to the point of crisis to reach it before the French attack developed impetus, to meet it with controlled fire and to turn it back again. As the musketry duel swelled Wellington rode on again, behind and round his infantry, to order the artillery of the left flank to deploy at right angles to the French line and fire into its exposed flank. A round shot from one of these guns hit the French general commanding this sector and cut him in half. His death was but one of the many which in accumulation broke the spirit of the French initiative, turned it in its tracks and so gave Wellington a victory.

He himself was narrowly spared. Though he had put himself at the head of none of the attacks – 'taking trouble' precluded that – he was constantly within range of cannon and frequently of muskets, perhaps as close as 200 yards. When giving orders to one of the Napier brothers, 'a ball passed through his left holster and struck his thigh; he put his hand to the place and his countenance changed for an instant, but only for an instant; and to my eager enquiry if he was hurt, he replied, sharply, "no", and went on with his orders'. The narrow escape discomposed him not at all. Napier saw him again 'late in the evening . . . when the advancing flashes of cannon and musketry stretching as far as the eye could command [in fact across a front of about six miles] showed in the darkness how well the field was won; he was alone, the flush of victory was on his brow and his eyes were eager and watchful, but his voice was calm and even gentle'.

Bussaco and Salamanca, representing the early and late Wellingtonian method in the Peninsula, tell us together as much about it as we need to know. Each demonstrates his essential methods: the careful matching of tactical intentions to topographical conditions, strict precautions to limit casualties by sheltering his troops behind cover as long as possible, hawkeyed scrutiny of enemy manoeuvring to watch for an advantage, resolute seizure of the chance when it occurred, on-the-spot supervision of each successive phase of the battle and refusal to delegate any responsibility central to the outcome of the engagement. That, in essence, was 'taking trouble'.

Observation and Sensation

Wellington observed now stands forth a clear-cut figure. He was certainly that to his officers and even to his men. Time and again they had seen him riding among them, taut, aloof and supervisory in bivouacs or on the line of march, passionately intent and oblivious of personal danger in the thick of battle. His clipped and utterly unambiguous style of speech was familiar to all who had heard it: 'Go on' – 'now's your chance' – 'stand up' – 'drive those fellows off' – 'don't give them time to rally' – 'steady' – 'forward'. Incisive, decisive, distinctive, Wellington's few and firm words leap from the page in the memoirs of all who recorded them.

But what did Wellington hear and see himself? Alexander on the battlefield, once in the heat of action, can have seen or heard little that might be dissected afterwards, by himself or anyone else. His experience must have been a boiling of bodies, sword-arms and horseflesh, a clamour of voices, urgent or terrified, animal screams, a clang of metal on metal. Physical pressure stronger or weaker would have told him how combat went immediately around him; a thinning of the dust cloud which fighting threw up would have signified that the enemy's line was breaking or broken through.

Wellington, standing back from action, itself much more rarely the hand-to-hand business of the edged-weapon age, and riding constantly from place to place, would have seen a great deal more. We actually have his own version of what he saw of his counterparts: he did not see Napoleon at Waterloo ('No, I could not – the day was dark – there was a great deal of rain in the air') but he did see Marshal Soult at Sorauren in July 1813 during the Battle of the Pyrenees ('I made out Soult most plainly. I had an excellent telescope. I saw him come up – all the officers took off their hats as he turned towards them. I saw him spying at us – write and send off a letter. I know what he was writing (laughing), and gave my orders accordingly; but so plainly did I see him that I am sure I should have known him again anywhere').

The view of Soult he caught would, of course, have come before the eruptions of gunpowder smoke closed off vision from one side of the field to the other. Discharges of musketry and cannon enveloped infantrymen and gunners in white clouds so dense that they could not see before their noses. But such eruptions were intermittent and local so that Wellington, although seeking to penetrate a generally obscure atmosphere, would not, from his rearward position and mounted height, have been blinded as they were. He could shift position, moreover, while remaining close to any particular chosen station, in order to improve his view; vision would often be better, for example, slightly to a flank. He also certainly rode forward, when need be, even though that increased his exposure to enemy fire. He was often exposed in such a way on a crest where he had made his soldiers lie down on the reverse slope.

The range at which he observed the enemy varied. In manoeuvring before a battle, the armies might be separated by several thousand yards and yet still within sight of each other; that was often so in Spain – Salamanca is the excellent example – where ridge lines determined their lines of march and so their intervisibility. In initial deployment for action they would rarely have stood more than 1,000 yards apart, that being effective cannon shot. Two days before Salamanca, when the armies were counter-marching at deployment distance, a cannon ball fell close to Wellington as he talked with his staff; he changed position, still talking. Once deployment gave way to action, distances would shorten rapidly; infantry could cross 1,000 yards of ground in five minutes, cavalry a good deal quicker. Wellington might find himself then at 200 or even 100 yards range from the enemy; if, as at Waterloo, he had to take refuge in a square from cavalry attack, much less. During the afternoon of Waterloo he may have been inside a square within fifty yards of the French cuirassiers.

What, in such circumstances, did he see and hear? More to the point, what did he look and listen for? Noise – its volume, quality, duration, bearing and range – was of the very greatest importance in signalling to him the course and intensity of action (never more so than at Talavera, a battlefield wreathed in mist). Individual rifle shots – only his sharpshooters were so equipped – would inform him that his skirmishers were engaged with the enemy's light troops; a crackle of musketry would signal closer contact; rolling volleys meant that the infantry masses were engaged at close quarters. If he were close enough, or the wind in the right direction, the carry of human voices might tell him a great deal. French troops were much more vocal than British, shouting old revolutionary slogans or cries of loyalty to the emperor as they advanced to the assault; officers, too, urged their men forward with a patter of well-worn phrases; and

bands might accompany a large-scale attack, brass having the quality
to carry through the crash of gunfire at a higher register (which
could be extremely unnerving for troops caught in its directional
cone).

This rise and fall of sound-waves would tell Wellington a great
deal, would indeed provide his main means of gauging the pattern of
events in sectors of the battlefield hidden from him by distance,
ground or fire. They would also help to convey how resolute or
battle-worthy were troops within visual range: half-hearted shouts
and ragged volleys implied uncertainty of purpose or lack of real
menace. But the evidence of his ears would count far less than that of
his eyes. Messengers from his subordinate commanders would, of
course, bring him word of passing events, particularly of real or
imagined crisis. But he counted on word of mouth less than other
generals of his age, because of his settled practice of 'taking trouble',
that is, going to see for himself. Such a practice required, if he were
not to be in constant and ineffective motion, that he should have
anticipated enemy initiatives by his battlefield predispositions. But
that, as his own description of his tactical system made clear, was at
the heart of his method. He expected to be able to anticipate when
and where danger would press, so that he could be on hand. And he
usually anticipated successfully. The occasions when he was caught
out – the loss of La Haye Sainte at Waterloo being one – were few.

Given that he was in the right place at the right time (perhaps
called there by tell-tale puffs of musketry smoke), Wellington would
search for visual reinforcement of aural impressions. First a glance
over his own men: what casualties had they suffered so far, were
their lines straight, their formations closed, distances between units
near enough for mutual support, tactical alignments conforming to
topography, reserves within call, artillery positioned to cover the
infantry? Then an inspection of the enemy: how steady was their
musketry (if infantry), how close-ranked their formation (if cavalry),
how unhesitant, in either case, their advance? He was perhaps never
close enough to scrutinize the expression on individual faces as the
fighting soldiers were in the culmination of an advance, but he
would have gathered a great deal from the general bearing and
posture of the enemy's front ranks. Ducking heads or an exaggerated
forward lean – the latter instinctive in soldiers advancing against fire
– would have suggested potentially disabling nervousness. So, too,
would a hasty pace: for some reason, a firm and unhurried tread is

far more intimidating in an attacker than a trot or run.

Finally a judgement about distance. Normally Wellington would leave the giving of the order to fire or charge to the commander on the spot; that was his role and was not to be usurped. But occasionally, if Wellington's sense of tempo dictated it, he would override, decelerating or hastening the necessary order of events. He acted so, for example, towards the end of the battle of Talavera, when he launched the 23rd Light Dragoons and King's German Legion Hussars against French infantry unwisely deployed; the decision, as it turned out, was a bad one. He did so again at Waterloo, when he overcame the Guards commander's caution and urged him on against the breaking French; then his intervention completed the victory.

Wellington, then, certainly saw far more than Alexander did. But he preserved a caustic scepticism about the possibility of ordering visual impressions into a valid version of events. 'The history of a battle,' he wrote to Croker two months after Waterloo, 'is not unlike the history of a ball. Some individuals may recall all the little events of which the great result is the battle won or lost; but no individual can recollect the order in which, or the exact moment at which they occurred, which makes all the difference as to their value or importance.' 'I object,' he wrote to Lord Mulgrave in December 1815, 'to all the propositions to write what is called a history of the battle of Waterloo. If it is to be a history, it must be the truth, and the whole truth, or it will do more harm than good, and will give as many false notions of what a battle is, as other romances of the same description have.' And, in the same month to Lord Clancarty, 'The battle of Waterloo having been fought within reach, every creature who could afford it, travelled to view the field; and almost everyone who came wrote an account . . . This has been done with such industry that it is now quite certain that I was not present and did not command in the battle of Quatre Bras, and it is very doubtful whether I was present in the battle of Waterloo.'

It was a function of Wellington's extreme coolness of character that these denials of his guiding role should have caused him nothing but amusement. He knew his own worth. It was his judgement of himself, by his own austere standards of what was 'gentlemanlike', that determined how he reckoned his achievement and his place in the world. Self-satisfaction was the opposite of what he felt. Judicious self-regard, on the other hand, that pride in inherited talents and their meet application which Hume held should properly form an individual's opinion of himself, was at the centre of the Duke's character. The attitude is not strictly Christian: it conflicts with the doctrine of grace, taking a form of heretical thinking called Pelagian. But the Duke was devoutly Christian by his own standards, while Pelagianism (and Pelagius was, as it happens, British) has been called the most English of heresies. It certainly fitted perfectly with the Great Englishman's outlook, at once proud and humble, cold and affectionate, aloof and deeply sensitive, indifferent to the suffering of others and yet acutely moved by it. Wellington was the Iron Duke, but he was also a man of flesh and feeling. Can we guess how he felt about the terrible work the world had called him to do?

The young Wellington had been light of heart. Those who served with him in India record the fun and high spirits of his household. '[He] lived inimitably well,' remembered William Hickey of Calcutta days, 'always sending guests away with a liberal quantity of the best claret. They generally entertained from five to ten guests daily at their table.' Wellington's breaks from routine on campaign against the Mahrattas were equally merry. Mountstuart Elphinstone recalls: 'Camp Day. General at half-past four. Tent-pins rattle. Talk with the staff, who collect there until it grows light. The assembly beats and the General comes out. We go to his breakfast table in front of his tent and breakfast; talk all the time. It is bitter cold and we have our greatcoats on. At half after six or earlier, or later, mount and ride . . . The General rides on the dusty flank, and so nobody stays with him . . . When we get to our ground from ten to twelve we all sit, if our chairs have come up, or lie on the ground. The General mostly lies down. When the tent is pitched we move in, and he lies on the carpet, and we all talk . . . Then we eat fried mutton, mutton chops, curries . . . and sometimes talk politics and other priorities with the General . . . All this is very pleasant.'

The company of the young and high-spirited – Elphinstone was one of those gay blades who won India for the British – remained deeply attractive to Wellington throughout his life. He was happier with the Elphinstones of this world than with any other company, except perhaps that of the succession of handsome, intelligent women who consoled him for the unhappiness of his marriage throughout his middle and old age. But he did not believe that life could or should be lived inside a charmed circle. He understood and accepted the weakness of the multitude, their fears, their selfishness, their inclination towards the easy way, because he detected those tendencies in himself, knew the trouble it had taken to overcome them, recognized by what constant effort they were held at bay, conceded that birth and upbringing gave him a power to master himself greater than others possessed.

His concern for the afflicted was consequently strong. Self-control did not exclude compassion. Alexander had buried his dead and succoured his wounded because to leave a warrior's corpse unhonoured was sacrilege to the Greeks, while to disregard the wounded was, at very least, bad policy. Wellington, by contrast, buried his dead because it was good practice but tended the wounded because it was charitable as well as sensible to do so. The dead were not buried with ceremony or memorial; it was a matter of getting corpses underground to leave a battlefield decent, control disease and preserve the morale of the army lest if pass that way again. The proper care of the wounded was, on the other hand, a matter of morality. Hearing after the siege of Ciudad Rodrigo that many had been left without shelter, he rode thirty miles after dinner to expel some uncaring officers from their lodgings and install the wounded in their place. He made the same journey the following night to ensure that his orders had been obeyed, since they had been received 'in a sulky manner', and when he found they had not, he put the officers under arrest, marched them to headquarters and had them tried and cashiered.

In India, after the capture of Asseerghur in 1803, he sent stocks of his own wine to the hospital and was seen there 'making enquiries that are as honourable to his feelings as they are agreeable and gratifying to the poor invalids'. He was particularly affected by wounds among his friends and subordinates. Many of his letters are to relatives of those killed or injured, commiserating in their loss or encouraging them to hope for the best. These sentiments were entirely genuine. His grief at the death of Major Cocks, a promising Highlander, at Burgos in 1812 reduced him to speechlessness. His own account of the passing of Gordon, his trusted staff officer, is touching in its stoic grief:

When I was at supper at the village of Waterloo, he was brought in, and I thought, as he had only lost his leg, we should save him. I went to see him, and said I was sorry he was

so severely wounded, at the same time taking hold of his hand.
'Thank God you are safe,' was his reply. I then said, 'I have no
doubt, Gordon, you will do well.' He raised himself and then
fell back in the manner that indicated his being completely
exhausted. Poor fellow . . . he probably felt there was no
chance. He died next morning.'

To Lady Shelley, a month after Waterloo, he tried to summarize
the range of sensations that command inflicted upon him:

His eye glistening and his voice broken as he spoke of the losses
sustained at Waterloo, he said, 'I hope to God I have fought
my last battle. It is a bad thing always to be fighting. While I
am in the thick of it I am too much occupied to feel anything;
but it is wretched just after. It is quite impossible to think of
glory. Both mind and feelings are exhausted. I am wretched
even at the moment of victory, and I always say that next to a
battle lost, the greatest misery is a battle gained. Not only do
you lose those dear friends with whom you have been living,
but you are forced to leave the wounded behind you. To be
sure one tries to do the best for them, but how little that is! At
such moments every feeling in your breast is deadened. I am
now just beginning to regain my natural spirits, but I never
wish for any more fighting.'

The key sentence in this remarkable passage of self-revelation –
equivalents from other commanders scarcely exist – is the third:
'While I am in the thick of it I am too much occupied to feel
anything'. That, in a sense, is naïve. His perceptions and reactions
must, on the contrary, have been on a hair-trigger. His mind, at a
calculating level, had to carry an inventory of his own forces, their
dispositions in breadth and depth, their cumulative loss and their
persisting combat ability. Perceptively, he had to try to calculate
how the enemy stood by the same indices. Both sets of calculations
had to be run against a mental clock of the passage of time, since the
onset of darkness must bring battle to an end (Talavera, a two-day
battle, was an exception to the age-old convention that battles were
one-day affairs). And throughout he had to form estimates of the
fluctuating resolution of his opponents, both of those he could see –
the enemy soldiers in the front line – and of those he could not,
particularly the commander against whom he was pitting his will.

In that sense Wellington felt a great deal, risked indeed a mental and emotional overload which commonly brought lesser commanders to breakdown. He himself recognized how responsibilities lighter altogether than his own had come close to destroying his ironsided divisional commander, Picton. 'In France Picton came to me and said: "My lord, I must give up. I am grown so nervous, that when there is any service to be done it works upon my mind so, that it is impossible for me to sleep at nights. I cannot possibly stand it, and I shall be forced to retire." Poor fellow! He was killed a few days afterwards.'

But, at a deeper level, Wellington's self-portrait stands true to life. He did indeed succeed, between the ages of thirty and forty-five, in banishing feeling from his personality. The decision to do so was deliberate and the effort by which he achieved it intellectual. Wellington understood the world in which he lived. The dynastic nation state, of which he was the perfect servant, represented to him supreme value. 'Beginning reform,' he told his confidante, Mrs Arbuthnott, 'is beginning revolution' – his own succinct version of the more familiar perception of Tocqueville's. Britain, he said in the same year, 1830, which saw the final overthrow of the Bourbon dynasty in France, 'should be more and more satisfied with its own institutions'. An established church, a parliament elected by limited franchise, a constitutional monarchy, an independent judiciary, a regular army – these were guarantees of that separation of function from feeling which he believed to be the bulwark of liberty. The army he commanded was, in a way, a microcosm of society as he thought it ought to be ordered, a hierarchy of classes, in which the best ruled, but with justice, regularity and regard for the liberties to which those beneath them were entitled. His conception of liberty was not a modern one, though he knew what the radicals of his day desired – to transform the equality of individuals under the law into equality of political rights. He did not deny that popular feeling supported that desire. 'But,' he asked in 1831, 'if we are to rely upon that feeling of the people . . . why do we not, at once, adopt the measure that we know the people prefer – universal suffrage, vote by ballots and annual parliaments?'

The argument against indulgence of that feeling he believed unanswerable. 'If you increase but a little the democratic power in the state, the step can never be withdrawn. [You] must continue in the same course until you have passed through the miseries of a revolution, and thence to a military despotism.' The step from indulgence of the feelings of the many to acquiescence in the feelings of a tyrannical individual was thus, in the Duke's view, short and unavoidable. It had been the chief experience of Europeans in his lifetime, and he had dedicated his life to opposing and then correcting it. Napoleon was to him not simply an opponent. He was an enemy, the embodiment of that principle of personal will to which his own austere cultivation of the anti-heroic personality was the antithesis. Not for him popularity, public adulation or the trickery of rhetoric, theatre and display. Heroism to the Greeks, Professor Moses Finley has explained, contained 'no notion of social obligation'. It was ultimately self-indulgent, self-flattering, solipsistic. '*Pothos*', Alexander's 'burning desire' to do something as yet not done by other men, perfectly encapsulates its ethos. Such a notion was abhorrent to the very centre of Wellington's being. 'Never forget,' Napoleon once wrote to his brother Jerome, 'your first duty is to me, your second is to France.' Wellington, sailing to Portugal as a subordinate commander in 1806, reproved a friend for urging that he deserved a higher place by an exactly contrary statement of obligation. 'I am *nimmukwallah*, as we say in the East; that is, I have eaten of the King's salt, and therefore I conceive it to be my duty to serve with unhesitating zeal and cheerfulness, when and wherever the King or his Government may think proper to employ me.'

He was to risk his life on thirty battlefields in performance of that duty. Through its discharge he would eventually become commander-in-chief of the army, Chancellor of the University of Oxford, Prime Minister of England and idol of every last common man in the country. 'Not once or twice in our rough island story,' went Tennyson's ode for his funeral. 'The path of duty was the way to glory.' For the notion of glory as the common man comprehended it, the Duke reserved one of the most cutting dismissals from his famously caustic repertoire. Asked if he were pleased to have been mobbed by the ecstatic population of Brussels on his return from Waterloo, he rejoined, 'Not in the least; if I had failed, they would have shot me.'

CHAPTER 3

Grant and Unheroic Leadership

In the early light of a spring morning during the presidency of Abraham Lincoln, a small man on a large horse was galloping through the dense woodland beside the Tennessee river that led inland from its western shore. The brim of a battered slouch hat nearly met the whiskers of his tight, determined, bearded face. A rough soldier's coat covered his shoulders. Only the knot of staff officers riding in his headlong wake marked him out as a commanding general from the throng of Union soldiers, some ranked in formed units, many leaderless and fugitive, that filled the clearings and broken ground through which all moved. The air was charged with the sound of heavy gunfire, sharpshooting, haphazard volleys, ripples of ordered musketry and the boom of artillery firing salvoes at pointblank range. Overhead the leaves pattered with the ripple of passing shots.

The small man was Ulysses Simpson Grant, commanding the District of West Tennessee, the date, April 6, 1862, and the noise, the opening exchanges of the battle of Shiloh, which had broken out some two hours earlier. Behind Grant lay the steamer that had just brought him from his headquarters eight miles downstream. Ahead raged an encounter between the Union and Confederate forces in the western theatre of operations of the American Civil War that had caught him by surprise, cast his army into disorder and thrown the outcome of the North's campaign on the Mississippi headquarters into sudden doubt.

For many men on both sides this was their first battle; for some it was the first occasion on which they had handled firearms. Hundreds of the Northerners had already found the experience of close-order, close-range fighting too much for their manhood and were streaming back, in numbers too large for any intervening officer to check, to temporary safety under the high banks of the Tennessee. Others had stood their ground or yielded it with soldierly reluctance, but in many places they kept their place in the line only by cowering in the shelter of earthworks stout enough to breast the hail of shot that swept the ranks. At one spot an observer saw thirty or forty Northerners, each clutching the belt of the man in front, tailing back behind a single thick tree 'while a distracted company officer, unable to control himself or his men, paced insanely back from end to end'.

The cry at many points was for ammunition. The Southern attack had caught the Northerners with what ball and powder they had had in their pouches, sixty rounds at most, and much of that had been shot off or spilled in the first hour of attack. The Northern army, which could draw on the copious output of New England industry, was careless with ammunition at the best of times. In crisis, it expended its ready stocks prodigally. It had done so now and Grant, as he began his ride around his stricken front, heeded the cries for ammunition first. He knew that the Southerners, always strapped for supplies, could win a firefight only as a result of bad Northern management of their own superior resources.

The necessary orders given, Grant turned his horse to ride along his front and survey its state. He found confusion that threatened collapse. The fighting had begun before dawn, when patrols from his leading divisions, expecting an unopposed advance into Southern-held territory, had bumped into strong forces of Confederates advancing to attack his main body in its encampment. The patrols had exchanged fire with the Confederate vanguard and then fallen back on their main line. That was composed of regiments almost all fresh to battle, led by officers as innocent of bloodshed as their men. One of them, the 53rd Ohio, had lost its colonel after the second volley. Howling 'Fall back and save yourselves,' he beat many of his soldiers in the race to safety. Another, the 71st Ohio, saw its colonel put spurs to horseflesh the moment the enemy appeared. The colonel of a third, the 6th Iowa, was palpably drunk, unable to give orders and had to be put under arrest by his brigadier. Whether he had been drunk all night or got drunk over breakfast was not established. Either state was perfectly credible in the first year of the Civil War.

Even the best of Grant's subordinates were in trouble. Sherman, who would go marching through Georgia two years later, had had a horse shot under him and suffered a wound in his hand. The Confederates were trying to work round the open flank of his division and were pressing him hard. Prentiss, in the centre, was already being forced back. The divisions on the left were giving ground along the river bank. At Pittsburg Landing, where Grant had disembarked, runaways were pressing for shelter into an ever tighter mass under the high bank. There would be 5,000 there by mid-afternoon – some said 15,000 – perhaps a fifth of Grant's entire army, many weaponless and none with any stomach for more fighting.

Those whom bravery, coercion or lack of opportunity to flee kept in the line – many more would have run but for the presence of cavalry or broken ground to their rear – were undergoing the most horrible of experiences. One regiment, the 55th Illinois, that did try to break back across a narrow ravine were caught in the hollow and shot down in dozens. 'I never saw such cruel work in the war,' said a Mississippi major. He spoke for a Confederate army which scented victory and was led forward by a general, A.S. Johnston, whose star stood as high as any Southern soldier's. Its infantry whooped and yelled their way through the woodland; even the artillery, pushing their guns to the edge of the firing line, were fighting like skirmishers. One gun team, unlimbering amid the broken ranks of a fleeing Union regiment, poured salvoes of grape into the fugitives as they streamed past, its victims too terror-stricken to halt, though there were enough of them 'to pick up gun, carriage, caisson and horses and hurl them into the Tennessee'.

Grant's artillery showed no such spirit. One demoralized gun crew flogged its horses bloody in an attempt to free a cannon jammed solid with a tree trunk between wheel and barrel. A whole battery, terrorized by the detonation of the ready-use ammunition in a limber, put their horses to and galloped clean off the battlefield. Where Grant saw such disorders he intervened to check them. But he could not be everywhere at once and his line, throughout the late morning and early afternoon, was pushed steadily backward, pivoting on its river flank and threatening eventually to be driven into the waters.

He had sent urgently for reinforcements, whose arrival would turn the tide. But the nearest were half a day distant and quite unalerted to the danger with which he coped meanwhile. Until they arrived, he could only gallop here and there, dealing with each crisis as he came to it. This was not one of those battlefields on which European generals expected to practise their craft, a swarth of grassland or open plough, like Waterloo or even Gaugamela. It was a tract of territory, indeed, on which no European army would ever have offered or given battle, a tangle of forest and scrub that denied a discerning eye all chance to survey the fighting line in its entirety. Smoke filled its rides and hollows, thickets distorted and deflected the noise of gunfire that shredded leaf and branch, streams and swamp separated unit from unit. There were no landmarks, no inhabitants to point the way, no *Feldherrnhügel* from which commander and staff could catch a prospect of friend and foe locked in combat. It was an entirely American landscape, one of those wildernesses which settlement as yet had scarcely touched, and Grant, like a native trapper, pioneer or man of the woods, had to deal with it in an entirely American way. A European general would have sounded retreat at the first hint of trouble, thinking to regroup on safer ground and fight another day. He, oppressed by the knowledge that the Union could afford to take 'no backward step' in its struggle with Southern rebellion, banished all thought of retreat and rode like fury from blind spot to blind spot, keeping his men in place.

Not all, even in the regiments that showed real fight, could stick their ground. Grant's centre division had been driven back early in the day but had then rooted itself on a spot that favoured defence. Its strength was whittled away in a succession of Confederate attacks. Its dead strewed its front, its wounded straggled away to the makeshift hospitals hastily organized in the army's rear. But its line remained unbroken. Grant visited it several times during the afternoon, bringing reinforcements when he could find them and heartening its commander with words of encouragement. But as the day wore on, its flanks became exposed, the Southerners working round on left and right to separate the division from its neighbours. Eventually it stood almost surrounded, reduced from 5,000 fighting men to little more than 2,000 and, when the enemy ran guns forward to sweep its front at close range, it could resist no longer. Grant had last visited it at 4.30. At 5.30 the white flag was raised and the survivors gave themselves up.

Fortune favoured the brave. The Southern commander had been

killed in the attack in the centre and his subordinates had not taken the trouble to impede Grant's closing of the gap in his line the capitulation had opened. They had not detected, either, that the Union artillery commander had been massing his surviving artillery on the river flank, where they chose to make what they judged would be the final assault. When unleashed, this assault was devastated by salvoes of grape at close range and dispersed in confusion.

The time was a little after 6. Grant then was close to the river himself, where the reinforcements he had urgently summoned nine hours earlier had begun to disembark in strength. Their appearance put new heart into him and the men about him. A fusspot subordinate, riding up with news that a third of the army was dead, wounded or fugitive, asked if he wanted to issue orders for a withdrawal. Grant dismissed him with curt contempt. Dark was falling, cold sheets of rain had begun to sweep the forest, the battlefield was filled with shivering, shelterless soldiers as anxious for a bite of hot food as they were for an end to the ceaseless bursts of firing which had driven them from one nameless spot to another throughout that awful day. But he, like they, could now glimpse hope of a change of fortunes.

Later that night, Sherman, his West Point classmate, found him standing under a dripping tree, coat collar round his ears, cigar clenched between his teeth. He had come, like the ill-advised subordinate earlier, to speak of retreat. 'Some wise and sudden instinct' prompted him otherwise. 'Well, Grant,' he said. 'We've had the devil's own day, haven't we.'

Grant took a pull on his cigar, the glow illuminating his neat, tight, determined features. 'Yes,' said Grant. 'Yes. Lick 'em tomorrow, though.'

So he did. The greatest general of the American Civil War had begun his ascent from obscurity.

Grant and the Progress of War

'War is progressive,' Grant was to write in his *Memoirs*. The idea would have been abhorrent to the Duke of Wellington, who feared progress in politics and stoutly denied its influence on the battlefield. 'Napoleon,' he said of Waterloo, 'just moved forward in the old style . . . and was driven off in the old style.'

But Wellington was fortunate – it was perhaps the only luck by which his generalship profited – to have commanded armies at the culmination of almost two centuries in which warfare had changed scarcely at all. Gunpowder had transformed the battlefield in the sixteenth century. The technical revolution it then brought about had dissolved all the old certainties by which war had been waged for 4,000 years, and with them the social systems they supported. Gunpowder, by substituting chemical energy for physical strength, put the under-fed and hastily trained on level terms with the muscular man-at-arms, whose *raison d'être* was fighting. It made the foot soldier the equal, if indeed not the master, of the cavalry-man, and robbed the overmighty subject of sanctuary from his overlord behind castle walls. It made those feudal rulers who had the wit to invest their revenues in cannon into kings and emperors and transformed simple seafarers who bought guns for their ships into world empire-builders.

But the gunpowder revolution was breathtakingly short-lived. By an effort of adaptation almost without parallel in human affairs, the Europe in which it occurred succeeded in little more than three generations in comprehending its nature and limiting its effect. The Renaissance and the Reformation are inconceivable without gun-powder. But by the end of the sixteenth century those two whirl-winds had been contained by the traditional aristocracies, whom Renaissance, Reformation and gunpowder together had threatened to rob of power, and absorbed into a new social order of which gunpowder was the controlling instrument. The ancient habit of bearing arms, universal but unmalign when real power rested with the 'strong man armed keeping his court', might by the gunpowder revolution have been translated into the 'right to bear arms', a genuinely seditious principle. That the right was withheld – at least until the coming of the 'Atlantic Revolutions' of 1776–1810 – derived from the resolutions made by rulers in Madrid, Vienna, Paris and London to monopolize the power unleashed by the gunpowder revolution and make that power the prerogative of the state.

The embodiments of that prerogative were to be the new state armies, the first Europe had known since the collapse of the Roman legionary system in the fifth century. They began to make their appearance in the sixteenth and by the seventeenth were full-fledged. All were characterized by a number of identical features. They were enlisted under a code of military law, usually ferocious in its sanctions. They were, in principle if not always in practice, regularly paid from central state funds, thereby imposing a charge on the revenues which required that tax-gathering become a bureaucratic procedure instead of an arbitrary exaction. They were uniformly clothed, by replacing with the king's livery that of the mercenary captains or the warrior's traditional motley. They were organized into units of increasingly standardized size and sub-division – regiments and battalions. But above all they were drilled. The origin of drill is held to be obscure. It is often said to be an expression of that urge to standardization of which uniform clothing and organization are also results. In fact the origin of drill is transparently obvious. Its development was a logical response to the danger inherent in the use of firearms by large numbers of men standing in close proximity to each other on a battlefield. Unsyn-chronized, the loading and firing of muskets by soldiers ranked next to and behind each other, bobbing, bending, turning, choosing their own targets and firing at will, must inevitably result in frequent and fatal accidents. The annual incidence of fatalities at the opening of the modern shooting season is proof enough of that danger. But partridge shooters and deer stalkers, wending their individual ways across the landscape, hit each other against the probabilities. Musketeers densely massed, as they had to be to maximize the firepower of short-range, slow-loading weapons, were trifling with the probabilities if they did not arrange all to fire at the same moment. Drill was no more than the institutionalization of such an arrangement. It ensured that each of the steps necessary to fill a musket with powder and ball – Maurice of Nassau, pioneer drill-master, stipulated forty-two – would be performed simultaneously, so that the culminating act, the pulling of the trigger, would occur only when each musketeer was standing upright and looking at the enemy. Accidents were not thereby precluded – drill will only minimize, not abolish self-centredness, clumsiness and over-excitement – but their incidence was very greatly reduced.

But drill had another effect. That was to act (whatever Grant said about inevitabilities) as an 'anti-progressive' influence on military technology and tactics. Initially such was not the case. The tendency of its influence was toward the refinement of weapon technology as a means of simplifying drill itself. Maurice of Nassau's total of forty-two steps was necessitated by the nature of the weapon he knew, the matchlock, whose handling required the management of quantities of loose gunpowder and a permanently smouldering fuse. Its transformation into the flintlock, whose characteristics did away first with the fuse and then with loose powder, both reduced the probability of accident – fuses and loose powder had a habit of getting together – and permitted the reduction of the number of drill steps from forty-two to about ten. An immediate effect was a greatly increased rate of fire, from one shot a minute to as many as three.

It was at this secondary stage that drill exerted its anti-progressive effect. The late seventeenth-century flintlock was amenable, even within the constraints of contemporary metallurgy and engineering, to considerable refinement. It might, for example, have been rifled, with high gains in range and accuracy. But rifled muskets, being more complicated as well as slower to load than smooth-bores, would have required a multiplication of drill steps and so imposed a retrogression on battlefield tactics. The same could be said of other gunpowder weapons, like siege and field cannon, whose management had also been reduced to standard drill sequences. Calculating costs against benefits (to apply a modern mode of thinking perhaps inappropriately to the past), seventeenth-century commanders arrived at the conclusion that simple drill and simple weapons served their purposes better than more refined weapons and less simple drill might have done.

The outcome, at any rate, is unarguable. Neither weapon technology nor drill sequences altered in essentials from the third quarter of the seventeenth century until almost the middle of the nineteenth. The British Tower Musket, popularly called the Brown Bess, equipped Marlborough's soldiers, Wolfe's soldiers and Wellington's soldiers alike. Its equivalents equipped the armies of Louis XIV, Peter the Great, Frederick the Great, George Washington, Napoleon and Bolivar, and the system of drill dictated by its simple technology won the battles of Blenheim, Poltava, Leuthen, Bunker Hill, Austerlitz, Waterloo and Carabobo. In every one of those battles the enemy 'moved forward in the old style and was driven off in the old style'.

But Grant was not born an American for nothing. In the long run, technology, as he rightly insisted, cannot be denied. The rifle, invented as early as 1615, was by 1815 a weapon whose time had come. Riflemen played a significant role at Waterloo, as they had done also in the Peninsula and as early as the American War of Independence, when the Kentucky breed had galled Redcoats at ranges that generals raised on European battlefields thought un-gentlemanly if not actually unethical. By 1842 British soldiers had been issued with a firearm whose firing mechanism superseded that of the old flintlock/matchlock for good. By 1853 this percussion musket had been rifled; as the 'Enfield' it would equip many soldiers of the American Civil War. And during the course of that war firearms engineered first to be breech-loading and then magazine-fed would come into use, thus inaugurating the technology which dominates infantry fighting to this day.

Wellington's certainty of touch in controlling his armies may thus be seen to have derived, in part at least, from the absence of technical and tactical change in warfare over the century and a half that preceded Waterloo. Eighteenth-century warfare has often been described as resembling a game of chess. Of course it did not, for the range and power of the 'pieces' available to the general were not arbitrarily limited by rules as are those of chessmen (even accepting that chess is a stereotyped war game). But his 'pieces' – infantry battalions, cavalry regiments – did nevertheless equate to each other in power and range of action to a quite remarkable degree. As a result good generals could 'play' a battle in a fashion not dissimilar from that by which a chessmaster plays his board; and a general of the intelligence and experience of Wellington, able to carry in his head an index of the speed at which his own and his opponent's units could move across the space separating them, the distance from each other at which their fire would prove effective, and the mutual loss they were likely to inflict, enjoyed against a commander not his equal something of the advantage that a grand master does against a merely competent challenger.

Stasis – the absence of change – conferred another, comple-mentary advantage on generals of the chessboard era: a certainty about the human equivalence of the armies they commanded. The impulsion to limit and control the gunpowder revolution was as much social as military or economic. And that was because it struck at the roots of the age-old connection between arms and landholding. For almost as long as men had gone to war, their leaders and their *corps d'élite* had been maintained by the ownership or tenancy of tillage and pasture. There had been exceptions to the principle. A few rulers – in Mesopotamia, in Egypt and in China – had succeeded in creating bureaucratic states where revenue could be raised directly from the cultivators and transferred through the central treasury to a royal standing army. The Romans had, over several centuries, transformed a militia of cultivators into a professional force. And the Islamic world had devised the unique institution of the slave army whose soldiers, until they took power for themselves, were sustained through the income of the Caliph's household. In almost every other warmaking society, however, land-holding and arms-bearing had always gone hand in hand.

An aristocracy was therefore by definition a class of both obligation and privilege, the one validating the other. Gunpowder, by invalidating the military usefulness of the European landholder – a man whose power on the battlefield derived from his horse, his retinue of followers and the skill-at-arms they learnt while peasants laboured to keep them in leisure – thereby challenged his privilege. It made the town-dweller or vagrant, who could be taught effective musketry by rapid schooling in drill, not only his equal but his superior. The crossbowman, his recent predecessor, had attracted the aristocrat's hatred for that reason, and all the more so because he had often been the employee of one of those nomad mercenary captains who, in the later middle years, kings and overlords were coming to find more immediately useful in the prosecution of their wars than the bucolic knight from the distant shires.

Confronted by the gunpowder revolution the knights of the shires might have given up the ghost. The mercenary captains – usually men of no birth, rarely men with land to their names – almost pushed them to that point. The captains' companies, officered at a subordinate level by a deputy (lieutenant or locum tenens) and superior servant (sergeant or sergeant major), formed units so readily marketable in the hire-and-fire business of late mediaeval and early modern warmaking that financial logic seemed to mark them as the force of the future. But two factors operated to inhibit the supplantation of the old landowning, 'feudal' hosts by the new mercenary armies (new only in a relative sense: mercenaries are as old as social upheaval in any settled society). The first was that employers found 'hire' a great deal easier than 'fire' in the mercenary market; some mercenary leaders, indeed (notably Francesco Sforza at Milan in the 1450s), objected so strenuously to 'fire' that they usurped power from the employers who threatened it and established dynasties of their own. That practice operated sharply to limit the number of sovereignties prepared to entrust their fortunes to hired soldiers. The second was that aristocrats, when compelled to opt for supplantation or adaptation, chose to adapt and made an excellent shift at acquiring mercenary skills.

By the mid-sixteenth century the sons of noble houses, who would not earlier have deigned to go warmaking unless mounted and armoured, were trailing a pike or shouldering a matchlock as if to the manner born. Soon afterwards their fathers were trading in the 'commission' market that bought the sons captaincies or lieutenancies, and so assured them military careers as if the purchase of title to warriordom were the most natural thing in the world. Military rank – a new concept – was thereby bought back into the aristocracy, thus on the one hand preserving the ancient nexus between land and arms and on the other reforging the old relationship between aristocracy and sovereign on a new basis.

Companies officered by 'sprigs of nobility', subordinated to the 'regiment' of colonels answering directly to the crown, recruited from the landless of the countryside and the jobless of the towns, clothed in the king's livery, paid from his treasury and armed from his arsenals, by the end of the seventeenth century provided the instrument through which the gunpowder revolution was bent to the service of dynastic statehood, harnessed to its wars and, at the same time, constrained from disrupting the social structures on which it subsisted.

Wellington was the inheritor of such an instrument. In the hands of Marlborough and Wolfe it had confronted its French equivalent on the battlefields of Flanders and North America and won. But their victories at Blenheim and Quebec owed nothing to differences in weapon technology, tactics or personnel, which were identical in the opposed armies; superior generalship alone underlay the outcomes. Wellington's triumph was therefore the greater for, though Napoleon's armies continued to resemble his at the material level, at the personal they had altered from those of dynastic statehood almost out of recognition.

Too much should not be made of Napoleon's boast that his armies offered 'a career open to talents'. Many of his officers were aristocrats or had held rank under Louis XVI. Many of his regiments were in origin an amalgamation of royal and revolutionary units. But some had been raised exclusively under the *tricolore*, while numbers of his generals had been mere sergeants under the old régime. Their experience in forging an army of the Republic out of that of the king on the one hand and the sovereign people on the other is an index both of the difficulty of their task and of the unique nature of what they created. Godart, for example, a former royal sergeant and future Napoleonic general, on being elected colonel of his revolutionary regiment in 1792 was denounced by his soldiers as 'a despot who despises liberty and equality' and threatened with hanging when he tried to teach them drill. Yet such regiments could, for all their hostility to traditional tactics, devastate armies of the old style through their sheer exuberance of spirit. A French royalist officer who fought against the Revolution denounced the 'hellish tactic' in which 'fifty thousand savage beasts foaming at the mouth like cannibals hurl themselves at top speed upon soldiers whose courage has been excited by no passion'.

The passion that animated the armies of the Revolution, and was transfused from them into the armies of Napoleon, derived from the idea that every man must, but also could, be a soldier. 'The general force of the Republic,' the Constitution of June 1793 decreed, 'is composed of the entire people . . . all Frenchmen shall be soldiers; all shall be trained in the handling of arms.' Two months later the Committee of Public Safety articulated this principle in even fuller form: 'Every Frenchman is permanently requisitioned for service with the armies. The young men shall fight; married men will manufacture weapons and transport stores; women shall make tents and nurse in the hospitals; children shall turn old linen into lint; the old men shall repair to the public squares to raise the courage of the warriors and preach the unity of the Republic and hatred against the kings.'

This detachment of military obligation from constraints of property, class, age or sex was truly revolutionary. It may indeed be regarded as the most revolutionary of the principal ideas put into circulation by the Revolution. 'Fraternity', after all, is a Christian virtue; 'Liberty' was the central value of the Greeks. 'Equality', on the other hand, was a principle not merely denied by most previous political philosophies, but rightly denied. For how may the individual become equal without the means to make himself so? Equality in law presumes a system of justice, equality of wealth a system of redistribution, and so in either case a superordinate authority. Authority had served the first patchily, the second never. But equality *tout court*, the notion that one man is as good as another, acquired real meaning if 'all shall be soldiers'. For, by that prescription, the right of the aristocrat or the property owner to ride roughshod over the peasant and artisan is abolished not only in theory but in fact. One soldier, in the age of the flintlock musket, *was* as good as another. His musket, issued him by the Republic, was a symbol not just of civic status but of personal power. It was certainly a brave officer who argued otherwise; hence the immediate abolition of corporal punishment in the French army at the onset of the Revolution in 1789. Hence, too, the right arrogated to themselves by the *'armées revolutionnaires'* – bands of armed political activists with a self-proclaimed authority to carry the revolution from Paris into the provinces – to bully and rob the ideologically half-hearted in the immediate aftermath of 1789.

But, as with so many political principles stringently applied, 'equality' in its military dimension proved to be a hollow idea. 'All shall be soldiers' does not translate readily, does not translate in any way, into 'All *can* be soldiers'. Older societies, which the Revolution claimed to have superseded, discriminated between warrior and non-warrior for a very good reason: that the soldier's trade is a harsh one – harsh emotionally as well as physically – which but a minority is fitted to perform. Only the young and strong can stand long marches, poor food, short sleep, scanty shelter, wet, cold, thirst and the constant burden of musket, knapsack and cartridge pouch. Only the tough and well-integrated can bear the risks of the battlefield, the callousness of combat, the agony of bereavement among friends and comrades. The Revolutionary and Napoleonic armies learnt those truths by hard practice. In the first flush of enthusiasm for revolutionary ideals or imperial glory, men flocked to their colours; exposed to the harsh reality of campaigning, men deserted in droves. The antidote was to be found in the imposition of disciplines altogether contrary to the ethos of the Revolution in its bright, confident morning: fines, imprisonment and execution.

The culmination of the French wars of 1792–1815 was therefore rich in portents for the future. Three elements in particular of the military system which had emerged from them rode in easy equilibrium. The first was the discovery that the pool of potential warriors that states could bend to their service comprehended a far larger proportion of the total population than they had earlier been willing or able to enlist. The second was that the pool required disciplining and drilling in a traditional manner if it were to obey orders. The third was that drill had begun to cede its central role in warfare to superior weapon power, represented primarily by the rifle, which promised to transfer advantage in warmaking to whichever society could most rapidly master the processes of technological change. That society would not be Wellington's. Fertile though New Britain was in the invention and production of machines by industrial process, Old Britain held its engineers at arm's length, excluded them from traditional society and stoutly preserved its central institutions for its own favourite sons. The army was one such institution. Wellington might describe it in 1828 as 'an exotic, unknown to the old constitution of the country . . . disliked by the inhabitants, and particularly by the higher orders, some of whom never allow their families to serve in it'. But the middle orders – the landed gentry, merchants and the professional class – looked to it to provide respectable employment for their male offspring. Through the purchase of commissions, the means by which the feudal aristocracy had contained the socially disruptive effect of the gunpowder revolution, their money continued to secure such employment until as late as 1871. And the trade was then abolished only in the teeth of fierce parliamentary opposition.

By that date, however, it was only the British who clung to the idea that an officer owned his rank as a piece of negotiable property. The French, their principal military competitors, had abolished purchase at the Revolution. At a much earlier date the other major European states had invested the right to commission in the sovereign. Qualification to hold rank varied from country to country. In Prussia and, to a lesser extent, Austria it was confined to those of noble birth. In Russia, the gift of rank reposed with the Tsar, who conferred guards and staff rank on the greater nobles, leaving ordinary regimental office to backwoodsmen. In only one advanced country was the title to military rank confined to those qualified to hold it by professional education. That country was the United States, which in 1802 founded what may well be regarded as the most significant of the world's officer-training institutions, its Military Academy at West Point. It was the school that was to produce Ulysses Simpson Grant.

The Professional Career of U.S. Grant

West Point! Who today among the visitors that tour its superb campus in their tens of thousands re-create in the mind's eye the tiny

college it was a century and a half ago? Then it was its strategic
location on the bluff above the Hudson River, dominating passage
from British-held Canada to the city of New York, that explained its
existence. Now West Point justifies itself. Its magnificent buildings
are one expression of its reputation. The roll call of its graduates is
another: among Presidents, Eisenhower and Grant, among great
Americans, Edgar Allan Poe and James McNeill Whistler ('Had
silicon been a gas, I would have been a major general,' so he ruefully
characterized one of his examination answers).

Grant's West Point, of which traces remain in the pretty Federal
houses lining one side of the Plain where the Corps of Cadets
parades in its 'long grey line', belonged to the second of the two
parallel traditions defining formal officer education since its inception in the sixteenth century. That second tradition was professional; its subject matter was ballistics, fortification and civil engineering. The first and marginally older was altogether different in
orientation; its purpose was both to civilize and to discipline the
existing warrior class.

That purpose had been served in the centuries of knighthood
much as it had in Macedonia before the accession of Alexander's
father, Philip. Stripling warriors were sent to court or to the
household of a great warrior to learn skill-at-arms and military
comportment. But just as Macedonia's transition from frontier
kingdom to imperial power prompted Philip to found a school for its
future leaders, so too did the gunpowder revolution drive the
European states that understood its impetus to replace the page
system with another that was formal, centralized and state-directed.
Their motives, in John Hale's words, were threefold: 'a desire to
moderate the lawlessness [of the traditional officer class]; an urge to
protect its status as the natural leader of society; and worry about its
decreasing militancy.' Of these the concern to moderate its lawlessness was the most powerful. Individualism had been an asset when
success in battle turned on brawn and bloodthirstiness. The onset of
drill called for different qualities, and above all the readiness to obey
orders. Hence the nature of the curriculum taught by the embryo
military academies founded in Elizabeth's England, Henry IV's
France, sixteenth-century Venice and early seventeenth-century
Germany. That at Siegen in Westphalia, for example, opened by
John of Nassau in 1617, taught a syllabus inspired by the innovations of the founder's relative, William: languages for the intellect,

riding and fencing for civility, but constant parade-ground drill for discipline.

None of these experimental institutions survived into the modern world. But those of their much later successors that did – Sandhurst in Britain, St Cyr in France, the Theresiania in Austria – clung to their informing principles. The intended purpose of the training in all of them was to produce young men who could obey the rules of polite society at home and the orders of their superiors on campaign. Competence in the higher technicalities of warfare counted for less or nothing at all.

The puzzling exclusion of the sciences of fortification and artillery from the syllabus is usually explained by a social factor: that engineering and gunnery had never been thought callings for the warrior. But that is to import into the sixteenth century the attitudes of the eighteenth. At the outset of the gunpowder revolution, guns were so few and inaccurate that gunnery was no science at all. It was regarded, John Guilmartin has pointed out, as a 'mystery', and its few expert practitioners as men endowed with an individual and unteachable gift. Fortification, on the other hand, pertained to architecture, thus to art, and so to a different tradition of education altogether. Michelangelo, trained in the studio of Ghirlandaio at Florence in the 1480s, actually argued in later life that he did not 'know much about painting or sculpture but [had] gained a great experience of fortifications', of his skill in which he was immensely proud. His boast was made to Sangallo, a member of one of a group of families, including the Savangnano, Antonelli, Peruzzi and Genga, which achieved a virtual monopoly over military architectural practice in northern Italy, home of the new 'artillery' fortification during the sixteenth century. Their members came to form an international cartel of fortification experts, jealously guarding their secrets, whose services commanded high fees from rulers as far distant as the kings of Portugal and the tsars of Muscovy. It was not until the end of the seventeenth century that the dominance of these commercial practitioners was broken and a sufficient pool of professionals emerged to be salaried as state employees. Once that step was achieved, it took only one more for governments to found national engineering academies, and so to put the training of their own engineering, and later artillery, officers on a permanent footing.

The British Royal Military Academy at Woolwich (1741) was one, the French École de Génie at Mezières another. With their foundation the social difference between engineer and artillery officers on the one hand and infantry and cavalry officers on the other began to make itself apparent. The latter group, still drawn from or claiming membership of the old warrior class with its philistine traditions, was disqualified by lack of formal education from competing for entry to the new schools. The former, who were less often warrior by breeding, were further disadvantaged by the aggressive dislike that the ignorant almost always feel for the educated. And that dislike was heightened, in the military context, by the extra dimension of danger that their skills added to the risks infantrymen and cavalrymen had always run on the battlefield. Artillery was a killer at longer ranges than those over which horse or foot could retaliate; fortification intensified to an almost unbearable degree the ferocity of close combat. There were understandable reasons, therefore, for warrior officers keeping their social distance from those of the 'scientific' corps, even if it was with the latter that the future of warfare lay.

These social distinctions expressed themselves in Britain and France by the continued separation of the warrior from the scientific academies until as late as the twentieth century; in other European states they took the form of a growling condescension towards sapper and gunner officers, whose uniforms were always dowdier, though their pay was higher, than those of the horse and foot. In only one advanced country did these corrosive snobberies not take root. That was the United States where, from the outset, a single military academy trained the army's embryo leaders in a stringently scientific discipline. West Point, though not the oldest surviving officer school in the world, was thus the first to be founded on lines that set the pattern for military education of the future.

The West Point that Grant entered in 1839 was, however, but the nucleus of the world institution it was destined to become. Its cadet body numbered fewer than 300; his class was only fifty-three strong. Like Grant himself, born to a tanner of Georgetown, Ohio, most of its members (they included Longstreet, McClellan, Buckner and Sherman), as Grant wrote, were 'from families that were trying to gain advancement in position or to prevent slippage from a precarious place'. The gentry of the New England cities and Southern plantations were sparsely represented; Lee, from the aristocracy of tidewater Virginia, was an exceptional figure among the academy's graduates. Grant, though of impeccable Pilgrim Father origins, probably indicated the horizons of most of his fellows when he wrote home in his first year that 'the fact is that if a man graduates here he is safe fer life' (his spelling was to remain endearingly erratic all his days).

Yet his Ohio origins may have been as significant to his generalship as his West Point education. Ohio in the 1840s was both the young republic's most secure bridgehead in the great interior of the continent that lies beyond the Appalachian chain, and a firm stronghold of Free Soil principles on the border of the slave states to its south. Ohio people's values were those that would come to dominate the American way: free enterprise rooted in personal property ownership, here represented by mixed farming and its associated trades, and passionate respect for education, already manifest in the foundation of a plethora of liberal arts colleges, of which it maintains a larger number of high quality to this day than any other state. It was also to prove a bastion of Northern military power when the Civil War engulfed the Union. Grant's Ohio birth was therefore both appropriate and at the same time formative in its influence on his outlook as an American.

For his formation as a soldier his West Point education was equally important. West Point taught little tactics and no more drill than was necesary for the Corps of Cadets to manoeuvre itself on the parade ground. The emphasis of the syllabus was on mathematics, engineering and science, the latter course broadened by Dennis Hart Mahan (father of the famous admiral) to comprehend the 'Science of War'. Mahan, a graduate of the French military engineering school at Metz (successor to Mezières), a devotee of the Napoleonic myth and an expositor of the idea of Napoleon's interpreter, Jomini, nevertheless added something distinctively American to his interpretation of the nature of war. America, it has been said, is a country dominated by the dimension not of time – as is Europe, trammelled by its history – but of space. It was to that concept that Mahan addressed himself in his lectures year after year when he argued that 'carrying the war into the heart of the assailant's country . . . is the surest way of making him share its burdens and foiling his plans'. Lee, a grandson-in-law of George Washington and a superintendent of West Point but not a pupil of Mahan, was never to strike nearer the heartland of the North than Pennsylvania. Grant, in his distant and at the time disregarded campaigning around Vicksburg on the Mississippi, was to give Mahan's dictum terrible force. By the doctrine of 'making the assailant share the burdens of war', and his contemporary, Sherman, tore the heart out of the Confederacy and restored its shattered parts to the government of the Union.

Grant's contemporaries might, however, have been forgiven for discounting the likelihood that he would rise to high place in the army. Physically slight, personally self-effacing, academically undistinguished, Grant left little trace of his passage through West Point or on the army during his brief professional career. Commissioned in 1843 into the infantry, when he would have preferred the dragoons (horsemanship was one of the few cadet accomplishments at which he excelled), he served first at St Louis and then at New Orleans. His regiment, the 4th Infantry, was then despatched to the Mexican border as part of the 'army of observation' with which the United States had decided to browbeat its neighbour into ceding all territory north of the Rio Grande. As Grant himself put it, the army's strategy was to 'provoke a fight, but it was essential that Mexico should start it'.

Grant strongly disapproved of this policy. A democrat and populist to his fingertips, he was possessed by the reality of American civilization and the difference between it and that of the Old World. When in May 1846 Mexico was provoked to war, he declared it 'one of the most unjust ever waged by a stronger against a weaker nation. It was an instance of a republic following the bad example of European monarchies, in not considering justice in their desire to acquire additional territory.' But for all his disapproval of it, the Mexican War taught Grant his business. He fought in four battles – at Palo Alto, Resaca, Monterrey and Mexico City, acted (very significantly for his future mastery of logistics) as a supply and transport officer, saw death at close hand, observed the behaviour in danger of soldiers high and low, took an acute measure of his own reactions and recorded what he saw and felt in a series of brilliant letters home to his fiancée, Julia Dent. They were to form the basis of his recollections of the war published in his magnificent *Memoirs* with which, though written when dying of cancer at the end of his life, he was to repair the last of many financial disasters.

'A great many men,' he said, 'when they smell battle afar off, chafe to get into the fray. When they say so themselves they generally fail to convince their hearers . . . and as they approach danger they become more subdued. The rule is not universal, for I have known a few men who were always aching for a fight when there was no enemy near, who were as good as their word when the battle did come. But the number of such men is small.' Grant may, as his biographer William McFeely suggests, have been such a man. Unerringly overtrusting of others in financial relationships, he looked at himself and all other soldiers going about their business with the keenest realism. Though he recognized a pang of anxiety in himself the first time he heard a gun fired distantly in anger, he found on face-to-face encounter with danger that he was not unmanned. This confidence in his physical courage – discovery of his moral courage would come later – was the foundation of his future generalship.

His baptism of fire was as gruesome as any soldier could have experienced. Low-velocity gunpowder weapons, though they did not reach to any great range, threw large pieces of heavy metal which, when they struck, could grossly disfigure without actually killing. Grant, at Palo Alto, was the witness of such an atrocity when 'a ball struck close by me killing one man instantly, it nocked Capt Page's under jaw entirely off and broke in the roof of his mouth . . . Capt Page,' he told Julia, 'is still alive.' In his *Memoirs* he recalled that 'the splinters from the musket of the killed soldier, and his brains and bones knocked down two or three others'.

Grant knew what he was risking, therefore, when next day he took over a company and led it in an attack against the enemy, and again at Monterrey when he joined voluntarily in a cavalry charge. In the assault on the city he made a daring single-handed dash to bring up a resupply of ammunition and felt a proper disgust that some 'poor wounded officers and men' he had pased on his ride 'fell into the hands of the enemy during the night and died'. Finally, in the capture of Mexico City, he achieved personal distinction. Spotting a vantage point, in a suburban church during the battle for the city walls, he installed a light howitzer in the tower and brought one of the Mexican bastions under fire. His divisional commander sent an officer (Pemberton, who would hold Vicksburg against Grant in 1863) to compliment him and got his name mentioned in despatches. He was also promoted lieutenant and breveted captain. He had had – Mexico City was the last battle – a good war.

But it was not by Grant's fastidious political judgement a good war at all. At the human level, of course, it had been a young man's wonderful adventure. 'The war was our romance,' said his classmate, friend and future opponent Simon Bolivar Buckner, and it can indeed be seen as the young American regular army's share in that extraordinary nineteenth-century romance lived out by European soldiers in the world's distant, hot and exotic corners. Grant was entranced in Mexico by the character of its landscape and people in exactly the same way as were British officers by the relics of Moghul India and the customs of the Sikhs, or French officers by the oases of the Sahara and the nomadism of the Tuareg. For the warfare of imperialism was a cultural exploration as well as an exercise of subjection, and it produced a literature of travel and ethnography of a quality that can distract the reader altogether from the purpose which brought the writer into touch with his subject in the first place.

The purpose, nevertheless, was conquest and annexation, and of both Grant the republican and democrat disapproved to his bones. 'The Mexican War,' he wrote in old age, 'was a political war and the administration conducting it desired to make political capital out of it.' It was political at a personal as well as party level. Its two most successful commanders, Taylor, the victor of Buena Vista, and Scott, the captor of Mexico City, both aspired on their laurels to the presidency, which Taylor actually secured in 1848. Worst of all, it was a war with dire political consequences for the United States itself. 'The Southern rebellion', Grant wrote in his *Memoirs*, 'was largely the outcome of the Mexican War.' He shared the view that the Democratic administration sought, by annexation of territory south of the Free Soil line, to find room for creating new slave states, as Texas would become, and so to circumvent the opposition of the Northern electoral majority to any extension of slavery. The consequences, he thought, were inevitable. 'Nations, like individuals, are punished for their transgressions. We got our punishment in the most sanguinary and expensive war of modern times.'

That lay thirteen years beyond victory in Mexico. In the interim Grant himself suffered much emotional punishment for no real transgression, except an inability to be hard-headed about money. A posting with the 4th Infantry Regiment to the Pacific coast involved a separation from Julia, who had become his wife on his return from Mexico in 1848, so painful that he was driven to resign his commission as a means of getting home to her. It was from that exile that his reputation as a drinker – probably exaggerated, though he became a chain-smoker of cigars – derives. Grant left the army on honourable terms in the permanent rank of captain, of which there were only fifty in 1854. But he brought no money back east, and there one business venture after another failed. Farming in Missouri, from a house called Hardscrabble which he built himself, yielded poor crops or none. He failed to get work as an engineer, an extraordinary rejection when West Point was the principal source of trained engineers in the United States. He failed as a debt-collector. He made no success even of working as a clerk in his father's leather business in Galena, Illinois.

In 1861, on the eve of the Civil War, Grant, aged thirty-nine, with four children at home and scarcely a penny in the bank, had made no mark on the world and looked unlikely to do so, for all the boom conditions of mid-century America. His Plymouth Rock ancestry, his specialist education, his military rank, which together must have ensured him a sheltered corner in the life of the Old World, counted for nothing in the New. He lacked the essential quality to be what Jacques Barzun has called a 'booster', one of those bustling, bonhomous, penny-counting, chance-grabbing optimists who, whether in the frenetic commercial activity of the Atlantic coast, in the emergent industries of New England and Pennsylvania or on the westward-moving frontier, were to make America's fortune. Grant, in his introspective and undemonstrative style, was a gentleman, and crippled by that quality.

The Civil War would, as perhaps only the Civil War could, rescue him from his social disability. For Grant was a gentleman in a distinctively American conformation. The Wellingtonian gentleman could conceive of no quarrel between himself and official society. 'I am *nimmukwallah*,' Wellington had said; he had eaten the King's salt. Grant, too, as a soldier had been *nimmukwallah*. But America, having no king, accorded its citizens a freedom to differ about its politics quite foreign to Grant's equivalent class in Europe. He clove to his own view of how the Great Republic should behave in its relations with weaker neighbours and dissident member states. That view was formed by a constitutionalism that might have been Washington's. The United States, as he saw it, was a country morally different from those of Europe. It should incur the stain neither of aggression in foreign relations nor of infidelity to the Union in domestic politics. The Mexican war had been a bad war for the first reason. For the second, a war against the 'Southern rebellion', as he called the secession of the slave states, would be a good war, even though his cold eye told him that war was a thing bad in itself.

His propensity to judge the politics of warmaking is an index of the changes in the commander's role that set Grant apart from Alexander on the one hand, and Wellington on the other. Alexander distinguished not at all between his role as ruler and his role as warrior. The two – in a world where states were held to be at war unless an agreement to observe peace specifically held otherwise, and in a kingdom whose court was also a headquarters – were identical. Judgements about the morality of any particular war would have been as alien to him as they would have been treasonable in a subject. Alexander was, in the strict sense, both the complete Hegelian and the perfect Nietzscheian. His state was the supreme expression of Reason and Will; he, as its ruler, Superman. Wellington, rooted in a society of law and institutions, would have been affronted by both notions; to him tyranny and *raison d'état* were equally repugnant. For all the power he exercised, he strictly circumscribed his own freedom to question orders or contest strategies. As a man whose highest ambition had once been to hold rank 'as a major-general in His Majesty's service', he drew the sharpest distinction between his political opinions and his military duties. Both in India and in Spain, distance and consequent delay in communication had shielded him from day-to-day interference in his conduct of the campaign. But he did not thereby conceive himself empowered to make policy. Grant's position was different again. Like Wellington, he rejected Alexander's identification of military with political power. Unlike Wellington, he fought for his country not because birth made him its subject but because he judged its cause just. 'The Confederates proclaimed themselves aliens, and thereby disbarred themselves of all right to claim protection under the Constitution of the United States, [becoming] like people of any other foreign state who make war upon an independent nation.'

The Confederates' proclamation of their alien status came when 'on the 11th of April [1861] Fort Sumter, a National fort in the harbour of Charleston, South Carolina, was fired upon by the Southerners and a few days after was captured'. The news reached Galena, Illinois, on April 15, prompted the town worthies to call for the recruitment of a Galena company and led to Grant's election as chairman of the recruitment meeting. The day changed Grant's life. 'I saw new energies in him,' recalled a neighbour. 'He dropped a stoop-shouldered way of walking, and set his hat forward on his forehead in a jaunty fashion.' Grant himself said, 'I never went into our leather store after that meeting, to put up a package or do any other business.' Within three years he would be General in Chief of the Armies of the United States. Within seven he would be President.

Grant's Army

Grant's election was one of thousands to take place all across the United States that April. In his case it was prompted by his fellow citizens' discovery that he was a West Pointer and a veteran of the Mexican War. Few towns were so endowed. The United States, already one of the most populous countries of the Western world, with more than 30 million inhabitants, was also one of the least militarized. Its regular army numbered only 16,000; Britain, with 27 million citizens and a navy larger than the next six put together, maintained an army of more than 200,000 men. Most of the American regular army, moreover, was stationed on and west of the Mississippi, guarding the settlement routes into Indian territory. There, in large measure, it was to stay throughout the Civil War, producing the odd effect that many of the country's few professional soldiers advanced their careers not at all by the one great professional chance the century was to offer them, simply because they were already in service when war broke out. It was largely on West Pointers like Grant who had taken their discharge in peace or who 'went South' in 1861 that the 'stars were to fall'.

Of some 2,000 graduates of West Point living in 1861, 821 were in service. Of these 197 'went South', together with 99 from the retired list. The Union retained the loyalty of 624 serving officers and immediately recruited another 122 from retirement. It was these men who, North and South, provided the Civil War armies with their seasoning of professional leadership. The armies themselves were almost wholly amateur and, until the introduction of conscription (1862 in the Confederacy, 1863 in the Union), voluntarily enlisted. They went about officering themselves in a uniquely American way. Some commanding officers of regiments were appointed by state governors, the regiments of both North and South being raised on a state basis; others, and almost all company and platoon officers, were elected by their men. Grant had experience of both methods. He first of all declined to stand for election by the Galena company, then later accepted from the governor of Illinois the colonelcy of a regiment which had thought better of its elected choice.

A Southern private in a Georgia regiment wrote home in 1861 to describe how it conducted its election of officers; the account must hold good for Northern regiments too: 'I could start out here and now and eat myself dead on "election cake", be hugged into a perfect "squish" by particular, eternal, disinterested, affectionate friends. A man is perfectly bewildered by the intensity of feeling that is lavished upon him. I never dreamed I was held so popular, fine-looking and talented as I found I am during the past few days.' The writer was not a candidate and found those who were, as so many Americans do their would-be leaders, figures of fun. In practice, many elected officers would perform competently in rank. Others would not. 'Colonel Roberts has showed himself to be ignorant of the most simple company movements. There is a total lack of system about our regiment,' wrote a Pennsylvanian private in the summer of 1861. 'Nothing is attended to at the proper time, nobody looks ahead to the morrow, and business heads to direct are wanting. We can only be justly called a mob and one not fit to face the enemy.' At the outset they were more dangerous to each other than to the Confederates; a regiment of cavalrymen drilling with swords frightened their horses into running away, reported the *Detroit Free Press* in September 1861, while infantrymen trying to execute the drill order to fix bayonets inflicted wounds on each other.

Drill, the fundament of success in gunpowder battle, had so little permeated the United States that Grant himself was uncertain of his recollection of the lessons taught at West Point. 'I had never looked at a copy of tactics from my graduation. My standing in that branch of studies had been near the foot of the class . . . The arms had been changed since then and [other] tactics adopted. I got a copy . . . and studied one lesson, intending to confine the exercise of the first day [with his new regiment] to the commands I thus learned. By pursuing this course I thought I would soon get through the volume.' Grant found his scheme both harder and easier than he hoped. Sticking to the rules, he saw, would lead to disaster. Reducing them to what he remembered from West Point would make them work. 'I found no trouble in giving commands that would take my regiment where I wanted it to go and carry it around all obstacles. I do not believe that the officers of the regiment ever

discovered that I had never studied the tactics I used.'
The eventuality was unlikely. A typical Union, or Confederate, regiment was formed of men wholly innocent of war in any form. Braggart though the regimental titles they adopted were – some Confederate units of 1861 called themselves the Tallapoosa Thrashers, Bartow Yankee Killers, Chickasaw Desperadoes, Lexington Wildcats, Raccoon Roughs and South Florida Bulldogs – the young men who joined them were more likely to know how to slaughter a pig than shoot a human being. In both armies half those enlisted gave their occupation as farmer; common labourers came next, and then tradesmen – carpenters, shoemakers, clerks, blacksmiths, painters, mechanics, machinists, masons and printers. A high proportion of Northerners were foreign-born, Germans, Irishmen and Scandinavians being the most numerous, a factor that complicated election. More Germans, who had done military service at home, and Irishmen, who might have served in the British army, had military experience than native Yankees. That made for no love lost in the ranks. 'I didn't vote for you,' jeered an Indiana private, 'and I wouldn't vote for any damned Irish son of a bitch. I don't care a damn for you.' He spoke from the frustration of 'first thing in the morning drill, then drill, then drill again. Then drill, drill, a little more drill. Then drill and lastly drill. Between drills we drill – and sometimes stop to eat a little and have a roll-call.' Work for those elected to rank went on when it stopped for the privates. 'Every night I recite with the other 1st Sergeants and 2nd Lieutenants,' wrote an Ohio sergeant in 1862. 'We shall finish Hardee's *Tactics* [the book with which Grant had had trouble] and then study the Army Regulations.' But for all their trouble, the volunteers continued to look like amateurs. 'Oh, father, how splendidly the regulars drill,' wrote a volunteer who had seen a regiment of the pre-war army on parade in 1862. 'It is perfectly sickening and disgusting to get back here and see our regiment and officers manoeuvre, after seeing those West Pointers and those veterans of eighteen years' service go through guard mounting.'

Such regiments were swamped by the unskilled masses that enthusiasm for the war brought to the colours at its outbreak. Volunteering quickly provided the South with nearly a quarter of a million men. Lincoln's call for 75,000 to serve for three months was instantly fulfilled. By August he had nearly 400,000 men under arms. But by then the first battles – Bull Run and Booneville – had been fought and some of the volunteers had thought better of their enlistment. Desertions were to plague both armies throughout the war and, in an essentially populist society, defy containment by punishment. That was particularly so in the South; a Mississippi judge wrote in 1864 that he knew many men 'now in desertion for the fourth, fifth and sixth times' who had 'never been punished'. Neither army had the resources to imprison the recalcitrants who, if really determined not to serve, could always make their escape to the open frontier or the immigrant-swollen cities of the North. Some 200,000 Union soldiers, out of 2 million enlisted, deserted temporarily or permanently during the war; only 141 of those caught actually underwent execution, the maximum penalty, for their crime.

That so many did run is not the least surprising in view of their unreadiness for the hardship of campaign and the horror of the battlefield. Of the march to Fort Donelson in February 1862 a Northern soldier wrote, 'Wee had a hard time getting to this place. I beleave that we endured the most intence sufering that an army ever did in the same length of time' [so much for the Grand Army's retreat from Moscow]. 'We were bound to lay for fore days and knights without sleeping and most of the time nothing to eat and raining and snowing a portion of the time with out any covering whatever was what I cald a bitter pill.' The experience of battle could drive men to triumphs of emotion over bare literacy. 'Martha,' Thomas Warwick wrote home to his wife after Murfreesboro in December 1862, 'I can inform you that I have seen the Monkey Show at last and I don't waunt to see it no more I am satisfide with ware Martha. I can't tell you how many ded men I did see . . . they were piled up one on another all over the Battel feel . . . Men was shot every fashington that you mite call for some had there hedes shot off and some their armes and leges . . . I tell you that I am tirde of ware . . . One thing shore I don't want to see that site no more.' An Alabamian told his sister after Chickamauga in September 1863, 'I have all ways crave to fite a lit[tle] gust to no what it is to go in to a battle but I got the chance to tri my hand at last anough to sad isfi me I never wan to go in an nother fite any more sister I wan to come home worse than I eaver did be fore.'

'I don't want to go that way if I can get home any other way,' he went on, 'but thare has been agrate meney soldiers runing a way lately.' In that juxtaposition lay the explanation of much of the generals' success, North and South, in keeping their armies intact.

In a land of immigration and free settlement, with the sketchiest of civil bureaucracies and a strongly egalitarian spirit prevailing among the soldiers of both sides, it was their willingness to accept discipline, rather than their officers' power to impose it, that ultimately kept them under arms. That willingness derived, when all allowance has been made for the inducement of regular rations and pay, from belief in the cause – Confederacy or Union, as the case was – thus making the Blue and the Gray the first truly ideological armies of history. No issue of personality blurred the quarrel, as it had in the English Civil War, and none of freedom or subjection to foreign rule, as in the struggles of Washington and Bolivar against Britain and Spain. The American Civil War was a civil war in the strictest sense, and its soldiers required to be led, not driven, to battle. Grant understood that, as his handling of his first regimental command clearly demonstrated:

> My regiment [the 21st Illinois] was composed in large part of young men of as good social position as any in their section of the State. It embraced the sons of farmers, lawyers, physicians, politicians, merchants, bankers and ministers, and some men of maturer years who had filled such positions themselves . . . The Colonel, elected by the votes of the regiment, had proved to be fully capable of developing all there was in his men of recklessness [i.e. indiscipline]. When there came a prospect of battle the regiment wanted to have someone else to lead them. I found it very hard work for a few days to bring all the men with anything like subordination; but the great majority favoured discipline, and by the application of a little regular army punishment all were reduced to as good discipline as one could ask.

'The great majority favoured discipline . . .' In those words, Grant discloses the touch that was to make him master of the Union armies. All who preceded him in the supreme command he would eventually inherit had tried to fight the American Civil War by methods inappropriate to its nature. Scott, the 'Giant of Three Wars' (but also 'Old Fuss and Feathers'), correctly foresaw in his Anaconda Plan that the South would have to be isolated and blockaded, but expected rebellion then to collapse from within. McClellan, the 'Young Napoleon', sought to wage war as he had seen it made by European armies in the Crimea; he would move nowhere without mountains of supplies and myriads of men, driving Lincoln to exasperate that 'sending reinforcements to McClellan is like shovelling flies across a barn'. Burnside (whose magnificent mutton-chop whiskers gave us 'sideburns') was much less fierce of heart than of face; he had twice refused the supreme command and when persuaded to accept it muddled his way into defeat. 'Fighting Joe' Hooker, who succeeded him, was unsuited to high command for different reasons. He would not take Lincoln into his confidence – a supreme failing in a political war – and commanded none among his colleagues. Meade, his replacement, could not grasp the political nature of the war at all; he resented the requirement for 'the war to be made on individuals' and wanted to win it by the old strategy of manoeuvre between armies. 'A proper Philadelphian who would "not even speak to any person connected with the press", [he] exasperated the War Correspondents and bored other Americans.'

Halleck, 'Old Brains', who acted as general-in-chief at Washington until displaced by Grant in 1864, comprehended the war's nature least of all. A pedant of the worst sort, he had translated Jomini, escape from whose narrow geometrical strictures was a prerequisite for victory on the vast campaigning fields of North America. As Grant's superior in the West, he was nearly to destroy that anti-Jominian's will to continue in service, so strongly did he deprecate Grant's urge to 'keep moving on'. A prisoner of his schooling at West Point, as in their different ways were also McClellan, Burnside, Hooker and Meade, Halleck held that 'moving on' was permissible only within limits defined by map and set-square. An army's 'base of operations', in his view, should also form the base of a right-angular corridor within which all manoeuvre should be confined.

But Grant knew, or was quickly to discover, that in a war of people against people, dispersed in a vast, rich but almost empty land, an army need have no permanent base at all. All that it required to operate was the ability to draw military supplies behind it by river and railroad, while it fed itself on the produce of the districts through which it marched. All that it then required to win was drill, discipline and belief in itself. Grant could supply all three.

Once established in command he would show himself at times as authoritarian as Wellington at his most iron ducal. 'Complaints have come in', he wrote toa subordinate general on January 20, 1863, 'of the outrageous conduct of the 7th Kansas . . . stopping to plunder the citizens instead of pursuing the enemy . . . If there are further

complaints well substantiated I wish you to arrest [the Colonel] and
have him tried for incompetency and his regiment dismounted and
disarmed . . . All the laurels won by the regiment . . . has been more
than counter-balanced by their bad conduct since . . . Their present
course may serve to frighten women and children and helpless old
men but will never drive out an armed enemy.' More impressive,
and far more revealing of his understanding of an ideological war,
was his handling of his soldiers before he had won laurels of his own
to substantiate his authority.

Discussing the failure of his subordinate, Carlos Buell, in the
Shiloh campaign, he recognized that he was a 'strict disciplinarian'
but suggested that, as a pre-war regular, 'he did not distinguish
sufficiently between the volunteer who "enlisted for the war" and the
soldier who serves in time of peace. One system embraced men who
risked life for a principle, and often men of social standing,
competence or wealth and independence of character. The other
included, as a rule, only men who could not do as well in any other
occupation.' During the Shiloh campaign, he himself had been
criticized for not putting his men to dig entrenchments, which might
have spared them the heavy casualties they suffered in the battle.
But he had decided that 'the troops needed discipline and drill more
than they did experience with the pick, shovel and axe. Reinforcements were arriving almost daily, composed of troops that had been
hastily thrown together into companies and regiments -- fragments of
incomplete organisations, the men and officers strangers to each
other.' He had seen the consequences of neglecting drill at the earlier
battle of Belmont. 'The moment the [enemy's] camp was reached
our men laid down their arms and commenced rummaging the tents
to pick up trophies. Some of the higher officers were little better
than the privates. They galloped about from one cluster of men to
another and at every halt delivered a short eulogy upon the Union
cause and the achievements of the command.'

No stronger Union man was to be found than Grant. But he
valued a day of drill higher than a week of oratory. He had been
rough with the 21st Illinois when he assumed their colonelcy,
knocking down a drunk with his bare fists, denying rations to men
late out of bed and tying others to posts for insolence. But he
preferred that his volunteers should learn the value of military
routine by experience rather than precept. Shiloh had horrified him.
'Many of the men had only received their arms on their way from

their States to the field. Many of them had arrived but a day or two before and were hardly able to load their muskets according to the manual. Their officers were equally ignorant of their duties. Under these circumstances it is not astonishing that many of the regiments broke at the first fire.' He had been driven to using his cavalry to stop men running away, a shift characteristic of the class-ridden armies of the European *ancien régime*. 'I formed [the cavalry] into line in rear, to stop stragglers – of whom there were many.'

It was necessities of that sort which drew from Joe Hooker the contemptuous gibe, 'who ever saw a dead cavalryman?' But Grant preferred not to use brother-in-arms against brother to keep men in the fight. Far more characteristic was his decision at Vicksburg to indulge his troops' desire to assault rather than besiege the enemy's fortifications. He knew they were misguided. 'But the first consideration of all was – the troops believed they could carry the works in their front.' He let them have their heads. 'The attack was gallant and portions of each of the three corps succeeded in getting up to the very parapets of the enemy and in planting their battle flags upon them; but in no place were we able to enter . . . This last attack only served to increase our casualties without giving any benefit whatsoever.' Grant, who was physically revolted by the sight of blood, bitterly regretted the loss. But his hard-headed understanding of the character of his citizen army told him that his soldiers 'would not [afterwards] have worked so patiently in the trenches' – work which inexorably advanced the victory he sought – 'if they had not been allowed to try'. By this ultimate readiness to command by consent rather than diktat Grant discloses the populist touch that made him a master of people's war.

Grant's Staff

The grindstone of war would, by the conclusion of the Vicksburg campaign, have given Grant's Western army a lethal cutting edge. Battle is the swiftest of all schools of military instruction and Grant's philosophy of war – 'Find out where your enemy is. Get at him as soon as you can. Strike at him as hard as you can and as soon as you can, and keep moving on' – had made veterans out of his amateurs in two years of campaigning. A survivor of the siege of Vicksburg testified to the transformation: 'What . . . stalwart, well-fed men, so splendidly set up and accoutred. Sleek horses, polished arms, bright plumes – this was the pride and panoply of war. Civilisation, discipline and order seemed to enter with the measured tramp of those marching columns.'

To make soldiers out of sod-busters was one thing; to turn city merchants into staff officers was another. 'With two or three exceptions,' wrote a contemporary, 'Grant is surrounded by the most ordinary set of plebeians you ever saw.' Another was far more scathing: 'Gen Grant has four Colonels on his staff . . . Lagow, Regan and Hillyer and I doubt whether either of them has gone to bed sober for a week. The other is not much better . . . although possessing more military talent he is . . . a sneaking Loco Foco of the N.Y. Herald Stripe.'

Grant, to Halleck in December 1862, gave some of these men a better character: 'Col Hillyer is very efficient as Provost Marshal Gen and relieves me from much duty that I have heretofore had to attend to in person. Col Lagow . . . fills the post of Inspector Gen . . . I am very much attached to [him] personally and can endorse him as a true honest man, willing to do all in his power for the service. My regular Aids are all persons with whom I had a previous acquaintance and were appointed by me for what I believed was their merit as men. They give entire satisfaction.'

But he admitted, 'Of my individual staff there are but two men who I regard as absolutely indispensable – Lt Col Rawlins, Assistant Adjutant General and Capt Boners, Aide de Camp . . . Rawlins I regard as the ablest and most reliable man in his Dept of the Volunteer Service. Capt Boners has been with me for fourteen months, first as a private soldier and clerk. He is capable [and] attentive.'

The nub of this letter is that his aides were 'all persons with whom [he] had a previous acquaintance'. What Grant had done, on his swift promotion from command of the 21st Illinois to rank as brigadier-general, was to cobble together a staff of men with whom he felt comfortable, most of them from Galena, Illinois, where he had worked in his father's shop, all of them with a background in small-town business or politics, none of them with any military experience at all.

The procedure was eccentric. It tells us a great deal about Grant's modesty of character and handsome-is-as-handsome-does approach to affairs. But it tells us more about the total unreadiness of

Americans in 1861 to wage a great war. Grant might have assembled a better staff had he cast his net wider than Galena main street. But it would have been a staff better in degree than kind. The United States in 1861 lacked altogether a pool of trained staff officers. There was, indeed, no staff college to produce one, West Point itself offering no more than officer training to a modest regimental level. The management of bodies of men larger than 1,000 strong had to be learnt in some informal way, either in the civilian world or by jumping in at the deep end. The South on the whole opted for men trained in the latter way. If we examine the careers of its dozen most prominent generals – Beauregard, Bragg, Ewell, Forrest, Hill, the two Johnstons, Jackson, Lee, Longstreet, Kirby Smith and Stuart – we find that eight had remained in continuous service after leaving West Point. Only Bragg, Forrest and the Johnstons had pursued careers outside the army (Jackson's professorship at Virginia Military Institute does not count). With the dozen leading Northerners, however, the proportion is exactly reversed. Buell, McDowell, Pope and Sheridan were serving officers. But Burnside, Halleck, Hooker, Grant, McClellan, Meade, Rosecrans and Sherman had all had civilian careers and several of them most successful ones. Halleck had been an influential lawyer, McClellan and Burnside respectively Vice-President and Treasurer of the Illinois Central Railroad, Sherman a prosperous banker and President of Louisiana State University.

There was, of course, no direct correlation between, on the one hand, civilian success or military obscurity and, on the other, victorious generalship. McClellan, outstandingly good at business both before and after the war, had no military dynamism at all. Jackson, the rustic college professor, possessed something like military genius. Grant's commercial incapacity we have already noted. Only Sherman, among the regulars, and Forrest, among the amateurs, showed both military and civilian competence. Sherman, Grant's protégé, took the Grant method of waging war against the enemy's people to ruthless extremes. Forrest, a self-made man who 'went into the army worth a million and a half dollars and came out a beggar', played Sherman at his own game, driving him to rage that Forrest must be 'hunted down and killed if it cost ten thousand lives and bankrupts the Federal treasury'.

But even if the pattern that emerges from these comparisons is not altogether clear, there is nevertheless significance in the wider

15 Ulysses S. Grant as Commander-in-Chief, 1865.

16 *Above* The Capture of Fort Donelson, February 16, 1862.

17 *Below* The Battle of Shiloh, April 6, 1862.

18 *Above* Grant's canal engineering towards Vicksburg, spring 1863.

19 *Below* The Siege of Vicksburg, 1863.

20 Grant accepting Pemberton's surrender, Vicksburg, July 4, 1863.

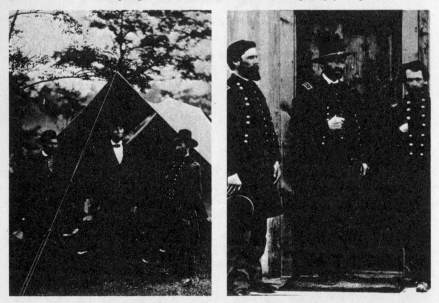

21 Lincoln with General J. A. McClernand, subsequently dismissed by
Grant, and Allan Pinkerton, of the Pinkerton Detective Agency, used
by Lincoln as an intelligence bureau, Antietam, October 3, 1862; one of
Alexander Gardner's photographs.

22 Grant with General John A. Rawlins (left) at the siege of Petersburg,
1864.

civilian experience of the Northern leadership. In a war of amateur armies, transported by railroad, controlled by telegraph, paid by taxes voted by democratic assemblies of which the soldiers were themselves electors, the likelihood was that men who had known the workings of commerce, industry and politics at first hand would be better attuned to the ends and means of the conflict than those who had spent their lives within barrack walls. The likelihood, moreover, is borne out by events. For all their operational expertise, Lee and Jackson proved men of limited imagination. Neither found means of forcing the North to fight on their terms, as they might have done had they tempted the Northern armies to enter the vast spaces of the South and manoeuvre out of touch with their railroad and river lines of supply. Both thought in terms of defending the South's frontiers rather than exhausting the enemy. The defeat of the Confederacy was in part the consequence of their essentially conventional outlook.

Grant's preference for 'persons with whom he had a previous acquaintance' at Galena may now look less parochial. The Galena gang were scarcely prepossessing. Lagow, his inspector-general, in charge of personnel, was a not very successful lawyer. Hillyer, the provost marshal in charge of discipline, had been in small-town real estate. Only Rawlins, the assistant adjutant general, and effective chief of staff, was a person of any quality. He had made his way from charcoal burning to a law office and then to city attorney and was active in politics as a Douglas Democrat. Grant valued his company because he could broach unmentionables without wounding or worrying. 'Rawlins,' said Cox, another member of the staff, 'could argue, could expostulate, could condemn, could even upbraid without interrupting for an hour the fraternal confidence and goodwill of Grant. He had won the right to this relation by an absolute devotion which dated from Grant's appointment to be brigadier-general in 1861, and which made him the good genius of his friend in every crisis of Grant's wonderful career. This was not because of Rawlins' great intellect, for he was of only moderate mental powers. It was rather that he became a living and speaking conscience of his general.' But, in a sense, all Grant's Galena and Illinois cronies served that function. Their small-town background, their unregulation way of doing things, their unmilitary garb, their slovenly speech, even their saloon-bar drinking style were a reassurance to Grant that he was in touch with the rough-and-ready manners and modes of thought of his citizen army. A staff of regulars would have been a barrier between him and his army. His staff of amateurs was a medium of communication, because it resembled the men he commanded almost to the point of mimicry.

There was, however, another reason why Grant was content to be supported in his work by a small group of amateurs (his staff never exceeded twenty). And that was that he preferred to do the work himself. He had discovered that, like Wellington, he had Herculean powers. He also knew that he was better at their jobs than any group of subordinates. Wellington could afford not to delegate because his army was always very small. Grant could afford not to because, though his armies were eventually very large indeed, they were composed of men used to shifting for themselves, which he encouraged them anyhow to do. The duties that their habits of self-sufficiency left him to perform were perfectly manageable by an individual, and he could therefore dedicate his staff not to bureaucratic routine but to acting as his eyes and ears.

When in supreme command, he outlined his desires to an aide, Lieutenant-Colonel Horace Porter, in these words (they might, as it happens, have been used by Moltke to his 'demigods' or Montgomery to his liaison officers):

> I want you to discuss with me freely from time to time the details of the orders given for the conduct of a battle, and learn my views as fully as possible as to what course should be pursued in all the contingencies which may arise. I expect to send you to the critical points of the lines to keep me promptly alerted of what is taking place, and in cases of great emergency, when new dispositions have to be made on the instant, or it becomes suddenly necessary to reinforce one command by sending to its aid troops from another, and there is no time to communicate with headquarters, I want you to explain my views to commanders and urge immediate action, looking to co-operation, without waiting for specific orders from me.

Grant could count on such response precisely because he ran his staff as a sort of barbershop meeting, where those with a place round the spittoon were as free to air their views as they were to spit tobacco juice or – depending how late the evening had drawn on – take a pull at the friendly bottle. Horace Porter describes just such an airing of views during the 1864 campaign when the headquarter cronies discussed in Grant's presence his practice of using the Commander of the Army of the Potomac as the medium for transmitting orders to its subordinate formations, even though, for personal reasons, he allowed that commander no effective freedom of action. Better, they argued, to deal direct with the men he trusted rather than prop up an undependable intermediary for the sake of appearances. Grant heard this insubordinate discussion out to its close before mildly observing that he preferred to go on as he did. But the passage had not been without value to him; it told him what common opinion was among ordinary Union officers. At the same time, it in no way suggested that the orders he gave failed to reach their appointed destination at the desired time, or that they were tampered with in transmission. He was reassured, in short, that his preferred custom of doing the work of command himself was working as he intended while the externalities of hierarchy were properly preserved.

That Grant did do the work of command himself is authenticated in a variety of ways. One is that we have his own throwaway dismissal of the thought that he valued the opinion of others. At the end of the siege of Vicksburg when the Confederate commander, Pemberton, was prevaricating over the terms of surrender, Grant communicated to his subordinates 'the contents of [his] letters, of my reply, of the substance of the interview, and that I was ready to hear any suggestion. This was the nearest approach to a "council of war" that I ever held.' Against 'the general and almost unanimous judgement of the council', he rejected Pemberton's prevarications altogether.

In amplification of this picture of independence, Porter testifies to the unvarying character of his method of work. On their return from a day of inspection during the Chattanooga campaign to which Porter had just been posted, Grant settled down to an evening at his desk:

> He soon after began to write despatches, and I arose to go but resumed my seat as he said 'sit still'. My attention was soon attracted by the manner in which he went to work at his correspondence. At this time, as throughout his later (and earlier) career, he wrote nearly all his documents with his own hand, and seldom dictated to anyone even the most unimportant despatch. His work was performed swiftly and uninter-

ruptedly, but without any marked display of nervous energy. His thoughts flowed as freely from his mind as his ink from his pen; he was never at a loss for an expression and seldom interlined a word or made a material correction. He sat with his head bent low over the table, and when he had occasion to step to another . . . to get a paper he wanted, he would glide rapidly across the room without straightening himself, and return to his seat with his body still bent over at about the same angle at which he had been sitting when he left his chair.

As he finished each page, he simply pushed it off the table on to the floor. When he had finished writing, he picked the pile up and sorted it for distribution. He then squared the corners of the sheets of paper, handed them to one of the staff, 'bid those present a pleasant good night and limped off to his bedroom'. Porter, who had been amazed by a procedure wholly new to him, was even more impressed to discover that the despatches were both models of lucidity and of the highest importance. They were 'directions . . . for the taking of vigorous and comprehensive steps in every direction throughout the new and comprehensive command'.

But all Grant's despatches were of that quality. Wellington was famed for his powers of literary expression; Peel, who was to succeed him as Prime Minster, thought him a supreme master of the English language. Grant, though his writing lacks the controlled passion to which Wellington's could rise at its best, was equally incisive. Meade's chief of staff once remarked that 'there is one striking feature of Grant's orders; no matter how hurriedly he may write them on the field, no one ever has the slightest doubt as to their meaning, or even has to read them over a second time to understand them'.

The six brief despatches written on the early morning of May 16, 1863, directing his four subordinates to concentrate their separated corps against Pemberton for what would be the battle of Champion's Hill, perfectly illustrate the clarity and force of his writing style. To Blair:

> Move at early dawn toward Black River Bridge. I think you will encounter no enemy by the way. If you do, however, engage them at once, and you will be assisted by troops further advanced . . . [Later] If you are already on the Bolton Road continue so, but if you still have choice of roads take the one

leading to Edward's Depot – Pass your troops to the front of your train, except a rear guard, and keep the ammunition wagons in front of all others.

To McClernand:

I have just obtained very probable information, that the entire force of the enemy has crossed the Big Black, and was at Edward's Depot at 7 o'clock last night. You will therefore disencumber yourself of your trains, select an eligible position, and feel the enemy . . . [Later] From all information gathered from citizens and prisoners the mass of the Enemy are south of Hovey's Division. McPherson is now up to Hovey and can support him at any point. Close up all your other forces as expeditiously as possible but cautiously. The enemy must not be allowed to get to our rear.

To McPherson:

The enemy has crossed Big Black with the entire Vicksburg force. He was at Edward's Depot last night and still advancing. You will therefore pass all trains and move forward to join McClernand with all possible despatch. I have ordered your rear brigade to move at once and given such directions to other commanders as will secure a prompt concentration of our forces.

To Sherman:

Start one of your divisions on the road at once with its ammunition wagons – and direct it to move with all possible speed till it comes up with our rear beyond Bolton. It is important that great celerity should be shown in carrying out this movement, as I have evidence that the entire force of the enemy was at Edward's Depot 7 o'clock yesterday evening and still advancing. The fight might be brought on at any moment – we should have every man on the field.

That evening he sent Sherman word of the result of his flurry of despatch writing: 'We met the enemy about four miles East of Edward's station and have had a desperate fight. The enemy were driven and are now in full retreat. I am of the opinion that the battle of Vicksburg has been fought.'

Such despatches equal those of Wellington at his crispest – as they did also in production of effect on the battlefield. But, as a writer, Grant exceeds Wellington in his powers of extended composition. His *Memoirs*, dictated (and, after his voice failed, written) while he was dying in agony from cancer of the throat, are not only a triumph of physical and moral courage – his family depended on their completion for rescue from bankruptcy – they are also an enthralling history of one man's generalship, perhaps the most revelatory autobiography of high command to exist in any language. For, despite his modest achievement at West Point, Grant possessed formidable intellectual capacity. He had the novelist's gift for the thumbnail sketch of character, dramatic setting of mood and introduction of the telling incident; he had the historian's ability to summarize events and incorporate them smoothly in the larger narrative; he had the topographer's feel for landscape and the economist's instinct for material essentials; and he had the philosophical vision to balance the elements of his story into the argument of his *apologia pro sua vita* – which was how a just triumphed over an unjust cause. The result is a literary phenomenon. If there is a single contemporary document which explains 'why the North won the Civil War', that abiding conundrum of American historical enquiry, it is the *Personal Memoirs of U.S. Grant*. What sort of soldier was it who composed this extraordinary record of an extraordinary career?

Grant on Campaign

He was certainly not a man to impress by either his appearance or his manner. A visitor to his headquarters in 1864 who sat for an hour beside his camp fire after 'a very hasty meal' described him as 'small . . . with a resolute square thinking face':

He sat silent among his staff, and my first impression was that he was moody, dull and unsocial. I afterwards found him pleasant, genial and agreeable. He keeps his own counsel, padlocks his mouth, while his countenance in battle or repose . . . indicates nothing – that is gives no expression of his feelings and no evidence of his intentions. He smokes almost constantly and, as I have then and since observed, he has a habit of whittling with a small knife. He cuts a small stick into small chips, making nothing. It is evidently a mere occupation of his fingers, his mind all the while intent upon other things. Among men he is nowise noticeable. There is no glitter or parade about him. To me he seems but an earnest business man.

A business man he, of course, was not. He was never to achieve that 'independence of all employment or office' which Wellington's accumulation of prize money in India won him. He was never to achieve settled capital wealth at all. The $6,000 his promotion to major general's rank brought him in 1863 was by far the largest annual income he had thitherto enjoyed; even so, to make it go round and save a little for the future was, as his frequent correspondence with Julia on financial matters shows, almost beyond him. Worry about money was one of the many anxieties he learnt to disguise behind the mask of equanimity he showed his soldiers, staff and superiors.

But everything else in the visitor's description of the camp-fire scene is acutely perceptive. Whittling, that American crackerbarrel habit, was a favourite displacement activity. Porter caught him at it during the battle of the Wilderness in 1864, wearing holes in a pair of cotton gloves Julia had sent him to replace the inelegant leather gauntlets she thought inappropriate to a general-in-chief. It was entirely harmless and 'helped him to think'. Smoking, on the other hand, probably killed him. A pipe smoker in youth, he now converted to cigars by chance. A newspaper account of his appearance during the fight for Fort Donelson in 1862 had him riding about the field with a cigar stub clenched in his teeth. Because victory at Donelson was good news when Northern victories were few, it brought him a cascade of cigars from admirers – 10,000 by his own reckoning – therefore he smoked nothing else and rarely stopped. On the second day of the Wilderness battle he started out with twenty-four: 'lighting one of them, he filled his pockets with the rest'. At the end of the day, when General Hancock came to his headquarters, Grant offered him a cigar and 'found that only one was left in his pocket. Deducting the number he had given away from the supply he had started out with in the morning showed that he had smoked that day about twenty, all very strong and of formidable size.'

A cigar was his habitual token of hospitality to a guest. An invitation to a meal at his headquarters was no treat. The food was simple and Grant often ate more simply than his staff. He liked cucumbers best of all, sometimes breakfasting off a cucumber soused in vinegar, washed down with coffee. He abhorred fowl and game ('I never could eat anything that goes on two legs'), was revolted by the sight of blood, human or animal, so that his beef had to be roasted black, and often chose to pick at fruit while his entourage tucked in more heartily. Soldiers' fare was his preference – corn, pork and beans and buckwheat cakes – though, oddly, he was also addicted to oysters.

Did Grant drink? Porter loyally asserts that 'the only beverage ever used at table besides tea and coffee was water . . . upon a few occasions, after a hard day's ride in stormy weather, the general joined the officers of the staff in taking a whisky toddy in the evening'. This assertion is disingenuous. 'The idea that Grant drank prodigiously,' writes William McFeely, 'is as fixed in American history as the idea that the Pilgrims ate turkey on Thanksgiving.' The truth seems to be that he was that horror of prohibitionists, not a steady imbiber but a sporadic and then spectacular drunk. McFeely, with other post-Freudians, believed that the trigger was sexual. Grant certainly drank heavily during his separation from Julia in California in 1852–4. In the aftermath of the Vicksburg triumph, which had kept him apart from Julia for two months, he went on a bender so dramatic that only the patriotic self-restraint of the *Chicago Times* reporter who manhandled him into bed kept it out of the newspapers. Rawlins, Grant's 'conscience', then took over, revealing perhaps why their intimacy was so essential to Grant's wellbeing. Rawlins was the son of an alcoholic, abhorred drink with the ferocity of an Anti-Saloon Leaguer and never hesitated to argue Grant off the bottle.

Drinking bouts furnished the only element of the spectacular in Grant's personality. When the clutch of the demon was not on him – and in 1864–5 he usually had Julia by him in camp – he showed the world that unvaryingly equable and self-contained exterior on which all visitors to his headquarters remarked. He was quiet in speech, though he had an impressively resonant voice, undemonstrative in manner, indiscriminately courteous to all callers, and a listener rather than a talker. He would not tolerate gossip or backbiting, choked whisperers into silence, never swore, though he was surrounded by profanes, was careful not to chide a subordinate in public and in general tried to command by encouragement rather than reproof. McClernand, the political general wished on him by Halleck during the Western campaign, irritated his professional sense, but he waited until the man inexcusably overstepped military proprieties before relieving him. The grounds he chose for his dismissal admitted of no argument, which he detested.

Sherman, his classmate and the one man whose talents he unreservedly admired, he always called by his surname, as Sherman did him. Otherwise he addressed subordinates by their military rank. His despatches to them were usually signed, 'respectfully' or 'your obedient servant'. He was equally courteous in his dealings with superiors, civilian and military. To Halleck, whom he rightly believed to have treated him unfairly after the victories of Forts Henry and Donelson, he showed nothing but dignified reproachfulness. To Lincoln, who very early perceived that he needed Grant ('he fights'), he accorded at all times a deep personal respect and the most proper constitutional subordination. McClellan, a busted flush, arrogantly opposed Lincoln for the presidency in 1864. Grant, a victor crowned with laurels, shrank from the political limelight: he was outraged when the Missouri electoral college wrote his name on the ticket, and successfully lobbied to have it withdrawn from the ballot.

Modesty pervaded the smallest details of his generalship. In April 1863 he was complaining to Julia of 'the want of a servant to take care of my things and pack up when we leave any place' which had 'left me now about bare of some necessary articles. I am always so much engaged in starting from any place that I cannot look after things myself.' The contrast with Wellington's personal entourage of cooks, valets and grooms, modest though it was thought at the time, is striking. The duty of arranging the cuisine at Grant's headquarters was shared in turn by the officers of his staff. And though he was latterly served by a personal attendant, Bill, a runaway Missouri slave, Bill's ministrations were sketchy. In February 1863 Grant wrote to Julia that his false teeth had been thrown away with the washing water.

But Grant's personal economy was so spartan that a servant was almost superfluous to his needs. His camp furniture consisted of canvas bed, two folding chairs, a wooden table; it was housed in a small tent. A larger tent served as his office and another as the staff mess. Grant bathed in a sawn-off barrel and transported his personal kit in a single trunk, which contained underclothes, a suit and a spare pair of boots. His unconcern for outward appearance was famous; though, like Wellington, scrupulous about bathing and changing his underclothes, he would not spare the time to shift uniforms. 'I like to put on a suit of clothes when I get up in the morning' – he dressed faster than anyone on his staff – 'and wear it until I go to bed, unless I have to make a change in my dress to meet company.' Riding hard and long he often came home mud-spattered and wet, but would do no more to get comfortable than thrust his boots towards the fire. Just as well that his accustomed outfit was a private's coat, on which he pinned his general's stars.

Grant's simplicity of speech, style and manners was not affectation. It was an expression of deep-seated character. If Wellington eschewed ceremony, theatre and oratory, Grant actively disliked all three, with rigorous distaste. On arriving in Washington in 1864 to be nominated general-in-chief, the longest speech he managed was, 'Gentlemen, in response, it will be impossible to do more than thank you.' While campaigning for the presidency in 1867 he managed to avoid making almost any speech at all. He appears never to have addressed his troops and thought it pointless to do so, an odd reservation in a political culture oiled by speech-making and populated by famous orators.

The attitude was partly temperamental; but it may have been reinforced by his low opinion of most of the political generals, great speechifiers, whom the party system inflicted on him, as well as by the feeling that talking had got the country into much of the difficulty out of which he was called to fight it free. Ceremony and theatre may have repelled him for the same reason. Both, in unmonarchical America, meant politics. The election parade was the only form of public ceremony most Americans knew, while mass military parades were simply too difficult for his undrilled armies to perform with any sureness or dignity.

In only one traditional display of leadership did Grant excel or take any pride. He was a magnificent horseman. He had been the outstanding equestrian in his year at West Point, effortlessly outrode his staff on campaign and was always mounted on horses others could not master. Cincinnati, his favourite, stood seventeen and a half hands high and carried him from Chattanooga to the end of the war. But his earlier horses – Jack, Fox, Kangaroo and Jeff Davis –

were also spirited, and his urge to ride them hard got him into trouble. On a night ride during the Shiloh battle he was fallen on by Fox and badly bruised. Luckily the tumble was on soft ground. In August 1863 he was thrown on to a hard roadway when his horse shied at a streetcar; the injury was to keep him on crutches until October.

These, fortunately for the Union, were the only injuries he sustained throughout the war. His health on campaign remained generally excellent, all the more remarkable in view of how roughly he camped and dined. He slept, like Wellington, without effort in any circumstances, always getting the eight hours needed, and generally turning in early. He caught a severe chest cold after Fort Donelson, complained of piles to Julia in April 1863, had stomach upsets before Shiloh and during the Petersburg siege and was struck down by a nervous headache in the tense hours before receiving Lee's surrender at Appomattox. But more commonly he rejoiced in an unaccustomed sense of wellbeing. 'I am well, better than I have been for years,' he wrote to Julia in March 1863. 'Everybody remarks how well I look. I never sit down to my meals without an appetite nor go to bed without being able to sleep.' And, three weeks later, in the swamps of the Mississippi where fever hovered over the army he inched towards Vicksburg, 'I never enjoyed better health or felt better in my life than since here.'

The truth was that war – or, more particularly, the American Civil War – suited Grant. He deplored the suffering it inflicted on his fellow-countrymen. He was deeply pained by every encounter with the wounded and dead and was physically revolted by the sight of blood. He had no taste at all for the conventional glories of war, for its parades and triumphs, for its honours and rewards. He shrank from crowds, hid from tuft-hunters, muttered inaudible replies to the thanks of Congress. He genuinely sought no high place and looked forward after victory to nothing grander than retirement as a gentleman farmer. But, while the war persisted, he drew the deepest satisfaction from the power he had found in himself to fight it as it ought to be fought. Where others dabbled in remembered classroom theory, aped their European counterparts, even sought to reincarnate Napoleon, he confined himself to practicalities: carrying the war into the enemy's heartland, making its people bear the real burdens of the conflict they had brought on the republic and meanwhile sustaining the spirits of an army of electors in a struggle

for constitutional orthodoxy. The struggle, he knew, would be won
not by a strategy of evasion, blockade or manoeuvre, but by fighting.
How did Grant fight?

Grant the Fighter

'I need this man,' Lincoln said of Grant. 'He fights.' So he did.
Chaplain Eaton, an intermediary of the President's, found the
general in the spring of 1863 'looking like half a dozen men
condensed into one'. Wearing an old brown linen jacket and trousers
worn through by constant contact with the saddle, 'his very clothes,
as well as the crows' feet on his brow, bore testimony to the
strenuousness of the life he was living'.

But Grant fought in a way that neither a hero like Alexander nor
an anti-hero like Wellington would have recognized as soldierly at
all. 'If he had studied to be undramatic,' said General Lew Wallace,
his subordinate at Shiloh, 'he could not have succeeded better.' The
theatrical was anathema to Grant. 'He confines himself,' reported
the *New York World* correspondent from the Vicksburg army, 'to
saying and doing as little as possible before his men. No Napoleonic
displays, no ostentation, no speech, no superfluous flummery.' His
soldiers for their part, reported Galway of the *New York Times*, 'do
not salute him, they only watch him, with a certain sort of familiar
reverence. [They] observe him coming and, rising to their feet,
gather on each side of the way to see him pass.'

Grant usually rode alone, and he was often alone on the battlefield, just as Wellington was at the close of Waterloo. But unlike
Wellington, and even more unlike Alexander, he felt no need to
share the risks of the individual soldier. Quite the contrary. To the
questions In front always? sometimes? or never? Grant would
probably have tried to avoid giving an answer but, if pressed, would
have uttered a grudging 'Never if I can help it.'

War, he might have explained, had become too important *not* to
be left to the general. Captains, colonels, even brigadiers might die
at the head of their men. The commander's place was out of range of
fire which, since the introduction of the rifle, swept the field in a
density and to a range which would have made Wellington's habits of
exposure suicidal. 'Those are bullets,' Rawlins at Shiloh had to
explain to Grant's paymaster, who had thought the noise in the trees

overhead rainfall pattering on the leaves. The bullets, Minie balls weighing nearly two ounces, could be projected 1,000 yards and still inflict the worst small-arms wound ever known in warfare.

Grant made it his practice to halt short of the edge of what riflemen call 'the beaten zone'. At Shiloh, on the second day, he gathered up some regiments at a spot where he detected the Confederate line was on the point of breaking, 'formed them into line of battle and marched them forward . . . After marching *to within musket range* [italics supplied] I stopped and let the troops pass,' he wrote. 'The command, *Charge*, was given, and was executed with loud cheers and a run; when the last of the enemy broke.'

Grant could not always keep out of danger. Later the same day he was riding with two staff officers when they inadvertently got within range of some Confederate riflemen. They instantly turned and galloped off but were under fire, by Grant's estimate, for one minute:

> When we arrived at a perfectly safe position we halted to take account of damages. McPherson's horse was panting as if ready to drop. On examination it was found that a ball had struck him forward of the flank just back of the saddle, and had gone entirely through. In a few minutes the poor beast dropped dead; he had given no sign of injury until we came to a stop. A ball had struck the metal scabbard of my sword, just below the hilt and broken it nearly off; before the battle was over it had broken off entirely. There were three of us; one had lost a horse killed, one a hat and one a sword-scabbard. All were thankful it was no worse.

At Petersburg, on October 27, 1864, things were nearly worse. Grant was riding with an aide when 'a shell exploded just under his horse's neck. The animal threw up his head and reared, and it was thought that he and his rider had been struck. They had not, but the horse entangled its foot in some broken telegraph wires lying on the ground, and by struggling prevented the general's escape.' It was some time before he could be disentangled and retire 'to a less exposed position'. He had had a similarly narrow escape at Vicksburg on May 10, 1863, and was to have another at Fort Harrison on September 29, 1864. On both occasions a shell burst near him while he was sitting in the open writing a despatch. His composure drew from an observer, a private soldier of the 5th Wisconsin, the remark, 'Ulysses don't scare worth a damn.'

Nor did he. His physical no more than his moral courage was never in doubt. Danger of capture alarmed him as little as danger of assassination, to both of which he was exposed at different times. On June 23, 1862, riding in territory where Confederate sympathies were strong, he escaped a prepared ambush only by good fortune; and on August 9, 1864, during the Petersburg siege, he was close to an 'infernal machine' planted by a Southern infiltrator which detonated an enormous explosion in an ammunition dump. But, though Porter took private precautions to avert assassination attempts thereafter, Grant refused to practise caution. As the leader of a people's army he could no more hide himself from the population among which he conducted the war than Lincoln could from the nation in whose name it was fought. Their shared disregard for the killer instinct among their enemies nearly brought them to a common end; it was only Grant's distaste for publicity that caused him to decline the President's invitation to join him in the theatre box where Lincoln was murdered.

But since Grant refused to lead by example, he had to command by other means. What were they? First and foremost through the written despatch, often transmitted by telegraph. The introduction of the telegraph underlay the first clear technical transformation of the general's role since the beginning of organized warfare. St Arnaud, Napoleon III's commander in the Crimea, thought it the death of generalship; it spelt for him the loss of all independence in the field, linking as it did headquarters directly with the seat of government. His anxieties proved unfounded: governments quickly discovered that the telegraph, though providing them with the means to interfere, did not confer the power to oversee. The man on the spot continued to know best, as he continues to do even in these days of 'real time intelligence' and satellite and drone observation.

But, if the telegraph could not make politicians into commanders, it could enormously enhance the power of generals to collect intelligence, summon reinforcements, rapidly redispose their forces, and co-ordinate the movement of widely separated formations. 'During 1864,' for example, 'hardly a day passed that Grant was not in possession of Sherman's current situation report, though they were sometimes separated by more than 1,500 miles of telegraph route'; Grant was then stalled outside Petersburg while Sherman was marching through Georgia. The telegraph route they employed, moreover, was but a fraction of that at the disposition of the armies. Though invented only in 1844 and commercialized only in 1847, the telegraph extended already over 50,000 miles of line in the United States by 1860. An American invention, it was in a sense an American necessity as, in its time, would be the domestic airline: a means to make a single society out of a continental diaspora. The telegraph network grew apace during the Civil War. Originally operated for military purposes by the Signal Corps, that organization's incapacity drove the armies back to the commercial companies whose routes, following the railroads, were eventually monopolized by the military in the zones of operations.

For tactical purposes, spurs were laid off the main lines by signal troops, some of whom became 'so skilful', Sherman recorded, 'that by cutting the wire they could receive a message with their tongues from a distant station'. The length of these spurs, run on insulated wires between trees or specially erected poles, could not be made to exceed about six miles. But such was the efficiency of Grant's signal organization that permanent lines were strung to follow the advance of his army almost as quickly as it moved. He himself, a visitor to his headquarters at Nashville in 1863 noticed, 'had a telegraph in his office and spent much of his time talking by wire with all parts of his command'.

Grant's own accounts reveal his reliance upon the medium. 'Headquarters,' he wrote in his *Memoirs* of his campaign in Tennessee in 1862, 'were connected [by telegraph] with all points of the command.' 'Telegraph instruments and an operator have been sent from here to you,' was the conclusion of his despatch to General Washburn near Vicksburg on June 10, 1863. 'Pursue the enemy with all vigilance wherever they may go reporting whenever you can reach a telegraph office,' he signalled to the cavalry raider, Grierson, in December 1862. 'Telegraph will probably be working through by tomorrow and railroad within five days,' was his message to McClernand later the same month. An excellent example of his own telegraphese was sent the following day, December 26:

Van Dorn went to Bolivar pursued by our Cavalry, then struck south-east through Salisbury and Ripley. Our cavalry was still in pursuit at that point and has since been heard from. This was yesterday. They are now near Grenada. Two deserters

came in from Van Dorn today; they left him 10 miles north of
New Albany at 10 o'clock last night – still going south. If there
is any cavalry north of the Hatchie it must be some small
irregular band. Send cars to Davis Mills and I will order four
regiments more up to you. Collect all the bacon, beef, hogs and
sheep you can from the planters. Mount all the infantry you
can and drive Forrest east of the Tennessee.

The mixture of hard information, informed speculation and direct
command contained in this signal is evidence of how closely textured
was the flow of intelligence into Grant's headquarters, and so
testimony of how central was the telegraph to his methods of work.
It is testimony in addition of how the coming of the telegraph had
revolutionized the commander's role. We know that Wellington – we
can only speculate about Alexander, though their means of collecting
intelligence and transmitting orders were identical, despite the
centuries that separate them – was chronically afflicted both by
message delays and by uncertainties about when a message had left
its destination and how fresh was the information on which it was
based. The Duke, for example, complained at the Duchess of
Richmond's ball that Blücher had sent him news of Napoleon's
invasion by the fattest officer in his army, who had taken thirty
hours to ride thirty miles. Telegraph operators, who automatically
included a 'time of transmission' (time, moreover, centrally
standardized thanks to the telegraph network itself) in the prefix of
all their sendings, might eat themselves circular without its affecting
the journey time of their messages one jot.

The telegraph did not, of course, confer any personal advantage
on Grant himself; it was the means by which all other generals,
North or South, articulated their commands. He simply had a
particular aptitude for the instrument, an aspect of his belief in the
'progressive' nature of warfare which was central to his generalship.
Other aptitudes of his were quite traditional. Like Wellington, who
could always outguess his officers as to what lay 'the other side of the
hill', Grant had an acutely developed feel for landscape. He had
always been fascinated by maps which were, of course, much more
freely available in the nineteenth than the eighteenth century, even
in a land as recently surveyed as North America. West Point taught
mapping and officered the Topographical Engineers, a major agent
in the mapping of the United States. Grant was a map collector and

in Mexico he provided Scott, Taylor and, by chance, Robert E. Lee
with cartographic information they lacked themselves. Porter, his
staff officer in the 1864–5 campaigns, noticed that any map 'seemed
to become photographed indelibly on his brain, and he could follow
its features without referring to it again. Besides, he possessed an
almost intuitive knowledge of topography . . . and was never so
much at home as when finding his way by the course of streams, the
contours of the hills and the general features of the country.' Hence
his noted resistance to 'turning back', which he admitted himself.
Porter noticed that 'he would try all sorts of cross-cuts, ford streams
and jump any number of fences to reach another road rather than go
back and take a fresh start'. His steeplechasing was almost always
successful.

Grant's mind was not just a graphic one. It was also stocked with
an analytic knowledge of past campaigns. For all his insistence on
the 'progressive' in warfare, his brother officers recalled that, during
his unhappy time as a captain in California, he could reconstruct the
course of the operations in Mexico as if he had 'the whole thing in his
head'; when he returned east in 1864 he disclosed to Porter that he
had found the time to follow the fighting in Virginia in close detail;
and on his world tour in 1877 he entertained his companion John
Russell Young with precise dissertations of Napoleon's campaigns
from Marengo to Leipzig.

Campaign study had helped him develop the most valuable of all
his aptitudes, that of seeing into the mentality of his opponents. We
have his own account of how he began to trust this capacity he found
in himself. At the very start of the war, as Colonel of the 21st
Illinois, he set out to engage a Confederate regiment operating in the
vicinity. Expecting to find it waiting to engage him, he pressed
forward only because he lacked 'the moral courage to halt'. When he
found that the enemy had decamped, 'my heart resumed its place. It
occurred to me at once that [he] had been as much afraid of me as I
had been of him. This was a view of the question I had never taken
before; but it was one I never forgot afterwards. From that event to
the close of the war, I never experienced trepidation upon confronting the enemy.'

More than that, he began to guess how they would react to his
initiatives, and even how they would arrive at independent decisions. During the Fort Donelson battle, he recalled remarking to one
of his staff, 'Some of our men are pretty badly demoralised, but the

enemy must be more so, for he has attempted to force his way out, but has fallen back; the one who attacks first will be victorious and the enemy will have to be in a hurry to get ahead of me.' During the Shiloh battle, when numbers of his regiments had collapsed and panicked his colleague Buell into thinking the army must retreat, he guessed that had he 'come through the Confederate rear, he would have witnessed there a scene similar to that of our own. The distant rear of an army engaged in battle is not the best place from which to judge correctly what is going on at the front.' He overruled Buell's instinct for withdrawal, pressed forward to victory and 'later in the war . . . learned that the panic in the Confederate rear had not differed much from that within our own'. In short, he had been right.

Sometimes he was wrong. During the manoeuvring before Vicksburg, he was sure that Pemberton would attack him at a place called Clinton, because he had captured an order from his superior to that effect. Pemberton, exercising his own judgement, decided the order impracticable, so putting Grant in error. But the mistake was a rare one, into which he had been drawn by previous acquaintanceship. Knowing Pemberton, he expected him to obey orders rather than trust his instinct. More often his estimate of his old West Point and army comrades was correct. He did not share the widely-held esteem for A.S. Johnston, his opponent at Shiloh, and he had no opinion at all of his opponents at Donelson. 'Floyd, the commanding officer . . . was a man of talent enough for any civil position [but] no soldier and, possibly, did not possess the elements of one . . . Pillow, next in command, was conceited. I had known him in Mexico, and judged that with any force, no matter how small, I could march up to within gunshot of any intrenchment he was given to hold.' Lee, whom he respected and who respected him (Longstreet had warned him that Grant was 'a man we cannot afford to underrate'), was more puzzling to read. But, eventually, Grant entered his mind and anticipated one move of his after another. Appomattox was to prove as much a moral as a material victory.

Grant did not found his mind-reading on mere divination. He valued objective information highly and collected it from many sources. Operating in Southern territory, as he largely did, local intelligence was denied him by the population – unless black. 'I have just learned from a reliable [runaway slave],' he telegraphed to Washington on March 27, 1863, 'that most of the forces from

Vicksburg are now up to the Yazoo leaving not to exceed 10,000 in the city.' But such windfalls were unusual. 'We were in a country,' he wrote of the 1862 campaign in Tennessee, 'where nearly all the people . . . were hostile to us and friendly to the cause we were trying to suppress. It was easy therefore for the enemy to get early information of our every move. We, on the contrary, had to go after our information in force, and then often returned without it.' 'In force' meant cavalry reconnaissance, but he also collected intelligence through spies and from the press. 'I have a very reliable man now in Louisiana,' he wrote to Admiral Porter from Vicksburg in June 1863, 'for no other purpose than to discover what orders Smith Price, etc, are now executing.' Espionage during the American Civil War, as in any war, yielded, however, intrinsically dubious information. Double-agenting was endemic in a context where friend could not be told from foe, and those temperamentally willing to practise the peculiar profession perhaps often deceived themselves as to where their sympathies lay in any case. The press, of which Grant, democrat though he was, rightly nurtured a deep suspicion, could prove on occasion more reliable. It was from a captured copy of a Southern newspaper that in May 1863 he first heard of 'the complete success of Colonel Grierson's raid into the heart of the Confederacy'.

Grierson's raid was intended principally to inflict damage on the Confederate railroad system, railroads – with rivers – being the force-lines along which the action of the Civil War flowed. The American was already a railroad economy before the war began. About 31,000 miles of track had been laid in the United States in 1861, all but 9,000 of it in states that would remain in the Union. Since Grant's first three years of campaigning were set in the South, he was initially a river rather than a railroad strategist; indeed it was his easy use of waterways that first marked him out as an exceptional commander. But the culmination of his Southern campaigning, the victory at Chattanooga, derived its significance from his severing of the 'Chattanooga–Atlanta link' (the track connecting the Confederate systems west and east of the Appalachian mountain chain); and, even while operating along the river lines of the Cumberland and Mississippi in 1862–3, he had consistently used the railroads as a subsidiary means to strategic and even tactical mobility.

Railroads stood high on Grant's index of what made warfare 'progressive'; and his correspondence is full of strict and precise instructions about how they were to be used. On January 3, 1863, he

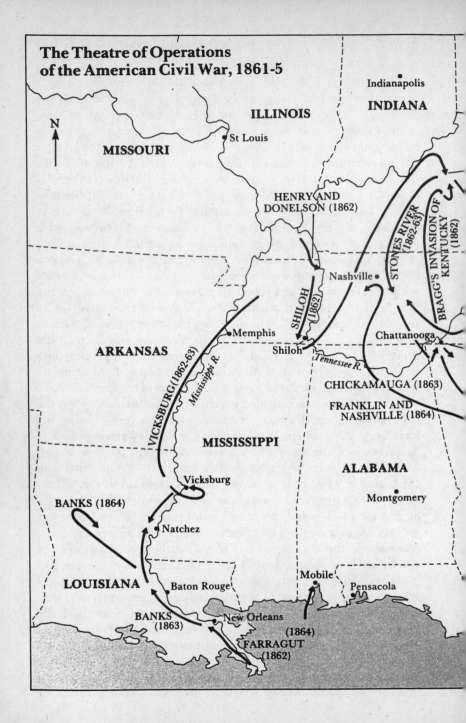

The Theatre of Operations
of the American Civil War, 1861–5

N

MISSOURI

ILLINOIS

INDIANA

Indianapolis

St Louis

HENRY AND
DONELSON (1862)

Nashville

STONES RIVER
(1862–63)

BRAGG'S INVASION OF
KENTUCKY (1862)

SHILOH
(1862)

Memphis

ARKANSAS

Shiloh

Chattanooga

Tennessee R.

CHICKAMAUGA (1863)

Mississippi R.

VICKSBURG (1862–63)

FRANKLIN AND
NASHVILLE (1864)

MISSISSIPPI

ALABAMA

Vicksburg

Montgomery

BANKS (1864)

Natchez

LOUISIANA

Baton Rouge

Mobile

Pensacola

BANKS
(1863)

New Orleans

(1864)

FARRAGUT
(1862)

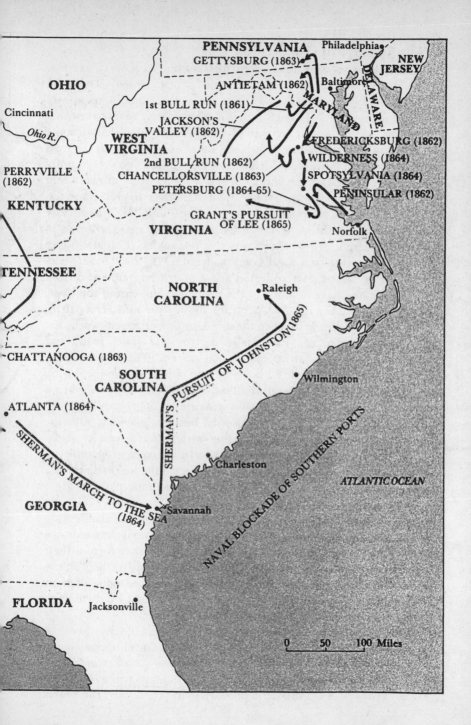

was instructing a divisional commander on the necessity of keeping the Memphis and Charleston Railroad open: 'some citizens of Memphis were overheard to say that there was a determination we should not run the ME–CRR – that it will be easier to interrupt that and force us to move the army to Memphis for supplies than to come here to fight the main army. It is my determination to run the road as long as we require it and if necessary I will remove every family . . . between the Hatchie and Cold Water rivers . . . For every raid or attempted raid by guerrillas upon the [rail] road I want ten families of the most noted secessionists sent south.' He was equally emphatic, and ruthless, in his orders designed to deny railroads to the Confederate army. 'Burn up the remainder of Black River Bridge,' he wrote to a local commander on May 29, 1863. 'Make details from the negroes collected about your camp, and also from the troops, and have as much of the road taken up, east of the river, as you can. Pile the ties [sleepers] up and lay the rails across them and burn them up. Wherever there is a bridge or trestle work . . . have them destroyed. Effectually destroy the [rail] road, and particularly the rails, as far east as you can go.' These instructions are pitiless. Rails heated red hot on a pile of burning ties could, by the insertion of bars through the bolt holes at each end, be given a corkscrew twist that nothing but passage through a rolling-mill would correct. As the South possessed but a single such mill, the Tredegar Iron Works located in the extreme north east in Richmond, Virginia, rails so vandalized were effectively irreparable.

During the Vicksburg campaign, Grant used the railroad network as an ancillary to the rivers, moving 'One (sometimes two) corps at a time to reach designated points out parallel to the railroad and only from six to ten miles from it.' This was a highly sophisticated logistic technique, ensuring that his trains of mules and horse-drawn waggons never operated more than a single day's march from their point of bulk-loading. Unlike Alexander's – and Wellington's – animal transport columns, they therefore consumed none of their own loads on the march and were no more fatigued by their work than drayhorses on a city delivery round.

Grant's real originality as a logistician, however, lay elsewhere. In his first two years in command he had based his line of operations on the rivers. It was a technique that came easily to a man raised in the Mississippi basin where the Father of Waters and its tributaries – the Ohio, Tennessee, Cumberland and Missouri – had fixed the routes of settlement and trade since the pioneers, French and English, had first penetrated the interior in the seventeenth century. But rivers, like railroads, confine almost as much as they further a strategist's freedom of action. Their course determines whither an army that ties itself to waterborne supplies may go and not go. The Confederates had exploited that limitation by a strategy of holding the river choke points – Forts Henry and Donelson, Port Hudson, Vicksburg – and to forcing the Union to work against the grain of the country instead of swooping down the lines of least topographical resistance. In an effort to outwit them, Grant spent much of the Spring of 1863 unavailingly exploring back waterways for short cuts and was eventually driven to the labour of digging a canal across the Vicksburg loop of the Mississippi in the hope of bypassing it.

None of these shifts succeeded. In May, 1863, therefore, he came to a momentous decision. 'I finally decided to have [no communications] – to cut loose altogether from my base and move my whole force without a rear link.' He had experimented already with this bold technique and had been heartened by the results. 'It should be remembered,' he wrote, not with total accuracy, 'that at the time I speak of it had not been demonstrated that any army could operate in an enemy's territory depending on the enemy for supplies.' He was forgetting that Napoleon, for example, had made foraging the basis of the French army's provisioning in Spain and elsewhere. But the technique had never been tried in a country as productive as the Confederate States, and it yielded astonishing results. 'I was amazed at the quantity of supplies the country afforded,' he wrote of his first experimentation in November 1862. 'It showed that we could have subsisted off the country for two months instead of two weeks without going beyond the limits designated. This taught me a lesson which was taken advantage of later in the campaign when our army lived twenty days with the issue of only five days' supply by the commissary.'

And to this strategy of making the enemy give him what he wanted he added the twist of denying the Confederates what they wanted for themselves. In November 1862 he had already obliged Southern civilians, starving in an area he had picked bare, 'to emigrate east, or west, fifteen miles and assist in eating up what we left'. During the siege of Vicksburg, he sent his subordinate, Blair, into the surrounding neighbourhood which was 'rich and full of supplies both food and forage. [He] was instructed to take all of it. The cattle were to be driven in for the use of our army, and the food and forage to be consumed by our troops or destroyed by fire.' These were measures that other generals had taken before; as by Marlborough on his despoiling of Bavaria in the summer of 1704. But Marlborough's motive then had been to bring on a battle with the French. Grant's was strictly materialist. 'Rebellion,' he had written to one of his divisional commanders in April 1863, 'has assumed that shape now that it can only terminate by the complete subjugation of the south or the overthrow of the government. It is our duty therefore to use every means to weaken the enemy by destroying their means of cultivating their field . . . You will encourage all negroes, particularly middle-aged males, to come within our lines [and] destroy or bring off all the corn and beef cattle you possibly can.'

The strategy of 'baseless' campaigning was one of immense daring – so daring that it alarmed even Grant's protégé, Sherman, who a year later would take it to extremes that Grant had not yet contemplated. In late May 1863 Sherman requested a private interview with Grant and warned that, 'I was putting myself in a position voluntarily which an enemy would be glad to manoeuvre a year to achieve.' In a textbook statement of Jominian theory Sherman argued that it was 'an axiom in war that when any great body of troops moved against an enemy they should do so from a base of supplies'. Grant was unmoved. 'To this I replied, the country is already disheartened over the lack of success . . . if we went back it would discourage the people so much that bases of supply would be of no use . . . The problem for us was to move forward to a decisive victory, or our cause was lost. No progress was being made in any other field, so we had to go on.'

Rivers and railroads were the means by which Grant brought his armies to the battlefield, spies, scouts and the telegraph the media through which he informed himself of the enemy's own movements. How did Grant conduct himself when planning or chance – it was usually planning – had brought the two sides to contact?

Not for him, as we have seen, the theatricalities of war. He suffered no wounds, lost only one horse in action and, though he was insistent on keeping the enemy under his eye, was also careful to keep at a safe distance from enemy gunshot. But none of that meant that he was content to command from a fixed point, articulating his army by orders issued through subordinates. His personal staff was anyhow too small to allow for that. Instead, he did things himself, galloping from place to place on his large strong horses to rally shaken regiments, encourage subordinates and send reinforcements to the front.

His style demanded all the more of him because of the ever-extending span of the battlefronts over which his armies operated. Alexander, who in any case kept to a fixed place of honour in the centre of the vanguard, fought on battlefronts two miles wide at most. Wellington at Waterloo, admittedly a small though not unusually small battlefield for the period, had about a mile of ground to cover. At Fort Donelson in February 1862 Grant's front extended over three miles, at Shiloh about five miles, at Chattanooga in 1864 about eight miles and, in the eastern campaign of 1864–5, ten miles at the Wilderness and twelve at Five Forks. These extensions marked an irreversible trend. As armies grew to consume the whole manhood of nations, fronts would span frontiers, making it impossi- ble for generals to see for themselves the course of events, confining them to central headquarters for most of the time, and determining that 'in front never' was the answer they had to give to the question about where a commander should station himself. But in 1861–5 it was still just possible for a general with the will to do so to ride about his line while his army was in action. Grant had the will.

We have his own accounts of his conduct at the three battles on which he built his career, Belmont, Fort Donelson and Shiloh. The first (November 7, 1861) was little more than a skirmish, chiefly notable because it was a success and because, for the only time in his career, he had a horse shot under him. At the second (February 15–16, 1862) he was fighting an enemy who had strong defences to his rear and enjoyed the option of retreating within them if defeated in the field; here he was, uncharacteristically, taken by surprise and forced to contrive a victory under the pressure of events. Both episodes perfectly exemplify his methods of command.

Grant, at Fort Donelson, first tried to subdue the enemy by using his attached fleet of gunboats to overwhelm the Confederate shore batteries along the Cumberland River. 'I occupied a position on shore,' he wrote, 'from which I could see the advancing navy.' As so often, however, army metal proved to outweigh naval and the gunboats were driven into retreat. 'The enemy had evidently been much demoralised by the assault, but they were jubilant when they saw the disabled vessels dropping down the river entirely out of the control of the men on board. Of course I only witnessed the falling

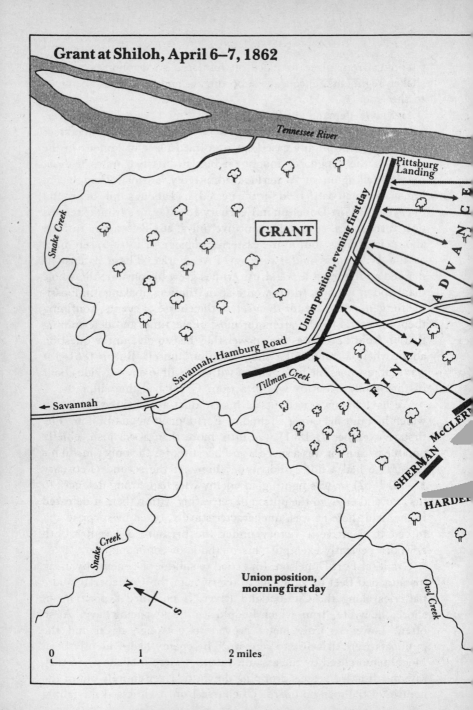

Grant at Shiloh, April 6–7, 1862

Tennessee River

Pittsburg Landing

GRANT

Union position, evening first day

FINAL ADVANCE

Savannah-Hamburg Road

Tillman Creek

← Savannah

Snake Creek

Snake Creek

SHERMAN

McCLER

HARDE

Owl Creek

Union position, morning first day

N
S

| 0 | 1 | 2 miles |

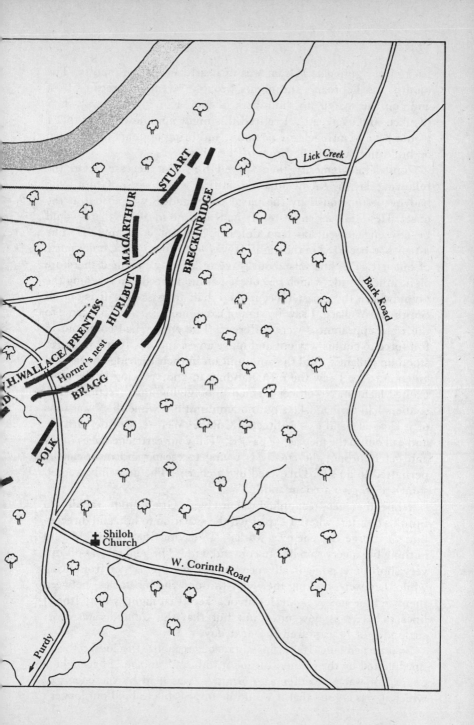

back of our gunboats.' Grant was disheartened by the repulse. The month was February, the nights brought twenty degrees of frost and, on the march up, 'numbers of men had thrown away their blankets and overcoats'. 'I retired this night not knowing but that I would have to intrench my position, and bring up tents for the men or build huts under the brow of the hills.'

Confederate temerity then spared him that necessity. On the following day the enemy attacked, at first with success. Grant, who had been summoned by the naval commander, was absent at the onset. He rode back in haste. 'I [had] had no idea that there would be any engagement on land unless I brought it on myself.' The attack had occurred in the night. 'I was some four or five miles north of our left. The line was about three miles long.' He had therefore eight miles to ride, which he covered at high speed. 'In reaching the point where the disaster occurred I had to pass the divisions of Smith and Wallace. I saw no sign of excitement . . . when I came to the right appearances were different. The enemy had come out in full force to cut his way out and make an escape . . . [Our] men had stood up gallantly until the ammunition in their cartridge boxes had given out . . . I saw the men standing in knots talking in the most excited fashion. No officer seemed to be giving any directions. The soldiers had their muskets but no ammunition, while there was tons of it close at hand . . . I directed Colonel Webster to ride with me and call out to the men as we passed, "Fill your cartridge boxes quick and get into line; the enemy is trying to escape and must not be permitted to do so." This acted like a charm. The men only wanted someone to give a command.'

While the men resupplied themselves, Grant 'rode rapidly to Smith's quarters where I explained the situation to him and directed him to charge the enemy's works . . . saying that he would find nothing but a very thin line to contend with. The general was off in a very short time, going in advance himself to keep his men from firing while they were working their way through the [obstacles] between them and the enemy . . . [He] bivouacked [that night] within [their] lines. There was now no doubt but that the Confederates must surrender or be captured the next day.'

So it turned out. Grant's instantaneous response to a local setback, unexploited by the enemy, turned it to his advantage. That night 'a council of war' – anathema to Grant – 'was held by the enemy at which it was argued that it would be impossible to hold out longer'.

Forrest, one of the toughest spirits in the Confederacy, succeeded in swimming his cavalry across a backwater to safety. The last of the Confederates, bar a few thousand who escaped otherwise, surrendered to Grant on his terms. They were unconditional, as he would insist throughout the war, thereby making the first of his distinctive contributions to its waging.

Two months after the capture of Fort Donelson – which with that of neighbouring Fort Henry gave control of the Cumberland and Tennessee rivers to the Union – Grant fought the battle of Shiloh. It was a fight wished upon him by the Confederates, who hoped thereby to reunite their armies, which the Henry–Donelson defeat had driven apart, by surprising him in the salient that separated their two wings. Surprise him they did. General A.S. Johnston got word that Grant was encamped near a small riverside church on the Upper Tennessee called Shiloh, made a cross-country march, through dense woodland, to reach his positions and encamped undetected within artillery range on the night of April 5–6, 1862. The next morning his men advanced to the assault, their opening salvoes being Grant's first warning that he was in trouble.

'While I was at breakfast,' he wrote in his *Memoirs*, 'heavy firing was heard in the direction of Pittsburg Landing and I hastened there.' The time was about 6.30. He was aboard his headquarters gunboat, *Tigress*, together with his staff and horses. At Pittsburg Landing they disembarked and he plunged into the frenzy of restoring order to a military situation that already threat .ed disaster. Many of the men of his five divisions – he commanded about 35,000 to Johnston's 40,000 – had already broken and men huddled under the bank of the Tennessee river in a compacted mass that would swell throughout the day. There was nothing, at this moment, he could do with them. Ordering the fresh regiments that had just landed to the front, he galloped off to confront other crises. The first, as at Donelson, was want of ammunition. Since the army had been surprised, it had only what was in the men's pouches. That matched the variegated weapons with which they were armed. Six different sorts were required by Sherman's division alone, and had to be sent forward to the right directions from the divisional ammunition waggons.

Grant then turned to gallop along his front and visit each of his five embattled subordinates, from left to right Hurlbut, Prentiss, Wallace, McClernand and Sherman. Choosing a woodland road –

the time was about 9.a.m. – he went first to McClernand, whose divisions were supposed to be in reserve in the centre but would soon be drawn into the fight, and then to Prentiss. He had already been driven back to a sunken lane, with a field of brambles to its front, which the Confederates, making their main thrust against it, would call the Hornets' Nest. Grant told Prentiss he must 'maintain that position at all hazards' and then rode off to see Wallace.

He was concerned about the security of a bridge across Owl Creek, a tributary of the Tennessee, to his rear. Across it must come the reinforcements he desperately needed, his sixth division, which he had left upriver, and the larger force under Buell at Savannah. Ordering Wallace to post infantry at the bridge, he sent a cavalry detachment with a note to Buell which he penned in the saddle:

> The attack on my forces has been very spirited since early this morning. The appearance of fresh troops on the field now would have a powerful effect both by inspiring our men and disheartening the enemy. If you can get upon the field, leaving all your baggage on the east bank of the river, it will be a move to our advantage and possibly save the day to us. The rebel force is estimated at over 100,000 men. My headquarters will be in the log building on top of the hill, where you will be furnished a staff officer, to guide you to your place on the field.

This note is deeply revealing of Grant's frame of mind and philosophy of war. Though written within sound of heavy gunfire and under heavy pressure of units, it is perfectly phrased and severely practical – it identifies where Grant's staff will be found, promises a guide and suggests a sensible means to press the march. On the other hand, it reveals acute anxiety; the figure of Confederate strength specified is too large by more than double. And yet, though material inequality is clearly his chief concern, it urges a moral point: that the battle will be won or lost in the minds of the combatants. Grant, so often characterized as a mere butcher, is thinking not of blood but of fears and hopes.

Of fears he was outwardly showing none. Soon afterwards he and his staff drew up in a clearing from which he could survey the front. Shot was cracking overhead and one of the staff nudged another to say, 'Go tell the old man to leave here for God's sake.' He got the answer, 'Tell him yourself. He'll think me afraid and so I am, but he shan't think so.' Eventually a third officer put it to Grant that,

'General, we must leave this place. It isn't necessary to stay here. If we do we shall all be dead in five minutes.' The general, who appeared quite unruffled, turned his gaze on his followers, said, 'I guess that's so,' and led them away.

His line by midday was under pressure at every point and he spent the afternoon riding from place to place encouraging his commanders, sending forward such uncommitted regiments as he could find and turning back others which were dropping out of the fight. At 1 p.m. he was at Pittsburg Landing, where Buell had just arrived by steamer, and he urged him to hurry on his reinforcements. But generally he was close up behind the front, as the soldiers of several regiments remembered. He led the 15th Illinois, which had been taken under fire by its own supporting artillery, back into position. The 81st Ohio, retreating from the Hornets' Nest, was twice stopped by Grant and sent back. So too was the 11th Iowa. The 15th Iowa, driven out of the line, was redeployed by Grant to another threatened spot.

Despite all his efforts, the situation steadily worsened. At 4.30 he was with Prentiss behind the Hornets' Nest, where the Confederate leader, A.S. Johnston, had been killed ten hours earlier. But Wallace, who was supporting Prentiss, had been killed also, both their divisions had been exposed by the retreat of the Union troops on their flanks and at 5.30 p.m. Prentiss, now commanding only 2,000 men, was forced to show the white flag.

Grant had contrived to close the gap in Prentiss's rear by shortening his line. Had the Confederates, however, not themselves been suffering disorganization, and had they had that superiority of 100,000 over 35,000 Grant imagined was theirs, they would certainly have won Shiloh on the first day. As it was, Grant, by giving ground, assembling a grand battery of fifty guns on his left flank, trusting to Sherman's unflappability on the right, and above all keeping his own nerve, saw the day out. A newspaper correspondent, catching Grant alone as the evening closed in, plucked up courage to ask if the prospect was not dark. 'Oh no,' said Grant. 'They can't break our lines tonight – it is too late. Tomorrow we shall attack them with fresh troops and drive them, of course.'

Drive them he did. The dead Johnston's army had, by the evening of April 6, itself suffered such casualties as to reduce its strength to 20,000. Grant's own army, reinforced by 25,000, then twice outnumbered it. The Southerners fought throughout the morning of

April 7 with a bravery that, it is said, changed Grant's view of the quality of the Southern cause for good. Thitherto he had thought its soldiers the dupes of demagogues. Thereafter he knew them to be patriots, never again to be underrated in action. But outnumbered patriots cannot carry a field by force of feeling. By early afternoon, when, as General Lew Wallace observed, 'the two armies as a general thing [had] degenerated into mere fighting swarms', over which neither Grant nor his new opponent, Beauregard, could exercise detailed control, the Southerners were beaten. Soon after 2 they received the order to retreat and were shortly gone. Grant 'rode forward several miles the day after the battle, and found the enemy had dropped much, if not all, of their provisions, some ammunition and the extra wheels of their caissons, lightening their loads in an effort to get off their guns'. Beauregard's account was more succinct. 'Our condition is horrible. Troops utterly disorganised and demoralised . . . No provisions and no forage; consequently everything is feeble . . . Our artillery is being left along the road by its officers; indeed I find but few officers with their men.' A little later he reported to higher command. 'If we are pursued by a vigorous force we will lose all in our rear. The whole road presents a scene of a rout, and no mortal power could restrain it.'

Grant had tried to organize a 'vigorous force' to pursue, but his army also was exhausted. It had lost 13,000 men killed, wounded and missing, of whom 1,700 men were dead, making the battle by far the bloodiest thus far fought in the war in either the eastern or western theatres. He was to suffer vilification both for the casualties his army had incurred and for the incontestable fact that he had exposed it to surprise attack. But Shiloh was equally incontestably a victory, won at a time when Northern victories were few. He would survive the attacks on his reputation. Physically he was unmarked by the ordeal. Emotionally, though worn by the knowledge of the suffering inflicted – 'the sight was more unendurable than encountering the enemy's fire' – he had the resilience to recover. Morally he had been vindicated by the result.

Above all, he now knew how to fight and win a battle. Battles far larger than any he had yet fought – the siege of Vicksburg and its prodrome, Champion's Hill, Chattanooga, Spotsylvania, North Anna, Cold Harbor, the long siege of Petersburg – lay ahead. But none would teach him to add to his store of skills as a commander of men and events. No future experience would alter the vision of reality he had now conceived for himself. The face he showed his soldiers at Shiloh would be the same face he showed the world at Appomattox and in the White House. It was a face that the essayist Henry Adams would later compare to Garibaldi's: 'Of the two, Garibaldi seemed to him a trifle the more intellectual, but, in both, the intellect counted for nothing; only the energy counted. The type was pre-intellectual, archaic, and would have seemed so, even to cave-dwellers'. This comparison is profoundly interesting, in part because it is wrong – Grant's intellectual powers were large and counted for a very great deal – in part because it translates Grant from a context purely military and American to one ideological and universal. Garibaldi was apotheosized by the Victorian world because his military bravado reverberated with its liberal ethos. In our own time, his assaults on order would have made him notorious; in his time his use of violence in pursuit of an ideal made him famous and admired. Grant, too, found the means to put generalship at the service of a cause. In the moment of victory his political understanding would be quite overshadowed by his soldierly achievement. But in retrospect, great though Grant's generalship is seen to be, it is his comprehension of the nature of the war, and of what could and could not be done by a general within its defining conditions, that seems the more remarkable. He had sought through warmaking, as the conclusion of his *Memoirs* sets out, 'a commingling of the people'. It would take more than a century after Appomattox for such a commingling at last to materialize. As it does so, Grant's precipitating role in the process begins to emerge as being as important as Lincoln's.

Grant and American Democracy

A 'commingling of people' is one, though not the only, definition of a state. The United States, uniquely among the polities of its age, had begun its existence as a fully-formed state, of which its founding fathers had fixed at the outset the exact and respective powers of its executive, legislative and judicial authorities. By that constitutional donation, America was brought at the moment of its birth to a situation which older societies had taken centuries of internal struggle to achieve, at which, indeed, many have still not arrived. 'Commingling' is a gentle word, implying compromise and consent.

State making, in practice, is a bloody business. Britain, of which the United States may be seen as a philosophically consistent duplicate, had rough-cut the pattern of 'separation of powers' taken by the founding fathers as their constitutional matrix only as a result of repeated internal conflicts, of which its own seventeenth-century civil war was but the most politically explicit.

For all its high-mindedness, however, the United States constitution is sprinkled with blood, not only that of the British redcoats who fought to deny the colonists their independence but also of the loyalists who opposed independence as an ideal. The reasons for which they chose to do so were complex, and by no means all were extinguished by Washington's victory. 'Sectionalism' was one: the belief that the interests of any one region of settlement would not necessarily be best served by a sovereign government planted elsewhere on American soil. The dispersion of settlement, already vast in 1776, underlay that calculation. Its enormous extension during the nineteenth century lent that calculation renewed force. It was felt most strongly of all in the Southern states, bedded in their slave economies, which they were neither willing nor able to transform, which they knew were repugnant to their fellow citizens of other sections, and which they could defend only by a manipulation of the constitutional machinery which a growing majority of Americans thought alien to its informing principles.

America was thus brought, in the 1860s, to confront an internal contradiction in its politics, of a sort all too familiar to the Europeans whom the New World denounced as sunk in sin, which proved to be capable of resolution only by the bad, old method of violence. Here is not the place to discuss whether slavery provoked the American Civil War, or whether that war might have been avoided. The war happened and we are discussing Grant's part in it. Let him speak for himself.

'The cause of the great War of the Rebellion against the United States will have to be attributed to slavery,' he wrote in his *Memoirs*:

> Slavery was an institution that required unusual guarantees for its security wherever it existed; and in a country like ours where the larger portion of it was free territory inhabited by an intelligent and well-to-do population, the people would naturally have but little sympathy with demands upon them for its protection. Hence the people of the South were dependent

upon keeping control of the general government to secure the perpetuation of its favourite institution . . . This was a degradation which the North would not permit any longer than until they could get the power to expunge [slave] laws from the statute books. Prior to the time of these encroachments the great majority of the people of the North had no particular quarrel with slavery, so long as they were not forced to have it themselves. But they were not willing to play the role of police for the South in the protection of this particular institution.

'It is probably as well,' he went on, 'that we had the war when we did.' Grant thus concedes his acceptance that the only means by which the North could 'get the power' to resolve its difference with the South was by fighting. But he did not always think so; writing to his father in November 1861, he was still inclined to see his duty as that of the suppression of rebellion, not as the remaking of the United States as a society without contradictions. 'My inclination,' he explained, 'is to whip the rebellion into submission, preserving all constitutional rights. If it cannot be whipped in any other way than through a war against slavery, let it come to that legitimately. If it is necessary that the Republic may continue its existence, let slavery go. But that portion of the press that advocates the beginning of such a war now, are as great enemies to their country as if they were open and avowed secessionists.'

Grant's views were changed by his exposure to Southern sentiment after his penetration of the upper slave states in 1862, reinforcing his discovery, made as early as Shiloh, that Confederate troops fought out of conviction, not bravado. From that time onwards he knew that Americans were two peoples, and could be made one only through the defeat of the minority by the majority. Even after he had come to that conclusion, however, he persisted in seeing beyond the war's end to the necessity of victors and vanquished learning to live together in harmony. That was the vision of 'commingling' he held thenceforward to the end of his life.

Grant's achievement of that vision entailed three dependent decisions, the first of which might seem flagrantly at odds with the other two. It was the decision that the war must be made total. As early as April 1863, as we have seen, he was writing that the war must achieve 'the total subjugation of the south' and that the army's duty was 'therefore to use every means to weaken the enemy' by destroying not only their armies in the field but their economy at home. Grant's title as 'first of the moderns' among generals derives from that gospel of frightfulness. Christian though he was, he had persuaded himself that the Just War doctrine of 'proportionality' – restraint of violence within the bounds necessary to make an enemy desist from it – did not apply in a war of principle. Even before his protégé Sherman had begun to make his name as a burner and breaker, therefore, Grant was burning and breaking with a will, turning recalcitrants out of their homes once territory was captured and ruthlessly carrying the war into the hearts of the Southern people.

But there was a limit which even he was prepared to set to ruthlessness: he would not countenance private law-breaking in the use of violence, either against property or the person. Grant was law-abiding to his fingertips. Hence the second of his decisions about how 'commingling' must be achieved: he must never, however great the powers invested in him as commander, infringe the authority of Congress or the President. The 'little scared-looking man' an observer watched receiving the revived rank of lieutenant-general from Lincoln in the White House on March 9, 1864, managed only a few words in reply, but they were words expressing thanks and recognizing responsibility. When one of his first meetings as commander-in-chief with Stanton, the Secretary of War, produced impasse and Stanton warned that he would have to take Grant 'to the President', Grant answered, 'That is right. The President ranks us both.' President and general had already established the proprieties of their relationship. 'All [I] had wanted,' Lincoln had told him at their first private interview, 'and had ever wanted was someone who would take the responsibility and act, and call on [me] for all the assistance needed, pledging [myself] to use all the powers of government in rendering such assistance.' Grant, for his part, assured the President that he would do 'the best I could with the means at hand, and avoid as far as possible annoying him'. Doing the best he could did not mean deferring to the President over strategy; he had already made it a principle that 'I did not communicate my plans to the President'. It did, on the other hand, mean deferring in all non-strategic matters. Ordered to recruit blacks into the Union army – a contentious policy – Grant answered Lincoln, 'You may rely upon it . . . I would do this whether arming the Negro seemed to me a wise policy or not, because it is an order that I am bound to obey and I do not feel that in my position I have a right to question any policy of the government.'

His third decision was an extension of the second. Just as he saw that legal propriety required humility to the authority of government, so too did he see that American propriety required humility to the sovereignty of the people. Grant was probably not, in his heart of hearts, a humble man. The truly humble flee power, even when it is thrust upon them; Grant refused no power that was offered him and, by every report of outward appearance, was gratified and enlarged by it. That, by his own account, he 'never felt better' than when exercising command in the fever swamps of the Mississippi suggests very strongly that his achievement of high rank satisfied a profound inner estimation of his own worth. It was an estimation, nevertheless, that he kept strictly within the bounds of decency, as his American contemporaries conceived it to be. Lesser men of similar rank did not. Frémont gave himself absurd airs – European they were thought. McClellan basked in the title of 'the young Napoleon' and believed it ensured him the presidential election of 1864. Halleck cultivated an Olympian aloofness. Longstreet played the prima donna and indulged in nervous breakdowns when crossed (notably at Gettysburg when Lee could have done without histrionics). In aping importance, these men – and many like them – were surrendering to an impulse which elevation to high command makes difficult to resist. Generalship is bad for people. As anyone intimate with military society knows only too well, the most reasonable of men suffuse with pomposity when stars touch their shoulders. Because 'general' is a word which literature uses to include in the same stable Alexander the Great and the dimmest Pentagon paper-pusher, perfectly well-balanced colonels begin to demand the deference due to the Diadochi when promotion carries them to the next step in rank. And military society, that last surviving model of the courts of heroic war leaders, regularly does them the favour of indulging their fantasies.

Grant resisted fantasy with republican sternness. When applying for appointment to adjutant-general at the outset of the Civil War, he pitched his ambitions at the most modest level: 'Feeling it the duty of everyone who has been educated at the Government expense,' he wrote, 'to offer their services for the support of that Government, I have the honour, very respectfully, to tender my services, until the close of the war, in such capacity as may be offered.' He indicated that he thought himself fitted at best for the command of a regiment; elevated beyond that level, he continued to maintain an establishment no grander than a regimental colonel's, and the same suited him until the end of the war.

The legend of Grant's modesty was almost as important as the fact of his triumphs in making him first the North's military hero and eventually the reconstructed Union's president. But more important still, as a dimension of this study of generalship, was the 'familiar reverence' which his conduct of high command evoked from his soldiers. 'Familiar reverence' is about as far as Americans think it proper to go in saluting a hero, while Grant's unheroic heroism was perfectly adjusted to the populism of the society he led to victory. A divergence from either style would have been untruthful to what Europeans recognize as distinctively American in the civilization of the New World and regrettably, in that respect at least, resistant to transplantation. In the Old, surrender to the appeal of the hero as leader, war chief and superman remained a possibility rooted in the subconscious of its traditional societies. In the mid-twentieth century, that possibility was to become a disastrous reality.

CHAPTER 4

False Heroic: Hitler as Supreme Commander

Few today think of Hitler as a soldier. But it was as a soldier, quite as much as a politician or an artist – strangest of his delusions – that he thought of himself. His political testament, dictated in the Berlin bunker on April 28, 1945, while Russian shells rained into the garden of the Reich Chancellery overhead, opens with the sentence, 'Since 1914, when as a volunteer, I made my modest contribution in the World War that was forced upon the Reich . . .' and those words echo directly the promise he gave the German people at the outbreak of the Second World War on September 1, 1939: 'I am asking of no German man more than I myself was ready to perform during the four years of the [First World War] . . . I am from now on nothing more than the first soldier of the Reich. I have once more put on the coat that was most sacred and dear to me. I will not take it off again until victory is assured, or I will not survive the outcome.' Thirty-six hours after signing his name to his political testament, still dressed in his personal version of the German soldier's field-grey tunic he had indeed worn throughout the war, he put a loaded service pistol to his temple and pulled the trigger.

It was not merely by outward symbolism or the nature of his death that Hitler lived the life of the sword. By his accession to the German presidency in 1934 he became titular chief of the German army and navy. In 1938, by his creation of the 'Oberkommando der Wehrmacht' (OKW), he invested himself with supreme operational authority over the armed forces. And on December 18, 1941, when he dismissed Brauchitsch from command of the German army, he himself acceded to that post and thereafter exercised direct control of the German armies in the field. He was, moreover, to hold high command for a longer continuous period than any other German during the Second World War. All three of the Army Group commanders in post at the outbreak, von Leeb, von Bock and von Rundstedt, had been dismissed before the end, as had eleven out of the eighteen field-marshals he had created and twenty-one of his thirty-seven colonel-generals. None of his four wartime chiefs of staff – Halder (September 1939–September 1942), Zeitzler (September 1942–July 1944), Guderian (July 1944–March 1945) or Krebs (killed in the battle of Berlin) – held office for more than three years. Keitel and Jodl alone equalled him in length of duty at OKW; and they were his functionaries, not independent decision-makers. Hitler was, therefore, supreme commander not only in name but in fact, and so indeed 'the first soldier of the Reich'.

But Hitler's five and a half years of high command, as he so constantly emphasized, were not his first experience of the military life. His service in the First World War had been almost as extended – August 1914 to October 1918 – and honourable enough for any German of his generation to have taken pride in it as a record of duty. *Frontkämpfer* – front fighter – was what he called himself, and with perfect accuracy. Thrice wounded – once by shrapnel in the face, once by a shell fragment in the left thigh, once by gas which temporarily blinded him – he took part in twelve battles, served twenty-five other spells of duty in the trenches and was five times distinguished or decorated, finally with the Iron Cross First Class. Two spells of home leave and five months in hospital apart, he was continuously with his regiment, the 16th Bavarian Reserve Infantry, at the Western Front from October 1914 to October 1918. 'Good Soldier Hitler' was a title he might have borne without any imputation of irony at all.

The circumstances of his war service have a significance, moreover, that almost all his biographers have missed or passed over without emphasis. They concern the regiment in which he served and the duty which he performed. The regiment first: its character helps to explain why Hitler would speak years afterwards of 'the stupendous impression produced upon me by the war – the greatest of all experiences', and how he could recall that 'individual interest – the interest of one's own ego – could be subordinated to the common interest'. All Hitler's biographers do agree in seeing him, from early manhood, as an individual set apart from others by his sense of difference, of unrecognized talent and frustrated fulfilment. He is, to social psychologists, a classic example of the lower middle-class male enraged by the constrictions and closed doors of a settled social order which will make no room for anyone struggling to enter it from below except by the passport of connections and credentials that Hitler either lacked or disdained to acquire. The consequent squalor and misery of his Vienna years may be seen as self-chosen: the odd jobs, the postcard hawking, the nomadism of furnished rooms and bachelor's hostel, the keeping up of appearances, the yearning to be accepted as what he clearly was not – artist, architect, intellectual, bohemian of good family, cadet of the empire's German élite. It was the Austrian empire's insistence on seeing him for what he was, a near down-and-out who sought to evade military service – which would have meant soldiering with the Czechs, Croats and Jews he shunned and despised – that drove him in 1913 to flee from its reach to the German city of Munich. There, where he succeeded in obtaining exemption from Habsburg military service, he found both physical and a sort of psychological refuge. He was later to describe the months he spent as lodger in the family house of a tailor as the 'happiest and most contented' of his life. But it was a transient contentment. He remained a man on the margin, surrounded by the *Germantum* – Germanness – he so much admired, but not part of it.

And then came August 1914, war and the sound of the trumpet. Hitler, as an Austrian subject, was not liable for military service in the Bavarian army (Bavaria, by the terms of the imperial association of 1871, maintained an army separate from though within the German military establishment). He determined to enlist none the less, directly petitioned the Bavarian king for permission to do so on August 3, the third day after the outbreak, and immediately received it. On August 16 he was enrolled in the 16th Bavarian Reserve Regiment.

His selection for the 16th Bavarian Reserve must be seen as a key ingredient of Hitler's life, for the regiment was composed of exactly that class of young Germans to which Hitler had so long aspired but failed to be granted admission. They were, in high proportion, high-school boys, university students and trainees for the professions who, by deliberate policy of the German military authorities, had not thitherto been drafted for military service. So much higher was Germany's birth-rate before 1914 than that of France, its chief potential adversary, that the army, prompted by the Reichstag's desire to tax at a level guaranteed to sustain industry's programme of heavy investment, had taken 30 per cent fewer than the French of its annual class of conscripts into training, allowing the surplus to accumulate in a so-called 'replacement reserve'. In August 1914 this reserve was immediately tapped to form fourteen new divisions of war service. The 6th Bavarian Reserve Division, to which the 16th Bavarian Reserve Regiment belonged, was one. Staffed by officers and NCOs of the standing army, its ranks were filled by recruits as wholly untrained as Hitler was himself.

It may seem an oddity of Hitler's personality that among his cargo of resentments no complaint of having been denied an officer's commission ever featured. It was not even a grievance with which as Führer he taxed the professional officer class, so ready though he was to find with it every other sort of fault. Two reasons may explain the omission. The first, well known to him, was that the German army promoted from the ranks of its war entrants a far smaller proportion of officers than did the British or French. Even at the height of the fighting, it strove to preserve the professional exclusivity of the officer corps, relying on the dedication of NCOs holding title as 'officer deputies' or 'sergeant-major lieutenants' to provide the cadre of leadership supplied in opposing armies by the commissioning of graduates of the *grandes écoles* or old boys of public schools. Hitler may therefore have been able to accept without rancour his consignment to the ranks, because he knew that his lot was no different from that of tens of thousands of other moderately well-educated young Germans. The second reason flows from the first. Assignment to the 16th Bavarian Reserve put Hitler among contemporaries whose comradeship he might count as social acceptance, even social promotion. The regiments of the 'replacement reserve' were the equivalents, in composition and ethos, of those British battalions of office and club 'Pals' who in 1916 sacrificed themselves in tens of thousands at the battle of the Somme. Their private soldiers were not, as some of the Pals' battalions advertised them to be, gentleman rankers chivalrously forswearing officer rank. But, like the Pals, they were certainly from the best and brightest of the country's manhood and, like them, were fated to be a lost generation.

That, above all, must explain why Hitler found the war 'the greatest of all experiences', just as Pal survivors of the Somme found it also. For the replacement reserve regiments of the German army were to undergo their Somme experience, two years earlier than the

Pals, in a battle against the British, French and Belgians in Flanders which came to be known in Germany as the 'Massacre of the Innocents' (*Kindermord bei Ypern*). In October 1914, desperate to keep open the closing gap in what threatened to become a continuous line of entrenchments from Switzerland to the sea, the high command plucked nine of the replacement reserve divisions from training in Germany and rushed them to the front. One of them was Hitler's, which on October 29 found itself in line between Hollebeke and Messines, a little south of the town of Ypres which was to give its name to the *Kindermord*. Its opponents were the soldiers of the British Expeditionary Force, dreadfully depleted in numbers by three months of fighting, but all veteran professionals in seasoned units. When the German conscripts, none with more than two months' parade-ground training, attacked the British trenches, they were cut down in hundreds. Of the 3,600 men of the 16th Bavarian Reserve (usually known as the List Regiment, after its commander, killed on the second day of the first battle), 349 died in the attack. Four days later, only 611 survived unwounded. Hitler's own company of 250 men had been reduced by early December to 42. He himself had been promoted lance-corporal and recommended for the Iron Cross Second Class.

The *Kindermord bei Ypern* had a profound effect on German feeling, comparable to that to be exerted in Britain two years later by the massacre of the Pals of the Somme. Between a third and a half of the infantry of nine divisions, about 40,000 men, were killed or wounded in twenty days of fighting. Earlier battles had been as costly, but the losses had fallen on troops trained and prepared for war. It was the military innocence, youth and, perhaps most of all, superior background of the Flanders victims which made their deaths cut so deep, destroying what belief remained in the possibility of a short war and providing a warning of yet worse damage to come to the social future of Germany. The *Kindermord* marked the moment when the Germans first confronted the reality of total war. But it was a watershed in the life not only of the community but of individual survivors. Hitler was one of them. Most of the comrades – can we call them Pals? – with whom he had left Munich in October 1914 he was never to see again. The brief brotherhood with his 'Young Germany' of dreams had been immediately shattered. The aloofness, the 'loner' behaviour, recalled by all his trench comrades – replacements for the casualties of 1914 – from the subsequent war years may well testify to the shattering of Hitler's own brief, cherished sense of belonging.

The protraction of the war heightened the singularity of his survival. Throughout its course the List Regiment was to lose just over 100 per cent of its paper strength, 3,754 men killed in all. This index of agony, unparalleled in the experience of any previous military generation and scarcely credible at all to the late twentieth-century mind, was not at all out of the ordinary among regimental casualty lists of the First World War. By 1917 the infantry units of all armies that had fought at the front since 1914 had, if wounded are counted with killed, suffered 100 per cent casualties, and by the end some units and formations would have suffered over 200 per cent casualties. The Newfoundland Regiment of the British Army suffered nearly 100 per cent casualties on the first day of the battle of the Somme, July 1, 1916, while the 7th Royal Sussex Regiment, on November 11, 1918, counted among its officers only two of the twenty-eight who had gone to France with it in May, 1915. Four out of nine Frenchmen who served with fighting units between 1914 and 1918 were killed or wounded; nearly 2 million, perhaps as many as 4 million, out of 35 million German males lost their lives in the same period. If those of military age are reckoned as 15 million, it may be seen that one out of four of that generation was buried somewhere in France, Belgium, Russia or the Balkans.

Hitler's survival may appear, in that context, all the more remarkable. And his was not the survival of a shirker or 'soft job' soldier. There were duties, even in an infantry regiment, that spared a man danger. Those of cook, clerk, groom were some of them. None came Hitler's way nor, apparently, would he have accepted one. All who served with him, officer and fellow soldier alike, testify to his uncommon conscientiousness as well as personal courage. In 1922, long before there might have been any profit in lending him praise, when Hitler indeed was still no more than a ranter on the fringe of nationalist politics, three of his officers recorded their wartime memories of him in terms of highest esteem. General Pietz, who had commanded the List Regiment, wrote of his 'exceptional pluck . . . and the reckless courage with which he tackled dangerous situations and the hazards of battle'. Colonel Spatany remembered that he 'set a shining example to those around him. His pluck and exemplary bearing throughout each battle exerted a powerful influence on his comrades and this, combined with his admirable unportentousness, earned him the respect of superiors and officers alike.' Lieutenant-Colonel von Tubeuf recalled him 'volunteering for the most arduous and dangerous tasks' and that 'of all my men he was closest to me in the human sense . . . The views he expressed in our private conversations . . . testified to his profound love of his country and to his altogether upright and honourable nature.'

Years later, in the closing stages of the *Kampfzeit* which brought Hitler to power, opponents seeking to wound him would sneer that for all his claim to have belonged to the ranks of the *Frontkämpfer*, he had been no more than a *Meldegänger* – messenger. It was not an insult that any *Frontkämpfer* would throw in the teeth of another. Messenger – 'runner' was the exact equivalent in the British army – was an appointment of uncommon risk. True, the runner was not what survivors of trench assaults in the British army would call a 'parapet popper'. He did not brave the awful moment of scaling a trench-ladder to launch himself into attack across no man's land. He did not know the dribble of unmanning fear in the night or morning that preceded it. But, equally, he knew nothing of the many longer days of relative safety when a company kept to its dugouts between attacks or stood out of the front line in support or reserve trenches. As a runner at battalion headquarters – Hitler belonged to the III Battalion of the List Regiment – he was at the disposal of its staff whenever it was in line, and liable to be sent forward, below or above ground, as the needs of communication with the front trench required. Hitler has left his own perfectly convincing account of what such continuous liability to exposure entailed: 'In Wytschaete during the first day of the attack three of us eight runners were killed and one badly wounded. The four survivors and the man who was badly wounded were cited for distinguised conduct.' While Hitler and those others waited outside the headquarters dugout for the battalion commander to decide which of them should be recommended for the Iron Cross, 'a shell hit the dugout, wounding Lieutenant-Colonel Engelhardt and killing or wounding the rest of his staff'. This episode, at the very beginning of Hitler's war, was repeated on countless occasions during its course.

Indeed, though we have nothing like a Hitler diary of the war, and a bare scattering of his letters from the front, it is by no means impossible to reconstruct an authentic version of what his experience as a *Meldegänger* may have been like. Battalion positions on the Western Front, of the sort occupied by III/16th Bavarian Reserve, occupied some 1,500 yards of front and extended to some 4,000 yards to the rear. Two lines of trenches, front and support, 2,000 yards apart, crossed the sector, with a third position 2,000 yards farther back. Battalion headquarters were located in the third position, at extreme range of enemy field artillery. Hitler, as a battalion messenger, would have spent his time at battalion headquarters going forward as duty required. Messages for the front line were marked XXX for 'urgent', XX for 'quick' and X for 'in your own time'. During quiet periods, X messages would be allowed to accumulate until a messenger went forward on a routine trip; XX messages had to be taken forward at once, XXX messages at all costs. The way forward to the front ran at first above ground; then, from the support line, communication trenches led to the front line. Under artillery or machine-gun fire, therefore, the worst of a messenger's two-mile run would be made 'below ground'. But communication trenches were often sketchy excavations, waterlogged and liable to collapse by shelling. Precisely when a runner most needed shelter, therefore, urgency might drive him above ground, forcing him to get forward by leaps and bounds from one point of dead ground or shell hole to another. Runner casualties, in consequence, were always heavy during heightened periods of trench warfare and very heavy during battles. Hitler's worst wound came to him in that way. Sent forward on October 7, 1916, near Bapaume, when the weight of British fire was so heavy that his officer had called for volunteers, he was hit in the left thigh by a shell fragment and disabled. His companion managed to struggle on. He was found by stretcher-bearers at the spot where he had been hit, and evacuated. The wound was so serious that he was sent to hospital in Germany, where he took five months to recover.

This wound came at the midpoint of Hitler's war, which was spent exclusively on the Western Front and almost continuously opposite the British sector in Flanders. A spell in the quiet sector in Alsace in the autumn of 1917 apart, he was otherwise always near Ypres, Lille or Laon, the dreariest, wettest and perhaps most dangerous sector of the trench line, and a focus of fighting that ranged in intensity from constant shelling and raiding to full-scale artillery and infantry offensives of the bitterest sort. Hitler's division opposed the British in three of the greatest battles of the Western Front, Ypres, the Somme and Arras. By the end of 1918, after the failure of the Ludendorff offensives which had been designed to win the war before American reinforcements consigned Germany to inexorable defeat, it had been so reduced in numbers that two of its three regiments had had to be amalgamated to make good losses. Shortly afterwards, on October 13, 1918, it was holding a position close to the point where it had started the war, at Werwick near Ypres, when a British gas bombardment caught Hitler in the front-line trenches. He had recently received his Iron Cross First Class for running a message across open ground under heavy fire. The gas, seeping unseen into his dugout, was a more insidious enemy. During the night he was overcome and at dawn stumbled towards the rear, blinded but carrying a despatch for battalion headquarters.

War and Hitler's World

The significance of Hitler's role as a *Meldegänger* in the List Regiment is not exhausted when its effect on his personal development or intermingling with the common *Frontkämpfer* experience on which the Nazi party was to draw so heavily has been dissected. Hitler, having been a soldier, was to become a commander. His *Meldegänger*'s function goes far to explain both the nature of the war he had undergone and, in direct contrast to it, that of the war he was to direct.

The First World War remains, to the Western mind even at the end of the twentieth century, *the* war, by reason not only of the destruction it brought to the primacy of the Old World and the agony it inflicted on the manhood and family feeling of a whole European generation, but of its abidingly mysterious character. '*How* did they do it?' the first question put to anyone confronted by the terrible reality of the trenches, gives way almost at once to a second, even more imponderable, 'Why was it *done*?' Why did the armies persist in the impossible, the breaking of barbed wire by breasts of flesh and blood? Why did the generals bind them to the effort? No armies ever before, not even in the worst passages of siege warfare, sustained courage or casualties with the suicidal relentlessness of those on the Western Front. The nature of Western Front fighting seems to defy nature itself. Whence that extraordinary defiance?

Explanations of the character of the First World War must derive from two sources, the first material, the second moral and intellectual. The material explanation returns us to and takes up from the end of the war that Ulysses S. Grant had directed in the United States fifty years before 1914. 'War,' he had then reflected in retrospective survey, 'is progressive.' What he had meant was that the rules by which the war of the past had been fought – edged-weapon and gunpowder alike – no longer applied to a military world penetrated by the railroad, the telegraph and the long-range firearm. Long-range firearms destroyed the age-old mathematics of the battlefield, those calculations of fight and flight distances that had held as good for Alexander's archers as they had for Wellington's musketeers. By the same token, the railroad and the telegraph transformed the mathematics of strategy. March rates could no longer be reckoned in terms of a foot pace, nor campaigning seasons measured by the rhythms of the harvest. Grant's armies might travel at commuter speeds and feed well in the field long after the grain had ripened in the ear.

But Grant's perception of military 'progress' was a more partial one than perhaps even he could have recognized. Fifty years on, the military world he had known was transformed once again. The temporary field forces he had commanded – 'mere armed mobs' by the contemptuous reckoning of his Prussian contemporary, Helmuth von Moltke – had given place in Europe to enormous standing armies permanently organized for war and backed by reserve organizations larger still. The Prussian army, committed in 1870 to war against France, like the Americans of 1861 improvised higher formations for the emergency. By 1914 the German army, together with the French, Austro-Hungarian, Russian and even the tiny British army, stood ready to take the field in higher formations – corps and armies – that were permanent elements of peacetime establishments. And because all, except the British, supplied the manpower of their peacetime armies by short-term conscription, they could also duplicate or triplicate those formations from their reservoirs of trained ex-soldiers.

The result of this military population explosion – it was nothing less – was to put under the hands of the generals of 1914 armies larger by exponential measure than any yet seen before. The French peacetime army of 1914 was almost as large as the Grand Army that Napoleon led to Moscow, 550,000 to Napoleon's 600,000. The German army, on its expansion to its war strength of 5 million, was larger by far than all the European armies of the Napoleonic wars put together. And it was packed and primped into formations so compact and uniform that its high command might parcel it hither and thither with the despatch of a postmaster sorting and sending the mails. At the height of the mobilization of August 1914 it was said that a loaded troop train crossed the Rhine to the concentration area of the German army in the west every six minutes. Mathematics demonstrated that, when concentration was complete, five German soldiers stood in notional file along each yard of the common Franco-German frontier.

But what to do with the enormous numbers thus assembled? They could be moved, fed, supplied; but could they be led to victory? Schlieffen, architect of Germany's war plan for 1914, tortured his fine military mind for fifteen years in a struggle to supply the answer. He drew his arrows on the map thus and then thus again, producing first a minor violation of Belgium's neutrality, then a major. He brought the German armies to the gates of Paris on paper, predicated the decisive battle they would fight there and finally confronted the probability of its failure. 'We must conclude,' he eventually confided to the pages of his military testament, 'that the enterprise is one for which we are not strong enough.'

Reality was almost exactly the contrary. The defect of the military organizations that went to war in 1914 was that they were too strong, so strong in both numbers and firepower that none could hope to defeat another in the open field, and all in consequence were fated to fight a stalemate warfare in static positions. Various characterizations of this state of affairs – all tautological – have been advanced. Liddell Hart's concept of the 'ratio of men to space' is the most straightforward. By it he demonstrates that the concentration of manpower on the fighting front from Switzerland to the sea was so dense and the capability for rapid reconcentration of reserves by lateral railroad along its length so large that no army, with the weapons and equipment then available to it, could hope to assemble a breakthrough force. By the time it had got together a concentration large enough by a general staff's calculations to force an entry, undisguisable signs of warning would have set counter-offensive reserves into motion. When it launched its attack, irresistible force would meet immovable object and stability, give or take a few thousand yards of front, must be restored.

Whence this ghastly equilibrium? Explanations must address two

situations, that of 'open warfare', so called, and that of the trench
warfare which followed it. Open warfare, the 'proper' activity of
armies since armies had made their first appearance in the second
millennium BC, had occupied the energies of American Civil War
soldiers from its outset almost to its close. But the open warfare of
1861–5 already displayed marked differences from that of the
Napoleonic wars, and the differences heightened rapidly thereafter.
At the root of the trend to divergence lay the factor of firepower,
enormously enhanced by the industrialization of weapon-making in
the nineteenth century. Two centuries of effective technical stasis in
military technology had come to an abrupt end in the twenty years
before 1861, when the time-tested blackpowder musket and smoothbore cannon were replaced in all advanced armies by rifled weapons.
Rifled weapons fired projectiles – explosive if from cannon – out to
unprecedented ranges and with an accuracy never before achieved.
An immediate effect was to drive cavalry, the bulkiest of tactical
targets, clean off the battlefield. Apart from the engagement between the Union and Confederates at Brandy Station in June 1863,
there were to be no cavalry battles in the American Civil War at all.
But rifled firepower also markedly altered the character of infantry
fighting.

Because losses began to accrue at distances from the enemy line
greater than any earlier known, and to rise more sharply as distances
shortened, battle lines themselves, by a natural effort at evasion,
tended to elongate. Generals, recognizing the futility of strengthen-
ing their formations at the places where casualties fell thickest, drew
reinforcements to the flanks, thereby both extending their fronts
and, like it or not, protracting the length of engagements. Two-day
battles, rare before 1861, thereafter became commonplace. In 1862
McClellan fought a seven-day battle; by 1864 Grant, in the country
around Richmond and Petersburg, was fighting ten-day battles –
Spotsylvania, North Anna and Cold Harbor – as a matter of course.
Such tactical protraction may be seen in part as a function of the very
large manpower reserves that national mobilization and rail trans-
portation made available to him. But it was to a greater degree
imposed upon him by the inability of flesh and blood, in the face of
firepower storms, to force a decision by the sort of moral effect – that
panique-terreur of eighteenth-century warfare – which musketeer
armies had consistently been able to achieve in a single day.

The effort to impose moral effect was to die hard. Belief in its battle-winning quality continued to animate the European armies of 1866–71, as it did, indeed, those of the opening months of the First World War. But a dispassionate military eye – some soldiers possessed one – could discern, nevertheless, a disquieting trend in the pattern of military operations after the end of the smoothbore age: that was the tendency for open warfare between large armies to resolve into close encounters around fixed points. Manoeuvre occupied the armies of the American Civil War for three of its four years; but the fourth was largely spent in siege operations outside Petersburg. The Franco-Prussian War began with six weeks of manoeuvre, followed by a five-month siege of Paris. The Russo-Turkish War of 1877 was little more than a single siege operation and the Russo-Japanese war of 1904–5, which opened with the largest manoeuvre engagements yet conducted, closed with 600,000 men confronting each other in impotence behind enormous trench systems.

Highly trained military minds grappled with the conundrum that increments of force served only to postpone the moment of decision. What, they asked, rested at the root of that contradiction? The answer seemed to lie in two directions: first, that the firepower which armies produced was not heavy enough; second, that the infantry must find, at the moment of final assault when supporting fire must necessarily fall away (or kill its own soldiers), an extra, almost superhuman, edge to their courage. 'Fire is the supreme argument,' lectured the future Marshal Foch to the French Staff College in 1900. 'The most ardent troops, those whose morale has been most excited, will always wish to seize ground by successive rushes. But they will encounter great difficulties, and suffer heavy casualties, whenever their partial offensive has not been prepared by heavy fire. They will be thrown back on their starting point, with still heavier losses. Superiority of fire . . . becomes the most important element of an infantry's fighting value.' But, at the same time, he and his contemporaries concurred in requiring of their subordinates something beyond even that which fire might supply. 'The chances of victory,' wrote the British Colonel Maude in 1905, 'turn entirely on the spirit of self-sacrifice of those who have to be offered up to gain opportunity for the remainder . . . The true strength of an Army lies essentially in the power of each, or any of its constituent fractions, to stand up to punishment, even to the verge of annihilation if necessary.'

The solution which the military intellectuals of the decade before the First World War proposed to the problem confronting them was, then, that fire should be heavier and soldiers braver. But more fire plus more courage was a recipe calculated, could they have but seen it, to postpone, not hasten, the battlefield decision they sought. So, at any rate, realities proved. The armies that marched to war in 1914 could produce volumes of firepower inconceivable even by the expectations of moderns like Grant or Sherman. Cannon, apportioned in Napoleon's army in a ratio of three to a thousand men, not only had doubled in proportion but fired twenty times faster. The infantryman's personal weapon fired eight times faster, to a range ten times as great. And, in supplement, each infantry battalion deployed two machine guns that duplicated the fire of eighty of its riflemen put together. A brigade of infantry, 3,000 men, when supported by its third of the divisional artillery, could in consequence discharge each minute a volume of fire at least equal to that of the whole of Wellington's army of 60,000 firing volley and salvo at Waterloo.

The consequences not only were to be expected, but might have been calculated. Hitler, indeed, in the only letter of his which has survived from the period of open warfare at the beginning of the First World War, perfectly describes the results. The 16th Bavarian Reserve was attacking near Ypres in October 1914:

> Shrapnel was bursting left and right of us, and the English bullets came whistling through the shrapnel, but we paid no attention to them. For ten minutes we lay there, and then once again we were ordered to advance. I was right out in front, ahead of everyone in my platoon. Platoon leader Stoever was hit. Good God, I had barely any time to think, the fighting was beginning in earnest. Because we were out in the open, we had to advance quickly. The captain was at the head. The first of our men had begun to fall. The English had set up machine guns, we threw ourselves down and crawled slowly along a ditch. From time to time someone was hit, we could not go on and the whole company was stuck there. We had to lift the men out of the ditch. We kept on crawling until the ditch came to an end, and then we were out in the open field once again. We ran fifteen or twenty yards and then we found a big pool of water; but it was no place for lying low. We dashed out again at full

speed into a wood that lay about a hundred yards ahead of us
. . . we crawled on our bellies to the edge of the wood, while
the shells came whistling and whining above us, tearing tree
trunks and branches to shreds. Then the shells came down
again on the edge of the wood, flinging up clouds of earth,
stones and roots, and enveloping anything in a disgusting
sickening yellowy-green vapour. We can't possibly be here
forever, we thought, and if we are going to be killed, it is better
to die in the open.

Most of the young soldiers of the List Regiment found death or
wounds in the open then or a few days later, sharing the fate of
hundreds of thousands of their German comrades and French
enemies all along the line of what was becoming the Western Front.
Trenches had already appeared on much of its length; barbed wire –
invented by an American in 1874, ten years too late to add its share
of horror to the Civil War – had begun to appear also. A month after
Hitler's baptism of fire at Ypres, trenches and barbed wire ran in a
continuous line for 500 miles from Switzerland to the sea. Courage
and fire, expended in torrents, had both failed to deliver the decision
that would have averted the stalemate thus imposed. The problem
thenceforth was to dissolve stalemate. How did the generals, cheated
of their decision, propose to do so?
    More courage, of which there was still a surplus, would contribute
to the recipe. Even more firepower, of which there was a temporary
deficiency, was to supply the greater part. The First World War, it
has become a convention to state, was an artillery war. But the
dimensions and evolution of the artillery effort are rarely defined.
The German and French armies each began the war with some
seventy artillery pieces in each of their infantry divisions, supplemented by heavier guns held at the disposal of the higher
commands. In total, the guns available to each side numbered about
6,000, most of which were light field pieces. Artillery doctrine
dedicated these guns to 'preparing' infantry attacks by deluging the
enemy's position, at the moment of assault, with hailstorms of
shrapnel.
    While the armies manoeuvred in the open, doctrine worked more
or less as ordained. German, French and British infantry all suffered
disabling losses from shrapnel while defending improvised positions
in the field, but losses were even heavier among troops forming up

for an attack. Once defensive positions were entrenched and wired, as they were everywhere by November 1914, infantry who braved the risk of assault began to suffer more heavily still. The Germans, who opted for a defensive strategy in the west while seeking to defeat the Russians in the east, were spared the worst. Their French and, as numbers grew, British attackers learnt the worst with each passing month. A quietus in the winter of 1914, imposed by bad weather and an ammunition dearth, was succeeded in the spring by a flurry of trench offensives that caused 150,000 casualties. Those of the autumn, in Artois and Champagne, caused more than a quarter of a million. None brought any appreciable gain of ground; none, even by the most optimistic estimate, threatened the German line with breakthrough.

The Allies, taking stock of their failure, ascribed it to insufficient artillery effort and sought means to redouble it. Two solutions suggested themselves: the first was to increase their number of heavy guns, with the aim both of causing greater destruction to the enemy's trenches and of 'interdicting' the routes by which enemy reinforcements might reach the threatened sector; the second was to enclose the attacking infantry in a 'barrage', or moving envelope, of shellfire, designed to prevent the defenders of that sector from manning their positions.

Enormous industrial effort and extreme ingenuity were harnessed to this solution, which persisted from early 1916 until the end of the war. By then the Royal Artillery exceeded in size that of the whole British army of August 1914; the Germany artillery, by comparison, grew in size elevenfold. The weight of preliminary bombardments increased consonantly. In the week before the battle of the Somme in 1916 the British fired 1 million shells; before Messines in 1917, a much more limited offensive, they fired nearly 4 million. Barrages meanwhile had been invested with extraordinary complexity. Gunners had learnt to 'creep' a line of exploding shells 100 yards ahead of advancing infantry, and at a foot's pace, to stop it, bring it back, and take it forward again, meanwhile playing at right angles to it curtains of shellfire so as to create a three-sided box.

The theory was that the infantry advancing inside such boxes would find the defenders either dead or cowering impotently in their dugouts. Reality proved different. As the attacker lengthened the reach of his artillery, the defender increased the depth of his trench system. As the attacker shortened the distance at which the barrage moved ahead of his infantry's advancing wave, the defender taught his own infantry to race even more quickly from their dugouts to the trench parapet. Flailed by an ever-heavier weight of fire, the carapace of the trench system, like the scar-tissue of an irritated wound, merely grew thicker by the effort to tear and open it.

General staffs were anguished at their inability to resolve the conundrum – a conundrum that was costing a million deaths a year by 1917. The tank, deployed by the British and French in 1916, provided a local remedy; German infiltration tactics, developed in 1918, offered another. But at the root of the problem, unperceived by those closest to it, was a structural defect in the artillery approach to warmaking. Those who wielded the weapon could not direct its impact. Generals, who as late as 1862 could directly observe the effect of their orders on the fighting, had now been driven, by the very intensity of the fire they unleashed, so far from the seat of action that the power to influence its ebb and flow had been taken from their grasp.

The familiar First World War photographs of kings, prime ministers and generals peering myopically through giant binocular periscopes from the rear of the fighting lines tell their own story. The high commands, commonly located in headquarters fifty miles from the front, could not see what was passing in the offensives they had set in motion. Information, when it reached them, arrived hours late in 'real time'; orders based on out-of-date information returned to the front later still by that crucial measure. And what held true for the generals did so also for the artillery commanders who were the principal agents of their plans. Bombardment and barrage plans could be pre-ordained. They could not be altered once the fighting had begun.

Artillery warfare was, in fact, self-defeating. The enormous preliminary bombardments gave a defender all the warning he needed to bring reinforcements forward to the threatened sector. The weight of fire unleashed actually added to the obstacles the attacking infantry had to negotiate, lashing barbed wire into impenetrable entanglements and churning no-man's-land into a moon landscape of shellholes. And the barrage, whether of the attackers or of the defenders, comprehensively destroyed the fragile network of telephone cables that offered the only means by which stricken infantry could request assistance from the artillery it counted upon to help it forward.

Hence the peculiar significance of Hitler's wartime role as *Meldegänger*. In the last resort, the success of operations in the First World War rested – as far as it could – with the humble individuals whose duty it was to run across the ground that broken telephone lines traversed, taking news of the worst from the front to the guns, in the hope that they might shift their fire in time to stem an enemy assault or help their own infantry forward to take an objective denied by the enemy's. Twenty years later the magic, unbreakable filigree of radio transmissions would substitute for the trench telephone networks that, bury them however deep the army engineers would, shellfire always found out. Until a dependable wireless set came, it was the brave runner, hurrying with his XXX messages between the shellholes, who had to knit up the ravelled sleeve of communication between front and rear. Hitler won his Iron Cross First Class on just such a mission, having volunteered to run with a message calling off German artillery fire that was falling on the List Regiment's own trenches and killing his comrades. The citation, written by his regimental colonel, perfectly encapsulates both the runner's lot and the central dilemma of commanders in the First World War: 'As a despatch runner,' Baron von Godin wrote, '[Hitler] has shown cold-blooded courage and exemplary boldness both in positional warfare and the art of movement, and he has always volunteered to carry messages in the most difficult situations and at the risk of his life. Under conditions of the greatest peril, when all the communication lines were cut, the untiring and fearless activity of Hitler made it possible for important messages to get through.'

Hitler's survival of the great dangers he ran was not entirely haphazard. A regimental comrade recalled that, unlike other runners who trusted to luck, he was a close student of the trench maps – revised and issued on a monthly, sometimes weekly, basis – and always tried to work out the safest route to his objective. Whether he looked further into the nature of his predicament, or whether he perceived the essential contradiction of seeking to articulate and control armies of millions by the medium of lance-corporal messengers, is more difficult to say. But we do know that, in his years of power, it was a constant refrain of his reproaches to his generals that he knew more about war than they did. And such was often the exact truth. A high proportion of the generals with whom he began the Second World War had been staff officers, or gunners, or both, during the First. Gunners by the nature of their role were at the wrong end of the tortured line of communication between front and rear and could not fully comprehend what misery lay at the other end. Staff officers, meaning members of the inner élite of the Great General Staff, had by army policy been kept out of the fighting altogether, their military gifts being thought too precious to risk in the mindless mayhem of the trenches. Thus, of Hitler's three army group-commanders of 1939–41, Rundstedt, a staff officer, Bock, on the staff from 1914–16 and Leeb, a gunner, all brought back from the First World War an unbalanced view of its nature. So, too, did his longer-serving chief of staff, Halder, a gunner who had been a staff officer throughout, while even his two most talented field-marshals, Manstein and Kesselring, had been staff officers also.

It may have been because Zeitzler had served as an infantry subaltern in the trenches that Hitler promoted him to be Halder's successor, and it was certainly in part because Rommel, Dietl, Model and Schörner had been outstanding junior leaders – significantly all were believing Nazis or popularly associated with the party – that he held them in such high regard. For Hitler was, in a sense, an anti-clerical in the church of war, a devotee of its practices but a root-and-branch critic of its high priests. He had witnessed at first hand the bloody outcome of their rituals – the taking of omens, the dedication of victims, the performance of sacrifice – and he had seen that the god of victory was not propitiated. He was in consequence to give high priests short shrift after 1939. By December 1941 Bock, Leeb and Rundstedt had all been sent packing, as was Halder shortly afterwards. And he was to accord no soldier thereafter equivalent status. If there was to be a high priestly successor, it would be himself. But he had determined to be a high priest with a difference. His predecessors had trusted to age-old doctrine to do their work – belief in the strategies of manoeuvre, deception and concentration of force. From the externalities and instruments of war, its weapons and equipment, they had withheld their imprimatur. He, as a man of the future, would accord the instruments his amplest blessing. Whether Hitler should be regarded as a fascist in the ideological sense is extremely doubtful. The construction of a corporate state was to him clearly a paltry thing beside the re-creation of a triumphal Germany. But to the aesthetics and dynamism of fascism he gave the fullest assent. Marinetti's manifesto of the Futurist creed, central to the fascist *Weltanschauung*, might have been written by Hitler himself. Like Marinetti he subscribed to 'a new beauty', could have argued that 'a roaring motor-car that runs like a machine-gun is more beautiful than the *Winged Victory of Samothrace*' and, with him, wished 'to glorify war'. He was electrified by his first view of a tank in 1934 (he had not seen one on the Western Front), subscribed throughout the war to a trust in the power of new and 'secret' weapons to reverse its course and died believing that it was only the failure of German inventors and German industry to deliver his 'victory weapons' that had brought him low. On February 13, 1945, only six weeks before his suicide, he confided to a visiting doctor that 'in no time at all I'm going to start using my victory weapons and then the war will come to a glorious end.'

Hitler's faith in the capacity of weapons rather than human power to bring victory set him at the far side of a divide from the German generals who had directed the First World War. They had chorused their contempt for their enemies' resort to *Materialschlacht* – 'the battle of material' – to win where the courage of their soldiers and genius of their staffs could not. Even Ludendorff, the 'silent dictator' of the last two years of the war, by whom German industry and manpower were harnessed to the outdoing of the allies in their chosen strategy, had conceived the *Materialschlacht* as an expenditure of brute force. Hitler's conversion to a vision of warfare as an exercise in the precise and controlled release of military power was not one in which he could have followed.

Nevertheless, Hitler was not ultimately an opponent of Ludendorff's nor even of the German generals who had preceded the silent dictator in high command. Like them all he conceived of war as a test of will and national character, a Darwinian struggle for the survival of the fittest, and therefore an enterprise from which the outpouring of blood in streams could never be separated. In his political testament, dictated on the eve of his suicide, he proclaimed that he died 'with a joyful heart in the awareness of the immeasurable deeds and achievements of our soldiers at the front, of our women at home, the achievement of our peasants and workers, and the contribution, unique in history, of our youth'. That the war he fought had caused 'millions of grown-up men to suffer death and hundreds of thousands of women and children to be burned and bombed to death in the cities' was not a reality from which he shrank. Having willed the ends, he accepted that he willed the means, for all that both had proved unavailing.

Should we seek an explanation of this appalling vision and its catastrophic outcome, we shall find it in Hitler's weird, perverse but not ultimately solipsistic philosophy. Hitler thought, with less precision but more force, very much as dozens of other anti-Marxians of his generation did. Like them, he resisted the idea that the 'scientific laws of history' predicted a future triumph of the masses. Unlike most of them, he proposed a programme to resist its realization. 'The Jewish doctrine of Marxism,' he wrote in *Mein Kampf* – his identification of Marxism with Judaism was both to heighten the local appeal of his critique and to devalue its ultimate force – 'rejects the aristocratic principle of Nature and replaces the eternal privilege of power and strength by the mass of numbers and their dead weight. Thus it denies the power of personality in man, contests the significance of nationality and race, and thereby withdraws from humanity the premise of its existence and culture.' To the Marxian belief in the triumph of the many, therefore, Hitler opposed the challenge of contest with the best. The challenge was, in essence, Nietzschean but was informed, as Nietzsche's purely academic celebration of the superman could not be, by Hitler's personal experience of contest at the front. He, even as a humble *Meldegänger*, had been superman himself, in a sense, had seen the supermen of the original List Regiment of October 1914 give up their young lives in an epic of self-sacrifice, and thereafter he never accepted that impersonal historical laws – least of all because their force was vaunted by Jews and Slavs – promised the inevitable victory of the mediocre many over the selected few. To the economic theory of Marx, Hitler opposed the military philosophy of Clausewitz – again a name cited in the political testament: in the path of 'progress' and 'history' he would plant the warrior, his weapons and the force of human will.

Hitler's determination to resist what even anti-materialists have come to accept as the dominant force in modern history – the trend, that is, for mass political movements and their economic interest to overcome all other groupings and values – seems to mark him as a man of reaction; a reaction, moreover, doomed to defeat. It is perfectly possible, however, to interpret modern history in a quite contrary way: to see the mass movements as marching in contraflow to another, quite as important and perhaps almost as powerful, development in which Hitler stands in midstream. For, parallel to and contemporaneous with the rise of mass political movements in Europe from the mid-nineteenth century onwards, there was an equivalent and opposed rise of mass military movements. Some – the creation of armies recruited by universal conscription – were state-sponsored; some – the spontaneous emergence of volunteer 'sharp-shooter' and 'rifle' associations – were not. The combined effect of the two was to achieve as marked a militarization of peoples as the impact of revolutionary and democratic ideas fostered their much more widely remarked politicization. And because the burgeoning force of nationalism jibed as well with militarism as it did with revolution – arguably even better – its power was consonantly enhanced.

Certainly it cannot be denied that, by the end of the nineteenth century, European armies had achieved the extraordinary and thitherto unprecedented feat of making military service popular. 'Did you ever hear of a man serving in the army at his own expense?' St Paul asked the Corinthians, defining an absurdity self-evident to the subjects of any centralized state at any time. But by 1900 millions of young Europeans were doing exactly that – given that conscription is a tax on man's time and earning power – and not only without complaint but with good cheer. By so doing, they not only gravely undermined the Marxian doctrines of alienation and class conflict – military service and its structure of leadership being, by Marxist analysis, instruments of exploitation and class warfare respectively – but also thereby lent their mass power to that agency most precisely designed to repress revolution wherever it should show itself. Marx, whose ideas became fixed at a moment when European military institutions hovered at an uncharacteristically low ebb – following their association with the failure of Bonapartism, the 1830 failure of legitimacy in France and, paradoxically, the failure of Decembrism in Russia – neglected to include in his analysis the reactionary, essentially emotive power of armies to control proletariats. Later, in the *Communist Manifesto*, which urges the masses to militarize their own organizations, he attempted to correct his mistake. But by then – the publication of the *Manifesto* anticipated the defeat of the 1848 revolutions by the Prussian and Austrian armies by a bare year – he had left things too late. While the movements to which his philosophy had given birth, the Social Democratic Party in Germany and Austria, the SFIO in France, struggled to adopt the centralism, hierarchy and discipline which Marx had belatedly identified as the keys to revolutionary victory, the armies with which they competed for influence over the masses effortlessly outstripped them. To voluntary party membership the armies opposed compulsory enlistment; to the political education of the parties' recruits the armies opposed military indoctrination; to the parties' efforts at 'heightening consciousness' the armies opposed the heightening of instinct – instincts of comradeship, loyalty and masculinity. Unsurprisingly the contest between these two value systems was found, in 1914, to be no contest. Confronted by the reality of proletarian militarism and patriotism, all the great socialist parties of Europe simply abandoned their effort to characterize the growing war as 'capitalist', a conflict between class-brothers, and cast their weight unprotestingly behind the parliamentary majorities of nationalists, conservatives and liberals who supported it.

The outbreak of the First World War may therefore be seen, in some sense, as the triumph of a silent reaction by Europe's armies against the ethos of liberty, equality and fraternity with which they had been taunted ever since the original Bastille day – the first naked defeat of an army by a popular movement – 125 years earlier. For all its ambiguous attitude to war, the Revolution – whether as reality in 1789, or idea, in the writings of Marx – stood for principles anathema to the military class. It was anti-officer, anti-order, and anti-discipline. The armies made every effort to reverse every one of those principles between 1914 and 1916, but, through the effects of defeat in Russia, Germany and Austria, failed and so conceded the Revolution a second chance. So complete was the collapse of the army in Russia, destroyed from within by the 'contradictions' of trench warfare, that in that country the reborn revolution took root. In Germany and Austria enough of traditional military structure and values survived to crush it in the making, but the outrage that embryo revolution aroused led in both countries to the rise of political movements whose stated purpose was to deny it by violence a third chance. Uniforms and banners were their outward symbols, 'front fighters' their self-appointed leaders. The Nazi party and Hitler, both insignificant at the moment of their entry into such politics, exemplified the phenomenon. Of the two, Hitler was by far the more significant. The infant Nazi party was flotsam in the tidewrack of defeat. He – for all the half-educated rhetoric of his writings and speeches, his psychological tophamper of rancours, insecurities and imagined injustices, and the muddled hatreds of what he called his philosophy – was a man in touch with a mainstream of life. He knew the power of the appeal to manhood, comradeship and warriordom, knew how to articulate it and knew how to bend it to his political purpose. That purpose, manifest in everything he said and wrote from the moment of his return from the trenches, was to refight the world war but bring it to the conclusion of a German victory.

The War Hitler Made

One of the amnesiac spots in modern memory of the First World War is the nearness by which Germany had indeed come to victory in 1918. In mid-June of that year, only four months before the armistice, German armies or those of their allies controlled more of Europe than they had at any stage since the outbreak. The whole of the Balkans lay within the German orbit and a German expeditionary force was fighting the French and British in northern Greece. The richest regions of northern Italy were under Austrian occupation. A German expeditionary force opposed the British in Palestine and another occupied Finland. In the west, German armies menaced Paris at a distance of fifty miles while in the east, where Russia had recently concluded an enforced peace, the German military frontier ran from Rostov-on-Don in the south to Narva in the north, encircling Kiev, the rich grainlands of the Ukraine, most of White Russia, the Baltic states and the whole of historic Poland.

The Kaiser's armies controlled more of Europe at that time than Napoleon's had ever done and almost as much as Hitler's were to do at the height of their conquests. Who can doubt that it was the recollection of what the *Meldegänger*'s sovereign had so nearly achieved that drove the Führer to emulate and then outdo him? The Second World War, in a sense, was fought to realize the victory that had nearly been Germany's in 1918. Apportionment of responsibility for its outbreak does not belong here. What can be said without contention is that Hitler never shrank from conflict either at home or abroad – direct confrontation with the German army excepted, after the disastrous failure of the Munich putsch of 1923 – that he courted war in the full knowledge of its risks from 1936 to 1938 and that, when it came in 1939, he accepted without demur its necessity to the realization of his foreign policy.

To argue this is to take issue neither with A.J.P. Taylor's now famous insistence that Hitler harboured no long-term war plan, nor with other historians' convincing demonstrations that Germany was unprepared for any long-term war at all. Hitler's calculation in 1939 was that he could defeat Poland before the French and British mobilized a serious counter-offensive – thereby guessing right about the dynamics of a two-front war when Schlieffen had guessed wrong – that diplomacy should then settle things in the West but that, if it did not, he stood an excellent chance of fighting himself out of trouble. The Ribbentrop-Molotov Pact of August 22, 1939, which assured Russia's non-intervention, secured his back. His front he could hope to secure by negotiation, the West Wall or, failing all else, Blitzkrieg.

Blitzkrieg was not a concept directly of Hitler's making nor, strictly, was his Polish victory an exercise in its form. The Polish army, surrounded on three sides by one enormously superior in men and equipment, was doomed to rapid defeat in any case; Russia's stab in the back merely sealed its fate. The three-week Polish campaign nevertheless practised the forces of Blitzkrieg – the panzer divisions and ground attack squadrons – in the operations of war itself so that when, in May 1940, they were committed to the test of Blitzkrieg proper they already enjoyed an advantage over their unpractised French and British opponents. But Blitzkrieg compounded that advantage. Essentially a doctrine of attack on a narrow front by concentrated armour, trained to drive forward through the gap it forced without concern for its flanks, Blitzkrieg was a formula for victory which owned no single father. The German tank pioneers, Lutz and Guderian foremost among them, had been avid students of the writings of the British 'apostles' of armoured warfare, Fuller and Liddell Hart. But it is a long step between the literary advocacy of a revolutionary doctrine, even from the conversion of influential individuals, and its acceptance by an organization as monolithic and set in its ways as the German army. The truth is, indeed, that the German army never was formally converted to Blitzkrieg, essentially a headline word applied retrospectively to spectacular events. What it adopted in reality was a form of organization, the large all-armour force, and a code of practice, the concentration of effort behind it, whose effect on the battlefield surprised no one more than many of those at its head.

So set in their ways were some of these generals, Beck, chief of staff until 1938, foremost among them, that the doctrine of armoured concentration might have found no acceptance at all had the army's tactical innovations of 1918 – called 'infiltration' – not anticipated what Guderian and his confederates preached. In that year the German army in the West abandoned its war-long reliance on the heavy artillery preparation and rigid barrage in favour of tactics altogether more fluid and instantaneous. Its gunners were belatedly trained to 'neutralize' the enemy's moral powers of resistance with a brief hurricane of fire, thereby denying the enemy the warning on which defenders had thitherto counted to reinforce a threatened trench sector. The infantry, meanwhile, were schooled to 'infiltrate' rather than occupy the enemy's positions as the neutralizing bombardment closed. 'Stormtroops' – Hitler's brownshirts both adopted their title and recruited many of their veterans – led the assault; élite 'interlocking' (*Eingreif*) divisions penetrated the gaps made and consolidated the ground won.

In four offensives, in March, April, May and June, these tactics worked brilliantly – up to a point. Even traditionalists of the stamp of Beck conceded that they would have worked absolutely had the follow-on forces been able to keep pace with that of the spearhead. But plodding, horse-drawn formations simply could not; by an effect to which Clausewitz had taught all offensives were liable they expended so much of their energy in mere movement that, when a culminating effort was called for, it proved beyond their power to deliver. Tank divisions, however, were not afflicted by 'friction' as marching forces were. By their nature they were 'storm' and 'follow-on' forces in one. It was this evident capacity of theirs to fight and advance at the same time that palliated opposition to the ideas of Guderian and his like; Hitler's support for these Young Turks dissolved it altogether. By May 1940 their beliefs were in the ascendant. A new plan inspired by one of them, von Manstein, had, with Hitler's endorsement, supplanted another, much less adventurous, proposed by the traditionalists of the general staff. The freshly blooded field army stood in the slips. Victory beckoned on the far side of the West Wall.

Its dimensions exceeded the expectations even of those most committed to the Blitzkrieg idea. The original general staff plan, codenamed 'Yellow', had proposed that, were Hitler to insist on attack in the West, it should have as its objective no larger piece of territory than the frontier area occupied by the French field army and its allied British Expeditionary Force. 'Sickle Stroke', as the Manstein-Hitler variant was codenamed, had a far more ambitious

23 Hitler at Breslau, March 1936.

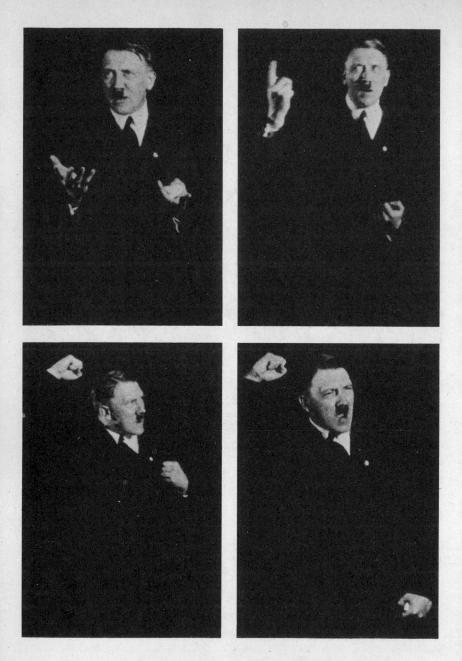

24 *et seq*. Hitler rehearsing his oratorical technique; the sequence was taken
by his private photographer, Hoffman, for Hitler to study so that he could
improve his performance.

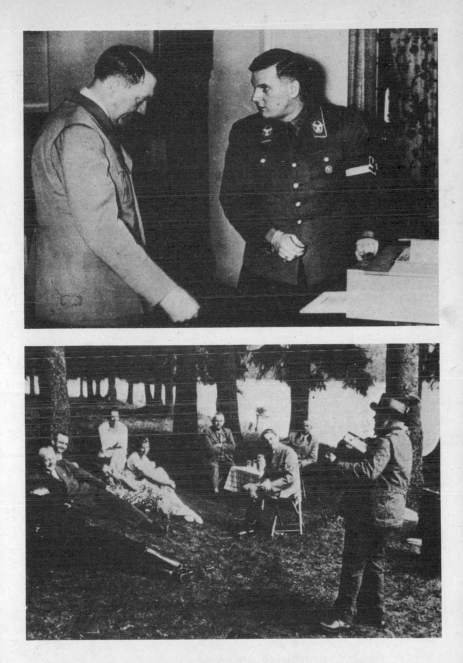

25 *Above* Hitler and Baldur von Schirach, the Hitler Youth Leader, examining an architectural model.

26 *Below* A pre-war Hitler picnic.

27 *Above* Hitler at the map table with Jodl (left) and Keitel.

28 Hitler decorating Hitler Youth defenders of Berlin, April 22, 1945; the last photograph taken in life.

aim. It committed the armoured forces to drive a corridor from the Ardennes in southern Belgium to the Channel coast near Abbeville, so cutting off the Anglo-French defenders from their base in the heartland of France, while a second armoured thrust through the Low Countries encircled them in a pincer movement.

Ironically the Allied war plan might have been designed precisely to further the success of this bold enterprise. It enjoined that the Anglo-French field army should, at Germany's first violation of Belgian neutrality, advance headlong into the Belgian Lowlands, trusting to the strength of the Maginot Line to protect them on their Ardennes flank. 'Sickle Stroke', however, located the German centre of armoured effort exactly at the point where the Maginot Line stopped, in territory deemed 'untankable' by the Allied high command, and therefore at a point where neither fortification nor troops of high quality opposed it. The troops occupying the threatened sector, General Corap's Ninth Army, were, by the worst of bad luck, troops of the poorest quality. Hitler, whose decision to risk war in the West was taken in November 1939, boasted to his generals that he was going 'to smash France to smithereens'. To smithereens was what three days of fighting reduced the Ninth Army in mid-May 1940. By May 19 the German tank spearheads were at Abbeville. Two weeks later the British Expeditionary Force had fled the coast of France, the French field army was encircled and defeated and the French heartland lay open to Hitler's panzer columns.

What ensued was scarcely war – so little so that on June 15, ten days before the paralysed French government accepted an unavoidable armistice, Hitler had already issued orders for the disbandment of thirty-five divisions, about one-quarter of the army's war strength. During the rest of the summer he tinkered with plans for the invasion of Britain, believing meanwhile that she would sue for peace. When it became clear she would not, he committed the Luftwaffe to the destruction of the Royal Air Force and, as that effort faltered, to direct attack on the British cities. But his real commitment during the glorious mid-months of 1940 was to exultation in his astonishing victory.

Its fruits were all the sweeter for the evident consternation it caused his generals, twelve of whom on July 19 he casually elevated to the rank of field-marshal. No such number had ever been created before – except by Napoleon, to whose mass promotion on May 19, 1804, Hitler's was a conscious reference. But no campaign of

Napoleon's, not even Austerlitz, had been so spectacular in its results as Hitler's of September 1939–May 1940. In twelve weeks of fighting – perhaps a little more if the Norwegian byblow of April is included – the Germans had destroyed two major European armies, gobbled up four smaller and inflicted on Britain the greatest humiliation in its history since the secession of the American colonies 170 years earlier.

Little wonder that he set himself to enjoy the summer of 1940. It was the first holiday he had permitted himself since the ecstatic early days of power. Then he had bathed in the adulation of simple people, as he and his inner circle toured the mountain villages and market towns of South Germany on pastry-eating expeditions. Now he indulged his taste for history and pomp, revisiting the billets of the List Regiment in Flanders, inspecting the Maginot Line and making his first trip to Paris, 'the dream of my life', where he brooded over Napoleon's tomb, exclaimed at the magnificence of the Opéra – opera-house designs were his favourite doodle – and paused at the Panthéon and the Arc de Triomphe.

But, if outwardly at ease, Hitler was inwardly preoccupied. Britain, though refusing to make peace, could not enlarge the war. Russia, pacified by a division of the spoils in the east, was a war-making power as great as Germany. The threat it posed to German primacy in Europe, characterized as the 'Red' or 'Slav menace' in his ranting years, never ceased to obsess him; it took equal and sometimes greater place beside his crazed denunciations of Jewry. At a meeting with his generals on July 31, called to consider the invasion of Britain, he alarmed them by advancing stronger arguments for invading the Soviet Union. As summer drew into autumn, the arguments for what would be codenamed 'Barbarossa' grew to seem more compelling. Britain, he was convinced, was postponing a settlement in the expectation that she would be saved by the United States; but the United States would abandon its neutrality only if Russia continued to pose the threat of a two-front war.

In November 1940 Hitler came to his decision. A visit to Berlin by Molotov, the Russian Foreign Minister, on November 12–13 dissolved any remaining hope that he would come to a satisfactory understanding with the Soviet Union. Its appetite for influence in the unapportioned sphere of the Baltic, Balkans and Near East was revealed to equal his own. On November 27 Hitler issued orders to the commander of his air-force mission in Bulgaria that left no doubt he had decided to attack Russia in the spring. Thereafter all that remained to fix was the operational plan for her defeat. At the July 21 meeting he had already sketched the outline: a drive to Moscow, coordinated with encircling movements in the north and south, followed by an offensive to capture the oilfields of the Caucasus. During December he presided at discussions between his own OKW staff and the army high command (Oberkommando des Heeres, OKH) over the refinement of the details. He and OKW laid greater emphasis on the encircling movements; OKH insisted on the centrality of the push to Moscow. This difference of opinion, which would re-emerge with disastrous consequences in the course of the campaign, was temporarily and cosmetically elided in the final drafting. On December 18 Hitler issued Führer Directive 21 for the attack on Russia. These directives, of which he signed fifty-one, were his means of outlining broad strategies; significantly, the last was issued in November 1943.

Hitler envisaged a short war and ordered preparations for Barbarossa to be complete by May 15. In the meantime, disturbances in the Balkans supervened to postpone its inception. Mussolini's decision to attack Greece in October, of which he had deliberately given Hitler no warning, so embarrassed the Führer by its failure that he was prompted to consider lending the Italians assistance – as in the following February he was to do in the Western Desert by sending Rommel and the Afrika Korps to bolster their defence of Libya against the British. An anti-German coup in Yugoslavia in March then made up his mind for him. It smacked of British influence, also strong in Greece, and was therefore not to be tolerated. In April he unleashed a Blitzkrieg against both countries, which culminated in a spectacular, though costly, airborne capture of Crete in May.

Whether or not the Balkan diversion robbed Hitler of the time and good weather in which he might have brought his 'short war' against Russia to a successful conclusion in 1941 is now disputed. Close students of his strategey in those months, like Martin van Crefeld, have argued that Barbarossa could, for strictly operational reasons, not have started any sooner than it did. Certainly it seems more significant to striking a judgement that Barbarossa was itself a flawed plan; like Schlieffen's, it hovered uncertainly between the aim of destroying the enemy's armies and the aim of neutralizing his capital. Barbarossa, when eventually unleashed, at once achieved enormous encirclements. By July 1, von Bock's Army Group Centre had surrounded 300,000 Russians at Minsk, and by July 19 it had encircled 100,000 more at Smolensk. Army Group North (von Leeb) destroyed or captured some 200,000 Russians in the same period, and, after a slow start, von Rundstedt's Army Group South was eventually to make the largest encirclement of all. The surrender of Kiev on September 26 put nearly 700,000 Russians in German hands (as many as three-quarters of the prisoners taken in these early battles were to die of neglect in German captivity).

But even before the Kiev encirclement had been completed, the inconsistencies of the Barbarossa plan had begun to emerge. As early as July 16 Army Group Centre had come to a halt on the direct route to Moscow, which lay only 200 miles ahead. Yet, though it had advanced 400 miles in a month, Hitler preferred to divert its two panzer groups, those of Hoth and Guderian – veterans of the 1940 triumphs both – to assist Leeb and Rundstedt on the northern and southern axes respectively. So outraged was Guderian by this decision that he risked confronting Hitler face-to-face in his East Prussian headquarters with a demand that it be reversed. Hitler refused, sent him south and did not redeploy his panzer group on the road to Moscow until early October. On October 3, he assured the German people that 'the foe was broken and would never rise again'. Events were to prove that the Russians were far from broken. Assisted by a delayed winter, which left the approaches to Moscow bogged in autumn mud, they reinforced the central front, fought the Germans to a standstill and in early December turned them back the way they had come.

'It it any less cold fifty miles back?' was the gibe with which Hitler taunted generals who begged for permission to retreat before the Russian counter-offensive. His soldiers, who had stuffed their service uniforms with torn-up newspapers, were scarcely capable of movement, forward or rearward, in any case. Somehow, though almost bereft of cold-weather equipment, they halted the Russian counter-offensive and redeployed for a resumption of their own. In early May, when the ground had dried after the spring thaw, it began. The objectives were the Volga near Stalingrad, the Caucasus and the oilfields of the Caspian Sea. A Russian counter-attack at Kharkov was defeated in mid-May, the Crimea occupied by early June, Rostov-on-Don, southern benchmark of the German military frontier of 1918, invested by July 22 and the Volga north of Stalingrad reached on August 23. By that date the spearheads of Army Group South were pushing into the Caucasus, had planted the German flag on the summit of Mount Elbrus, highest peak in Europe, and were only 300 miles from Baku, the centre of Russian oil production. In thirteen months Hitler's armies had advanced 1,200 miles, taken nearly 4 million Russian soldiers prisoner, driven the Soviet government to the brink of flight from Moscow, caused the relocation of one-third of Soviet industry east of the Urals, and brought the richest areas of Russia's agricultural land under occupation and exploitation. So certain did victory seem during that year that Hitler had, even as the Russians began to deliver their December counter-offensive, almost casually and certainly quite unnecessarily, declared war on the United States as a token of solidarity with his Japanese allies in the wake of their attack on Pearl Harbor.

Unseen hands, nevertheless, were plucking at the German armies' coat-tails. 'Follow-on' had proved, in the enormous spaces of Russia, altogether less easy than in the close countryside of France. There the infantry had lagged at most a few hours behind the tanks. On the steppe, the infantry, even by marching twenty-five miles a day, might not catch up with the spearhead for days at a time. And the bag and baggage trailed even farther to the rear, crowded onto roads never meant for heavy traffic, or waiting for carriage on the sparse and devastated rail network. While the distances lengthened, however, the front broadened, so that at the operational edge a few hundred men might find themselves 'holding' a dozen miles of ground; Army Group A (ex-South), for example, had its twenty divisions spread along 500 miles of the River Don in early August. Farther south, on the Kalmuk steppe, sectors fifty miles wide were 'held' by roving patrols.

The Russians had seen, and now took, their opportunity. On November 19 and 20, they penetrated the German line north and south of Stalingrad, in which bitter fighting had raged since September, and encircled the city. Thus began the Sixth Army's struggle for survival, which was to endure in conditions of mounting deprivation until the following February. While the battle lasted Hitler had thoughts for no other concern. Believing Göring's assurance that the Luftwaffe could supply the Sixth Army by air, and refusing to issue its commander Paulus (redactor, ironically, of the Barbarossa directive), with authority to break out, he devoted all his energies to retrieving his lost prize. But an effort by Manstein to break through to the city in December failed, the Russians widened the scope of their attacks and by February 1, as the Sixth Army's resistance came to an end, the southern army groups had been pushed back behind the Don, retaining only Rostov as a bridgehead in the great swathe cut by their summer advances.

Stalingrad marks in broad retrospect both the high point and end of Hitler's war. Certainly his confidence in his power to command either the enemy or his generals was so shaken by the defeat that he gave little of himself to the discussions on how best to recoup the army's fortunes in 1943. Kursk, the eventually abortive and by Hitler much postponed offensive which resulted, was the brainchild of his new chief of staff, Zeitzler, rather than his own. Defeats and setbacks in other sectors shook his confidence also: the destruction of Rommel's army in Africa, the reversal of fortune in the Atlantic battle, the beginning of co-ordinated Allied air attacks on the Reich, the Anglo-American invasion of Italy and the overthrow of Mussolini. But it was the humiliation in Russia that cut deepest.

The proof supplied by Kursk that his military instinct was superior to that of his generals, as represented by Zeitzler, restored some of his confidence; he bolstered it with his growing trust in the war-winning qualities of secret weapons his scientists were developing. Vilification of his faithless and gutless allies also served as a ready reinforcement of his sense of solitary indispensability. And the physical isolation of his headquarters ensured that he confronted reality only in self-administered doses. Somehow or other, as the disasters of 1943 gave way to the looming crises of 1944 – deeper Russian advances in the east, the menace of Anglo-American invasion in the west – he sustained his capacity to think, plan, command. The officers' plot of July 1944 sealed his conviction that he could trust no one but himself to fight the war to its end. Thereafter all military decisions were made by him alone. Many were made in the closest detail. Even in the last week of his life his staff were radioing precise operation orders from the Berlin bunker to units – by then mere fragments, if not figments – whose movements he continued to plot on his situation map. Late in the evening of April 29, 1945, nineteen hours before his suicide, he signalled OKW to ask five categorical questions: 'Where are Wenck's spearheads? When do they attack? Where is the Ninth Army? In which direction is Ninth Army breaking through? Where are Holst's spearheads?'

The nominal size of the formations concerned apart, these were messages of the sort with which Hitler the *Meldegänger* might have dodged from shellhole to shellhole across the List Regiment's sector of the Flanders front thirty years before. Hitler on the eve of death, indeed, endured circumstances scarcely different from those he had undergone in the four years of his youthful life on the Western Front. The world for him had come full circle. Incarcerated in an underground shelter, with enemy shells turning the soil above his head and infantry fighting across narrow no-man's-lands only a few hundred yards distant, he was surrounded by the paraphernalia of military command, maps, map tables, talc, chinagraph, field telephones, and by worried officers in field-grey who, as in the List Regiment's dugouts, looked to him to bring relief from the ordeal. Then they had taken it for granted that, on orders, he would risk his life on the run back to the guns with a message for counter-bombardment. Now they looked to him for a different relief – an end to things altogether, by a decision for flight, surrender or his own extinction. Flight or surrender they knew he would not countenance. The consequent expectation of his suicide permeated every corner of the bunker as the Battle of Berlin approached its climax. He would represent his suicide as a soldier's death, 'the fate that millions of others have taken upon themselves'. Those who attended him to his last moment in retrospect saw it otherwise – the bankrupt gambler's leap into the void. Few, if any of them, succeeded in explaining, even to themselves, how the greatest of German institutions, the instrument by which the state had been created, enlarged, unified and sustained, the tabernacle of universal military philosophy and the *maison mère* of the world's modern armies, had consigned its fate to the sleepwalker instincts of a sometime lance-corporal and battalion runner. It is an explanation many others have sought since. What was the nature of Hitler's obsessive, intensive and eventually superordinate relationship with his soldiers?

Hitler's Soldiers

The essence of Hitler's achievement of dominance over the German army may be briefly stated: finding it humbled and diminished, he gave it back its strength and so its pride, but he took from it in compensation, though in scarcely perceptible instalments, its independence and autonomy and so eventually its dignity and conscience.

The German army of 1933, the year in which Hitler achieved power, was still subject to the limitations of its size and strength imposed by the Allies at the Versailles settlement. Restricted in numbers to 100,000 men, who were all bound to serve twelve years (a measure designed to preclude the accumulation of trained reserves), it was forbidden to possess tanks, heavy artillery or an aviation arm; the very small navy was equally denied submarines or any surface ship larger than a heavy cruiser. The army Staff College had been closed in 1920 and the general staff abolished, the allies having hoped thereby to extinguish the intellectual life of the German military leadership, to whose vitality and inventiveness they ascribed the glittering successes of its field armies since 1866.

Externally the Versailles restrictions had achieved their object. The army's seven infantry and three cavalry divisions were a threat to no neighbour, were scarcely even an instrument of national security, as the officers who yearly rehearsed the strategy of 'yielding defence', ordained by current training regulations, ruefully reflected. Internally, however, Versailles had missed the mark. Designed to stunt the German army by making it ridiculous, it contrarily succeeded in transforming it into an élite. Enlistment in the ranks was eagerly competed for in an economy where steady jobs were few; officers' commissions, far from losing their cachet, attracted an even higher proportion of candidates from the nobility than they had under the last Kaiser; in 1913, for example, only 27 per cent of junior officers had the 'von' to their names, while in 1931–2 the percentage of lieutenants commissioned with that distinction was 36 per cent. Nor were those the dimmer younger sons; the Reichsheer set a high academic level of entry and got those it wanted. Their motivation, it seems, was largely traditionalist. Under a despised republic, the nobility saw service in the army as a sort of substitute monarchism and eagerly espoused it. *Innere emigration* – 'internal emigration' – is the term used by sociologists to describe the phenomenon. Its reality is conveyed by the aging Hindenburg's gesture at the ceremony of Hitler's installation as Chancellor in the garrison church at Potsdam on March 21, 1933. Arrayed in the full-dress of an imperial field-marshal, he turned on reaching the head of the aisle, where he had first stood as a lieutenant in the 3rd Foot Guards on his return from victory over Austria in 1866, and saluted the Kaiser's empty throne with his ceremonial baton.

But fine gestures butter no parsnips. The Reichsheer's officer corps may have been rich in titles but it was poor in pay and promotions. The average age of a colonel in the German army in 1933 was fifty-six; four years later, in Hitler's Wehrmacht, it was thirty-nine. Hitler, in decreeing rearmament and an end to Versailles, transformed the regular officer's career prospects, as a direct function of his enormous expansion of the army's size. From seven it expanded to twenty-one and then thirty-six divisions, to include heavy artillery and tank units, as well as, of course, a separate air arm, the Luftwaffe. By 1939, thanks in part to the incorporation of the Austrian army the previous year, its strength stood at 103 divisions, of which six were tank, four mechanized and ten motorized.

Expansion was paid for, however, at a heavy cost to the regular officers' role and status. Not only had the army's inner core of carefully selected, largely rustic, long-service enlisted ranks, dutiful in manner and army-centred in outlook, been swamped by waves of young city-dwelling conscripts, many of them enthusiastic Nazis or at least ex-members of the Hitler Youth; the officer corps itself had been diluted by a flood of entrants of similar outlook if different background. In 1932 the Reichsheer admitted 120–180 cadets annually; in 1937 the intake had increased to 2,000. Many of these appeared, to the increasingly self-conscious élite of the pre-Hitler army, as less than their social equals, a division that was to have the gravest of consequences as the Hitler years drew on. The Reichsheer élite continued, by reason of seniority, to dominate the high command. But its formerly easy relationship with the rest of the army had suffered also. The young thrusters among its own thought the old generals were out of touch with modern war; with the new officers they themselves were ideologically out of sympathy; and with Hitler they found themselves at a constantly increasing disadvantage, which damaged their standing and sapped their own self-confidence.

The German *Generalität*, unlike that of other European countries, had never been brought wholly under the sovereign authority of the state. The Prussian nobility from which it was drawn had abandoned the life of their estates for that of military service reluctantly; in compensation it had won from the Prussian crown an effective veto over the management of the military affairs of the state itself. In the nineteenth century that veto had been exercised largely to safeguard the nobility's military, and so social, privileges. In the twentieth it had been extended into politics proper. The army had been the agency of the Kaiser's abdication, which it had enforced as a means of rescuing Germany and, as it thought, itself from the consequences of defeat in 1918. Thereafter, under Weimar, it had elevated itself 'above politics' but, by insisting on its right to nominate the Minister of War from its own ranks, had retained the power to withhold a mandate from any parliamentary party of which it disapproved. By nominating a War Minister to Hitler's first cabinet it had acquiesced in his chancellorship. But its belief that it might contrive to preserve ultimate authority under a dictatorship as it had under a democracy was thereby falsified. Blomberg, its nominee, was a vain and weak man; Fritsch, the army commander-in-chief, was a narrow traditionalist. When in 1938 both were compromised by impropriety, Hitler not only removed them from office but altered the officer structure in a way that ensured the army's political veto was ended for good. The Ministry of War was abolished and replaced by the Supreme Command (OKW), of which he made himself chief; from that position he nominated another narrow traditionalist, Brauchitsch, to replace Fritsch, but with greatly reduced powers. Furthermore, as executive head of OKW, he appointed a man, Keitel, of no independence of character at all; told by Blomberg, when enquiring if Keitel was a suitable candidate, that the Minister of War had used him merely as an office manager, Hitler exclaimed, 'That's exactly the man I am looking for,' and used him thereafter as nothing else.

Even before he came to assume title as commander-in-chief of the army in December 1941, therefore, Hitler had so disposed authority over the armed services that, for the first time in the history of the German state, it led directly to himself as its head. OKW, his own headquarters, had at its centre a National Defence Section that functioned as an operations staff; from the outbreak of war until the end it was headed by a former gunner officer, Alfred Jodl, a man of exceptional ability and energy. To it reported the chiefs of staff of the three armed services. Relations with those of the air force and navy were bureaucratically correct. With the army chief of staff they were professionally and emotionally complex. Not only did Germany's status as a land power invest the operation of the army with primary significance; the fact that OKW's principal officers were all drawn from the army made for jealousies, competitiveness and ill-feeling.

They were compounded as the war drew on. Brauchitsch, Fritsch's successor as commander-in-chief, was a man of brains and breeding; he belonged to the freemasonry of the 3rd Foot Guards, Hindenburg's old regiment, which had supplied the high command with a disproportionate share of its leaders; Hammerstein-Equord, a former commander-in-chief, and Manstein had also both begun their careers in it. But, though an excellent linguist and a student of world affairs, Brauchitsch lacked the strength of character to steer the army away from the strategic choices Hitler, through OKW, imposed on it. 'Hitler,' he was to say after the war, 'was the fate of Germany, and this fate could not be stayed.' This fatalism, even defeatism, marked him down for contempt in Hitler's eyes. On the one hand he was ready publicly to laud what Hitler had done for the country and the army; on the other he would stage, but then lose, arguments with Hitler over critical tactical and strategic decisions. 'Our leader of genius,' he told officers in 1938, 'has recast the great lesson of the front-line soldier in the form of the National Socialist philosophy' – in itself a fascinating perception of the wellsprings of Hitler's inspiration. 'The Armed Forces and National Socialism are of the same spiritual stem. They will accomplish much for the nation in the future, if they follow the example and teaching of the Führer, who combines in his person the true soldier and National Socialist.' But on May 24, 1940, outside Dunkirk, in exercising the old Great General Staff officer's right to withhold his signature from an order in testimony of his professional disapproval – the order was for the disastrous 'halt' of panzer forces committed to the destruction of the British Expeditionary Force – he kept silence when Hitler overrode him. He had already offered but withdrawn his resignation over a plan to attack the French in the Saar. Yet though he expressed frequent dissent from Hitler's strategy of postponing the attack on Moscow during the summer of 1941, he did not take his opposition to the point of resignation and was eventually obliged to tender it at Hitler's irate insistence when the failure of the resumed Moscow offensive had put him in the right.

Brauchitsch's dismissal – accompanied by that of Rundstedt,

Guderian and Hoepner, the panzer group commanders, and the retirement of Bock and Leeb – made almost a clean sweep at the head of the army. It also instituted changes of the most swingeing structural and psychological nature. 'Anyone can do the little job of directing the war,' Hitler said as he assumed Brauchitsch's responsibilities. 'The task of the Commander-in-Chief is to educate the army to be National Socialist. I do not know any Army general who can do this as I want it done. I have therefore decided to take over command of the Army myself.' This to Halder, Chief of Staff, who barely escaped the sack himself and would suffer it anyhow in the September. To this contemptuous dismissal of the general staff's professional significance, Hitler added the insult of usurping only its operational functions; the 'remaining powers of the army commander-in-chief,' he decreed in his order of December 19, were to be exercised by Keitel 'as the supreme commanding and administrative officer of the army.' Hitler, in short, was to be chef; the generals bottle-washers. They were to be left to find, train and equip the army's soldiers; he was to commit them to and command them in battle.

Nor did the army high command's humiliation end there. As early as January 1940 Hitler allotted responsibility for the planning and execution of the attack on Norway and Denmark, as a tri-service operation, to OKW. Following the brusque success of that attack, Scandinavia was left within OKW's sphere of authority and, as Hitler's 'peripheral strategy' extended, to it were added other smaller conquered territories and theatres of intervention – the Balkans, Greece and Libya. The list was enlarged to include France in 1941 and, after Hitler's assumption of commander-in-chief of the army in December, effectively deemed to comprehend all theatres except the Eastern Front. Germany thereafter was to fight two wars – OKH's in Russia, and OKW's everywhere else. The result of this division of responsibilities was to ensure that only Hitler had a full oversight of strategy. In disputes with OKH, represented on visits to his headquarters by the army chief of staff, he could always win by emphasizing that the army did not grasp the importance of the campaigns in Africa or the West – to say nothing of the U-boat or air war. And even in disputes with OKW, which did maintain a detailed supervision of the course of operations in the east, he could argue that it lacked the ultimate responsibility he bore, as commander-in-chief, for the fortunes and welfare of Germany's principal concentration of military manpower.

This playing of both ends against the middle was to result in the most spectacular and damaging of all his breaches with his soldiers – before, that is, the military treachery of July 20, 1944, cast the whole regular officer caste irredeemably into disgrace. In September 1942, anguished by the spectre of impending defeat in southern Russia, he devoted days to railing against Halder, the chief of staff, for his failure to bring the advance into the Caucasus to a swift conclusion. Jodl, whom he had sent to see the cause of the delay, made the brave mistake on his return of endorsing the local commander's insistence that further progress was impossible. He had already enraged Hitler by demonstrating from written sources that Halder's orders to the Caucasus force were in origin Hitler's own. He now suffered the full weight of the Führer's temper. Calling the meeting to an end, Hitler refused to shake hands with either Jodl or Keitel – a mark of disfavour he sustained for the next five months – and banished them thenceforth from meals at his table. Moreover, as a precaution, he said, against further misquotation, he ordered that stenographers should henceforth be present at his twice-daily situation conferences to take down every word uttered.

By the autumn of 1942, therefore, even before the catastrophe of Stalingrad and the declaration of war against America had robbed him of what remained of the strategic initiative, he was already enmeshed as a supreme commander in a web of rancour, mistrust, divided counsel and competing responsibilities entirely of his own making. Four separate military staffs – his own (OKW), the army's (OKH), the air force's (OKL) and the navy's (OKM) – supervised the conduct of operations in their own spheres uncoordinated by any higher intellectual directive than his own. The armaments industry was controlled by a separate ministry again. The collection and analysis of intelligence was the responsibility of several – some say twelve – separate agencies, among which OKW's own Abwehr was only one voice. And meanwhile, in ever more persistent competition with the army for the cream of manpower, the pick of equipment and the cachet of prestige, Himmler's party army, the SS, grew in size and influence. At a time when his enemies sought, by painful administrative and diplomatic effort, to bridge differences between their own armed forces and their national interests, Hitler, impelled by the logic of the dictatorship principle – *Führerprinzip* – was hellbent on enlarging and compounding the divisions implicit in his own system. His life, once so simple, even in the days of headlong

Gleichschaltung – Nazification – grew more complex and demanding
with each passing month of his terrible war. By what methods and
routine did he seek to cope with the burden of labour he had created
for himself?

Hitler's Headquarters

Hitler, as Alexander did at the outset of the Persian expedition, cut
himself off from the seat of civil government at the inception of the
Second World War, and thereafter returned to it only for intermittent and brief intervals. Unlike Alexander, however, and for reasons
of leadership philosophy which we shall approach later, he did not
fix the location of his headquarters at any place where he risked
sharing the dangers and privations of the soldiers on whom the
execution of his orders fell. This is not to say that Hitler directed the
Second World War in luxury. On the contrary, unlike Roosevelt,
whom British visitors to the White House were horrified to note
would conjure up a highball to accompany weighty strategic debate,
or Churchill, whose daily breakfasts of partridge or pheasant
cheerfully exceeded the weekly protein intake of British schoolchil-
dren, Hitler lived the war years on miserable fare in bleak surroundings. Vegetarian gruel and mashed apple were his ration, wooden
barrack huts or concrete bunkers his dwelling. Occasionally the
oppressiveness and isolation of his command centres would drive
him to seek relief of spirit in Munich or his pre-war haven on the
Obersalzberg; but the greater periods were spent in the mosquito-
infested forest of Rastenburg, East Prussia, at Vinnitsa in the
remoteness of the Ukraine or underground at the Reich Chancellery
in Berlin.

Hitler had constructed, though he did not in every case occupy,
more than a dozen wartime headquarters, and also used an impressive (and uncharacteristically quite luxurious) headquarters train, the
Führersonderzug, 'Amerika'. It was in 'Amerika' that he travelled in
successive stages – Bad Polzin, Illnau and Lauenburg – to the Polish
front in September 1939 and to Yugoslavia in April 1941. In 1940 he
occupied three western headquarters: *Felsenest* (Crag Nest), May
10–June 5; *Wolfsschlucht* (Wolf's Gorge) June 6–28; and *Tannen-
berg*, June 28–July 7. He went back to Crag Nest for a Christmas
visit to the troops in 1940, spent one day at Wolf's Gorge II on June

17, 1944, during the Normandy campaign (the impact of a German rogue flying bomb directly overhead drove him from it) and part of December 1944 at *Amt 500* in the Eifel to oversee the Ardennes offensive. Otherwise he was at *Werwolf* in the Ukraine (July 16–November 1, 1942, and February 17–March 13, 1943), at *Wolfsschanze* (Wolf's Camp), Rastenburg (from June 24, 1941, on and off, to November 20, 1944), and then, except for the Ardennes visit, continuously at the Reich Chancellery until his suicide. Engineers also prepared unused headquarters designated *Riese* (Giant), *Wolfsturm* (Wolf Attack), *Wolfsberg* (Wolf Mountain) and, after the Nordic gods and heroes, *Hagen*, *Lothar*, *Brunhilde*, *Rudiger* and *Siegfried*; Hitler, even given that he had used the *nom de voyage* 'Wolf' before the war, had unerringly bad taste in codenames. In duration of residence, it may be seen, *Wolfsschanze* was his principal headquarters. Its location, layout and routine typify those of the war.

Hitler's choice of a location as remote as Rastenburg, a forest site in the depths of East Prussia (Poland since 1945), was dictated by two considerations: personal security; and proximity to the eastern front, in accordance with the tradition of transferring headquarters from the capital to the war zone at the commencement of hostilities – the Kaiser had spent most of the First World War at Spa, in Belgium. A third reason may be deduced: Hitler's wish, once war began, to detach himself from the business of civil government the better to concentrate on the direction of operations. Rastenburg certainly was a military headquarters pure and simple. It had an excellent communications centre and its own airfield, to which civil functionaries frequently flew, but its staff and discipline were military. The inner compound, where Hitler lived, contained offices for the Reich press chief, a Foreign Office representative and the Armaments Minister (when visiting), but otherwise accommodation was provided only for liaison officers of the navy and air force and for OKW; OKH maintained a separate headquarters at Mauerwald, eight miles from Führer Headquarters and connected to it by light railway.

The staff of the inner compound – the outer chiefly housed the personnel of the elaborate security service – was small (Picker, who belonged to it, says twenty-six), consisting of little more than Hitler's personal servants and secretaries and the operations section of OKW. Hitler's personal staff was important to him. Like many

Hitler's Empire and the Location of his Headquarters, 1939-45

NORWAY
Oslo

NORTH SEA

IRELAND

ATLANTIC OCEAN

GREAT BRITAIN
London

Stockhol

DENMARK

Copenhagen
Zoppo

NETH.
Amsterdam

Goddentow-Lanz

BEL.
Brussels

Polzin

GERMANY

Bruly de Peche
Soissons
Paris

Rodert
Berlin

Gross-Borr

POLAN

Ziegenberg

Wars
Illnau

Kniebis
Berchtesgaden

CZECHOSLOVAKI
Prague

PORTUGAL
Lisbon

FRANCE

SWITZ.

Schloss
Klessheim

·Madrid

AUSTRIA
Munichkirchen

HUNGAR

SPAIN

ITALY

Rome

Belgrade·
YUGOSLAVIA

Sofi

MOROCCO

Algiers

ALBANIA

GREECE

ALGERIA

Tunis

Athens

TUNISIA

MEDITERRANEAN SEA

Tripoli

Germany's frontiers in 1937

■ Hitler's headquarters

■ Furthest penetration of German troops

--- Present-day country boundaries

LIBYA

Tobruk·

0   200 miles

others who used the power to kill on the largest scale without pity, he was elaborately considerate of the welfare and feelings of people around him. The deaths of those present in the conference room on July 20, 1944, moved him deeply; his mortally wounded stenographer, Berger, he hastily promoted in the Civil Service so that his widow might draw a pension. To Frau Schmundt, widow of his chief adjutant killed by the conspirators' bomb, he wept, 'It is you who must console me for mine was the greatest loss.' And when word reached him that Traudl Junge, one of his secretaries, had lost her husband in Normandy, he kept the news to himself for some days, brooding on the pain he knew he would have to inflict. 'Ach, child, I am so sorry; your husband had a fine character,' he said when he eventually told her; Captain Junge, his former orderly, had been an officer in the SS.

His secretaries were more than helpmeets. They were also companions and confidantes. Hitler had always intermingled work with long, shapeless bouts of chatter, tea-drinking and pastry-eating. Before the war his chosen companions had been men – old party faithfuls, newer hangers-on, people he regarded as fellow 'artists' and friends of friends. At Rastenburg he had no chosen companions and the secretaries substituted as intimates. It was an attraction that they were women; Hitler, whose sexual life remains a mystery and who, in any case, did not allow his companion, Eva Braun, to reside at Rastenburg, had a strong inclination towards *Schwarmerei* in his relations with the opposite sex – that sort of semi-physical sentimentality more characteristic of friendship between a younger man and an older woman than of passion between lover and mistress. The company of approving women provided him with the opportunity to be listened to, to air his less gruesome prejudices, to play the student of history and critic of art, to ramble, reminisce, repeat himself, in brief to bore his listener stupid without risk of losing her friendship. At Rastenburg he made the fullest use of it. The routine he had adopted there kept him busy with the soldiers twice in the twenty-four hours for long periods and out of bed until after midnight. Lunchtime and the early hours were breaks in the timetable which he devoted to 'table-talk' or 'teahouse' chats with the secretarial circle.

In the early Rastenburg time, when the war was still going well, some of them were actually able to enjoy the claustral isolation, spiced as it was with the excitement of great events. One of the private secretaries recorded a typical day in June 1941, soon after Barbarossa had begun:

> We girls are accommodated as well as the men are. The blockhouses are scattered in the woods grouped according to the work we do. Each department is kept to itself. Our sleeping bunker, big as a railway compartment, is very comfortable-looking, panelled with a beautiful light-coloured wood. [Rastenburg] is wonderful except for an appalling plague of mosquitoes. My legs have been stung to bits and are covered with bumps . . . The men are better protected by their long leather boots and thick uniforms; their only vulnerable point is the neck. Some of them go round all day with mosquito nets on . . . the temperature here is a pleasant surprise. It is almost too cool indoors . . . the forest keeps out the heat; you don't notice until you go out . . . where the heat clamps down on you.
>
> Shortly after 10 a.m. we go to the mess bunker, No. 1 Dining Room – a long, whitewashed room, half sunk half-underground, so that the small gauze windows are very high up. On its walls wood engravings, one of baskets, another of Henry I, etc. A table for twenty people takes up the entire length of the room; here the Chief takes his lunch and supper with the generals, his general staff officers, adjutants and doctors [this was before the breach with Keitel and Jodl]. At breakfast and afternoon coffee we two girls are also there. The Chief sits facing the maps of Russia hanging on the opposite wall and this naturally prompts him to make repeated remarks about Soviet Russia and the dangers of bolshevism . . . He makes a clean breast of his apprehensions, again and again emphasising the enormous danger bolshevism is for Europe and saying that if he had waited just one year longer it would probably have been too late.
>
> We wait in this No. 1 Dining Room each morning until the Chief arrives for breakfast from the map room, where meantime he has been briefed on the war situation. Breakfast for him, I might add, is just a glass of milk and a mashed apple . . . Meanwhile we get the Chief to tell us what the latest war situation is.
>
> Afterwards we go at 1 p.m. to the general situation

conference in the map room, where either Colonel Schmundt
or Major Engel does the briefing. These briefing situations are
extremely interesting. The statistics on enemy aircraft and
tanks destroyed are announced – and our troops' advance is
shown on the maps.
After the situation conference it is time for lunch, which is in
the No. 2 Dining Room for us. As this is often just a hot pot we
mostly pass it up. Anyway that's what we do when it's peas and
beans. If there is nothing important to be done, we sleep a few
hours after lunch so we are bright and breezy for the rest of the
day, which usually drags on until the cows come home. Then,
around 5 p.m. we are summoned to the Chief and plied with
cakes by him. The one who grabs the most cakes gets his
commendation. The coffee break most often goes on to 7 p.m.,
frequently even longer. Then we walk back to No. 2 Dining
Room for supper. Finally we lie low in the vicinity until the
Chief summons us to his study where there is a small
get-together with coffee and cakes again in his more intimate
circle . . . I often feel so feckless and superfluous here. If I
consider what I do all day, the shattering answer is: absolutely
nothing. We sleep, eat, drink and let people talk to us, if we are
too lazy to talk ourselves.

Hitler's work habits, formerly alarmingly erratic, at least to
bureaucrats and professionals schooled in the Prussian tradition,
were in fact becoming more disciplined as the time of easy victories
passed. But this secretary's picture of a still haphazard, café-terrace
approach to war-making is all too well borne out by the transcripts of
his table-talk – recorded by a notetaker, Heinrich Heim, at the
behest of the party secretary, Martin Bormann – which began to be
taken down in the following month, July 1941. ('We must remember,' notes Albert Speer, 'that the collection includes only those
passages [thought] significant. Complete transcripts would reinforce
the sense of stifling boredom.') In the early weeks of Barbarossa, the
pastry-eating circle had to listen to monologues – Hitler's preferred
conversational form – on the treasures of the Leningrad Hermitage,
the origins of Spartan gruel, the future of monarchy, British power
in India, the iniquity of lawyers, the Swiss as hoteliers, meteorology,
typewriting in primary schools, the standardization of electrical
voltages, the prophetic sense of Emperor Julian the Apostate, the

re-employment of old soldiers as tobacconists and the human aversion for snakes, bats and earthworms.

The record for the night of July 21–2, 1941, conveys the flavour of these tergiversations with reasonable exactitude, if allowance is made for the absence of the recurrent diatribes against Jews, Slavs, Christianity and Bolshevism:

> When all's said, we should be grateful to the Jesuits. Who knows if, but for them, we might have abandoned Gothic architecture for the light, airy, bright architecture of the Counter-Reformation. In the face of Luther's efforts to lead an Upper Clergy, which had acquired profane habits, back to mysticism, the Jesuits restored to the world the joy of the senses . . . Fanaticism is a matter of climate – for Protestantism, too, has burnt its witches. Nothing of that sort in Italy; the Southerner has a lighter attitude to the matter of faith . . . It's remarkable to observe the resemblances between the evolution of Germany and that of Italy. The creators of the language, Dante and Luther, rose against the ecumenical desires of the papacy . . . I must say I always enjoyed meeting [Mussolini]. It's curious to think that, at the same period as myself, he was working in the building trade in Germany. Our programme was worked out in 1919, and at that time I knew nothing about him . . . If the Duce were to die, it would be a great misfortune for Italy. As I walked with him in the gardens of the Villa Borghese, I could easily compare his profile with that of the Roman busts, and I realised he was one of the Caesars . . . Italy is the country where intelligence created the notion of the state. The Roman Empire was a great political creation, the greatest of all. The Italian people's musical sense, its liking for harmonious proportions, the beauty of its race. The Renaissance was the dawn of a new era, in which Aryan man found himself anew . . . The smallest palazzo in Florence or Rome is worth more than all Windsor Castle. If the British destroy anything in Florence or Rome, it will be a crime. In Moscow, it wouldn't do any harm; nor in Berlin unfortunately [a rare Hitler joke]. I've seen Rome and Paris, and I must say that Paris, with the exception of the Arc de Triomphe, has nothing on the scale of the Coliseum . . . There's something queer about the Paris buildings, whether it's those bull's-eye

windows, so badly proportioned, or those gables that obliterate whole façades . . . Naples, apart from the castle, might be anywhere in South America . . . My dearest wish would be to be able to wander about in Italy as an unknown painter.

As the war drew on, the Führer would play the polymath a good deal less and his *Kaffeeklatschen*, postponed ever later as worsening situation conferences protracted, would become scarcely bearable ordeals to those obliged to keep him company. Morell, his doubtfully-competent but trusted personal physician, was allowed to slumber while the miasma of autodidacticism drifted over the gathering. The professional listeners, secretaries and adjutants, relieved themselves with internal screams of tedium when the talk turned once again, at 3 in the morning, to the future settlement of the Ukraine, the sapping effects of Christianity on Nordic hardihood, the virtues of vegetarianism and old times in the trenches. 'It's all so convincing what the Chief says,' the girl secretaries recorded in July 1941:

> He explains how Christianity by its mendacity and hypocrisy has set back mankind in its development, culturally speaking, by two thousand years. I really must start writing down what the Chief says. It's just that these sessions go on for ages and afterwards you are just too limp and lifeless to write anything. The night before last, when we left the Chief's bunker, it was already light . . . A strange calling like ours will probably never be seen again: we eat, we drink, we sleep, now and then we type a bit, and meantime keep him company for hours on end. Recently we did make ourselves a bit useful – we picked some flowers, so that his bunker does not look too bare.

But on New Year's Eve, 1941, her diary records that the strain of the eastern front was already beginning to tell on both the Supreme Commander and his soothing and echoing claque. 'We were all in a cheerful enough mood at supper in the No. 2 mess. Then we were ordered over to the regular tea session where we found a very weary Chief, who nodded off after a while. So we accordingly kept very quiet, which completely stifled what high spirits we had been able to summon up. After that the Chief was away for three hours in conference, while the menfolk who had been summoned to offer New Year greetings hung around with doom-laden faces, not daring to allow a smile to pass their lips.' Nine months later, after Stalingrad and Kursk, temporary gloom would have given way, Albert Speer, the armaments minister, recorded, to permanent irritation:

> Before Hitler appeared, someone might ask, 'So where is Morell this morning?'
> Someone else would reply crossly, 'He hasn't been here for the past three evenings.'
> One of the secretaries: 'He could stand staying up once in a while. It's always the same . . . I'd love to sleep too.'
> Another: 'We really should arrange to take turns. It isn't fair for some to shirk and the same people to be here all the time.'

Early in the war, as always at the Berghof in days of peace, Hitler had lightened the evening tedium with film shows; his taste was for current commercial successes. Later he gave them up, 'out of sympathy for the privations of the soldiers', and substituted the playing of records, but in very stereotyped programmes: 'First he wanted a few bravura selections from Wagnerian operas, to be followed promptly by operettas,' Speer recalled. 'He made a point of trying to guess the names of the sopranos and was pleased when he guessed right, as he frequently did.' In private Hitler also put Beethoven and Bruckner on the gramophone. But his only real relaxation at Rastenburg was in walking and training his dog, an Alsatian bitch called Blondi. Eventually by insisting that no one else feed her, he made himself her master. Until then she had been notoriously insubordinate during Hitler's post-prandial walks – until late 1943, when his strength began to go, he made a point of walking several miles a day – the only living creature, the few sceptics who visited Rastenburg reflected, to display any consistent independence of spirit in his presence.

Blondi was also the only Rastenburg resident to wrinkle a nose at the unfailingly awful cuisine; when allowed to table, she shrank from the paps and vegetarian slops on which Hitler dined. Although the Führer did not try to impose his vegetarianism on anyone else (and, after Hess's flight to England in 1941, none of his circle aped it), he insisted on the observance of rationing regulations. The menu was the military field meal, there was little butter or meat served, and little alcohol; second-rate sparkling wine, Speer observed caustically, was deemed a treat. Smoking, of course, was absolutely forbidden in Hitler's presence. 'I'm convinced that, if I had continued to be a smoker,' he reflected complacently on March 11, 1942, 'I'd not have held out against the life of incessant worry that has for so long been mine. Perhaps it's to this insignificant detail that the German people owes my having been spared to them.'

Incessant worry had never, in fact, been Hitler's lot until the Moscow setback of December 1941. He had undoubtedly had severe attacks of nerves on several occasions during the war before that time. On November 14, 1940, in the first week of his attack on Norway, he had so overpainted to himself the threat of British counter-attack that he actually ordered Dietl, subsequently to become one of his favourite generals, to withdraw. 'The hysteria is frightful,' Jodl noted in his diary. But, after Jodl had uttered his remarkable reproof – 'My Führer, there are times in every war when the Supreme Commander must keep his nerve,' striking the map table with his knuckles between each word – Hitler composed himself and allowed Jodl to draft an order instructing Dietl to hold on. There had been a similar crisis during the Dunkirk episode, one so intense that David Irving, not an historian to diminish Hitler's military stature, describes it in his monumental study of his generalship as a 'nervous breakdown'. But those early falterings Hitler subsequently put behind him. He showed no self-doubt before the attack on Yugoslavia and Greece nor, even more surprisingly, in the weeks before Barbarossa itself. Insomnia, to which he was endemically prone, returned in the few nights before the attack. But he seems to have determined to quell his daytime worries by fatalistic acceptance of its dangers. 'Barbarossa is a gamble like anything else,' he remarked on May 29, three weeks before the Russian expedition. 'If it fails, then it will all be over anyhow. If it succeeds it will have created a situation that will probably force Britain to make peace. What will the United States say when all at once Finland is on our side? When the first shot is fired the world will hold its breath.'

He was scarcely ever again to deal so boldly with the prospect and consequences of risk. To local crises he would react with energy and decision and was greatly heartened when a threatening situation was thereby restored. The success of the Kharkov counter-offensive in February 1943 was one (though the credit was really Manstein's); the containment of the Anzio bridgehead in Italy in January 1944 another. At least twice more he found the nerve for a genuine strategic gamble, once at Mortain in August 1944, when he struck to behead the Allied breakout from Normandy, and again in the Ardennes in December, when he tried to repeat the success of 1940. Both were catastrophic failures, entailing the destruction of irreplaceable armoured reserves and hastening rather than postponing the onset of Germany's defeat.

But by that stage of the war he was a man living with the knowledge of inevitable defeat, a knowledge that marked his face, hair, gait, posture and gestures with ghastly evidence of the stress he bore. The worst of his fears he kept at bay with bold expressions of belief in the tide-turning powers of his secret weapons; but they must have co-existed with the anticipation, growing within his consciousness like a psychic tumour, of the death he knew he would ultimately have to inflict upon himself. For the last two years of his life Hitler was a breathing, walking, talking, calculating corpse, destined as certainly for the grave as any of the millions he marked for death in that terrible climax of his dictatorship. The power to kill was, indeed, the only power left to him after mid-summer 1943. Peace he knew his enemies would never concede to Germany while he remained at its head; surrender meant, he must have guessed, trial and execution as a war criminal. After Kursk, therefore, his generalship partook of nothing more than reflexive reaction to his enemies' initiatives. Strategic choice had slipped from his grasp, never to be restored. If we wish also to perceive something of the means by which he exercised it, therefore, we have to return to the earlier period of his time as *Feldherr* – lord of the field. In the first period – characterized, as we have seen, by attacks of severe indecision – he lacked both the competence and the confidence to conduct operations on a day-to-day basis (though not to override the general staff when, as over 'Yellow', he thought its plans defective). In the period intermediate between the fall of France and the attack on Russia he and Germany rode so high that decision-making was fraught neither with stress nor risk. It is in the months that followed the inception of Barbarossa but preceded the onset of disaster at Kursk that we should look for example of how the *Feldherr* grappled with command in the circle of conflicting but free choice. Stalingrad – the decision to fight, the conduct of the battle, the bearing of the consequence – reveals the nature of Hitler's generalship as well as, perhaps better than, any other campaign. How did Hitler come to wage and lose this decisive battle?

Hitler in Command

That Hitler accepted the concept of decisive battle we may take as given. It is central to the philosophy of Clausewitz, to whom Hitler uniquely granted the title of intellectual master. 'Not one of you,' he threw at a Munich audience in 1934, 'has read Clausewitz or, if you have read him, you haven't known how to relate him to the present.' 'My generals,' he taunted a group of them in August 1941, 'I know Clausewitz and his axiom: one must first destroy the enemy's armies in the field and then occupy his capital.' That Hitler thereby conflated something Clausewitz did say with something he did not – Clausewitz actually thought the enemy's capital an entirely second-ary objective in war – does not falsify his assertion that he was a disciple. Clausewitz has been more widely misquoted than not, and the Führer is in good company in getting only part of his teaching right. What is important is that he chose a major, not minor, doctrine of the master's on which to act, thereby validating his assertion, supported from other evidence, that he was a long-time student of war with a well-informed grasp of its essentials. The apparently empty Vienna years had been spent in quite strictly directed reading, at least about war – as a fellow down-and-out who ran his literary errands testifies – so that he had already learnt, well before 1939, both what Clausewitz said about the centrality of battle and, from wide browsing in military history, what battle en-tailed. His own trench experience had invested theory with dreadful reality. When, in the summer of 1942, he was obliged to turn to the question of whether or not he should fight at Stalingrad, there can have been no doubt in his mind about the consequences of choosing to do so.

Stalingrad (formerly Tsaritsyn, now Volgograd) is an industrial city on the lower Volga, Russia's greatest river, which flows thence into the Caspian Sea. In terms of human geography, the river marks, better perhaps than the Urals, the boundary between European and Asiatic Russia, and was therefore an objective of the greatest psychological significance, a significance reinforced by its economic importance. The Volga is a major artery of long-distance transport-ation in the Soviet Union; Stalingrad is, and already was in 1942, a major productive centre. For Hitler it had an additional ideological significance: Leningrad and Stalingrad he regarded as the eponymous capitals of Bolshevism. The former he held under siege in mid-1942, of the latter he prized the capture.

Yet at the outset of the campaign in 1942, which began on May 8, no plan to take Stalingrad had been drafted. The objects of the offensive were laid down on April 5 in Führer Directive No. 41: to destroy Soviet forces west of the River Don, so as to open the way to the capture of the Caucasus oilfields; and to make 'an attempt' to reach Stalingrad. The operation was entrusted to Army Group South, commanded by Field Marshal von Bock.

Three preliminary operations were necessary, however, to clear the ground before the drive east could begin: at Kerch and Sevastapol, to complete the occupation of the Crimea; and at Kharkov, to open the way to the Don. Subsidiary as they were, they entailed fighting on a scale that caused half a million Soviet losses. Hitler was meanwhile also preoccupied with the Leningrad front, which the army high command would have preferred to make the principal focus of effort for 1942, and distracted by events in the Mediterranean, where he feared the Western allies might reinforce the British army that was locked in battle with Rommel and the Italian-German army of Africa, and was momentarily alarmed by the rumour of a cross-Channel invasion.

The Crimean preliminaries were successfully completed. The Kharkov battle, however, developed in a way that was to distort the unfolding of Bock's southward drive with cumulatively disastrous results. His capture of Kharkov had so devastated and disorganized the Soviet defenders that their front collapsed across a wide sector, allowing him to advance almost unopposed to the Don. There he was supposed to turn south towards Stalingrad and the Caucasus, using the river as flank protection against enemy forces on the other side. Bock's assessment of the local situation in the first week of July, however, was that he risked being attacked from across the river by Russian troops which were evidently concentrating at Voronezh, a major rail and road centre. Acting on his own initiative, therefore, he moved to capture Voronezh, thus committing Army Group South both to cross the river and to drive east, when the plan dictated he should stay on his own side of it and march south.

Hitler's reaction was not to insist on Bock doing as the plan ordained, but (July 7) to divide his army group into two: Bock remained in command of the new Army Group B, Field Marshal List was given charge of a new Army Group A, comprising the units on the southern half of the old army group's front. Hitler's reasoning seems to have been that Bock, to whose local judgement he partly deferred, could deal as he thought fit with the situation around Voronezh, while List sustained the drive south towards the Caucasus. The scheme, however, did not work. Bock allowed himself to be dragged further into fighting around Voronezh, while List's southward movement opened a gap between the flanks of the two new formations. On July 13 Hitler decided to dismiss Bock (for the second time: a victim of the previous December's mass sacking, he had been reinstated when Reichenau, of Army Group South, had died of a heart attack) and to replace him with General von Weichs. He, by his own interference, now began to exaggerate the divergence of advance by Army Groups B and A, ordering A to shift its tank forces ever more southward as a means of completing the destruction of the Soviet forces on the German side of the Don with which the summer campaign had opened.

His professional subordinates, notably Halder, the army chief of staff, objected; Halder attempted to point out that Hitler was now trying to fight a major battle both on the Don and, by extension, on the Volga and at Stalingrad, while simultaneously seeking to capture the Caucasus. One or the other, was his contention; there was not enough force, particularly in tanks, to do both. Hitler dismissed his objection as cavilling. On July 23 he promulgated a new Führer Directive, No. 45, which may be regarded as the most disastrous of all issued over his signature. While ordering Army Group A (List) to complete the battle of annihilation on the Don and then proceed to the Caucasus, it simultaneously directed Army Group B (Weichs) not merely to advance to but also to capture Stalingrad.

Hitler was straining after the impossible. Not only were the distances involved in his strategy enormous – 200 miles to Stalingrad, 600 miles to the Caucasus – thereby creating a front 800 miles wide (from Baku in the Caucasus to Stalingrad city), but the forces available, already stretched, were quite inadequate to cover such expanses or to hold the ground if it could be won. The two army groups between them had only sixty-five divisions, of which fewer than ten were tank. The rest, like those Hitler knew so well from 1914, were foot infantry divisions whose artillery and transport were horse-drawn; in many the only motor vehicle was the general's staff car. Divisions like these could, by the utmost physical effort, cover twenty-five miles a day, a pace that exhausted the men and killed the horses. If opposed they could not manoeuvre; if counter-attacked, they could only stand and wait for help or break. The gap that would inevitably open between their plodding advance guards and the tank spearheads could be filled, at best, by thin screens of cavalry and armoured cars.

Hitler's grasp of the difficulties to which he had consigned Army Groups A and B was not strengthened by his decision to move headquarters from Rastenburg to *Werwolf* at Vinnitsa, in the Ukraine, on July 16. In theory the move put him closer to the front, though it left him 500 miles from Stalingrad and 1,000 from Baku; in practice, it created several days' confusion, during which a vital piece of intelligence was overlooked. Foreign Armies East, the branch of the Abwehr that watched the Soviets – with considerable skill and success – reported on July 15 that the Soviet leadership was preparing measures for the firm defence of Stalingrad. By the time Hitler was established at Vinnitsa, this snippet had got 'buried' in a flood of further information and no notice was taken of it.

The disruption caused by this move was to be repeated on October 30 when headquarters returned to Rastenburg and was effectively out of action for two days; and then again on November 11, when Hitler abandoned Rastenburg for the Berghof until November 23, a physical dislocation that implied psychological withdrawal. By that time the battle for Stalingrad had begun to go very badly indeed.

Throughout August Army Groups A and B slogged forward, while Hitler juggled with operations on the adjoining fronts of Army Groups Centre and North, the first to enlarge the salient north of Moscow, the second to bring the siege of Leningrad to an end. Slow progress in both made for worsening relations with Halder, whom Hitler caught out time and again in apparent insubordinations. Orders given for the movement of divisions often could not be carried out because of local Russian resistance; the Führer always ascribed the failures, when he discovered them, to Halder's incompetence or disobedience. News received on August 23 that Fourth Panzer Army, the cutting edge of Army Group B, had reached the Volga north of Stalingrad brought a lightening of the atmosphere. But it was offset by worries about the Moscow and Leningrad fronts and slow progress in the Caucasus.

These dissensions were about to come to a head. Hitler was already considering Halder's removal. At the end of the first week of

September he contrived to fall out with all his closest military advisers, those of both OKH and OKW, simultaneously. On September 4 he threw at Halder the taunt that he had not even been wounded in the First World War, that his military experience was limited to sitting 'on the same swivel chair' and challenged him to say if he knew anything about fighting soldiers at all. Five days later Halder was summarily sacked, to be replaced by the ex-infantry subaltern, Zeitzler, who had not been a general a year earlier. List was also dismissed for lack of drive and Hitler assumed command of Army Group A himself. Meanwhile he moved to consummate the breach with Jodl also. Sent to gather proof validating Hitler's suspicion that slow progress in the Caucasus was the fault of Halder's insubordination, Jodl returned with evidence that it was the result of objective inconsistencies in Hitler's strategy. It was from that moment, on September 8, that Jodl – and his superior, Keitel, whose eternal sycophancy did not offset the taunt of association with his clever and outspoken junior – were banished from the Führer's social circle and heaped with marks of disfavour.

Jodl might have made this humiliation the pretext for resignation. Hitler had, in fact, contemplated his, and Keitel's, dismissal. But when he did not proceed with it, Jodl preferred to soldier on, explaining later to his deputy, Warlimont, that the source of a dictator's power was his self-confidence, which must not be sapped by disloyalty. Two months later, when Warlimont himself was subjected to dismissal (subsequently revoked), Jodl stated flatly, 'for us the Führer's will is the supreme law of the land'. Yet the atmosphere at Führer headquarters, already charged with mistrust, had overnight become intolerable to any man of honour. The tradition of the German general staff was that of easy intimacy between chief and helpmate. Now, records Warlimont of the days after September 8, 'the entire existence and work of the headquarters seemed paralysed':

> Hitler shut himself up in his sunless blockhouse and apparently only left it after dark, taking care not to be seen. The map room, which, during the preceding days and weeks, had daily been the scene of prolonged discussions and furious arguments, lay deserted. The briefing conferences now took place in Hitler's own hut; they were limited to the smallest possible number of essential reporting officers and the procedure – or

lack of it – was quite different. Not a word more than necessary was spoken; the atmosphere was glacial . . . The briefing conferences were eventually resumed in their old form but Hitler never appeared in the mess again. His chair in the dining room stood empty for some time and was then taken on by Bormann. Forty-eight hours after [September 8] ten to twelve shorthand typists from the Reichstag appeared in the headquarters, were put into uniform, took the oath of allegiance to Hitler himself and subsequently, two at a time, were invariably present at all military discussions.

Until routine was gradually restored, Hitler interviewed Zeitzler – the close friend of his chief adjutant, Schmundt – in his private quarters. Zeitzler, a straightforward combat soldier, did not make the mistake, as Halder had done on August 20, of confronting Hitler with Russian tank production figures. Halder's warning that these amounted to 1,200 a month – an underestimate, but even so over twice those for Germany – cast the whole of the Eastern Front strategy into such doubt that it is little to be wondered Hitler chose to denounce him as a defeatist. The Führer found Zeitzler's narrow-focused concern with the simplicities of moving units here and there much more to his taste. Together they could pore over small-scale maps of the front. Hitler used a magnifying glass, as he did spectacles for reading documents – discussing when this or that battalion might arrive at a chosen position with a sense of deeds done and fate averted never possible when a general staff pedant might intervene to invoke considerations of higher strategy or, heaven forbid, the purpose of the war. Moreover Zeitzler had the 'front-fighter's' nerve to stand up to Hitler when the two were together in the company of other generals. Soon after his appointment, Hitler launched at him one of his now familiar diatribes about the academicism of the general staff, culminating in the gibe, 'What do you know about troops?' Zeitzler replied that, like Hitler, he had marched off to war in 1914 in an infantry platoon. 'For bravery in the face of the enemy, I was promoted lieutenant. For three years I commanded a company and for one year I was regimental adjutant. I was wounded twice. I think my combat experience was as good as yours.' Hitler, it was noted, paled and treated him with circumspection thereafter.

This theatre of temperament and dramatic exits at Führer

headquarters contrasts shabbily with the consequences for ordinary soldiers of what was – or was not – decided at the Rastenburg and Vinnitsa situation conferences that summer and autumn. Far away in the Caucasus, it was the ordeal of intermittent supply and rough going that afflicted them. At Stalingrad it was the resistance of the Red Army itself. The Fourth Panzer Army's advance to the outskirts of the city on August 23 had drawn the largely infantry Sixth Army into fighting for its houses and public buildings. By mid-September a fullscale street battle of the most bitter sort was in progress in the sixteen-mile strip of built-up area that ran along the west bank of the Volga.

A letter from a Russian soldier to General Zhukov, commanding the Sixty-second Army defending the city, conveys the intensity of the fighting in September. His post of duty was in a grain elevator:

> In the elevator the grain was on fire, the water in the machine-guns evaporated, the wounded were thirsty, but there was no water nearby. This was how we defended ourselves twenty-four hours a day for three days. Heat, smoke, thirst – all our lips were cracked. During the day many of us climbed up to the highest points in the elevator and from there fired on the Germans; at night we came down and made a defensive ring around the building. Our radio equipment had been put out of action on the first day. We had no contact with our units.

The lot of their German enemies, also oppressed by heat and thirst, was similar. It was shortly to grow worse. On September 9 Stalin had asked Generals Vasilevsky and Zhukov to prepare plans for the restoration of the situation in the city. In the weeks that followed the plans grew into a scheme for a far more ambitious operation, nothing less than the total envelopment of the Sixth Army inside Stalingrad by convergent pincer movements from north and south. Diligently and secretly the Soviet Don and Stalingrad Fronts gathered reinforcements and prepared disguised attack positions, waiting for the coming of the cold to freeze the Volga and allow their assault columns across without bridging. Early in the morning of November 19, conditions and preparations having matured, they struck. Their chosen points of penetration were held by weak elements of Army Group A, contingents from Germany's Romanian and Italian allies. Both collapsed in the first day of fighting and by November 23 Stalingrad was surrounded.

Hitler, whose responsibility for the management of the battle was total – every link in the chain of command from Supreme Commander of the Armed Forces to Commander-in-Chief of the Army to Commander of Army Group A was held by him at this moment – was 1,300 miles away when the storm broke, taking a break from Rastenburg at the Berghof in Berchtesgaden. It was an extraordinary disinvolvement at a moment not only of crisis but of multiple and pre-existing crises, since at the beginning of November it had become clear that Rommel had lost the battle of Alamein and on November 8 the British and Americans had invaded North Africa. Not until November 23, however, did Hitler order the OKW operations staff, which had trailed after him to South Germany, to return to Rastenburg and not until November 25 had its re-assembly been completed. He simultaneously divested himself of command of Army Group A to Kleist and ordered Manstein to form a new Army Group Don, which was to force its way back into Stalingrad.

The consequences of that decision determined two others: one of November 23 that Paulus, commanding the Sixth Army in Stalingrad, should not try to break out, and one of November 24 that the Luftwaffe should meanwhile supply his twenty-two divisions by air, as Göring assured him it could. Of these three decisions, one – that Paulus should stay put – could be made to stick; the other two would not. Paulus required 300 tons of supplies a day simply to survive, while the average the Luftwaffe was able to deliver was something under 200. Manstein could find reinforcements – just – for the break-in effort, code-named 'Winter Storm', but could not be rushed to his objective in the teeth of ferocious Russian resistance.

Hitler, at the December situation conferences to which news of his efforts was brought, maintained an outward air of confidence that 'Winter Storm', which began on December 12, would succeed. But, as he neither would allow Paulus to strike towards Manstein in assistance, nor could conjure up fresh reinforcements to strengthen Manstein's thrust, he must inwardly have felt hope in a victorious outcome draining from him. An analysis made by Geoffrey Jukes of his reactions to requests and suggestions during the crucial period reveals that they were wholly negative:

Date	Subject	Outcome
December 13	Withdrawal of Army Group A from the Caucasus.	No decision
	Request from Manstein for reinforcements.	No decision
December 15	Relief force comes to a halt.	No decision
December 17	Request for Sixth Army to be allowed to break out.	Refused
December 19	Request repeated urgently. (Manstein in fact ordered Paulus to break out, but he would not do so without Hitler's assent.)	Refused
December 20	Contradictory orders on movement of SS panzer division.	Confusion
	Withdrawal of Sixth Army discussed.	No decision
December 21	Sixth Army ordered to break out if it can also hold Stalingrad.	Confusion
December 22	Further request for Sixth Army break-out.	Refused
December 23	'Winter Storm' abandoned.	

Such an analysis, revealing though it is, conveys no flavour of the atmosphere in which such critical issues were discussed, shelved or rejected. Albert Speer, who as Armaments Minister was present at many of them, sets the scene:

Every day around noon [there was a later meeting at early evening and, as the war worsened and Hitler's insomnia with it, another at midnight] the grand situation conference took place. Hitler was the only one who was seated – on a plain armchair with a rush seat. The other participants stood around the map table . . . Desk lamps with long swinging arms illuminated the maps. First the eastern theatre was discussed. Three or four strategic maps, pasted together, were laid out on the long table in front of Hitler. The discussion began with the northern part of the eastern theatre of war. Every detail of the events of the previous day was entered on the maps, every advance, even patrols – and almost every entry was explained by the Chief of Staff. Bit by bit the maps were pushed farther up the table, so that Hitler always had a comprehensible segment within reading distance. Longer discussion was devoted to the most important events, Hitler noting every change from the previous day . . . The situation in the western theatre of war, at that time still centred in Africa, was taken up next by General Jodl. Here, too, Hitler tended to interfere in every detail . . . Once the 'army situation' had been discussed, reports of the events of the last twenty-four hours in the 'air situation' and the 'naval situation' . . . were reviewed. On questions of air and naval warfare Hitler left his commanders-in-chief the broadest freedom of choice.

As it happens, the degree to which Hitler interfered in the tactical detail of any operation is conveyed by one of the stenographic reports, all but fragments of which were burnt before capture at Berchtesgaden in May 1945, which has survived. It is that for the opening day of 'Winter Storm', December 12, and it fascinatingly reveals the banal, rambling, discursive, sometimes microscopic, sometimes 'world historical' nature of Hitler's supreme command discussions with his generals:

Midday Conference, Rastenburg, 12.45

HITLER.   Has there been some disaster?

ZEITZLER.   No, my Führer, Manstein reached the obstacle and captured a bridge. The only attacks were on the Italian front. One regiment here was alerted during the night and reached its battle position at 10 a.m. That was good because the Italians had already put in all their reserves.

HITLER.   I've had more sleepless nights over this business in the south than anything else. One doesn't know what's going on.

     . . .

ZEITZLER.   Field-Marshal Manstein called me early this morning. He has captured the bridge at this place. There is a little pressure starting against 23rd Panzer Division. Those are probably the forces they brought up. Resistance here was not very great. Very heavy fighting flared up here during the course of the day. The enemy captured Ritchev. That's most unfortunate because of the bridge. That was the line of communications we used to bring forces up . . . we intercepted a radio message from the [Soviet] VIII Cavalry Corps saying that they were taking up a defensive position. It is still not clear what the enemy is doing up here. It may be merely a reaction to our radio traffic. Before we moved this was very high. It may be, however, that he is preparing something. The main attack on Sixth Army was in this area.

. . .

HITLER.   Looking at the big picture I've thought of one thing, Zeitzler: under no circumstances must we give [Stalingrad] up, we should never get it back again. We know what that means. I can't lay on any surprise operations. Unfortunately it's too late now. It would all have gone quicker if we hadn't hung about at Voronezh. Then we'd have got through in the first rush, but it's ridiculous to imagine that we can do it a second time after having withdrawn and abandoned our equipment. We couldn't take everything with us. The horses were worn out. They can't pull anything any more. I can't feed a horse off another horse. If it was Russians I'd say that one Russian could eat another. But you can't get a nag to eat another nag.

. . .

HITLER.   Of course, it's most important to see how the Italians get on today. One thing I don't see and that is how I can possibly get away from here [to the Berghof at Berchtesgaden] today, Jodl. I can of course cancel everything.

JODL.   There will be a lot of other problems left in the air too.

HITLER.   I agree. We can make up our minds at the last moment. What are the train connections?

JODL.   In general there's a connection every two hours.

	It's very seldom necessary to go as much as three hours without a connection; as a rule it's every two hours, sometimes more often.
BODENSCHATZ.	If the radio is functioning we can keep in touch that way.
HITLER.	Can we get anything like a proper picture by radio? Is that possible and how long will it take? Everything has to be encoded. How long will it take to deal with even a minor question?
JODL.	That's no good.
HEWEL.	One can telephone from the station.
HITLER.	From every station?
JODL.	It's a bit more difficult from the temporary stations than the permanent ones. But you will get through in any case.
HITLER.	If I do go, I will cut out Berlin. We'll see today and tomorrow.
ZEITZLER.	We're going to have some very important days with very important developments.

. . .

ZEITZLER.	Everybody's very pleased with the 297th Division just now; it's first-class. There was a lot about it in the report. But I don't think the enemy will attack here just yet; he has moved everything away. The whole attack depends on whatever we can punch a hole through here.
HITLER.	Yes, 206th Division is covering up but has one regiment detached. It has three regiments.
JODL.	It's 100 per cent complete right up to the last man. Nine battalions.
HITLER.	But one regiment's detached. It has nine 75-mm self-propelled, or hasn't it?
JODL.	No, towed.
HITLER.	It's got six and 22nd Division has eighteen.
ZEITZLER.	Yes, it's been reinforced.
HITLER.	That one's pretty weak; one 75-mm and two 76-mm and he's bringing down one regiment from 294th Division. That means there's no reserve up there.

. . .

HITLER.   Except in the last resort, where the general must be
                 the standard bearer because it's a matter of life and
                 death, he must be back behind. In the long run you
                 can't command in the rear of battle . . . Once a unit
                 has started to run, the ties of training and organisa-
                 tion quickly go unless there is iron discipline. It's
                 miles easier to go crashing forward with an army
                 and win victories than to bring one back in good
                 order after a setback or a defeat. Perhaps the
                 greatest feat of 1914 was that they managed to get
                 the army back after making fools of themselves on
                 the Marne and to get it to stand and reorganise on a
                 definite line. That was perhaps one of the greatest
                 feats. You can only do that with very high-class
                 disciplined troops.

JODL.   We managed to do that here too with the German
                 troops.

HITLER.   We managed it with the Germans but not with the
                 Italians; we never shall with them. So if the enemy
                 breaks through anywhere there will be a catas-
                 trophe.

Catastrophe ensued on February 1, 1943, when Paulus decided to
surrender the starving and frozen remnants of his army to the
Russians and himself with it. Hitler, at the midday situation
conference for that day, the transcript of which also survives, voiced
the worst of his fears for what would follow – and contempt for
Paulus, whom he contrasts with a woman whom the newspapers had
recently reported making a sensational suicide:

HITLER.   They have finally and formally surrendered there.
                 Otherwise they'd have concentrated, formed
                 square and shot it out, using their last bullets on
                 themselves. When you think that a woman's got
                 sufficient pride just because someone's made a few
                 insulting remarks to go and lock herself in and
                 shoot herself right off, then I've no respect for a
                 soldier who's afraid to do that but would rather be
                 taken prisoner.

ZEITZLER.   I can't understand it either. I still wonder whether it's true. Whether perhaps he [Paulus] isn't lying there badly wounded.

HITLER.   No, it's true . . . I had my doubts before. It was at the moment when I heard he was asking what he should do. How could he even ask such a thing? . . . A revolver – makes it easy. What cowardice to be afraid of that! Ha! Better to be buried alive! And in a situation like this where he knows well enough that his death would set the example for behaviour in [the rest of Stalingrad]. If he sets an example like this, one can hardly expect people to go on fighting.

ZEITZLER.   There is no excuse; when his nerves look like breaking down he must shoot himself first.

HITLER.   When one's nerves break down there is nothing to do but say, 'I can't go on' and shoot oneself. In fact you could say that the man ought to shoot himself. Just as in the old days commanders who saw that all was lost used to fall on their swords. Even Varus told his slave: 'Now kill me!'

ZEITZLER.   I still think they may have done that and that the Russians are merely claiming to have captured them all.

HITLER.   No! . . . Any minute he'll be speaking on the radio – you'll see . . . And there's this beautiful woman, a really very beautiful woman, who is insulted by some words. Straightaway she says – it was only a triviality – : 'So I can go; I'm not wanted.' Her husband answers: 'Get out then.' So the woman goes off, writes a letter of farewell and shoots herself . . . What hurts me most is that I went on and promoted him field-marshal. I wanted to give him his heart's desire. That's the last field-marshal I promote in this war . . . No, they'll all talk on the radio themselves. You'll hear it soon enough. They'll all speak personally on the radio. First they'll call on the [rest of the Stalingrad garrison] to give themselves up and then they'll say the meanest things about the German Army.

Hitler's instinct for the weaknesses in human nature was absolutely accurate. Paulus would shortly join the 'Seydlitz' group of 'anti-Fascist' German officers in Russian hands and contribute to its propaganda effort. Hitler himself, however, had made a misjudgement: his last-minute promotion of Paulus had been calculated to drive him to suicide, since no German field-marshal had ever surrendered to the enemy. That ultimate omission apart, neither Paulus nor the Sixth Army failed Hitler. One of his last messages, transmitted on January 22, 1943, blankly communicated its predicament: 'Rations exhausted. Over 12,000 unattended wounded in the pocket. What orders should I give to troops, who have no more ammunition and are subjected to mass attacks supported by heavy artillery fire?'

Hitler had no orders to give, except that 'surrender is out of the question'. Paulus's personal decision for survival he dismissed as 'an aboutface on the threshold of immortality'. There were to be many more before the tide of Allied advance would ultimately roll over the Reich. By May 1945 every single surviving German field-marshal – Model, a late creation, took the way out from which Paulus had flinched – would be a prisoner in British, American and Russian hands. Many of their coevals had mentally given up the fight well beforehand; of the colonel-generals who had held the post of chief of the general staff, Guderian had retired after a blazing row in March 1945, Zeitzler had broken down after July 1944 and Halder was in a concentration camp. Among the leading field commanders, Bock, Leeb, Rundstedt, Manstein, Hoth, Kleist and Weichs had been dismissed. Rommel had committed suicide to spare his family the consequences of his complicity in the July plot. Hoepner had been executed as a result of it and Kluge driven to suicide by suspicion of involvement. Several others had died or done away with themselves under the stress of command – Reichenau, Dollmann (both heart attacks) and the Luftwaffe generals Udet and Jeschonneck (suicides).

Yet of the 1,400 men who held general rank in the army and Luftwaffe from 1939 to 1945, no fewer than 500 had been killed or gone missing in action, an extraordinarily large proportion, perhaps without parallel in any other war fought by an advanced country. Hitler's generals, by the token of faithfulness until death – is there any higher? – had served him well. He, by the token of victory or defeat, had served the offices of supreme commander disastrously badly. How, when his early generalship was so brilliant, did he succeed in leading Germany to catastrophe?

The brief answer is that the Second World War, when widened to include the Soviet Union and the United States among Germany's enemies, was a war that Germany could not win. A fuller answer needs deeper analysis. First and foremost there is the issue of Hitler's command style. He decided from the outset, as we have seen, to centralize decision-making at a point far from the front and thence to supervise the control of operations in the closest detail. *Führerprinzip* provided the motivation that underlay this choice: if he was to exercise supreme power, he must do so in the military as well as civil sector. But he could not have realized that ambition, had not current technical developments, unfortunately for the German army, made available to him the instruments which, superficially at least, endowed him with the means to do so.

Radio – 'wireless' better communicates its crucial military quality – had, by its perfection in the 1930s, dissipated the cloud of unknowing which had descended between the fighting soldiers and their commander ever since long-range weapons had driven him from the focus of combat. Wireless generated a flow of information from the point of critical contact between friend and foe which, properly used, did allow headquarters at successively higher levels of command to monitor the progress of events and moderate their course by sensible intervention. But 'sensible intervention' implied a division of responsibilities. On the Allied side it was generally and scrupulously observed. Churchill, for example, took the closest interest in the conduct of battles but had, or was talked by his advisers into, the sense not to interfere with his generals when crisis at the front transfixed their attention. Hitler, as we have seen, did not. It may, to the layman, seem impressive that Hitler could dispute with Zeitzler exact details of one or another regiment's complement of equipment – so many guns of this calibre, so many of that. To the professional such pettifogging is evidence of necessarily dangerous meddling. For radio did not bring to the Führer's headquarters all the other information of an immaterial but much more important kind – the look of the battlefield, the degree of heat and cold, the variation in intensity of enemy pressure, the level of noise, the flow of wounded backward, the flow of supply forward, the mood of the soldiers, to be judged by the expression of their faces and the tone of their answers to questions – which only a man on the spot would gather. Without recourse to such essential impressions (it is of the greatest significance that Hitler served exclusively in the West from 1914 to 1918, and so never experienced either the climatic extremes or spatial vastness of the Eastern Front) he was skimming the surface of generalship and, for all his ostentatious display of technical expertise, no more 'commanded', in the full sense of the concept, than he had as corporal in the List Regiment.

Hitler's mastery of technical detail, the fruit of an excellent memory and regular study of technical manuals, was a principal means by which he imposed his judgement over his generals. Albert Speer describes how he acquired it: 'He obtained his information from a large book in a red binding . . . a catalogue, continuously brought up to date, of from thirty to fifty types of ammunition and ordnance' (he had also been the devotee since Vienna days of the *Flottenkalender*, a German *Jane's Fighting Ships*, which he had by heart). 'He kept it on his night table' (and had a habit of abstracting what he regarded as key changes of information on scraps of paper, which he then ostentatiously discarded). 'Sometimes he would order a servant to bring the book down when in the course of military conferences an assistant had mentioned a figure which Hitler instantly corrected. The book was opened and Hitler's data would be confirmed, without fail, every time, while the general would be shown to be in error. Hitler's memory was the terror of his entourage . . . By tricks of this sort [he] could intimidate the majority of officers who surrounded him.'

But his expertise, Speer points out, had a narrowing rather than broadening effect on his method of command. '[His] tactical horizon . . . just like his general ideas, his views on art and his style of life, was limited by the First World War. His technical interests were narrowly restricted to the traditional weapons of the army and the navy. In these areas he continued to learn and steadily increased his knowledge, so that he frequently proposed convincing and usable innovations. But he had little feeling for [as opposed to exaggerated faith in] such new developments as, for example, radar, the construction of an atom bomb, jet fighters and rockets.' Moreover, though he dealt fluently with technical experts, the judgements in which he led them to agreement were shallow. Speer says of his relations with his soldiers: 'He knew how to distinguish key matters from those of lesser importance . . . His questions showed that he would grasp the essentials of complicated subjects. However, there was a disadvantage to this of which he was unaware; he arrived at the core of matters too easily and so therefore could not understand them with real thoroughness.'

As the tide of war turned against him, his earlier readiness for debate and give-and-take diminished. 'From about the autumn of 1942,' Speer observed, 'it became almost impossible to oppose Hitler on important questions.'

> . . . Hitler would not stand for objections from those who constituted his daily entourage . . . if a controversial point arose in the course of the discussion, [he] usually evaded it skilfully, postponing clarification of it skilfully to a subsequent conference. He proceeded on the assumption that military men were shy about giving in on points in front of their staff officers. Probably he also expected his aura and his persuasiveness to operate better in a face-to-face discussion with an individual. Both these elements came across poorly over the telephone. Probably that was why Hitler always showed a distinct dislike for conducting important arguments on the telephone.

The ultimate cause of his inflexibility may, however, be judged to have a different source, lying in his fixed perception of how high command ought to be exercised. In essence, it derived, as with so much else, from his trench experience. From those years he had brought the conviction, rooted in the German army's own First World War doctrine, that unless going forward an army is safest if it stands firm, holding to 'the rigid defence of a line', as Falkenheyn's general staff memorandum of January 1915 ordained. To it he added, once he had acquired the self-confidence to impose his operational judgement on that of his generals – and he had begun to do so even before the opening of the battle of France – the belief that 'remote control', insensitive to the tactical ebb-and-flow though it had been in the First World War, served better than direct involvement once radio communications allowed direct touch with troops in the fighting line. 'In the long run you can't command in the roar of battle,' he had preached on December 12, 1942. 'Gradually [a man] loses his nerve. It's different in the rear.'

But, as even front commanders, like Rommel, Guderian and Montgomery were discovering, one also thereby loses touch with the 'feel' of battle – a loss of sensation that drove them, at the precise moment when Hitler was justifying his increasing disengagement from the events of war, to find ways of involving themselves more closely. Rommel, in the Western Desert, was commanding from a tank, keeping contact with his main headquarters by radio through which he transmitted simple pre-arranged cypher groups that indicated a change of direction or thrust. Montgomery created a forward headquarters, to which a trusted band of young liaison officers brought tactical information and impressions, fresh almost by the standards of 'real time', direct to his command caravan. And Guderian, as the famous photograph of himself sharing a radio truck with his signallers and Enigma cypher machine operators reveals, was moving with the leading waves of his panzer army, while it felt for weak spots in the enemy's line and exploited them at his direction. Hitler, in short, had come only halfway into the modern world. For all the cosmetic Futurism of his style, he remained a creature of his youth and its vanishing background, in which command emanated from an unseen All-Highest to whom the simple soldier owed the duty of strictest obedience and by whom was owed nothing in return but the guarantee that his orders would bring victory. In a favourite quotation from Clausewitz, on which he hinged the culminating chapter of *Mein Kampf*, he predicated his perception of the commander's supreme obligation: 'The stain of a cowardly submission can never be effaced . . . This drop of poison in the blood of a people is passed on to posterity and will paralyse and undermine the strongest of later generations.'

Hitler and the Theatre of Leadership

Yet Hitler never supposed that he, Mikado-like, could command loyalty-unto-death from behind the walls of a Forbidden City. Neither Rastenburg nor any other of his headquarters was conceived as sanctuary; *Führerhauptquartier* was a monastic retreat – his admiration for the machinery, as opposed to the doctrine, of the Catholic Church was strong throughout his life – not a funkhole. After the Stauffenburg assassination attempt of July 20, 1944, he understandably insisted on the imposition of strict security measures in his immediate vicinity. Theretofore he had been philosophic about personal risk. 'There was no known remedy for an idealistically minded assassin,' he observed at table on May 3, 1942. 'He therefore found it quite understandable that ninety per cent of historical assassination attempts had succeeded . . . Since [that was so] he stood calm and erect in his car. In this way the saying that the world belongs to the courageous was confirmed over and over again. If an assassin intended to shoot him down or kill him with a bomb, then there was no defence possible even if he was sitting down.'

His acute understanding of the popular mind led him to perceive, however, that the reality of isolation from danger, conferred by the remoteness of all Führer headquarters, must be offset by the illusion of shared risk. Hitler's was certainly not unalert to the ancient and central dilemma of the general: Where to stand, how often to be seen? In front always, sometimes or never? were questions on which he had pondered privately and publicly since the first days of his ascent to power. 'By virtue of a natural order,' he had written in *Mein Kampf*, 'the strongest man is destined to fulfil the great mission . . . yet the realisation that this *one* is the exclusively elect usually comes to the others very late . . . their fellow men are usually able least of all to distinguish which among them – being solely endowed with the highest ability – deserves their sole support.' In his political life, particularly in the 'years of struggle', Hitler had seen the need and usually chose to be 'in front always'. His conduct at the Odeonplatz during the failure of the November putsch of 1923 may not have been as bold as Ludendorff's, but it was certainly not shameful. And he had shown time and again before and thereafter that he would risk physical danger in the fulfilment of his self-appointed mission to resurrect Germany from the grave of defeat. The question remained, nevertheless, whether in wartime, after he had decided that 'never' was to be his answer to the question 'in front?', he could persuade his soldiers that he partook of their exposure and therefore understood their predicament.

Propaganda – though no such crude encapsulation was ever applied to the means of his public representation – was the solution. Hitler had had an acute grasp of the importance of propaganda from an early age, had applauded the superiority of Allied over German propaganda in the First World War in *Mein Kampf* and had there singled out its didactic essentials: the selection of a few simple messages for endless repetition. 'The receptivity of the masses is very limited,' he wrote, 'their intelligence is small, but their power of forgetting is enormous; in consequence of these facts, all effective propaganda must be limited to a very few points and must harp on these in slogans until the last member of the public understands what you want him to understand by your slogan.' Goebbels, the propaganda minister – 'enlightenment' minister was his exact title, a brilliant pilfering from the age when to the world Germany meant Herder and Goethe – had already burdened the German public consciousness with a kaleidoscopic image of Hitler as his people's mentor and protector, the unsleeping guardian of their interests, the lonely helmsman of their destiny, the orphan of their collective sufferings, and the guarantor of their future return to greatness. To that image he added, from the outset of war, the picture of a Hitler unwillingly re-outfitted in the battle gear of a frontfighter, marching to victory as if – not wholly present in body but totally in spirit – at the head of troops. Not even Goebbels, however, for all the brilliance of his propaganda instinct, could find as exact a metaphor for Hitler's illusory physical ordeal as the Führer could himself. Just as Hitler returned again and again, in the intimate circle of his situation conferences, to the theme of his four years at the front, loading on his generals, in the knowledge that none dared a rejoinder, reminder after reminder of his experience of the common soldier's lot, so, too, on those occasions when he spoke directly to his people during the war, did he evoke time after time the past he shared with so many of them – mothers of fallen heroes, widows of the lost generation, fathers of the next, old frontfighters themselves – as a survivor of the First World War, in validation of his comradeship with the new generation who wore field-grey.

No message of his more brilliantly conveys the shameless invocation of his title to heroic leadership – for it was as hero that Hitler struggled to represent himself with even greater shrillness as his claim to that role passed – than his public explanation of his decision to assume personal command of the German army on December 22, 1941:

> Soldiers – the battle for the liberty of our people and for the security of its future existence . . . is now approaching its culminating and turning point . . . I know war from the mighty conflict in the West from 1914 to 1918. I experienced personally the horrors of almost all the battles as an ordinary soldier. I was wounded twice and then threatened with blindness.
> It is the army which bears the weight of the struggle. In

these circumstances I have therefore decided, in my capacity as Supreme Commander of the German Armed Forces, to assume personally the leadership of the army.

Thus nothing that torments you, weighs upon you, and oppresses you is unknown to me. I alone, after four years of war, never for a second doubted the resurrection of my people. With my fanatical will, I, a simple German soldier, succeeded after more than fifteen years of labour, in uniting once more the whole German nation and in freeing it from the death sentence of Versailles.

My soldiers, you will therefore believe that my heart belongs solely to you, that my will and my work serve unflinchingly the greatness of my people, that my mind and my resolution are directed only towards the destruction of the enemy – that is, towards the victorious conclusion of this war.

What I can do for you, my soldiers . . . by way of care and leadership, will be done. What you can do for me and what you will do, I know you will do with loyalty and obedience until the Reich and our German people are finally saved.

Shameless though Hitler's manipulation of the heroic value system was, its effectiveness was borne out by results. The German army of 1945, unlike that of 1918, fought unquestioningly to the end. An inner circle of regular officers of the 'old' army apart – Catholic aristocracy like Claus von Stauffenberg, Prussian and Pomeranian feudatories like Quirnheim and Yorck von Wartenburg – the run of the mill officers and common soldiers gave him their total loyalty and surrendered at the last only when ordered to do so. Yet Hitler had scarcely ever spoken to any of them directly during the war or shown them his face. In the victory campaign of 1939–40 he toured the front after the fighting finished; in December 1940 he paid a Christmas visit to his SS bodyguard in the West. Otherwise, as an almost complete lack of appropriate photographs reveals, he held himself aloof from his faithful *Landsers*, communicating with them only by written order of the day and the very rare broadcast. Indeed, as Albert Speer recalls, on an isolated occasion when his journeying brought him into direct contact with the human instruments of his supreme command, he shrank from its reality. 'In earlier years,' Speer noted of the encounter, which took place on the transfer of headquarters from Rastenburg to the Berghof on

November 7, 1942, 'Hitler had made a habit of showing himself at the window of his special train whenever it stopped. Now these encounters with the outside world seemed undesirable to him; instead, the shades of the station side of the train would be lowered.' Late one evening he sat with Hitler 'in his rosewood-panelled dining car':

> The table was elegantly set with silver, glass, china and flowers. As we began our meal, none of us at first saw that a freight train had stopped on the adjacent track. From the cattle car bedraggled, starved and, in some cases, wounded German soldiers, just returning from the east, stared at the diners. With a start Hitler noticed the sombre scene just two yards from his window. Without as much as a gesture of greeting in their direction, he peremptorily ordered the servant to draw the shades. This, in the second half of the war, was how Hitler handled a meeting with ordinary front-line soldiers such as he himself once had been.

Hitler was never to starve; one of the eeriest elements of the mise-en-scène of his suicide was that a last lunch of spaghetti and vegetarian sauce preceded it by only half an hour. Yet, if we are looking for psychic rather than physical penalties of Hitler's calculated distortion of the heroic ideal for his crazed and ultimately criminal generalship, they are not hard to find. For already by the end of 1943, under the stress of the ordeal his command inflicted upon his soldiers but spared himself, he was a man far advanced in physical decay. In that year he was only fifty-three years old. His health throughout his political life, hypochondriac worries notwithstanding, had been excellent. It had remained good – and why, indeed, should it not have done? – during the period of easy victories. Morell, his personal physician, diagnosed hardening of the arteries in early 1942, but the condition was kept under control by one of the numerous medications – mostly for flatulence, about which Hitler had an obsession – he dispensed. Insomnia, which had troubled him in political crises before the war, and during the preliminaries to Barbarossa, returned during Stalingrad, as did a notable shortness of temper. In the immediate aftermath he developed external symptoms of stress. Guderian, on a visit to Vinnitsa in February 1943, noticed that his 'left hand trembled, his back was bent, his gaze was fixed, his eyes protruded but lacked their former lustre, his cheeks were flecked with red'. But his physical, as well as his intellectual, powers remained intact. Though Speer noticed a growing apathy in his manner and torpidity in his thought, the two men still took walks together on Speer's visits to Rastenburg in the autumn of 1943, and Hitler still exercised the Alsatian bitch, Blondi. Then in 1944 physical deterioration began to set in with extraordinary rapidity. He had found the first white hairs on his head in early 1942. By the spring of 1944 a visitor who had known him of old saw 'a tired, broken and elderly man, dragging his feet and stooping so low he seemed to bow. His features were sunken and lined with worry and anger. His eyes stared with almost a reproachful gaze. [His] secretaries noticed that sometimes his knees would begin to shake, or he had to grasp his trembling left hand with his right; the tremor when he had to lift a cup to his lips was too marked to be concealed.' The bomb explosion of July 20, 1944, added other disabilities, notably a ruptured eardrum, but from that he made a good recovery. Physical senility raced on unabated. By the end of 1944 he could walk only thirty or forty yards without stopping for a rest. By the spring of 1945 he was on the edge of total decrepitude:

> [His] face was ashen, puffy and deeply lined and his eyes seemed to be glazed over with a mucous film, without life in them. His right arm sometimes trembled violently and at such times he would clutch it impatiently with his left . . . Age, and the stooping of his shoulders, had given him a shrunken look . . . But the most noticeable change in him was the strange, lurching walk, like a drunken man. He would walk for a few paces and then stop, holding on to the edge of a table. In six months he had aged ten years.

Whence this terrifying disintegration? Insomnia was one explanation, but it was an insomnia rooted in a deeply destructive self-reproach and anger with fate. 'I keep seeing staff maps in the dark,' he told Dr Erwin Giesing in February 1945, 'and my brain goes grinding on and it takes me hours on end to drop off. If I then switch on the light, I can sketch exactly where every division was at Stalingrad. Hour after hour it goes on, until I eventually drop off around five or six.' Other images may have swum into his consciousness to torment him. Like all infantry soldiers of the First World War, Hitler had brought back from the trenches mental mementoes with which few had ever been cursed before – memories of bodies strewn like logwood on the battlefields or stacked in cords for burial in mass graves. The human connection between the holocaust of the First World War and the holocaust of the concentration camps must seem undeniable to anyone who can confront the visual evidence; without the anterior conditioning of the trenches to accustom men to the physical fact of industrialized killing, how would the necessary numbers have been found to supervise the processes of extermination? Hitler, by all the testimony, closed his mind to that side of his warmaking. To the physical extermination of his soldiers he could not. For he, as supreme commander, bore the ultimate responsibility for it; his responsibility was unalleviated by any gesture, let alone actuality, of shared risk; and ultimately it could be expiated only by the delivery of victory. By the spring of 1945 the last shred of hope in victory had been dissipated. He, the frontfighter, was left with the guilt of having delivered the sons of his own generation to death in millions and Germany to a second defeat. Feebly he ranted that, if the war were lost, it would be because the German people had not been worthy of him, but inwardly, if any rationality remained – and all observers testify that he retained his rationality to the end – he must have known that precisely the contrary was true: it was *he* who had not been worthy of the German people, and his progressive physical disintegration was the outward sign of his inward collapse under that knowledge.

For Hitler's supreme command had been – and may have appeared to him as he passed it in retrospect – no more than a charade of false heroics. It had been based, as he himself trumpeted in his days of power, on the concept of lonely suffering, on his internalizing of his soldiers' risks and hardships in the fastnesses of Rastenburg and Vinnitsa, on the equation of their physical ordeal with his psychological resistance, on the substitution of 'nerve' for courage, ultimately on the ritual of suicide as the equivalent of death in the face of the enemy. Few suicides are heroic, and Hitler's was not one of them. Among all the epitaphs that have been written for him since April 30, 1945, 'hero' is a word that finds no place among them. Nor is it probable that it ever shall. Heroes, in the last resort, die at the head of their soldiers and find an honoured grave. Hitler died in the presence of no man and his ashes are scattered in a place that today cannot even be found.

CONCLUSION

Post-Heroic: Command in the Nuclear World

Hitler's squalid and ignominious death brings to an end this survey of the transformation of command across 2,000 years of Western history. Can we draw from it any general reflections on the nature of military power, the means by which it is exercised and the process by which its effects are invested with political value?

It is of overriding importance to recognize that military achievement is not an end in itself. Primitives may fight in blissful unconsciousness of performing any larger function than masculine self-expression. The professional warriors of advanced states may deny that they are anything more than simple soldiers doing their duty as they see it and dying when duty demands. Even their leaders may decry political purpose in strategy, claiming to be moved by military imperatives that stand at the furthest extreme from the dictates of diplomacy or the statesman's perception of national interest. 'A la guerre comme à la guerre,' say soldiers; by which they mean that war changes how warriors look at the world, altering their priorities and submerging the preoccupations that animate peaceful society. Those – the profit motive, respect for property rights, obedience to the law, propitiation of the great, conciliation of minorities, performance of ritual and observance of custom and common courtesy – have no place, or only the very smallest, on the battlefield. There the race is indeed to the swift and devil take the hindmost. But, remote though the battlefield is from the market-place and the court of law, its pre-existence, or the potentiality of recourse to it, underlie all assumptions citizens make about the order of things as they find them. Force, blind themselves to its sanction as the right-thinking may, provides the ultimate constraint by which all settled societies protect themselves against the enemies of order, within and without; those with the knowledge and will to use it must necessarily stand close to or at the very centre of any society's power structure; contrarily, power-holders who lack such will or knowledge will find themselves driven from it.

There can, however, be nothing mechanistic about the exercise of power through force, whether naked or implicit, long though the power-holding and power-hungry have sought such a secret. Force finds out those who lack the virtue to wield it. Such virtue, in theocratic societies, is deemed to descend from God or the gods, and rulers by divine right may in consequence despatch their subjects to the battlefield without thought or imputation of need to lead them there. Secular rulers enjoy no such moral exemption; in their worlds the virtues that attach to force are those by which it is resisted – resilience, tenacity, hardihood but, above all, courage. They must therefore either go in person or else find the means of delegating the obligation without thereby invalidating their right to exercise authority outside the battlefield and in times of peace.

In the preceding pages we have surveyed the practices by which four different societies dealt with the dilemma of command. By the heroic ethos of the Alexandrian world – an ethos that was widely to persist or later re-emerge elsewhere – command was simply subsumed within the art of government itself, if the latter were not indeed subordinated to the former. No more distinction was made in Alexander's Macedonia between his roles as king and war-leader than between those of his leading subjects as electors and warriors. The legitimacy of all their roles was established and sustained by readiness to go to the battlefield and fight with courage once there; Alexander's function differed from that of his followers only in that he was expected to lead them to victory.

Not even defeat, if paid for by a kingly death, could rob such a ruler of a hero's title. A heroic death, indeed, both glorified the victim and best legitimized his blood-heir's succession to his title. But it was in that cyclic rededication of the warrior ruler to legitimization by battle that the sterility of the heroic society lay. No development from it – political, cultural, intellectual or economic – was possible as long as its élite's preoccupations were consumed by the repetitive and ultimately narcissistic activity of combat. All societies which achieved escape from the constrictions of heroism did so by separating the hero from the rest of society and according equal or superior prestige to functions more creative than his – those of the judge, scholar, diplomat, politician and merchant.

Two routes which seemed to promise such escape proved in the long run to be dead ends: the mercenary and slave soldier systems. By the second, favoured in early Islam, the function of warriordom was delegated to men who were the ruler's property. The logic of force, however, acting as it might have been expected to do, worked over time to reverse the property relationship, transforming those who exercised force into the possessors of power by fact if not title. The Mameluke kingdom that resulted was heroic by every test of that ethos, proving to be incapable of civic development and so rooted in their traditional style of warmaking as to fail even militarily when confronted by the armies of societies which had achieved adaptation. The mercenary system, on the other hand, revealed its undesirability by contrary effect. Only those societies which had achieved a considerable degree of economic development could afford to hire rather than breed soldiers; it was their own wealth which made the devolution of military duty so attractive to them and, conversely, to those who agreed to perform it on a commercial basis. The logic of force then working, however, to persuade the mercenary that he might take all that was available rather than the share he was offered, states which had opted for hired defence tended to discover that they had sold their birthright. The social outcome proved to be either a reversion to heroic leadership or, when enthroned mercenaries became softened by wealth and ease, a resort to mercenarism all over again.

Successful escape from heroism was, therefore, to be by one of two other routes. The first, epitomized by the society of which Wellington was a paragon, lay through the creation of a military class compensated for its isolation from political power by an apparatus of established rewards and privileges. Such classes emerged in few societies and at rare periods in history, and the process by which they did so remains deeply mysterious. The Roman empire's class of professional soldiers is one example of the phenomenon; its evolution continues to engage the dedicated interest of historians of antiquity. Western Europe's regular armies are another. They are, indeed, an historical phenomenon in their own right, but the stages by which they detached themselves from the muddle of feudal levies, royal retainers and hired freebooters who had served the mediaeval kingdoms are still shrouded in obscurity. All that can be said with confidence is that by the eighteenth century they existed in a finished form and that, by their liberation of their rulers' other subjects from the performance of military duty, they had released the energies of the rest of society for the tasks of creation – commercial, industrial, intellectual and artistic – which were to make Europe the master of the known world, and the conqueror of the globe's hidden parts, in their own time.

But even a professional military class, however stern the self-restraint by which it lives, must in the last resort act to confine the scope for development of the society it serves. Military culture, central though it is and must be to the heroic ideal, can successfully adapt to the progressive separation of sovereign power from the person of the sovereign, even when the principle of the sovereign as hero on which it turns may have become a fiction. What it cannot accommodate is the formal transfer to the fact of sovereignty from ruler to ruled, that necessary process by which absolute states become democracies. Soldiers who have gone to the battlefield as the sovereign's surrogates and risked their lives in the name of the king instinctively recoil from the demand that they shed blood in the name of 'the people', a figment which can never be brought to represent the hero in any form. All peoples who have attempted any rapid transition from monarchical to representational rule have, in consequence, encountered military opposition, the manifestation of which is called revolution.

By extraordinary ideological determination, as in the United States at its founding, or by subtle gradualism, as in nineteenth-century Britain, a few have nevertheless succeeded in creating democratic constitutions to which soldiers could give their professional obedience. But the achievement of peaceful revolution does not dissolve the requirement for heroic leadership when a popular state calls on its people to die in battle. Then the eternal questions voice themselves again: 'Where is our leader? Is he to be seen? What does he say to us? Does he share our risks?' And the same questions in different form confront the leader himself: In front always, sometimes or never? is a dilemma that the elected statesman can ultimately no better escape than the heroic leader himself.

An elected leader who sticks to the rule 'never', perfectly proper though his decision may be by constitutional and practical judgement, will pay a terrible price if he inflicts on his people burdens heavier than they can or will bear: the disappearance of the French government of 1940 into one of history's *oubliettes* is a warning to that effect; the political extinction of President Lyndon Johnson at the height of the Vietnam war may be another. 'Never' may, in the last resort, stand even an unelected ruler with absolute power of repression at his disposal in no better stead. Hitler's suicide may be perceived as the due he had to pay the German people for leading them to defeat in 1945, and his foreknowledge of its inevitability appears, in retrospect, as a spectre with which he had long lived. The halfway house of 'sometimes' or 'I have shared such risks in my time' may not answer well either. Napoleon III's presence at the battle of Sedan could not rescue him from obloquy; Jefferson Davis, who had been severely wounded in the Mexican War, lost all hope of heroic epitaph when he cravenly fled from Richmond in 1865 at the appearance of Grant's army.

All such men of power may be judged to have met the fates they did and to deserve the reputations they enjoy from simple failure to understand the demands levied on them by the imperatives of command. Government is complex; its practice requires an endless and subtle manipulation of the skills of inducement, persuasion, coercion, compromise, threat and bluff. Command, by contrast, is ultimately quite straightforward; its exercise turns on the recognition that those who are asked to die must not be left to feel that they die alone. But the relief of the warrior's ultimate loneliness is achieved by means quite as complex as those that attach to government. The successful leader – given that he is not doomed to fight an unwinnable war – is the person (women can lead as well as, if not better than, men) who has perceived command's imperatives and knows how to serve them. Those imperatives are few – but not all will necessarily yield to discovery, even under assault by a mind as possessed by the urge to power as that of Hitler himself. How are they to be enumerated?

The Imperative of Kinship

Command, the cliché has it, is a lonely task. But so it must be. Orders derive much of their force from the aura of mystery, more or less strong, with which the successful commander, more or less deliberately, surrounds himself; the purpose of such mystification is to heighten the uncertainty which ought to attach to the consequences of disobeying him. The taskmaster who eschews mystification, who makes himself, his behaviour and his responses familiar to his subordinates, must then evoke compliance either by love or by fear. But love and fear, strong though the role of each is in the masculine world of war, are emotions ultimately self-limiting in effect. True love is felt by two parties; it can rarely be simulated by either over the lifetime of a relationship. The commander who shows the love he feels when he gives orders must eventually cripple his will to expose his loved ones to danger. Fear, on the other hand, operates only if it is felt more keenly than the fear that it opposes. In the short-term, it can drive men to self-sacrifice ('Dogs,' Frederick the Great demanded of his grenadiers, 'would you live for ever?'). In the long-term it loses its power to compel by reciprocal mechanistic effect. Caught between two fears, the subordinate will eventually seek escape from both.

Mystification supplies the medium through which love and fear, neither ever precisely defined, cajole the subordinate to follow, often to anticipate, the commander's will. But mystification is a function of distance, real or illusory, which the commander must impose or contrive. Hitler and the château generals,* on whose command style he modelled his own, created mystification by imposing distance, of fifty or so miles in their case, hundreds in his, between themselves and their subordinates. Alexander contrived a sense of distance by living within his aura of kingship, reinforced as it was by the priesthood whose offices he alone, as the Macedonians' sovereign, could perform. Wellington and Grant, in the very different societies to which they belonged, contrived distance in appropriate ways: Wellington, scion of a society dominated by gentlemen, created and maintained a gentleman's household of servants, hounds, horses and hunting companions wherever the vagaries of campaign took him, living a country-house life in the heats of India or the snows of the Sierras; Grant, a small-town American, took the companionship of his own small town into the field, delimiting the distance necessary to his emotional comfort by setting a barrier of Main Street cronies between himself and the larger world of the army outside it.

Distance is, nevertheless, a negative dimension. The man who

---

* Higher commanders at the Western Front in the First World War generally established their headquarters in châteaux at some distance behind the lines.

insists on it becomes a recluse, and the reclusive commander achieves nothing. Distance must be penetrable by access either inward, outward or both. Hitler allowed occasional inward access: Guderian, for example, had the self-confidence to insist on personal confrontations with the Führer at Rastenburg when he felt that strategic crisis required it. Alexander thrived on outward access: he constantly moved among his subordinates, showing himself to his Macedonian subjects, dramatizing his kingship and playing the hero to the ever ready audience his army provided. Wellington and Grant, by contrast, freely encouraged access both inward and outward. They were often seen by their subordinates in the field, as they moved among them in an environment of shared danger – all too closely shared by Wellington; they were also easy hosts, Grant even more so than Wellington, receiving guests from the body of the army in the small society of their headquarters, making visitors feel at home and letting them go with the sense of having shared the vital intimacy of the commander *chez soi*.

The most important medium of penetrability, however, was supplied not by personal access but by the diaphragm of intimates and associates which surrounded the commander. Their selection and quality was crucial to the relationship that the general established with those to whom his orders were transmitted. Hitler, isolated by real distance from his fighting and suffering armies, needed his aloofness to be mediated by men with whom the common soldier could identify, warriors who had also starved, thirsted, shivered, sweated and bled with the man in the front line unlike the château generals of 1914–18. He signally failed to surround himself with anyone of that sort. Keitel, his principal subordinate, wobbled with the pounds of easy living and mindless sycophancy; Jodl, his brainbox, was marked by the stresses of the map table, not the foxhole; Schmundt, his chief army adjutant, and so its principal representative at Führer headquarters, babbled to his old comrades-in-arms when they met of the spell Hitler had cast over him, never of his chief's concern for the welfare or preoccupations of the men under his command. As a result it was only by the genius of Goebbels's propaganda efforts in representing the Führer to the Wehrmacht as a front-fighter with the best of them that the force of his orders was sustained to the end.

Alexander's army was suffused by his personality from the outset of his anabasis to his death; the role of his intimates, who became the

Diadochi, in interpreting and transmitting the nature of that personality is undeniable. But the limitation of his relationship with them is
defined by their subsequent behaviour. The Diadochi were as much
competitors in heroism with Alexander as mediators, and the
posthumous fragmentation of his empire was the result of their
desire to equal his achievement rather than propagate it. His
essentially unstable system was held in equilibrium only by his
day-to-day efforts; when his death disturbed the balance, both army
and empire fell apart.

Wellington and Grant, representatives rather than embodiments
of a system, used their circle of intimates to much more fruitful
effect. Their intimates fulfilled the role on the one hand of remem-
brancers to the commander of his responsibility for the army's
welfare, and on the other of witnesses to the army of the commander's concern for it. The extent of their success is borne out by the
excellence of relations pertaining between headquarters and troops
throughout all their campaigns, a success in the last resort attributable to the commanders' skill in selecting men who provided
windows to both worlds.

Grant and Wellington both succeeded, in short, in creating a bond
of kinship between themselves and their followers by surrounding
themselves with men who posed no threat to their primacy yet were
of sufficiently soldierly quality to command the army's respect.
Alexander, on the other hand, was fated to be surrounded by men
who, while their soldierly qualities were not in doubt, so powerfully
shared his ethic of heroic individuality that he could never truly rest
at ease with them. Hitler went to the other extreme: his intimate
circle was selected by the test of sycophancy, which made for perfect
domestic ease at headquarters but denied him any bond of understanding with the fighting men at the front.

The Imperative of Prescription

Understanding between commander and followers is not assured
solely by the mechanisms of kinship. A commander must not only
show what he feels for his soldiers by the quality of their representatives he chooses to keep at his side. He must also know how to speak
directly to his men, raising their spirits in times of trouble, inspiring
them at moments of crisis and thanking them in victory. The more

directly heroic the nature of his leadership – and therefore in all likelihood the more extreme the predicament to which he exposes them – the stronger that imperative. Wellington and Grant, leaders of constitutional armies in inter-state wars, were bound comparatively lightly by that imperative and both were notably poor communicators. Hitler on the other hand – a demagogue fighting a demagogue's war – though he rarely spoke directly either to army or people during its course, controlled a propaganda machine of the highest sophistication and was acutely sensitive to its operation. And Alexander was, of course, a master orator, a brilliant stage-manager of his own speaking performances and a supreme psychologist in his choice of rhetorical devices – challenges, threats, cajolery, bribes, appeals to pride, evocations of past achievements, promises for the future. The means by which he brought the force of his personality and intellect to bear on his army remain obscure; no human voice, without artificial amplification, has the power to reach the whole of an army as large as he commanded. In consequence, he sometimes spoke only to his officers, and at others repeated his speech, or variations on it, to fractions of his army in turns. But it is quite possible that he occasionally paraded it in a natural amphitheatre where echo would make him heard simultaneously by all.

Whatever the means he employed to make himself understood, Alexander had grasped from the outset the imperative of prescription – the need of every commander to convey an impression of himself to his troops through words, to explain what he wants of them, to allay their fears, to arouse their hopes, and to bind their ambitions to his own. It is a mark of the depths to which the art of command fell in the era of château generalship that this need was served barely, if at all, by any of the generals of the First World War. Their armies were, by an ironic twist of social and constitutional development, the most literate and politically conscious mass forces ever to have taken the field. By an equally ironic twist, the Staff College culture which informed their leadership had, by a bogus scientism, so sanctified the importance of purely theoretical principles of warmaking, and consequently so depreciated the importance of human emotion, that the common soldiers were not thought worth the expenditure of their commanders' breath.

The lesson of that fatal misjudgement was to be widely drawn by the generals of the Second World War, many of whom were to become as adept at self-presentation and prescription as Alexander himself. Hitler may have scarcely ever been photographed among his soldiers; photographs abound of his subordinates – Guderian, Rundstedt, Dietl, Model, Student – among theirs. The dislike felt for Montgomery by his more blinkered contemporaries was largely provoked by his remarkable theatrical gifts, much appreciated by his audiences of ordinary soldiers. And the art of self-preservation became in the post-war years a positive cult in two armies committed to struggle against the odds, the Israeli and the French. 'When I give difficult orders,' an Israeli general is remembered as saying, 'I like to do so in person, so that I can meet my soldiers' eyes.' 'Whatever else you may say about me,' General de Lattre de Tassigny assured the young officers of the army he was rescuing from the Indo-China disasters of 1950–1, 'you will not be able to say that you were not *commanded.*'

For all the importance of prescription, military literature is curiously deficient in discussion of how it should be done. What German classical scholars call the *Feldherrnrede* – the general's speech before battle – was a well-known literary form in antiquity. In the modern world Raimondo Montecuccoli, the imperial general of the Thirty Years' War, is almost the only writer to have addressed the subject. His remarks are extraordinarily penetrating, many of them still closely relevant to the manipulation of soldierly emotion on the contemporary battlefield.

'Exhortation of the host' is how he describes the imperative of prescription, 'when the general speaks publicly to his soldiers in order to urge them to demonstrate *virtu* and to infuse them with courage.' He suggests four main ways by which those objects may be achieved.

The first is by 'arguments of use':

. . . captains can incite soldiers to fight wars by indicating the necessity of battle, which deprives men of all hope of saving themselves except through victory and which forces them either to conquer or die. The same result may also be achieved by depicting the justice of one's cause, by appealing to patriotism and love of the captain, and by evoking disdain for the enemy; by showing that the enemy is saying ignominious things about one's own troops; that he wants to take away their property, religion, liberty and lives; and that it is better to die generously than to languish under tyranny.

'Exploiting the fear of infamy' is the second:

. . . make soldiers see that they are in the presence of illustrious persons. In order that they may abhor cowardice and exalt valor and so that they will have witnesses to their actions, they should fight under the watching eyes of the general or the prince . . . In order that the men will be prepared for the fray in a manner they can comprehend easily, the commander will declare that it is not the army of the fatherland but the fatherland itself that is endangered because it will have nothing left if the army is beaten.

'Exciting the desire for riches and prestige' is the third: 'It is also possible to make soldiers resolute by raising the hope of great rewards and prizes if they succeed, whereas they must be brought to dread severe punishment if they fail.' But it is Montecuccoli's fourth method which has the most convincing ring to modern ears, 'Developing confidence'. Let the captain, he says, show that

he himself is lighthearted and full of hope by means of his facial expression, his words and his dress. His visage should be severe, his eyes intrepid and luminous, and his clothing flamboyant. He should banter with his men, be clever and witty. They will then deduce that their general could not jest and enjoy himself like that if there were any real danger, if he did not think that he was much stronger or if he did not have good reason to scorn the enemy. The troops are bound to take confidence.

'The first quality of an officer,' wrote the future Marshal Lyautey in 1894, 'is gaiety,' independently echoing the point that Montecuccoli makes. Among the imperatives of command, that of speaking with all the arts of the actor and orator to the soldiers under his orders stands with the first.

The Imperative of Sanction

It is self-deluding to expect, however, that men can be led to fight solely by encouragement, flattery or inspiration. Words supply an uncertain antidote to fear. Fear must be opposed by fear itself or by a material factor as strong or stronger, and the commander who shrinks from threatening his troops with punishment or who will not deign to bribe or reward them will make easy meat.

Grant, among our four commanders, had least recourse to either sanction, the result of his access to very large reserves of manpower, from which the depradation of desertion could easily be made good, and also of his sensitivity to the populist ethos of contemporary America.

Outrage – rape or pillage – aroused his ire, as did treason or selfish profiteering, and he would punish peremptorily in such cases. But he did not regularly hang or imprison for cowardice or disobedience, because his citizen armies themselves tolerated such divergences from good military practice, recognizing them to be inseparable from their amateurism. For the same reason neither he nor his soldiers placed any high value on decoration or exceptional payments; service freely undertaken for a cause (the North did not conscript until 1863) was held in itself to be a badge of honour, to which others were superfluous, if indeed not odious.

Wellington, on the other hand, commanding men brought into the army by want and serving in it without sense of public duty, punished ferociously and conceded reward, in the form of loot, as a necessity. His philosophy of sanction had been that of European armies since time immemorial and differed from that of mediaeval hosts or mercenary companies only by the stricter regularity with which it was enforced by military law and standing orders. In the aftermath of his wars, however, when military service was established throughout Europe on a footing of social obligation rather than hired enlistment, the basis on which both reward and punishment were administered was consonantly transformed. Punishment lost such barbaric features as flogging (a voter could scarcely be triced up at the triangles), though it retained the ultimate sanction of death for cowardice, desertion or mutiny. Reward, on the other hand, was enormously elaborated.

Napoleon, the first leader to command something approximating to a citizen army, had early grasped that the dignity of the citizen soldier required that he be rewarded for exceptional conduct not by the arbitrary prize of loot (falling though it naturally does to soldiers foremost in the fight or breach) but by tokens of society's esteem. The Legion d'Honneur, instituted in 1802, was the first decoration for bravery to be created in any army for which all soldiers, irrespective of rank, were eligible. In a sense, it demonetarized reward in the field, and with such success that by the middle of the nineteenth century all Western armies had followed the French suit. The British Victoria Cross, the Prussian Iron Cross, the Russian Order of St George, the American Medal of Honor were all modelled on the Légion; their institution was followed by the creation of additional medals for lesser acts of bravery or devotion, so that by 1915, for example, a British general had at least six grades of decoration for which he could recommend soldiers under his command.

Decoration is a particularly potent tool in the management of a commander's direct subordinates, his staff officers and generals. Alexander had rewarded loyalty and success by marks of personal favour. Wellington and Grant, controlling armies formally structured by rank, arranged for their better subordinates to be promoted; a great deal of Grant's correspondence with Washington was devoted to that matter. Hitler, having the apparatus of both rank and decoration at his disposal, freely distributed promotion and rewards among his successful generals. Cunningly, and by a reversion to the conquering style of old, he also made so-called 'donations' to the favoured few, grants of land or money given privately and secretly to the very senior. It was a deliberately calculated means of compromising the integrity of the *Generalität*, sowing disunity and disarming opposition.

Yet, until his outright breach with the army after July 1944, Hitler was curiously lenient with the unsuccessful, even with the contrary. Like any strong-minded generalissimo before him – Joffre, for example, in 1914 – he dismissed on a large scale if combat efficiency required it; the mass purge of December 1941 showed how ruthless he could be if he chose. Yet, despite causing the Reichstag to accord him, in April 1942, absolute powers, he used such powers sparingly. Hoepner was deprived of his pension for his mishandling of his panzer group in 1942, von Wietersheim reduced to the ranks for incompetence, von Sponeck sentenced to be shot for abandoning the Kerch peninsula (the sentence was later commuted to imprisonment) and Falay and Stumma both dismissed outright as a result of breaches of documentary security in their commands. Until the Bomb Plot, however, Hitler's personnel policies were substantially no harsher than those of Churchill's, and a good deal less draconian than Stalin's, who, having murdered half the senior officers of the Red Army in 1938, had no compunction about executing unsuccessful generals in the crisis of 1941; several anticipated their fate by committing suicide.

Speer, a civilian observer of proceedings at Hitler's headquarters, was indeed surprised by the apparent lack of awe in which the professional soldiers held their supreme commander. 'I had expected respectful silence during the situation conferences,' he wrote,

> and was therefore surprised that the officers who did not happen to be participating in a report talked together freely, though in low voices. Frequently the officers, showing no further consideration for Hitler's presence, would take seats in the group of chairs at the back of the room. The many marginal conversations created a constant murmur that would have made me nervous. But it disturbed Hitler only when the side conversations grew too excited or loud.

It was only when 'he raised his head disapprovingly [that] the noise . . . subsided'.

The treachery of the traditional military class in July 1944 put an end to the easy ways for good. Mistrust came to pervade all intercourse between Hitler and his generals and, as the tide of defeat engulfed the Reich, suffused the army at large. During the retreat from France, Hitler threatened *Sippenhaft* – punishment of family – against commanders who surrendered fortified places. And in the last days of the war all ordered discipline was thrown to the winds; 'flying' courts-martial summarily executed soldiers suspected of seeking to surrender and even those found separated from their units.

These were measures of desperation and, given the inevitability of impending defeat, anyhow quite fruitless. But the nakedness of the expedient nevertheless exposes in a peculiarly stark form the necessary ambiguity of the relationship by which leader and followers are bound. Coercion is as essential a component of command as prescription or kinship. Ideally it should remain implicit, and when made explicit should manifest itself as rarely as possible as physical force, except in extreme emergency never falling arbitrarily or threatening the majority. Once a commander becomes as much an enemy to his followers as the enemy himself – and what else is a commander who breathes fire and sword against his own men? – the mystification of his role is destroyed and his power, essentially an artificial construct, dissipated beyond hope of recall.

The Imperative of Action

Kinship, prescription, sanctions are all preconditions of command. They do not amount to command itself. There are, indeed, times when a commander must watch and wait, and then it will be by prescription and sanction that his authority is sustained. But in the last resort a commander must act. How should he do so?

Action without forethought or foreknowledge is foolhardy. Commanders must know a great deal before they act and see what they are about when they do. These prerequisites are defined in the military vocabulary as intelligence and control and form two of the major elements of what analysts of strategic affairs have recently come to call C^3I; Command, Control, Communication and Intelligence. New definitions, however, do not change old realities. The essentials of action by the commander are *knowing* and *seeing*.

All four commanders whose methods we have surveyed grasped the central importance of *knowing*, both in general and in particular. Alexander's youthful obsession with the human geography of the Greek and Persian worlds – Who lived where? What did they grow? How did one travel from here to there? – was to be matched by Wellington's appetite for topographies and Grant's fascination with maps; even Hitler, indiscriminate as he was in choice of reading, the wordy frothings of racialist philosophers and the simple story-line of cowboy writers having an equal capacity to entertain him, took trouble to supply himself with exact military knowledge, if of a strictly limited usefulness. He certainly knew a great deal about the equipment of his armies and believed he knew all that was essential about soldiering; but he had an ignorance of climatic and terrain difficulties in the east, where he had never served, which was to prove fatal. Alexander, Wellington and Grant, on the other hand, knew their armies inside out, their theatres of campaign, and also a great deal about their enemies. Grant, of course, was privileged by special access to his opponents' minds; he had served with many of them, if he had not indeed known them as fellow cadets at West Point. Alexander's and Wellington's intimacy with the enemy was less complete. Both, however, understood a good deal about the forces they opposed, Alexander because the backbone of the Persian army was Greek, Wellington because he had been educated in France.

General knowledge is ultimately limited in its usefulness, however, precisely by its generality. Particular knowledge – of the enemy's whereabouts, strength, state, capabilities and intentions – is by contrast the material on which effective command thrives. Its value is recognized by the simplest minded. The difficulty is to acquire it and, once acquired, to put it to use. Martin van Crefeld, in his study of staff systems, advances a reflection in this regard of the most acute insight: that in pre-industrial society, particular knowledge was generated in quantities small enough to be handled by an individual, but reached him at a speed not much faster than armies moved and so tended to be out of date when received – and was not therefore 'real time' intelligence, as communication experts now characterize the commodity; but once industrial technologies – of which the telegraph was the first – allowed intelligence to outpace the movement of armies, its volume at once increased to exceed the capacity of any one man to collect and digest it. The rise of general staffs – essentially collections of subordinates expert enough to process particular knowledge on the commander's behalf – almost exactly coincides with the appearance of the telegraph, thus bearing out the point that van Crefeld makes. But, as he goes on to emphasize, the delegation of information-processing to subordinates imposes a remove between the commander and his besetting realities, beyond those that already exist.

Château generalship – in some sense, an acceptance of the logic of circumstance – was one reaction to this development. But superior generals, of whom both Wellington and Grant were types, had always resisted the logic of circumstances, had been keenly alert to the danger of distancing themselves from reality that even the comparatively primitive technologies and staff systems with which they worked threatened. The antidote that they applied was an insistence on *seeing*. Grant, making allowance for the recently and very greatly heightened danger of moving exposed within the missile-zone on his battlefields, managed to see a great deal. Wellington, who gambled recklessly with the lesser but still acute dangers of the missile-zone in his time, saw as much as was possible for any individual horseman. Both acquired crucial 'real time' intelligence in large quantities, processed it instantly, gave necessary orders immediately and were able to monitor the effects almost as they watched.

Alexander, because of his direct involvement in hand-to-hand fighting, an inevitability of the heroic ethic, had been able to do no such thing. Nor, paradoxically, could Hitler. He, deluded by the apparent instantaneities of the radio, telex and telephone (though he disliked the latter instrument, which minimized his magnetism), believed that he saw with the immediacy of the men on the spot. He was, however, wrong, and the workings of Führer headquarters were afflicted by all that was and is worst about both the château generalship of his own youth and the elaborately mechanized and automated command centres of our day. Floods of information, collected and transmitted apparently in 'real time', arrived at his situation conferences with significant delay; precise and detailed orders, seemingly attuned to realities, returned from him to the point of action only after realities had moved on. The disjunction between intention and effect resolved itself in the undignified and impotent tirades to which the Führer subjected his subordinates, both in headquarters and at the front, when events were revealed to have escaped his direction.

The problem of 'real time' intelligence probably defies solution. Armies are, in a sense, mechanisms designed to allow the will of an individual to bear directly on outcomes; that purpose is the justification for the hierarchy and discipline by which they are articulated. If the long experience of war demonstrates any one thing, however, it is that those moments when the scope of action and the size of armies lie in optimum relationship to each other – those moments, that is, when the flow of information upwards and orders downwards will most nearly match the pace of events – are very, very few. The masters of gunpowder warfare, among whom Frederick the Great and Wellington were outstanding, operated at such optima; because the tactics and strategy then prevailing obeyed rules of almost mathematical constancy, the clever commander could use whatever privileged information came his way to predict, anticipate and influence outcomes with uncanny certainty. At almost all other times before or since, however, such disequilibrium has normally prevailed between the size of armies and the scope of action that outcomes have yielded no certainties at all. Armies have either been too small for a commander seized with a vision of outcome to achieve it; or too large for any commander, however elaborate his information-gathering means, to grasp where the opportunity for outcome lay. Strategic indecision – by far the most common end of all campaigns – results in the first case; painful and bloody attrition, the all too frequent product of modern warmaking, in the second.

The insolubility of the 'real time' intelligence dilemma accepted – the dilemma is as great today, allowance for relative velocities of force being made, as it ever was and far more crucial in importance – the actual issue of command may now be seen to confront us. In front – always, sometimes, never? is, I have suggested, the question which must lie at the heart of any commander's examination of conscience. Those, like Alexander, to whom 'always' was the instinctive response, solved the 'real time' intelligence dilemma by dismissing it; their response to the challenge of events was to determine outcomes by direct, personal intervention. Those, like Hitler, the château generals and the denizens of contemporary situation rooms, who choose to say 'never', do so because of their belief that the dilemma is solved by artificial vision – that supplied by telegraphic, telephonic and, today, televisual communication; their response to the challenge of events was and is to demand more information and to issue stronger orders. It is the third group, formed of those giving the answer 'sometimes', whose response to the dilemma is most fruitful. Wellington and Grant – but also Caesar among their predecessors, Guderian and Montgomery among their successors – accepted that neither *knowing* nor *seeing* alone return an answer to the challenge of events. Sometimes a commander's proper place will be in his headquarters and at his map table, where calm and seclusion accord him the opportunity to reflect on the information that intelligence brings him, to ponder possibilities and to order a range of responses in his mind. Other times, when crisis presents itself, his place is at the front where he can see for himself, make direct and immediate judgements, watch them taking effect and reconsider his options as events change under his hand.

The proof of the pudding is in the eating. The 'sometimes' generals, among those we have considered, achieved a notably more consistent record of success than the 'always' or 'nevers'. Alexander, for all the dramatic immediacy of his style, put the future of his army at risk whenever he took the field, since its survival depended upon his own, and he trifled with his survival as a matter of honour. Hitler exposed his whole army to constant risk of disintegration, once the tide turned against it, simply because he refused to contemplate the reality of its predicament, to which he insisted his own was superordinate. Grant and Wellington, on the other hand, by walking the narrow path between extreme and false heroism, succeeded in constricting the ambient risks both to themselves and their armies and thereby in 'leading' – if from the rear – their soldiers to victory.

But Wellington and Grant did more than obey the imperative of action – of selecting and performing, that is, the correct function for themselves in the context that the military circumstances of their time dictated. They also succeeded in obeying the best and greatest of imperatives – which Alexander had obeyed to the unsafe exclusion of all others – that of conspicuous participation in the dangers that confront the lowliest soldier most keenly; in short – the imperative of example.

The Imperative of Example

The first and greatest imperative of command is to be present in person. Those who impose risk must be seen to share it, and expect that their orders will be obeyed only as long as command's lesser imperatives require that they shall. Presence may with limited and temporary success be simulated – by frequent visits to the danger zone at moments of quiescence or (what has been said about Jefferson Davis notwithstanding) by the invocation of a reputation for risk-taking in times past. Neither, however, guarantees that the seeming or one-time hero will thereby stimulate heroism in those he wishes to imbue with it. Legendary warriors like Churchill's Carton de Wiart, one-armed, one-eyed, seven times wounded on separate Sundays, or Franco's Millan d'Astray, founder of the Spanish Foreign Legion and also lacking an eye and an arm, may impel young soldiers to reckless deeds by the incontestable evidence of their own past contempt for danger; but few who have shown such contempt survive to infect others with their spirit. Old warriors who have survived risk intact seem to the young merely old; and would-be heroes not heroic at all. It is the spectacle of heroism, or its immediate report, that fires the blood.

Hence the collapse of so many armies whose commanders neglected to show themselves to their soldiers at the moment of danger. 'A rational army,' said Montesquieu, 'would run away.' And so, if we accept that self-preservation is the ultimate expression of rationality, we must agree it would. The thought is one that ought never to be far from any commander's mind. For the merest twitch of emotion stands between his exaltation and his descent to ignominy. At one moment he may, from his horse or headquarters, survey ten thousand, even a million men, ranked to heed his orders. At the next they may be streaming to the rear, obeying no order but 'sauve qui peut'. The transformation might sound over-dramatized; very large armies are as slow to disintegrate as they are to concentrate, since *panique-terreur*, the psychological state that eighteenth-century generals strove to create in the collective nervous systems of their opponents, can initially infect only those fractions of armies exposed to the enemy's main offensive effort. The rest will catch the infection indirectly, feeding their fears on rumour and sensation rather than the reality of rout at close hand, perhaps in consequence failing to find room on the roads to the rear, fighting rearguard actions willy-nilly or floundering in indecision until forced to offer their surrender when abandoned, encircled or marooned.

The sensation of defeat is, nevertheless, unmistakable and often uncontrollable. Few large modern armies have run with the instantaneity of Darius's at Issus or Gaugamela; parts of the Polish army preserved their integrity throughout the awful days of retreat from the frontier to Warsaw in September 1939, and the French defenders of Lille sustained such resistance in 1940 that their German opponents rendered them the honours of war when they eventually marched out to captivity. But when the germ of defeat takes a hold, even very large armies can fall apart with epidemic rapidity. Such was the fate of the Italian army at Caporetto in November 1917, of the bulk of the French army of the North-East in May 1940, of the German Army Group Centre in June 1944. The resulting humiliation of their commanders was pitiable. Cadorna, Georges, Busch had all been paladins; the first a general whose unapproachability struck fear into his subordinates, the second an Olympian of the generation of Foch, the third a victor of the French and Russian Blitzkriegs. Overnight they dwindled into despised nonentities. Cadorna was hurried into obscurity, Georges left weeping at his map table, Busch consigned to the pool of rejects unemployable even in the backwaters of Hitler's empire.

None wholly deserved his fate. The disorders which engulfed their armies were defeats that were waiting to happen, and perhaps no general could have averted them. But Cadorna and Georges had contrived to command in a fashion that ensured professional extinction would follow failure as night the day. Both were 'château generals' of the most extreme type, and though 'château generalship' was an understandable reaction to the recent appearance of long-range weapons, its effect on the relationship between leaders and led was so deadening that even the most arrogantly insensitive of generals should have taken steps to ameliorate it. By the time of Busch's disgrace in 1944 the more perceptive had already begun to do so. Cadorna and Georges appear never to have thought of attempting or even simulating heroic leadership themselves. To that extent they suffered their deserts.

Yet in their youth generals had shared risk with their soldiers as a matter of course, just as leaders had done for a hundred generations. Why the submergence of heroic leadership by château generalship, which was its antithesis? The answer is in part cultural and intellectual – and to this we shall return – but in greater measure technical. The trend of weapon development had for several centuries been acting to drive commanders away from the forward edge of the battlefield, but they had nevertheless resisted it. What occurred at the end of the nineteenth century was a sudden acceptance by the generals of all advanced armies that the trend could no longer be gainsaid and that they must abandon the post of honour to their followers.

The option of command from the rear had, nevertheless, always been open. Alexander had chosen not to exercise it because the values by which he lived and reigned forbade his incurring any taint of cowardice. Within 200 years of his death, however, his own society had advanced to a recognition that a general's station need not be fixed at the point of maximum danger, that he might indeed serve the cause of victory better from a place where he could observe and encourage rather than fire others by his example. But that recognition was not to extinguish the power of the heroic ethic altogether. On the contrary, what resulted was the marriage of the two, giving birth in turn to a code of compromise. By its dictates the general would seek to set as striking an example of risk-sharing as he could, consonant with the need to keep a distance from danger sufficient to allow his controlling the battle as a whole.

It was by those dictates that such commanders of professional armies as Caesar and Wellington adjusted their response to threat and crisis. Caesar, articulating a weapon system technically no different from Alexander's though superior to it by the index of drill and discipline, was often impelled to its frontier of contact with the enemy, and both dressed and behaved accordingly. He affected a distinctive red battle cloak and had ready prepared a repertoire of battlefield oratory with which to inspire and instruct his subordinates. The death of the legions with that of the Roman empire brought back the heroic style. But with the return of regular armies, of which Wellington's was the most perfected type, the compromise between prudence and exposure re-asserted itself. Wellington's close encounters with death were never haphazard, but the result of a mathematical calculation of the ebb and flow of danger. On the open battlefields where he and his opponents chose to give action, it was a consistent possibility, given the known ranges at which weapons took effect, to anticipate the fine tolerances when this position or that would become untenable by the commander and to move accordingly. Wellington did not represent his style of command in terms of the judgement of 'fight' and 'flight' distance by which a lion tamer exerts his mastery over his charges – and a spell over his audience; but it was calculated in almost exactly the same way. If one dimension of command is the theatrical, one would say that, while Alexander's performance was relentlessly Grand Guignol, Wellington's was brilliant melodrama, a succession of perfectly timed exits and entrances, each advancing the plot to its triumphant conclusion by spectacular and risk-fraught effect.

It was a performance, nevertheless, that literally diced with death, as his tally of minor wounds and disabled mounts testifies. Just forty years after his last appearance on the stage of battle, the pattern of risk-taking he had run would have swiftly exhausted an imitator's invulnerability. The tide of probability had then begun to run against anyone foolish enough to keep to the saddle within 500 yards of the firing line – he had survived long exposure at 100 yards or less – and wise generals reacted accordingly. Grant, as we have seen, was very wise. Confident in the power of other means to legitimize his authority, he unashamedly held himself rearward of all but the incalculable odds – stray shells, ambush – while sending his soldiers forward without compunction to face the danger he had decided it was not his duty to share.

Yet Grant did not think it proper to exempt himself from the environment of risk altogether. Though leaving the heroic role to his subordinates, he kept a place for himself on the stage of battle as a sort of actor-manager, prompting the principal players at need and intervening from the wings when crisis threatened the development of the action. The actor-manager role he created – few contemporaries learnt to function as he did – was to prove, however, a transient one, intermediate between Wellington's style, rooted as it was in the heroic tradition, and that of the château generals to come. Some commanders of the Prussian wars of 1866–71 would ride the battlefield as if none but a silver bullet could touch them. But the majority kept to or near their headquarters, communicating with the front by messenger and surveying it, if they could at all, by telescope. Fifty years later, their descendants – French and German indiscriminately – were not to think of quitting their headquarters at any time. Berthelot, Joffre's operation officer at the Marne in 1914, would indeed spend the whole of the battle literally *en pantoufles* – shod in carpet slippers – and sitting at his desk from which only the summons to a meal (he might have doubled as the fat man in a circus) could shift him. The hazards of the preceding Great Retreat had obliged him to set up his office in a succession of town halls and schoolhouses. With the stabilization of the front in October, however, he would be solidly established in château comfort at Chantilly and his opposite numbers in the allied and opposing armies likewise, the Germans having chosen Spa, a health resort in Belgium, and the British Montreuil, a charming little walled town close to the English Channel. It was from those secluded places that the great slaughter of the trenches would be directed, totally out of sight and, unless for a trick of the mind, also out of sound of all the headquarters responsible for it.

One of the inhabitants of British headquarters, Charteris, Haig's chief of intelligence, has left us a picture of life at Montreuil in 1916:

> Here at GHQ, in our own little town away back from the front line trenches [delicately put; Montreuil was fifty miles behind the lines], there are few visible signs of war. We might almost be in England . . . All the work in all the departments is now systematised into a routine. Most of it is done in office. One of the great difficulties of everyone at GHQ is to get away from the office often and long enough to get in close touch with the front. Few can ever get much further forward than the HQ of Armies . . . Forward of Army Headquarters, one is nearer the fighting, but even they are now mostly in towns or villages several miles behind the front line. Further forward still are Corps Headquarters, where there is generally plenty of evidence of war . . . but even Corps Headquarters are now pretty

big organisations and are almost always in a village. In front of
the Corps Headquarters the Divisions are mostly in farm-
houses, but well in the fighting line. One can almost always get
one's car up to them. But that is about the limit, and visits
forward of them consequently take up a good deal of time. We
all manage, anyhow, to see something of a division headquarters, but it is only when there is some particular object, more
than simply looking around, that one can give up the time to go
beyond them. I have not even seen a Brigade Headquarters in
the front line for the last month.

Since brigades stood a rank higher in the chain of command than
battalions, which actually occupied the trenches, it may be seen that
Charteris, whose duty was to form a picture of events at the front for
transmission to his chief, did so at best largely second-hand. Haig
himself, though his biographer, John Terraine, claims for him that
he visited the trenches frequently, was rarely observed to do so by
memoirists of the front line. Even at Montreuil he preserved an
Olympian detachment from the work of the staff; one of them recalls
that, as a special concession, staff officers were allowed to leave their
desks to watch him ride in and out from his office provided they did
not show themselves at the windows. Haig's residence was not even
in Montreuil; he preferred to seclude himself from its relative
hurly-burly at the château of Beaurepaire some ten miles away in the
heart of the countryside.

The simulated absolute monarchy of château generalship ultimately provoked the military equivalent of revolution in almost all
the armies on which it was imposed. In May 1917, after the failure of
some particularly heartless offensive plans, nearly half the divisions
of the French army downed tools, announcing their unwillingness to
attack the Germans again until their grievances were redressed. In
October of that year the Russian army, disillusioned by the point-
lessness of its sufferings, simply 'voted for peace with its feet', as
Lenin put it, allowing him to transform the power vacuum which
resulted into political revolution. In November the Italian army
effectively gave up the fight to which Cadorna had relentlessly
driven it, with consequences that almost brought Italy to defeat. It
was a crisis of morale in the German army in September 1918 that
prompted Ludendorff to tell the German government it must treat
for peace. And even the British army, in the aftermath of the March

retreat of 1918, suffered a collapse of morale so acute that Haig was impelled to subordinate his independence of command to the French, as the only means of securing reinforcements to shore up his shaken front.

At the root of all these spiritual crises lay a psychological revolt by the fighting soldiers against the demands of unshared risk. For two or three or, in the case of the German army in September 1918, four years, orders had emanated from an unseen source that demanded heroism of ordinary men while itself displaying heroism in no whit whatsoever. Far from it: the château generals had led the lives of country gentlemen, riding well-groomed horses between well-appointed offices and residences, keeping regular hours and eating regular meals, sleeping between clean sheets every night of campaign and rising to don burnished leather and uniforms decorated with the high awards of allied sovereigns. Meanwhile those under their discipline, junior officers and soldiers alike, had circulated between draughty billets and dangerous trenches, clad in verminous clothes and fed on hard rations, burying their friends in field corners when spells from the front allowed and kicking a football about farmyards by way of relaxation. The implication of such disparities can be suppressed in the short term; modern armies are, indeed, mechanisms of such suppression. Their elaborate hierarchies – fourteen ranks interpose between a private and general – act as a system of screens to camouflage the altitude at which dangerous orders are generated. Since the subordinates most exposed to the consequences, ordinary fighting men, receive those orders from someone scarcely less exposed than themselves, or perhaps even more so – the platoon or company leader – resulting dissatisfactions are dissipated at that level if they are indeed felt or expressed. It takes much time for a bad or inconsiderate general's qualities to diffuse downwards through the barrier layers of rank, and even more time for that diffusion to type him for what he is. Even when so typed, he continues to be protected by a parallel mechanism of suppression, the code of military law. Unlike civil society, military society makes dissatisfaction with a superior, once expressed in any form, a criminal offence; even 'dumb insolence' attracts confinement, while fomenting dissent is mutiny, in time of war an act punishable by death.

Yet, as even bad generals know, hierarchy and discipline cannot suppress the implications of risk disparities for ever. Even while the

First World War raged, some armies had begun to recognize the deficiencies of château generalship and taken steps to alleviate them. Pétain, appointed to rehabilitate the French army after the mutiny of May 1917, not only instituted enlightened measures of welfare, more generous leave, better food, provision for entertainment – but also took care to design a series of limited operations against the Germans whose small scale ensured their success. By learning that their commanders could lead them to victory – and some French generals, like Marchand, had always been models of the exemplary style – the disheartened *poilus* were gradually weaned back to optimism.

That the commanders of citizen armies should have so gravely abused the reasonable expectations of their followers is evidence of how artificial and unreal was the general staff culture in which contemporary commanders had been raised. That culture was modern and its intensity a function precisely of its novelty. The perception by which it had been created was not false. The sudden heightening of danger on nineteenth-century battlefields quite properly required the commander to withdraw himself, and the consequent delay in the acquisition of 'real time' intelligence rightly demanded that subordinates should act for him at times and places when and where he could not be present. The cultural mistake lay in elevating those subordinates to the status of an élite and their function to superior expertise. General staff selection and training, based on fierce competitive examination, produced in the years 1870–1914 côteries of military specialists whose professional exclusivity was overweening. A social chasm was thereby opened between those who thought and those who fought; worse, thinking came to be deemed more important than fighting in the conduct of war, the emotions of ordinary soldiers subordinate to the perceptions of staff officers and the making of plans superordinate to their execution.

'Knowing', of a limited and theoretical sort, thus came to dominate 'seeing' in the system of military values, with results whose undesirability was to be concealed until the spiritual revolt of European armies in 1917–18 made them stand plain. The history of the emotional life of armies ever since has been one of a retreat from that disjunction. Staff officers who, even when general staff culture flourished at its most intense, had nominally been required to alternate between staff appointments and troop duty, were subsequently and with increasing strictness actually required to do so. Staff training, formerly restricted to a minority, has progressively been extended to the majority of officers. The dynamics of combat – its stresses and psychological climate – have come to form an ever larger subject of consideration in that training. Those who undergo it have demonstrated the military society's change of heart by the enthusiasm with which they cultivate intimacy with the man in the ranks and the frequency with which they seek his company. Leadership, of a style sufficiently heroic to satisfy Alexandrian exigencies, is the command mode to which modern generals now aspire. Their armies perform accordingly. The Israeli army, animated by a code of which 'Follow me' is the central tenet, defeated its Arab enemies with a consistency that seemed routine until in 1973 the Egyptian army, its leadership transformed by an internal revolution inspired by the heroic ethic, very nearly succeeded in reversing the pattern. The Chinese and Vietnamese armies, outstanding among victors in the post-war years, both insist on the closest personal identification of leaders with led. The British army, once infected as badly as any by general staff culture, demonstrated how completely it had cured itself of the disease by its victory in the Falklands, a triumph of heroic leadership against odds. And the American army, trammelled by a theoretical approach to warmaking though it tends to be, has elevated the management of small groups to so high a place in its operational doctrine that its general staff culture may now be judged to persist only in a benign form.

And yet the cure to which so many armies have successfully subjected themselves may, with perspective, now come to appear irrelevant to command's current central problem. For armies have, by the nuclear revolution of 1945, been set aside from that central place in the defence of nations they have occupied since time immemorial.

'In order that the men will be prepared for the fray in a manner they can comprehend easily,' advised Raimondo Montecuccoli,

> the commander will declare that it is not the army of the fatherland but the fatherland itself that is endangered because it will have nothing left if the army is beaten; that it has entrusted all its resources and power to the soldiers; that they are the repository of all its hopes that they surely do not wish to be destroyed.

Montecuccoli's assumption that the army in war opitomized the state, so that its commander was therefore burdened with essentially sovereign responsibilities, is one which would have held good at virtually any moment of the twenty-four centuries which this book has surveyed. It holds good no longer. Armies are now but one means by which states of the first rank – those deploying nuclear weapons or belonging to an alliance which does – defend themselves, and not only that: they are a subordinate means. Truly critical command functions no longer belong to generals, but have emigrated to the centre of political power itself, have been returned into the hands of constitutionally sovereign authority itself and subject those who exercise them – president, prime minister, first secretary – to their burdens. Those burdens, always awesome, have been heightened by the dimensions of nuclear power, to the level of the almost unbearable. For it is not merely the 'resources and power' of the 'fatherland' – nation, *rodina*, *patrie*, call it what you will – that lie at risk should those exercising sovereign authority through nuclear weapons fail or miscalculate; it is the physical survival of the millions of human beings who have entrusted their wellbeing to him or her. Today the political leaders of the nuclear states have become Alexanders, the repositories of ultimate military as well as political responsibility in the polities they head, but with this unmanning – or unwomanning – difference: that those whose hands lie closest to the weapons by which society is defended are those who, in the eventuality of their use, would be placed furthest from the physical consequences of their impact. Nuclear war would expose every ordinary man, woman and child in every nuclear-armed nation to the risk of instantaneous disintegration or, failing that, to the inevitability of secondary irradiation. Presidents, prime ministers, first secretaries would, by contrast, belong to the only group – and that a tiny one – whose survival would in any way be assured against immediate or postponed nuclear extinction. The imperative of example would, in short, have been stood on its head; those least involved in the prosecution of war and least equipped to protect themselves against its consequences – suckling babes, nursing mothers, the sick, the lame, the very old – would stand in the front line; heads of government, by definition also nuclear force commanders, would be sheltered in deep headquarter bunkers or sequestered in airborne control posts. The weak would risk most, the 'strong' least of all. What are the implications of this extraordinary reversal of command ethic?

The Validation of Nuclear Authority

The sequestration of the commander from risk in nuclear-weapon states is, for all the paradox it entails, a perfectly proper procedural response to the dangers by which they are encompassed. The propriety flows from the anticipated nature of a nuclear war itself. For nuclear weapons may have three targets: the first is the civilian population and cities of an enemy state; the second are its weapons and weapon sites; the third its centres of command. Strategies dedicated to the destruction of each of them are called respectively counter-force, counter-value and decapitatory. The logic which underlies each may be characterized as follows: an attack on weapon systems (a 'first strike') would, if successful, win the war; but, weapons being numerous and well-protected, all opposed nuclear powers reserve their weapons – belief at any rate has it – for a 'second strike' against cities, the menace of which is held to deter the first. Nuclear weapons thus hold each in thrall by the logic of 'mutually assured destruction'. But the logic has a chink. If one side were able to outwit another's warning systems and destroy its command centres, it might thereby escape the retaliation of a 'second strike' – the authority to order which would have been paralysed – and proceed either to destroy the enemy's weapon systems or simply dictate peace under that or associated threats.

The spectre of this strategy of decapitation, long perceived and well understood by all nuclear states, explains and justifies the measures taken to protect their high commands from attack. There are many. One is that of direct defence, providing leaders with command shelters proof against nuclear strike. A second is escape, the provision of airborne command posts which would carry leaders away from points of nuclear impact at moments of danger. The third is alternative command, the empowering of nominated and instructed subordinates to exercise nuclear command authority in the case of death, disablement or isolation of the sovereign. The fourth, complementary to the other three, is redundancy, the multiple duplication of command centres and channels, so as to permit the free flow of orders even when the primary centres and channels have been interrupted.

The American nuclear command system, about which most has been revealed, is known to include all these features. A National

Military Command Centre in the Pentagon and a hardened underground Alternate National Military Command Centre collect and collate the intelligence – chiefly from satellite surveillance and ground radar sources – by which the danger of nuclear attack is monitored and transmitted to the President. He has a Situation Room in the White House to which he would go in the event of nuclear alert – two were caused by false alarm in 1979 and 1980 and there have been several deliberate alerts – and could, if time allowed and risk sufficiently threatened, transfer to a communications aircraft, the National Emergency Airborne Command Post, kept permanently ready at Andrews Air Force Base near Washington. Operational alert authority over nuclear forces is exercised by the North American Air Defense Command located inside Cheyenne Mountain, Colorado Springs (though it is not hardened to survive a major nuclear impact), while command of the strike forces themselves belongs to the Strategic Air Command, one of whose generals is permanently airborne in a 'Looking Glass' aircraft and which also deploys an Emergency Rocket Communication System, mounted in one or more Minuteman missiles, which (presumably) would broadcast attack orders if all other instruments of command had been destroyed. In the event of the President's death, disablement or isolation, however, his authority would devolve first on the Vice-President, followed by a succession of cabinet officers, in strictly specified constitutional order, and thence on commanders holding 'predelegated authority' whose identity is concealed (but are believed to number the six or seven exercising 'unified or specified' command). Serving all in the nuclear chain of command is a multi-branched communication network, which uses the national telephone network as its medium and assures, in the event of anything except a stateswide catastrophe, that legitimate nuclear launch orders would reach launch centres if ever issued.

So comprehensive is the American nuclear command and control system that the role of the man at its centre, the President, has been described as that not of implementing nuclear response (or attack) but of precisely the contrary: assuring that missiles will always remain in their tubes or silos, and aircraft within national airspace, unless he specifically orders otherwise. The President is, in short, like the wise elder of a pre-heroic society, an inhibitor of conflict, not its instigator, director or leader. The President's command centre, writes Paul Bracken, the major authority on the matter, has as its function 'not to act as *a trigger to launch nuclear weapons* but as *a safety catch preventing other triggers from firing*'. Between the pre-heroic inhibitor and moderator of conflict, however, and the nuclear-power President interposes a crucial difference of status: the former acts by open, the latter by secret method. The tribal elder who urges restraint does so through his links of kinship with his people, by prescription, sanction, direct action and, if necessary, example. The President who exercises restraint on behalf of his society does so, necessarily, by mysterious means. 'Detailed information on the procedures for using [nuclear control measures],' writes Paul Bracken, 'is one of the U.S. government's most closely held secrets. Information about which location the President would go to, which communication lines he would use, how much predelegated authority would be given to provincial commanders and which communication system would be selected for sending firing orders are all surrounded in much deeper secrecy than that surrounding the technical characteristics of the weapons themselves.'

'The reason for such secrecy,' he goes on, 'is not hard to fathom.' Indeed it is not. Nuclear command and control secrets are, more than any others of the strategic system, those that an adversary would most like to penetrate. For, if penetrated, an enemy would then be able to calculate if a decapitating strike was feasible and, if it were judged so (admittedly by no means a foregone conclusion), exactly how, when and where to target his missiles. Moreover such secrets are, in the last resort, the only ones that a nuclear power can realistically hope to deny to another. Everything else in the system – missile sites, radar stations, command centres, airbases, satellites – is physically substantial. Even the minute-by-minute locations of ballistic submarines and nuclear-armed aircraft are, in the last resort, ascertainable by surveillance methods because submarines and aircraft, being physical objects, return sonar or radar signals and are therefore identifiable, even if with greater or lesser difficulty, in time and space. The one insubstantial, physically immaterial component of the system – not identifiable or penetrable by surveillance systems – is the procedure by which its physical elements would be activated and operated. True, the communication links by which procedures are initiated are vulnerable to direct attack, as, by cryptology, is the coded language in which communications are transmitted. But, because of the high degree of 'redundancy' (which simply means large-scale duplication) in the links, and because, as far as we know, even the most advanced cryptology cannot break current cyphers in 'real time', the communication system may be judged for the present secure. What ought always to remain beyond the reach of anything the enemy can deploy against it, except the efforts of traitors or 'agents in place', is the nuclear command protocol itself – authentification codes, launch orders and the Single Integrated Operation Plan or its Soviet equivalent.

The necessary secrecy that surrounds these inner secrets, however, brings with it, at least in democracies, a central contradiction; that the single most important process of government – for what else is that by which the survival of a people is ensured? – is itself kept secret from the electors themselves. The existence of this contradiction may not, at first consideration, have the power to shock. Confidentiality is, after all, an admitted right of government even in the most thoroughgoing democracies – cabinet discussions, for example, are kept secret, as are the internal processes by which ministries and departments arrive at their decisions of policy – and for confidentiality to embrace the heart of national security procedures might seem a quite proper extension of that principle. The difference, however, between cabinet confidentiality and national security confidentiality lies in the fact that the first concerns what are indeed *discussions*, unpredetermined in their form, while the second are indeed *procedures*, having – presumably – the same formality and sequentiality as constitutional practices for the enactment of law, the appointment of officers of state and the declaration of war.

The development of such other procedures in the history of democracies is one of the progressive rolling back of the curtains of secrecy by which they were originally surrounded; an excellent definition of democracy is that it is a system of government in which rule is conducted by rulers in open view of the ruled. In the United States, for example, not only must Congress discuss the passage of bills in open audience and the President accept public endorsement, or disallowal, of his appointments of cabinet officers, ambassadors and judges; President and Congress are both bound to conduct debate over the declaration of war in open session. Yet, by an unprecedented reversal of the historic trend of democratic development, we now live with a state of affairs which surrounds a matter far graver than traditional declarations of war – a decision to initiate and respond to nuclear attack – with a secrecy so complete that we do not, for example, even know whether the launch procedure has been computerized or is still amenable to human check and balance. Consider what that obscurity implies: if launch procedures have already been computerized – if, that is, machines are now instructed to order the launch of missiles at some predetermined presentation of warning signals by the other machines of the surveillance system – then democratic government is already hollow at its centre, for the leader elected as the guardian of their security by the citizens of any democratic state that is also a nuclear power – the United States, Britain, France – is no longer empowered to exercise moderation, restraint or second thought in the matter which may determine whether it survives or not as a society. If the opportunity for moderation, restraint or second thought still pertains – if command procedures, that is, have not yet been computerized – democratic electorates may breathe again. But they are still left altogether uninformed – and therefore unable to express either their approval or disapproval – of the measures instituted by government to control and direct the weapons by which they expect to be defended.

There may be, given the intrinsic nature of the deterrent relationship which holds nuclear adversaries in mutual check, no way by which democracies can bring nuclear launch procedures within their system of accountability. Democracies may, in short, have to accept a permanent and unalterable diminution of their right to know, to criticize and to amend. But if that is the case, then the relationship by which the people of a democracy and their leader are bound together has not only been changed fundamentally and for good; the nature of that change requires that democratic leadership must in future partake of a style and a character altogether different from any that has prevailed before.

Let us briefly remind ourselves of the imperatives that have combined to define leadership in the past: they have comprised an element of *kinship*, by which the leader surrounded himself with intimates identifiable by his followers as common spirits with themselves, thus guaranteeing that their mutual humanity, in all its strength and weakness, will be constantly represented to each other; kinship has been bolstered by *sanction*, the reward – or punishment – of followers according to a jointly accepted value system; sanction has been reinforced by *example*, the demonstration of the personal acceptance of risk by the authority who requires others to bear it at his behest; example has been amplified by *prescription*, the explanation of the need for risk-taking by the leader, in direct speech, to his followers; and prescription has finally been made concrete – reified would be the technical term – by *action*, the translation of leadership into effect, of which victory was the desired result.

Power over nuclear weapons has undermined or invalidated all these imperatives. The exclusivity of the nuclear community, burdened by secrets it is legally forbidden to communicate, and physically isolated from the community it is charged to protect, has sundered all *kinship* between it and society at large; *sanction* has lost its force, since the proper management of a nuclear system will generate no occasion for either punishment or reward, or none at any rate that can be readily revealed; the opportunity for *example* is, as we have seen, denied by nuclear logic, which requires the leader to be at least risk among all members of his or her society; *prescription*, in consequence, is self-defeating, if not downright destructive of authority, since all exhortation to courage and fortitude invites the riposte, And What of You?; and *action*, the test by which leadership has always ultimately been validated, is, of course, denied by the necessity to avoid all outcomes in nuclear confrontation whatsoever.

The leaders of nuclear powers are therefore fixed in a dilemma: how to validate (legitimize, political scientists would say) their authority without recourse to any one of the heroic props always previously found necessary to that end? Autocracies, like the Soviet Union, confront this dilemma in a less acute form than democracies, since the autocrat does not shrink from using force to impose his will, up to the limit where force must rebound against his hold on power; but even an autocrat as extreme as Hitler took the precaution to employ reward, exhortation and a carefully contrived image of himself as hero as a means to palliate his dependence on direct coercion. Democracies, contrarily, have diluted the heroic appeal by adducing the principle of consent to justify disparities in risk-sharing. Thus Abraham Lincoln, with but a few days of bloodless campaigning against the redskins to his name, and Franklin Roosevelt, a man absolutely untouched by military experience, could both demand the ultimate sacrifice of their fellow citizens on the grounds that the voters had, by electing them president, willed them powers of war as well as peace, with all the consequences that flowed from that act.

Liberal democracy has never failed, none the less, to invoke the apparatus of heroic leadership when it could, its comparative brevity and localization as a form of government making consent alone too uncertain a means of legitimizing commands which regularly spared from their consequences those responsible for their issue. Thus Gladstone's anti-militarism could preserve its consistency because he was able to avoid leading Britain into blood-letting on any large scale. But the authority both of Asquith's government and of the *Union sacrée* of 1914–16 was undermined by the evident inconsistency of their pacific inclinations and their warmaking policies, to say nothing of the wholly civilian backgrounds of the ministers who composed them. Not only have the leaders of the democracies in the total war era subsequently taken trouble to publicize their individual military records, if they had any to claim – as Churchill, Kennedy and Eisenhower, for example, notably could and, more modestly, Truman, Nixon, Carter and even Reagan also; they have additionally – and the consent principle notwithstanding – regularly mobilized the imperatives of kinship, prescription, sanction, action and, where possible, even example to heighten their military authority.

Those expedients, it has been demonstrated, no longer avail. What therefore is to take their place? No programme of national reassurance can do so. The early efforts of the United States and British governments to 'educate' their populations in techniques of nuclear survival foundered on evident and quite rational disbelief, and were indeed inevitable victims of the complementary but contrary half of the same strategic argument: that security in a nuclear world derived from the *certainty* of retaliation, otherwise known as Mutually Assured Destruction. That being so, the governments of democratic states which are also nuclear powers – those of nuclear autocracies should also take heed, but are under less compulsion to do so – must establish a new form of military command. It is best characterized as 'Post-Heroic Leadership'.

Post-heroic leadership will require that most difficult of all feats, in government, a transition from one system of appeal to human responses to another and quite different one. Traditional leadership in all its forms, even the most liberal and humanistic, has always had to delve deep into what is instinctual and emotive in the collective psyche to find the elements which will lend it force. Democracy, in its fundamental dimension, is a means of limiting the egotism and waywardness of those who exercise power by replacing them with others when their pretensions become intolerable. The alternation of declared political positions is a superficiality of the democratic system; it is the popular right to deprive one constituent group of the political class of authority and invest it in another that makes democracy morally superior to autocracy – call it monarchy, aristocracy or oligarchy – in any of its forms. But traditional democracy, fragile flower that it is, has never derived its force from moral argument alone. Morality is, in the last resort, founded upon reason, but mankind in the mass does not choose or unchoose by purely rational process. The most successful democratic leaders have known as much and acted accordingly, buttressing their reasoned arguments with a carefully calculated appeal to material interest and emotional response and, with an elaborate 'presentation of self', contrived to personify the image of leadership closest to that which a people, at one time or another, seeks for its own. The wastepaper basket of democracy is filled with the lives of would-be leaders whose highmindedness led them to reject such artifices and rest their approaches to the electorate on pure rationality.

The advent of nuclear weapons has put a term to the semi- and anti-rational style. Mankind, if it is to survive, must choose its leaders by the test of their intellectuality; and, contrarily, leadership must justify itself by its detachment, moderation and power of analysis. Hopes of transition to such a style of leadership need not be based on mere wish. The history of the world's first and only acute nuclear crisis lends substance to the belief that it may be achieved.

That episode was the Cuban Missile Crisis of October 14–27, 1962, which brought the United States and the Soviet Union to the brink of war. It retains the keenest significance for the modern world for three reasons: it is the only nuclear crisis of which we have a detailed account written by an insider (*Thirteen Days* by Robert Kennedy, brother of the President and US Attorney-General); it was presided over, on the American side, by a leader who had revived the heroic style in an extreme form; it was conducted, nevertheless, in a strictly post-heroic manner and resolved with rapid and complete success.

What were the bases of that outcome? The first was President John F. Kennedy's determination that the three competing *velocities* of the crisis – the velocity of the Russian initiative, the velocity of the necessary American response, and the velocity of assessment and decision – should be identified and separated. The second was that assessment should be entrusted to a group of men, the Executive Committee (Ex Comm), chosen for their expertise and sagacity, relieved temporarily of other responsibility and convened to meet outside his presence. The crisis therefore developed, as far as was possible, in a way which ensured that the velocity of events did not accelerate the velocity of decision-making, with all the undesirable consequences of rushed and unconsidered judgement that might otherwise have ensued.

At the outset, the Ex Comm accepted the assessment that the deployment of Russian missiles to Cuba, the preliminaries to which had been discovered at an early stage, would take two weeks to complete while the appropriate American military dispositions required only forty-eight hours, thus leaving twelve days for rational consideration; the Ex Comm also quickly identified the three outcomes to which dispositions might lead – air blockade, bombardment and invasion of Cuba; and it finally and quickly agreed on how it should organize itself for the appropriate decision-making in the time it had decided was available.

The nature of the decision-making appears, in retrospect, the most impressive and significant feature of the crisis. The Ex Comm decided at the outset not to organize itself in a hierarchical way; it forswore 'leadership' from the start. 'We all spoke as equals,' Robert Kennedy recalled. 'There was no rank . . . we did not even have a Chairman . . . the conversations were completely unstructured and uninhibited. Everyone had equal opportunity to express himself or to be heard directly.' Some found the burden of equal responsibility too heavy to bear. Dean Rusk, the Secretary of State, underwent what Kennedy identified as a nervous breakdown early on and thereafter absented himself. McGeorge Bundy, the National Security Advisor, proved incapable of taking a consistent line. He was 'first for a strike, then a blockade, then for doing nothing'; finally for a strike again. But that at least demonstrates that the Ex Comm avoided 'groupthink'. In fact, and despite the insistence of its only military member, General Maxwell Taylor, on advocating military action, the Ex Comm took only three days to reach a majority decision for blockade. Another day was devoted to technical discussion outside the Ex Comm forum and a further two, October 21–2, to conferences with President Kennedy himself. By the sixth of the thirteen days available, therefore, a rational response to the Russian threat had been identified and endorsed. A week later the Russians also had accepted its logic and turned their missile-carrying ships away from Cuba to a homeward course.

The history of the Cuba crisis therefore offers both reassurance and hope that future nuclear crises may be resolved as rationally and harmlessly. But it must be remembered that the world has moved on since 1962, and moved on apace. Pace is, indeed, the crux. Of the three velocities which drove that crisis – velocity of events, velocity of response and velocity of decision-making – the last has remained static, as it must; the human mind and the human tongue work no faster in 1987 than they did in 1962 or, to cast back to Alexander, than in 334 BC. But the *reporting* of events, which feeds the pace of crisis, has accelerated significantly, and the velocity of response – military disposition and alert – even more markedly. The Soviet Union in 1962 was seeking to dispose missiles into a gap in the American warning system by ponderous sea transport, taking days to complete. Today its missiles are disposed on submarines from which their flight-times to targets within the forty-eight contiguous United States are measured in minutes.

A velocity of unvarying pace – that at which human beings receive, assimilate and discuss information and decide what must be done in its light – therefore competes with velocities which are constantly quickening. Because they concern activities which are also swelling in volume – more long-range, short-flight-time weapons, more information – the human beings who are hampered by the unvarying velocity of their own thought processes seek to equalize the imbalance by reducing the flow of information to more manageable proportions and bringing the weapon array under ever more centralized control. The desired end of this trend is for all weapons to be made obedient to a single command, which in its turn will be determined by a single 'go' or 'no go' reading from all incoming information. The modern supreme commander – president, prime minister, first secretary – is, in short, seeking to return from the complexities of strategy to the simplicities of tactics; to a situation in which the warrior both sees his target and, by direct observation of its behaviour, launches or stays his weapon accordingly.

But desire and circumstance meet here, alas, in irresoluble conflict. To reduce a large volume of complex information quickly to a simple 'read out' can be done; but only by interposing a dense filter of machines and intermediary personnel between the decision-maker and reality. Machines, in the circumstances, can make of information only what they are told or programmed to do; while intermediary personnel, as they assess the information that passes before them, inevitably encroach upon the ultimate function of the supreme decision-maker. The result may be to persuade the strategist that he enjoys the tactician's direct vision and freedom of action; but the sensation will be an illusion.

Worse, it will be an illusion pregnant with disastrous consequences. Not only will it tempt the supreme commander into decisions which programmed and mediated information may, all desire to the contrary, have made for him. It will also tempt him to act the tactician and – therefore – the hero. Kennedy, as we saw, managed to resist that temptation. But Hitler assuredly did not. And though Hitler's personality was grossly aberrant, the means by and the environment in which he exercised command were not so at all. Indeed they directly resembled those that prevail in Washington, Moscow, London and Paris today. That being the case, the possibility that the supreme commander of a nuclear weapons state will at some time in the future yield to the temptation of false heroics and seek to play the tactician, just as Hitler did, cannot be ruled out of account.

The prospect is potentially catastrophic. How can it be forestalled?

Two methods suggest themselves. The first is to decelerate the two velocities – of events and appropriate response – that drive the critical velocity of decision-making. Easier said than done is the obvious response. But efforts to decelerate are nevertheless afoot through the vast American (and Soviet) scientific enterprise called the Strategic Defense Initiative. 'Star Wars' is both seen and represented as a system of protection; President Reagan's depiction of the eventual SDI product as a missile-proof 'astrodome' best conveys that aspiration. But even his warmest supporters concede that the dream of an astrodome is an illusion. Total missile-proofing probably lies beyond the capacity of any scientific community to achieve. That is not to say, however, that Star Wars is without merit, political or military. On the contrary, it is an enormously hope-giving initiative, if it is seen, as it properly should be, as a mechanism to procure not total *defence* but relative *delay*. Deterrence, as we are currently reminded, derives its logic from its instantaneity, the certainty of instantaneous retaliation by second strike should a first strike fail. The outcome of that dialectic is called Mutually Assured Destruction. Because Star Wars threatens to dilute mutuality, assurance and destruction, it is seen as damaging to the deterrent principle. If, on the other hand, its influence is calculated not on the effect it might exert on outcomes but on the delay it could impose on decision-making, its desirability switches from negative to positive. Nuclear weapons strategy within a Star Wars system would, if a crisis boiled from menace to action, almost certainly result in some missiles reaching their target on one or both sides. But, horrible though such an experience would prove, the event would not only be bearable in a way that Mutually Assured Destruction would not. It would also allow the contestants to think and calculate rationally during the course of the exchange – to act, that is, as strategists instead of tacticians – and to perhaps extricate themselves from deepening trouble rather than be driven further into it by the velocities of event and response.

Star Wars therefore offers hope; but only through the prospect it promises of reverting from the diplomacy of the hair-trigger to the more traditional rhythms which animated international relations before the coming of nuclear weapons. The outcome of a nuclear war, even one mediated by SDI mechanisms, would still be so much worse than of any ever known to the world that no strategic theorist may properly portray the Initiative as man's best and last resort. Mankind needs not new hardware but a change of heart. It needs an end to the ethic of heroism in its leadership for good and all. Heroism, as we have seen, is not a necessary constant in the way that societies work. Heroism is an irrational and emotional response to challenge and to threat. In a world of riches and poverty, better and worse land, full and empty spaces, good and bad gods, true and false creeds, the appeal of heroism was a natural temptation to those who felt that it would lend the decisive cutting edge to weapons otherwise inadequate for victory over the stronger, the more fortunate, the better favoured by history. It was also a splendid cloak for the bully, the tyrant, the ideologue and the fanatic, not least when the urge to tyrannize came to possess whole peoples, rather than those given to or taken by them as leaders.

For much of man's known past, the heroic ethic, in some guise or other, has characterized the style of government by which he has conducted his affairs in most quarters of the globe. A few people in a few places have found other means to legitimize the authority under which they have lived. The theocracies of China and the Middle East represent one alternative form. The liberal democracies of the nineteenth-century West represent another. Both chose to preserve and cultivate the heroic ethic, none the less, in certain carefully isolated sectors of their societies, and to sustain the creed of struggle within their larger political philosophies. In the theocracies that creed belonged with the depiction of those 'outside' as barbarians or unbelievers. In the democracies the creed of struggle worked to energize politics from the inside, making 'heroes' of men and women simply through their advocacy of the opposed positions of right or left, red or white, us or them.

The concept of struggle, and its attendant ethic of heroism, broods over us all today. It lies at the heart of Marxism and hovers not far from the guiding belief of democracy in the values of human freedom and choice. Yet the spectre of risk, by confronting which the leader authenticated himself as hero, is no longer deflected from those who follow him by the singular role he takes for himself. On the contrary, it diffuses the whole arena of struggle, threatening everyone equally, if not indeed the led more directly than their leader. The traditional means by which the leader sought to validate his followers' sharing of the risk he led them to face – the cultivation of a sense of kinship, the use of sanction, the force of example, the power of prescription, the resort of action – now all fail. Indeed, what is asked first of a leader in the nuclear world is that he should not act, in any traditionally heroic sense, at all. An inactive leader, one who does nothing, sets no striking example, says nothing stirring, rewards no more than he punishes, insists above all in being different from the mass in his modesty, prudence and rationality, may sound no leader at all. But such, none the less, is the sort of leader the nuclear world needs, even if it does not know that it wants him. 'Post-heroic' is the title he might take for himself. For all is changed, utterly changed. Passing brave it may once have been to ride in triumph through Persepolis. Today the best must find conviction to play the hero no more.

Select Bibliography

Primitive Warfare

Bohannan P., ed., *Law and Warfare: Studies in the Anthropology of Conflict*, New York, 1967
Bramson, L. and Goethals, G., *War: Studies from Psychology, Sociology and Anthropology*, New York, 1964
Cohen, R., and Service, E., eds. *Origins of the State*, Philadelphia, 1978
Divale, W., *Warfare in Primitive Societies*, Oxford and Santa Barbara, 1973
Ferguson, R.B., ed., *Warfare, Culture and Environment*, London and Orlando, 1984
Pruitt, D., and Snyder, R., eds, *Theory and Research on the Causes of Wars*, Englewood Cliffs, 1969
Turney-High, H., *Primitive War*, Columbia, SC, 1949

Alexander the Great

Unless otherwise attributed, direct quotations from the life of Alexander the Great by ancient authors are from the Loeb Classical Library editions of:
Arrian, *History of Alexander and Indica*, ed. and trans. E. Iliff Robson, 1929
Curtius, *History of Alexander*, ed. and trans. J.C. Rolfe, 1946
Diodorus, *Diodorus of Sicily*, ed. and trans. C. Bradford Welles, 1963
Plutarch, *Life of Alexander*, ed. and trans. B. Perrin, 1919
Adcock, F., *The Greek and Macedonian Art of War*, Berkeley, 1957

Anderson, J., *Military Theory and Practice in the Age of Xenophon*, Berkeley, 1970

Badian, Ernst, *Studies in Greek and Roman History* ('Alexander the Great and the Loneliness of Power'), Oxford and New York, 1964

Berve, H., *Das Alexanderreich and prosoprographischer Grundlage*, 2 vols, Munich, 1926

Bieber, Margaret, *Alexander the Great in Greek and Roman Art*, Chicago, 1964

Burn, A.R., *Alexander the Great and the Hellenistic World*, New York, 1962

Dilke, O., *Greek and Roman Maps*, London, 1985; rpt. Ithaca, 1985

Ehrenberg, V., *Alexander and the Greeks*, Oxford, 1938; rpt. Hyperion, CT, 1981

Ellis, J.R., *Philip II and Macedonian Imperialism*, Princeton, 1976

Engels, F., *Alexander the Great and the Logistics of the Macedonian Army*, Berkeley, 1978

Finley, M.I., *The Ancient Economy*, Berkeley, 1973; *The World of Odysseus*, London, 1977; New York, 1978

Fox, R. Lane, *Alexander the Great*, London, 1973; New York, 1974

Fuller, J.F.C., *The Generalship of Alexander the Great*, New Brunswick, 1960

Garlan, Yvonne, *War in the Ancient World*, London, 1975; New York, 1976

Green, P., *Alexander the Great*, London and New York, 1970

Griffith, G.T., *Alexander the Great: The Main Problems*, Cambridge and New York, 1966

Hadas, Moses, *Hellenistic Culture*, New York, 1959

Hammond, N., *Three Historians of Alexander the Great*, Cambridge, 1983; New York, 1984

Marsden, E.W., *The Campaign of Gaugamela*, Liverpool, 1964; rpt. Atlantic Highlands, NJ, 1985

Milns, R.D., *Alexander the Great*, London, 1968

Olmstead, A.Y., *A History of the Persian Empire*, Chicago, 1948

Pearson, L., *The Lost Histories of Alexander the Great*, New York, 1960

Savill, A., *Alexander the Great and His Time*, London, 1959; New York, 1966

Snyder, J.W., *Alexander the Great*, New York, 1966

Tarn, W., *Alexander the Great*, 2 vols., Cambridge, 1948; rpt. Chicago, 1981

Tarn, W. and Griffith, G.T., *Hellenistic Civilisation*, London and New York, 1952

The Duke of Wellington

Direct quotations from Wellington, unless otherwise attributed, are from:

Lt-Col Gurwood, *The Dispatches of the Field Marshal the Duke of Wellington*, 12 vols, London, 1837–8.

Arthur Wellesley, *Supplementary Despatches and Memoranda of Field-Marshal Arthur, Duke of Wellington*, 15 vols, London, 1858–72

Philip Henry Stanhope, *Notes on Conversations with the Duke of Wellington*, Oxford, 1888; rpt. New York, 1973

Bell, D., *Wellington's Officers*, London, 1938

Brett James, A., *Wellington at War*, London and New York, 1961

Davies, G., *Wellington and His Army*, Oxford and San Marino, 1954

Gates, D., *The Spanish Ulcer*, London and New York, 1986

Glover, M., *The Peninsular War*, London and Hamden, CT, 1974

Glover, R. *Peninsular Preparation: The Reform of the British Army, 1795–1809*, Cambridge and New York, 1963

Howard, M., *Wellington Studies*, London, 1959

Larpent, F.S., *The Private Journal of Judge-Advocate Larpent*, London, 1853

Longford E., *Wellington: The Years of the Sword*, London, 1969; New York, 1970

Oman, C., *A History of the Peninsular War*, 7 vols, Oxford, 1930; rpt. New York, 1977; *Wellington's Army*, London, 1913

Rothenburg, G., *The Art of War in the Age of Napoleon*, Bloomington, 1978

Ward, S.G.P., *Wellington's Headquarters*, Oxford and New York, 1957; *Wellington*, London, 1963; New York, 1964

Weller, Jac., *Wellington in the Peninsula*, London, 1962; New York, 1963; *Wellington at Waterloo*, London and New York, 1967; *Wellington in India*, London, 1972

Wellesley, M., *The Man Wellington*, London, 1937

General Ulysses S. Grant

Direct quotations from Grant, unless otherwise attributed, are from *The Papers of U.S. Grant*, ed. John Y. Simon, Illinois University Press, 1967 – particularly volumes 7 and 8, and from the *Personal Memoirs of U.S. Grant*, 2 vols, New York, 1885–6

Ambrose, Stephen, *Duty, Honour, Country. A History of West Point*, Baltimore, 1966

Badeau, Adam, *Military History of Ulysses S. Grant*, New York, 1882

Bates, David, *Lincoln in the Telegraph Office*, New York, 1907

Bauer, Karl, *The Mexican War*, New York, 1974

Benedict, Michael, *A Compromise of Principle*, New York, 1974

Boatner, Mark, *The Civil War Dictionary*, New York, 1959

Burne, A.H., *Lee, Grant and Sherman*, Aldershot, 1938

Cadwallader, Sylvanus, *Three Years with Grant*, New York, 1955

Catton, Bruce, *U.S. Grant and the American Military Tradition*, Boston, 1954; *Grant Moves South*, Boston, 1960; *Grant Takes Command*, Boston, 1969

Conger, Arthur, *The Rise of U.S. Grant*, New York, 1931

Cunliffe, Marcus, *Soldiers and Civilians*, Boston, 1968

Donald, David, ed., *Why the North Won the Civil War*, Baton Rouge, 1960

Fuller, J.F.C., *The Generalship of U.S. Grant*, New York, 1929; *Grant and Lee*, Bloomington, 1957

Johnson, R.U., and Buel, C.C., eds, *Battles and Leaders of the Civil War*, New York, 1887–8

Lewis, Lloyd, *Captain Sam Grant*, Boston, 1950

Luvaas, Jay, *The Military Legacy of the Civil War*, Chicago, 1959

Macartney, C.E.N., *Grant and his Generals*, New York, 1953

McFeely, William, *Grant*, New York, 1981

McWhiney, Grady, ed., *Grant, Lee, Lincoln and the Radicals*, Evanston, 1964

Owens, Kenneth, *Galena, Grant and the Fortunes of War*, DeKalb, 1963

Porter, Horace, *Campaigning with Grant*, New York, 1897

Weigley, Russell, *Towards an American Army*, New York, 1962; *The American Way in Warfare*, New York, 1973

Wiley, Bell Irvin, *The Life of Johnny Reb*, Indianapolis, 1943; *The Life of Billy Yank*, Indianapolis, 1952; *The Common Soldier of the Civil War*, New York, 1977

Wilson, Edmund, *Patriotic Gore: Studies in the Literature of the American Civil War*, New York, 1962

Adolf Hitler

Direct quotations from Hitler, unless otherwise attributed, are from *Mein Kampf*, trans. R. Manheim, London, 1969, and from *Hitler's Table Talk*, ed. H.R. Trevor-Roper, London, 1953

Bezymenski, L., *The Death of Adolf Hitler*, London and New York, 1968

Bullock, A., *Hitler. A Study in Tyranny*, London and New York, 1964

Craig, G., *The Politics of the Prussian Army*, New York and Oxford, 1964

Domarus, M., *Hitler. Reden und Proklamationen, 1932–45*, 4 vols., Munich, 1965

Fest, J., *The Face of the Third Reich*, London and New York, 1970; *Hitler*, London and New York, 1974

Gilbert, G., *Nuremberg Diary*, London, 1948; New York, 1949

Halder, Franz, *The Halder Diaries*, 7 vols., ed. A. Lissance, Washington, 1950

Irving, D., *Hitler's War*, London and New York, 1977

Kehrig, M., *Stalingrad Analyse und Dokumentation*, Stuttgart, 1974

Kubizek, A., *Young Hitler*, London, 1954; New York, 1955; rpt. Westport, 1986

Leach, B., *German Strategy against Russia, 1939–41*, Oxford and New York, 1973

Maser, W., *Hitler*, trans. P. and B. Ross, London and New York, 1973

Milward, A., *The German Economy at War*, New York, 1964; London, 1965

Picker, H., *Hitlers Tischgespräche im Führerhauptquartier, 1941–2*, Stuttgart, 1963

Schramm, P., ed., *Kriegstagebuch des Oberkommando der Wehrmacht*, Frankfurt, 1961; *Hitler als militärischer Führer*, Frankfurt, 1962

Smith, Bradley, *Adolf Hitler, His Family, Childhood and Youth*, Stanford, 1967

Speer, A., *Inside the Third Reich*, London and New York, 1970

Trevor-Roper, H.R., *The Last Days of Hitler*, London and New York, 1956; *Hitler's War Directives*, London, 1964

Warlimont, W., *Inside Hitler's Headquarters*, London, 1962; New York, 1964

Command and Leadership

Barker, T., *The Military Intellectual and Battle*, Albany, 1975

Bracken, P., *Command and Control of Nuclear Forces*, New Haven, CT, 1983

Corvisier, A., *Armies and Societies in Europe*, Bloomington, 1979

Creveld, M. van, *Command in War*, London and Cambridge, MA, 1985

Dixon, N., *On the Psychology of Military Incompetence*, London, 1976; Topsfield, MA, 1984

Gabriel, R., and Savage, P., *Crisis in Command*, New York, 1978

Hittle, J., *The Military Staff*, Harrisburg, 1961

Luttwak, E., *The Grand Strategy of the Roman Empire*, Baltimore, 1978

McNeill, W.H., *The Pursuit of Power*, Chicago, 1982; Oxford, 1983

Mallett, M., *Mercenaries and their Masters*, London and Totowa, NJ, 1974

Parker, G., *The Army of Flanders and the Spanish Road*, London and New York, 1972

Quimby, R., *The Background of Napoleonic Warfare*, New York, 1957

Toolcy, R., *Maps and Map-makers*, London, 1952; New York, 1953

Vaché, A., *Napoleon en Campagne*, Paris, 1900

Verbruggen, J., *The Art of Warfare in Western Europe during the Middle Ages*, Amsterdam and New York, 1977

Index